13.75

DANUBE

DANUBE

CLAUDIO MAGRIS

Translated from the Italian by

Patrick Creagh

Farrar Straus Giroux

NEW YORK

Library of Congress Cataloging-in-Publication Data
Magris, Claudio.
[Danubio. English]
Danube / Claudio Magris; translated from the Italian by Patrick
Creagh.—1st American ed.
p.   cm.
Translation of: Danubio.
1. Danube River Valley—Description and travel.   2. Magris,
Claudio—Journeys—Danube River Valley.   I. Title.
DB449.2.M2713   1989   949.6—dc20   89-7942

To Marisa, Francesco and Paolo

They ride and ride until they come to the Danube . . .

The Flight of King Matthias, Slovenian folksong

CONTENTS

MAP   10–11

1   A Question of Gutters   13

2   The Universal Danube of
    Engineer Neweklowsky   55

3   In the Wachau   125

4   Café Central   165

5   Castles and Huts   217

6   Pannonia   239

7   Grandma Anka   289

8   Doubtful Cartography   335

9   Matoas   359

    INDEX   402

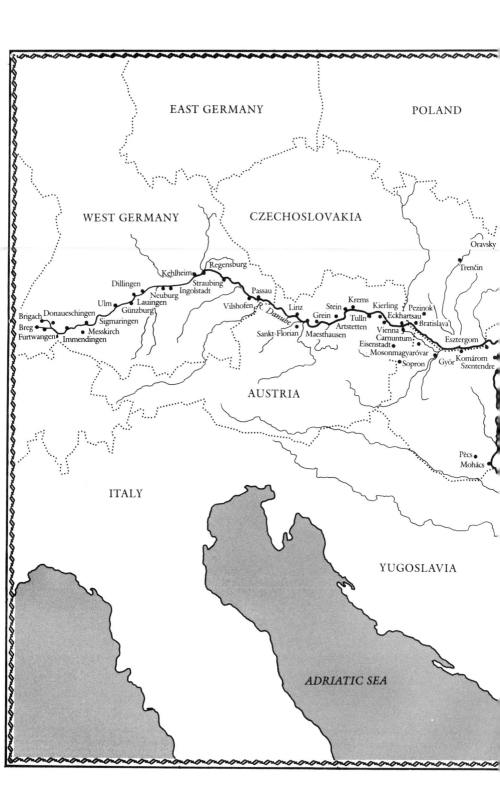

EAST GERMANY

POLAND

WEST GERMANY

CZECHOSLOVAKIA

Oravsky

Trenčín

Regensburg
Kehlheim
Dillingen
Straubing
Neuburg
Ingolstadt
Passau
Ulm
Lauingen
Vilshofen
Linz
Krems
Günzburg
R. Danube
Stein
Kierling
Pezinok
Donaueschingen
Sigmaringen
Grein
Eckhartsau
Brigach
Messkirch
Sankt-Florian
Tulln
Bratislava
Breg
Maesthausen
Artstetten
Vienna
Esztergom
Furtwangen
Immendingen
Carnuntum
Eisenstadt
Komárom
Mosonmagyaróvár
Szentendre
Sopron
Győr

AUSTRIA

Pècs
Mohács

ITALY

YUGOSLAVIA

ADRIATIC SEA

THE DANUBE

Miles
Kilometres
0   200   400

SOVIET UNION

drámok • Matiašovce
• Matliary
Tatranská Lomnica

Czernowitz

HUNGARY

RUMANIA

ödöllö
udapest
sepel

Cluj (Klausenburg)   • Bistrita
                • Sighişoara

Kalocsa
Szeged   Sibiu (Hermannstadt)   • Brasov (Kronstadt)   Galati   Chilia Veche
Baja.   Brăila   Tulcea   Sulina
• Subotica   • Timişoara   R. Danube
ombor
patin   Histria •
Novi Sad

R. Danube   Vršac   • Bucharest   Constanta
        Pančevo Bela Crkva   Adamclisi
Belgrade   .Turnu Severin
        Djerdap   Kladovo   Giurgiu
                            R. Danube   BLACK
        Vidin   Ruse
              Lom Kozlodúj   • Nikopol   SEA
        Belogradčik

BULGARIA

        • Sofia

        • Plovdiv

A Question of Gutters

I. A PLAQUE

"Dear friend!

Sig. Maurizio Cecconi, alderman of the city of Venice, has proposed that we organize an exhibition based on the enclosed prospectus, entitled 'The Architecture of Travel: Hotels, their History and Utopia'. The proposed location is Venice. A number of institutions and organizations appear willing to underwrite it. If you are interested in working with us . . ."

This cordial invitation, which arrived a few days ago, is addressed to no one in particular, and does not name the person or persons apostrophized with such rapture. The affectionate outburst sponsored by the municipality transcends the individual to embrace the general: humanity at large, or at least a vast and fluid community of the cultured and intelligent. The proposal attached has been drawn up by professors at the universities of Tübingen and Padua, drafted according to a rigorous logic, and furnished with a bibliography. It aims to reduce the unpredictability of travel, the intricacy and divergence of paths, the fortuity of delays, the uncertainty of evening and the asymmetrical quality of any journey, to the inexorable order of a treatise. The whole scheme is a first draft of a Statute for Living – if life is a journey, as they say, and we pass across the face of the earth as guests.

In this world administered and organized on a planetary scale, to be sure, the adventure and mystery of travel would seem to be dead and done for: even Baudelaire's Voyagers, who set out to look for the unheard-of and were ready to face shipwreck in the attempt, found in the unknown, and in spite of every unforeseen disaster, precisely the same tedium that they left at home. To be on the move, however, is better than nothing: one stares out of the window of the train as it hurtles into the countryside, one raises one's face to the breezes, and something passes, flows through the body. The air creeps into one's clothes. The ego dilates and contracts like a Portuguese man-of-war. A little ink overflows from the bottle and is diluted in an ink-coloured sea. But this gentle loosening of the bonds, which replaces the uniform with a pair of pyjamas, is more like an hour's break in the school timetable than the promise of the great demobilization. Vain fancies, says Benn, even when one feels the pitiless azure break open beneath a debatable reality. Too many self-satisfied, peremptory soothsayers have taught us that the "all-inclusive" clause in the price-lists of tourism includes even the rising of the wind. But luckily we are left with the adventure of classification, the thrill of diagrams, the allure of methodology. The professor from Tübingen engaged by the alderman may be aware that the world is humdrum enough to threaten the Odyssey, the real, unique experience of the individual; but he cheers himself by adorning page 3 with a quotation from Hegel, that great product of the theological seminary in his university town, and echoes him in asserting that method is the construction of experience.

This wooden bench, overlooking the narrow strip of water, prompts me to feel kindly towards the orderly plan which I found in the post-box shortly before leaving – towards the miniature Art of Fugue hidden beneath the bowstrokes of those logical passages. The wood of the bench has a good smell to it, a manly toughness reminiscent of the Rider of the Lone Valley, while the Breg – or the Danube? – is a flowing bronze ribbon, brown and shining; and, thanks to a few patches of snow in the woods, life seems cool and fresh. There is promise in the sky and in the wind. A happy conspiracy of circumstances and a benevolent state of relaxation – aided perhaps by the cordiality of that "Dear friend!" – prompt me to have faith, and even to accept the synthesis, formulated beyond all reasonable doubt by our German colleague in the Venetian project, between Hegel's Science of Logic and the various categories of hotel.

It is comforting that travel should have an architecture, and that it is possible to contribute a few stones to it, although the traveller is less like one who constructs landscapes – for that is a sedentary task – than like one who destroys them. This was the manner of Hoffmann's Baron von R., who travelled the world collecting views and, whenever he thought it necessary in order to enjoy or create a fine panorama, had trees cut down, branches stripped, humped surfaces smoothed, entire forests flattened and farms demolished, if any of these obstructed a fine view. But even destruction is a form of architecture, a deconstruction that follows certain rules and calculations, an art of disassembling and reassembling, or of creating another and different order. When a wall of foliage suddenly fell, opening out a vista towards a distant castle in the light of sunset, Baron von R. remained for a few minutes gazing upon the spectacle that he himself had staged, and then hurried away, never to return.

Every experience is the result of stringent method, even the transparence of a distant sunset for Baron von R. or the snow-fresh air that visits this bench in the Black Forest. It is in classifications that life flashes through so tantalizingly, in the registers that attempt to catalogue it and in so doing expose its irreducible residuum of mystery and enchantment. In the same way the project drawn up by these two effusive scholars, set out like Wittgenstein's *Tractatus* (1.1, 1.2, 2.11, 2.12 etc.), affords us in the truly minimal gaps between one number and the next a glimpse of the unlimited vicissitudes of travelling. It divides hotels into the classes of luxury, middle-class, simple, working-class, local, dockside, "charabancs welcome", peasant, princely, monastic, charity-supported, aristocratic, as well as hotels of the trade-guilds, the customs and excise, the post office and the carters' union. Only scientific tables really succeed in placing adequate stress on the metaphysical humour of everyday things and events, their connections and sequences. For example, in Section E, devoted to *Scenes* – such scenes, of course, as are likely to take place in hotels – at a certain point we read: "2.13. Erotica: – courtship – prostitution. 2.14. Ablutions. 2.15: Bedrooms. 2.16. Alarm-calls."

I have no idea which category of hotels would include the one at Neu-Eck in the Black Forest, only a mile or two from this bench; a hotel in which, twenty-three years ago, as I sat reading a small coaster, advertising Fürstenberg Beer (it was a cardboard disk with a sort of red dragon on a gold background rimmed with blue), the course of my life was decided. Departure and return, "le voyage pour connaître ma géographie", as that Parisian madman put it. The plaque, only a few steps from this bench, indicates the source of the Danube – or one of them. In fact it stresses the point that this is the principal source. River of melody: that is what Hölderlin called it: the deep-hidden parlance of the gods, the thoroughfare linking Europe and Asia, Germany and Greece, along which poetry and the word, in the times of myth, ascended to bring the sense of being to the German West. For Hölderlin there were still gods on the river-banks, hidden and misunderstood by the men of the night of exile and the alienation of modern times, but nonetheless living and present. Deep in the slumber of Germany, dulled by the prose of reality but destined to reawaken in some Utopian future, slept the poetry of the heart, of freedom, of reconciliation.

The river has many names. Among some peoples the words Danube and Ister were used respectively for the upper and lower courses, but sometimes for the entire length. Pliny, Strabo and Ptolemy wondered where the one ended and the other began: maybe in Illyria, or at the Iron Gates. The river, which Ovid called "bisnominis" or double-named, draws German culture, with its dream of an Odyssey of the spirit, towards the east, mingling it with other cultures in countless hybrid metamorphoses in which it finds its fulfilment and its fall. The German scholar who travels fitfully along the whole course of the river carries with him his baggage of fads and quotations; if the poet entrusts himself to his *bateau ivre*, his understudy tries to follow the advice of Jean Paul, who suggested that on the way one should gather and record not only visual images but old prefaces and playbills, railway-station gossip, epics and battles, funerary and metaphysical inscriptions, newspaper clippings, and notices pinned up in taverns and parish halls. *Memories, impressions, reflections and landscapes on a voyage to the Orient*, announces a title of Lamartine's. Reflections and impressions of whom? one may ask. When we travel alone, as happens only too often, we have to pay our way out of our own pocket; but occasionally life is good to us, and enables us to see the world, if only in brief snatches of time, with those four or five friends who will bear us witness on the Day of Judgment, and speak in our name.

Between one trip and the next we attempt to transfer the bulging files of notes onto the flat surface of paper, to get the bundles of stuff, the note-pads, the leaflets and the catalogues, down onto typewritten sheets. Literature as moving house; and as in every change of address something is lost and something else turns up in a "safe place" we had forgotten about. Indeed, we go almost like orphans, says Hölderlin in his poem on the sources of the Danube: the river flows on glittering in the sunlight like the current of life itself, but the feeling that it reflects back is an illusion afflicting the dazzled sight, like the non-existent luminous spots on the wall, the neon dazzle.

A tremor of nothingness sets fire to things, the tin cans left on the beach and the reflectors of motorcars, just as sunset makes the windows blaze. The river adds up to nothing and travelling is immoral: this is what Weininger said, as he was travelling. But the river is an old Taoist master, and along its banks it gives lessons on the great Wheel and the gaps between its spokes. In every journey there is at least a smattering of the South, with hours of relaxation, of idleness. Heedless of the orphans on its banks the Danube flows down towards the sea, towards the supreme conviction.

2. DONAUESCHINGEN VERSUS FURTWANGEN

Here rises the principal branch of the Danube, states the plaque by the source of the Breg. In spite of this lapidary claim the centuries-old dispute over the sources of the Danube is still raging, and is in fact responsible for heated contention between the towns of Furtwangen and Donaueschingen. To complicate matters, a bold hypothesis was recently set forth by Amedeo, highly esteemed sedimentologist and secret historian of red herrings. He proposes that the Danube is born from a tap. Without wishing to summarize the age-old library of publications on the subject – they stretch from Hecataeus, predecessor of Herodotus, to the issues of *Merian* magazine, on news-stands now – we should at least mention the aeons for which the source of the Danube was as unknown as that of the Nile, in whose waters it is in any case reflected and mingled, if not *in re* at least *in verbis*, in the comparisons and parallels between the two rivers which for centuries tread on each other's heels in learned commentaries.

The river's sources were the object of the investigations, conjectures or information of Herodotus, Strabo, Caesar, Pliny, Ptolemy, the Pseudo-Scymnus, Seneca, Mela and Eratosthenes. Its sources were imagined or located in the Hercynian Forest, in the land of the Hyperboreans, among the Celts or the Scythians, on Mount Abnoba or in the land of Hesperia, while other hypotheses mention a fork in the river, with one branch flowing into the Adriatic, along with divergent descriptions of the Black Sea estuaries. Whether it be from history or from myth – which has the Argonauts sailing down the Danube as far as the Adriatic – that we pass to prehistoric eras, our reconnaissance is left groping in the dark and lost in vastness, in geography on a titanic scale: the *Urdonau* in the Bernese Oberland, with its springs, where the peaks of the Jungfrau and the Eiger now rise, the primordial Danube into which flowed the Ur-Rhine, the Ur-Neckar and the Ur-Main, and which towards the middle of the Tertiary, in the Eocene Age, between sixty and twenty million years ago, had its mouth where Vienna now stands, flowing into a gulf of Thetis, primal mother of ocean, in the

Sarmatic Sea which covered the whole of south-eastern Europe.

Not particularly sensitive to the archaic and its Indo-European prefixes, Amedeo skips the Urdonau and joins in the present dispute between Furtwangen and Donaueschingen, two Black Forest towns standing 35 km apart. Officially, as is well known, the sources of the Danube are at Donaueschingen, the inhabitants of which guarantee their originality and authenticity in their by-laws. Even in the times of the Emperor Tiberius the little spring that bubbled out of that hillside was celebrated as the source of the Danube, and apart from this it is at Donaueschingen that we find the confluence of two rivers, the Breg and the Brigach; and according to the current opinion, confirmed by guide-books, Public Authority and proverbs, this meeting of the waters constitutes the beginning of the Danube. The start of the river that creates and encloses what is known as Mitteleuropa is an integral part of the ancient domain of princes, along with the Fürstenberg castle, the court library which contains the manuscripts of the *Song of the Niebelungs* and *Parsifal*, the beer also called after the local princes, and the music festivals which created the reputation of Hindemith.

"Hier entspringt die Donau," this is the source of the Danube, declares the plaque in the Fürstenberg park at Donaueschingen. But the *other* plaque, which Dr Öhrlein, who owns the land where the Breg rises, has displayed at the source of the Breg, explains that, of all other possible sources, this is the stream that starts farthest from the Black Sea – 2,888 km away to be precise – 48.5 km further upstream than Donaueschingen. Dr Öhrlein, whose river-source lies a few kilometres from Furtwangen, has brandished all manner of certified documents in his battle against Donaueschingen. This is a minor and somewhat tardy repercussion of the French Revolution in the backwoods of "German wretchedness": an example of the middle-class professional man and small landowner rising against the feudal nobility and its coats of arms. The good burghers of Furtwangen have backed Dr Öhrlein in a body, and everyone remembers the day when the Burgomaster of Furtwangen, followed by a swarm of his fellow-citizens, disdainfully poured a bottle of water from the Breg into the spring at Donaueschingen.

3. THE REPORT

Amedeo's report, contained in a minutely detailed letter – which I have brought with me in order to do a spot-check before talking to him about it when he joins us, which should be soon – accepts the Furtwangen claim, albeit with a few variants, according to which the source of the Danube is the Breg; and that therefore the Breg is the real Danube, while the Brigach, being less far from the Black Sea, is a tributary of the Breg. The report takes the form of an incisive epistle, the scientific exactitude of which is garnished with humanistic elegance and threatened by melancholy. In it we recognize not only the author of studies on landslides and vast shifts of terrain, milestones of sedimentology, but also the most retiring and elusive author of less well-known texts, such as the *Encomium of Absent-Mindedness*, and of troubled yet punctilious translations of German Romantic poetry.

One realizes from the report that what first attracted him must have been the inn, that *Gasthaus* with sloping roof and wooden walls which stands near the source of the Breg. There are many hostelries in his report, which is the true account of an expedition, like those made by explorers hunting for the sources of the Nile, and he therefore notes all the stages of the journey; there are inns with stone dwarves in the garden, or leafy branches above the door, or ancient pianolas, or wooden ladders leading to the loft. Between the lines of the report, written by a man otherwise so amiable and reassuring, there is a marked attempt at flight, the corrupt excursion of someone apparently in search of a hiding-place, a place in which to vanish. Those inns are cheerful spots for chatter and tippling, but in the somewhat darker corners of the *Stube* or in the bedrooms with their sloping ceilings the author is seeking something quite different: the witch's hut in the woods, the retreats of our childhood. But unlike Tristram Shandy, who feared he would never manage to catch up with himself, it is as if the author of the report wanted to lose himself and provide himself with misleading directions.

He arrived at the source from Furtwangen, where he had paused to visit the Clock Museum, and wandered about for a couple of hours among thousands of clock-faces of every shape and size, cogwheels and hands, robots and pianos set in motion by the passing of the hours, and "forests of pendulums", as he mentions with particular stress. In his letter, that isochronous movement that surrounded him on all sides seems the secret rhythm of life, the automatic scansion of a time that is perfectly pure and perfectly empty. Existence, in that letter, appears to be a motion self-contained and forever returning to the beginning, as if between the two extreme and recurring points of the pendulum's swing there were nothing at all, nothing other than the abstract oscillation itself and the force of gravity that draws it down; so that in the end, when the wear and tear of the years has done its work, the body attains an irrevocable state of quietude.

His little excursion to the springs was almost certainly a means of escape from that feeling of stalemate, a subterfuge used to skirt round his own tortuous depths with a good brisk walk in the open air. To distract your gaze from your inmost being, to apply it to analysing the identity of others or the reality and the nature of things – there is nothing better.

How is it that phenomena appear on the horizon of the world and of the mind? "This book is blue and this ashtray is a Christmas present," writes Paolo Bozzi in his book *Unity, Identity, and Chance* (1969). But he immediately stresses the difference between the two predicates, between the visible property of that blue – which reaches the cerebral cortex by way of electromagnetic waves and the impulses of the optic nerve – and the quality of being a Christmas present, which exists solely in the mind of the person who received it and simply does not exist for an uninformed observer coming into the room at that moment.

Is that water bubbling up on Dr Öhrlein's land really the source of the Danube? Or is it merely that it is known (thought, believed, claimed) to be the source of the Danube? Amedeo, clearly, wanted to go back to the things themselves and their initial impact on the consciousness. He therefore set out from Furtwangen determined to describe the sources of the Danube as they offer themselves to observation, so as to grasp them in their pure form, having already put brackets around all preconceived theories.

His report begins scrupulously and convincingly. The water of the Breg issues from the ground in a small dip in the hillside, the slope of which continues to rise above the spring for several dozen yards. Amedeo follows the upward slope, along with Maddalena and Maria Giuditta, and all three end up with sopping wet shoes, socks and trouser legs. The grass in that meadow is steeped in water; the whole surface of the soil is sodden and flooded by countless little rivulets. In those circumstances the two sisters move, and are drenched, with more grace than Amedeo, whose charm consists largely in his reassuringly massive bulk, much like that, for example, of Pierre Bezukov. His pen, however, is fully capable of such grace, settling lightly and precisely on details as a butterfly settles on flowers. Phenomenology is right: the pure appearance of things is good and true, and the surface of the earth is more real than its gelatinous inner hollows. St Augustine was partly wrong in exhorting us not to step outside our own selves; for anyone who remains constantly within loses himself in daydreams, and ends by burning incense to some genie arising from the refuse of his fears, as vacuous and insidious as the nightmares warned off by evening prayer.

In his pages about that meadow on the hillside our sedimentologist strikes a mighty vein. He finds the classical fertility of the epic writer who, in dealing with details, grasps the presence of a universal law binding them all into a single harmonious unity. The sciences help us not to lose our heads, to travel forward, and to find that the world, after all, is good and securely constructed. Anyone with a solid education in science eventually feels at home, even among things which change and continually lose their own identity.

Perhaps a little reluctant – maybe anxious – to belong to this category, Amedeo (as he says in his report) set himself to answer the question: "Which is the real continuation of the river uphill from the spring?" Ever since Heraclitus the river has been *the* image for the questioning of identity, beginning with that old conundrum as to whether one can or cannot put one's foot in the same river twice. Descartes, too, with his famous bit of hard, cold, white wax which, held near the fire, changed in shape, size, compactness and colour, while remaining a piece of wax: it was on this very river, on the Danube at Neuberg on November 10th 1619, in a room heated for the winter thanks to the generosity of the Duke of Bavaria, that he began to think in clear and distinct terms.

The water that emerges in the little hollow of the spring quite clearly comes from the sodden meadow a few steps further up the hill; evidence of this is a photograph showing Maddalena leaning on Maria Giuditta's shoulder and holding up a finely-proportioned, sopping wet foot. The soil digests the innumerable tiny trickles, filters them, and renders them back to the broad light of day where the spring itself rises, immediately beside Dr Öhrlein's plaque. The scholar Amedeo thereupon questioned himself about the source of the water which saturated the meadow, and which was therefore the Danube. He followed the course of the rivulets that trickle down the slope, and within a hundred yards he found that he had arrived at an eighteenth-century house, flanked by a woodshed. Also before his eyes was "a long, projecting gutter, or maybe even a pipe, which passes close to the woodshed and gushes out abundant water in the direction of the hollow", which is, of course, situated lower down. "There is no question about it," he continues, "the water that runs down the slope into the hollow where the spring is comes from the gutter, which is uphill from it. Water can only flow downwards; it cannot flow up a slope or a pipe (or is that the only place in the world where the most straightforward law in classic physics fails to function?)."

If the river is visible water, exposed to the sky and to the eyes of humanity, that gutter is Danube. So far the report is above criticism. If one goes to the banks of a river at different places and at different times, pointing one's finger at the water each time and saying "Danube" – we owe this theory of definition by demonstration to the logician Quine – we eventually arrive at the identity of the Danube. The Danube exists, there is no doubt about it. If Amedeo clambers panting up the slope, pointing his index finger and saying "Danube" over and over again, indicating the source of the Breg, the rivulets in the meadow which feed it, and the gutter which feeds the rivulets, then that is the Danube.

But who supplies the gutter? What invisible fluvial divinity? It is at this point that the report takes a tumble, because the scientist yields to a gossipy approximation: he makes use of hearsay. Maria Giuditta, he tells us, with her long legs, was the first to reach the house at the top. She looked in at a window on the ground floor and questioned the grumpy old lady of the house. From her she learnt that the water reaches the gutter from a basin, and that this basin is constantly full because of a tap that no one ever succeeds in turning off; and that this is in turn connected to "a lead pipe, which may well be as old as the house, and which ends up God knows where."

No need to comment on the rank amateurism of such language. It reminds one of the publications on the sources of the Nile penned by the reckless Captain John Speke, which – according to his rival Richard Burton, as well as James M'Queen, an authoritative and biased member of the Royal Geographical Society – were a downright discredit to geography. Our scholar, though perfectly accustomed to checking hypotheses by experiment, did not even take the trouble to check up on the existence of this tap; indeed, he only came to learn of it from someone else, who in turn had only heard it mentioned in passing by a third party, and one whose reliability is impossible to judge. Even Herodotus, all that time ago, trusted his informants only if they were eye-witnesses. It may be that Amedeo was put off the scent by a question shouted out by Maddalena, who was following along behind, lily-white and beautiful: "And what do you suppose would happen if the tap were turned off?" The mental image of Bratislava, Budapest and Belgrade completely waterless, of ancient objects and skeletons and the immense bed of the empty river, must surely have carried his mind towards metaphysical dimensions of causality. What will happen there if something happens here? Needless to say nothing will happen at all; but all the same . . .

4. MORALISTS AND GEOMETRICIANS AT THE SOURCES OF THE BREG

In the first place, that tap does not exist. It is not difficult to follow Amedeo's itinerary. I take the few steps from my bench downhill to the source of the Breg, then, sousing my shoes and socks, climb up through the meadow towards the house. The water glitters in the grass, the spring flows quietly out, the green of the trees is good, and so is the smell. The traveller feels rather clumsy and small, aware of the superior objectivity in which he is framed. Is it possible that all those little trickles in a field are the Danube, the river of superlatives, as it has been called, with its basin of 817,000 square kilometres and the two hundred thousand million cubic metres of water which it pours out into the Black Sea every year? A few hundred metres further down the valley the stream is fleet and swiftly shining, and already merits the epithet of "sweet-flowing", which Hesiod applies to the Ister.

My steps towards the house are like sentences on a sheet of paper; my foot tries out the waterlogged soil and avoids a puddle as the pen encircles and crosses the blank spaces of the page, circumventing a clot in heart and thought, and carries on. Writing ought to be like those waters flowing through the grass – full of spontaneity, fresh and timid but inexhaustible. Such a humble, bashful song of life resembles the absorbed, profound expression on the face of Maddalena, not the dryness and vexation of writing, a watercourse where the flow is often mismanaged.

The soul is a stingy thing, as Kepler chided himself, and takes refuge in the little corners of literature rather than inquiring into the Deity's design for Creation. Those who entrust their being solely to paper may discover in the end that they are mere silhouettes cut from tissue paper, likenesses that quiver and shrivel in the wind. It is this wind that the traveller longs for – adventure, the gallop to the hilltop. Like Kepler Mathematicus, he wants to fall in with God's plans and the laws of nature, and not just follow his own idiosyncrasies; and he would also like the short climb to the house to be some glorious advance, like the Tigers of Mompracem scaling the heights under enemy fire, to conquer and to free their native land. The wind, however, does not blow in our faces but at our backs. It thrusts us away, far from the house where we were born, and from the Promised Land. And so it is that the traveller plunges deeper into his own allergies, his own imbalances, hoping that through those chinks slashed in the back-cloth of daily living, there might be at least a puff of wind or a draught coming from what is truly life, though concealed by the screen of reality. Literary manoeuvres then become a strategy to protect those badly patched tatters in the stage-curtain of distance, to prevent those minimal chinks from closing up altogether. A writer's existence, said Monsignor Della Casa, is a state of war.

I climb the slope and reach the house. I climb it? I reach it? The use of the first person singular is decidedly questionable, and a traveller, faced by the objectivity of things, is especially hampered to find himself tripping over the personal pronoun. Victor Hugo, strolling along the Rhine, would willingly have thrown the thing away, fed up with this Stinking Egowort that sprouts and spreads from one's pen. And yet, another traveller no less illustrious, nor less hostile towards the egotism of words and pronouns (Stendhal touring France), said that it is, after all, a convenient way to tell a tale.

So I look at the house, I walk all round it, I scrutinize it, and I compare it with the description in the letter. The problem confronting any branch of knowledge is that of making the Southern Seas, the endless heaving extent of them, fit in with the blue map the "Southern Seas". Little inclined to exactitude, your man of letters prefers to ramble on a bit, to come up with a few moral critiques of the supposed exactitude of science. "We are perpetually moralists," said Doctor Johnson, "but we are geometricians only by chance."

The truth is, there is no tap in the house. It's an old enough house: the kitchen bears the date 1715. An old crone, springing into view on the doorstep, rather snappily warns us not to steal, but to listen rather (for two and a half marks per head) to a tape describing the blackened fireplace, the eighteenth-century implements, and the customs and usages of days of yore. We place five marks in the pit of her hand, which resembles the bark of a centuries-old tree and demands a certain respect, not to say awe. The kitchen is black all over, a cavern odorous with bacon-flitches and with the past. The voice on the tape-recorder is the voice of the woman herself, who thus saves herself the trouble of telling the same old story over and over again. In fact she confines herself to making authoritative gestures to put finishing touches to the discourse. She is old, irascible, lonely, and accustomed to her solitude, indifferent towards that passer-by called life and to the dark of the blackened kitchen where she has always lived. It is only when her own recorded voice mentions Sulina, the infinitely distant mouth of the Danube on the Black Sea, that her expression softens a little.

There is no tap, no tap at all, either in the house or outside. The water that drenches the meadow in which rises the source of the Breg comes out of a pipe stuck upright in the earth. Slightly higher up are a few patches of white, and it may be that the melting snow, along with other local rivulets, contributes to the volume of water which keeps the meadow sodden. In any case, the water rises through the pipe and overflows. The old girl has put a hollowed-out log under the outlet of the pipe, forming a kind of gutter. The tube pours water into this primitive gutter, which in turn empties into a bucket. Here the old woman collects what water she needs. The bucket is always full, and the excess water, pouring in unceasingly, streams down the slope, floods and inundates the meadow, and drenches the land from which, in the hollow down the hill, springs the source of the Breg, which is to say of the Danube.

This is not a new discovery at all. In his great work of 1785 the Danubian Antiquarius (pseudonym of Johann Herm. Dielhelm) speaks of a house on Mount Abnoba, from the roof of which one gutter pours water into the Danube, and the other into the Rhine. He also mentions, further, an inn at the highest point of the Freiburg road, known by the name of Kalteherberg, Cool hostel, the roof of which slopes two ways, one side pouring its water into the Rhine, the other into the Danube. So the matter of gutters has from ancient times been a *Leitmotif* in the debated question of the sources of the river. Certain it is that in the profoundly erudite discourse of the Antiquarius the gutters pour their water into a Danube that was already in existence, whereas according to Amedeo's theory, apart from his blunder about the tap, that gutter *is* the source of the Danube, is the Danube itself. We know so very little, and before getting on our hind legs and spouting about the truth, we ought to debate problems at least twice, as did the Goths who for this reason, so appealed to Laurence Sterne; that is, once when drunk and again when they had slept off their hangovers. Anyway, the Goths also took their oaths on the god Ister, and in some inscriptions in Rhaetia the god Danubius is put on the same level as Jupiter Optimus Maximus.

5. MITTELEUROPA: HINTERNATIONAL OR ALL-GERMAN?

Do we raise our hands and swear on the deity Danube that the gutter is the Danube? Well, what is missing in this business is the most basic factor of all. The gutter which feeds the spring is itself fed by the spring. So we find ourselves at once in the very midst of Danubian Culture, in the world of Parallel Action, the committee invented by Robert Musil. In order to celebrate the seventieth anniversary of Francis Joseph's reign it sets out to sing the praises of the founding principle of Austrian civilization – and indeed that of Europe *tout court* – but fails to find any such thing, thus discovering that the whole reality of the matter has gone up in smoke, that its elaborate edifice is built on thin air.

The gutter which bathes the soil from which it is fed may be the captious deduction of scholars taking the day off, but what is certain is that at Donaueschingen, the accredited source, the Danube flows into the Brigach, that is to say, into one of its own tributaries. In the round bowl which collects the waters of the spring there is a plaque which states that at one time the real Danube, the tiny original rivulet, ran parallel with the Brigach, after two kilometres joining the Brigach itself and the Breg, forming a single stream known, in fact, as the Danube. But it adds that since 1820 there has been an underground conduit which taps the waters of the primary source and channels them into the Brigach. The real Danube is therefore two hundred metres in length, a minute tributary of the Brigach, though the official Danube starts a little further on, at the above-mentioned confluence of the Brigach, the Breg and (strictly speaking) also the trickle of the Musel, a mere streamlet running down from Bad Dürmheim, that one can jump across. Moreover, 20 or 30 kilometres downstream, at Immendingen, the Danube disappears, at least in part: it falls into fissures in the rocks and re-emerges 40 kilometres further south, where it is called the Aach, and flows into Lake Constance and therefore into the Rhine (the sources of which are as disputed as those of the Danube). The Danube is therefore, in some measure, a tributary of the Rhine, flowing not into the Black Sea but into the North Sea – the triumph of the Rhine over the Danube, revenge of the Niebelungs over the Huns, predominance of Germany over Central Europe.

Ever since the *Song of the Niebelungs* the Rhine and the Danube have confronted and challenged each other. The Rhine is Siegfried, symbol of Germanic *virtus* and purity, the loyalty of the Niebelungs, chivalric heroism, dauntless love of the destiny of the Germanic soul. The Danube is Pannonia, the kingdom of Attila, the eastern, Asiatic tide which at the end of the *Song of the Niebelungs* overwhelms Germanic values: when the Burgundians cross it on their way to the treacherous Hunnish court, their fate – a Germanic fate – is sealed.

The Danube is often enveloped in a symbolic anti-German aura. It is the river along which different peoples meet and mingle and cross-breed, rather than being, as the Rhine is, a mythical custodian of the purity of the race. It is the river of Vienna, Bratislava, Budapest, Belgrade and of Dacia, the river which – as Ocean encircled the world of the Greeks – embraces the Austria of the Hapsburgs, the myth and ideology of which have been symbolized by a multiple, supranational culture. It embraces the Empire in which the sovereign addressed himself to "my peoples" and the national anthem was sung in eleven different tongues. The Danube is German-Magyar-Slavic-Romanic-Jewish Central Europe, polemically opposed to the Germanic *Reich*; it is a "hinternational" ecumene, for which in Prague Johannes Urzidil praised it; it is a hinterworld "behind the nations".

The Danube-Aach version of the story appears, on the other hand, to be the symbol of that all-German ideology which viewed the multinational Hapsburg monarchy as a branch of Teutonic civilization, a stratagem or an instrument of Reason for the cultural Germanization of Central and Eastern Europe. Such a thesis was maintained, for example, by Heinrich von Srbik, the great Austrian historian who sang the praises of Prince Eugène of Savoy, was averse to Frederick the Great and Prussianism, and ended up a National Socialist.

This "hinternational" Central Europe, nowadays idealized as the harmony between different peoples, was without doubt a very real thing in the latter days of the Hapsburg Empire, a tolerant association of peoples understandably lamented when it was over, not least when compared with the totalitarian barbarism that replaced it in the lands of the Danube between the two World Wars. All the same, the Central European mission of the Hapsburgs was in some measure a makeshift ideology, arising from the failures of Austrian policy in Germany. The wars between Maria Theresa and Frederick II of Prussia severed what Heinrich von Srbik, in a book published in 1942, called *Deutsche Einheit*, German oneness. The split between Austria and Germany widened increasingly during the period which followed – from the Napoleonic Wars to the Austro-Prussian War of 1866; a period that witnessed the decline of Hapsburg power and above all of its leadership in Germany. Incapable of bringing about the unity of Germany, an ideal now headed by Prussia, the Austria of the Hapsburgs sought a new mission and a new identity in the supra-national empire, the crucible of peoples and of cultures.

At the root of the Hapsburg myth, which contrasts the Danube with the Rhine, there lies this historical wound, and as the wound grows worse, the myth grows more elaborate. During the First World War, at the beginning of the end, Hofmannsthal extolled "The Austrian", praising his traditional ability to laugh at himself and his sceptical attitude towards history, and contrasting him with the state-worshipping Prussian, apostle of dialectical thought and virtuously fanatical. In the 1920s and 1930s the identity crisis of the tiny, newborn Austrian Republic, orphan of the Empire, stimulated and intensified categorical theory-mongering about "Austrian-ness", and disser-tations on "The Austrian Man", everlasting and utterly distinct from your German.

Austrian Fascism, in its attempt to stand up to Nazism, added to this tradition despite some profound inconsistencies. Refusal to be iden-tified with the German element gives rise to the Austrians' constant talk about their own identity; the drift of this is that there is no such thing as an Austrian nationality, as Baron Andrian-Werburg asserted in the last century. Such introspection is ultimately concentrated into an endear-ing self-denigration, the discovery that "being Austrian" is something indefinable. Indeed in this very factor they find their own essence – all the more gratifying for being anomalous.

Does the Danube lead further and further from the Rhine? Or else is it fated to appear as an emissary from those German waters to the east? The numerous political plans for Central Europe, put forward at

various times, oscillate between schemes for multinational confeder-
ations, such as those of Franz or Popovici, and programmes for
German supremacy, such as those of Naumann. Writers almost always
tend to see only the "hinternational" Danube, while historians also take
account of the German-ness of Danubian Austria, with the Rheingold
often gleaming in the blue Danube.

The vast debate on Austria among political scientists and historians
hinges largely on the role of the German element, on its relation to the
other nationalities in the Empire, on the proximity and/or distance
existing between "Germans" and "Austrians". The Austro-German
outlook does not simply mean German nationalism: at certain moments in history – as after the catastrophe of 1918, when it was the
democratic and socialist elements that were in favour of union with
Germany – it has indicated identification with the culture which
appeared likely to bring progress, as had happened in the times of
Joseph II and nineteenth-century liberalism. The *Anschluss* of 1938 is
the tragic, grotesque perversion of this symbiosis between German
leadership and the spirit of progress.

The disputed link between Central Europe and Germanism frequently becomes a dramatic theme, as Arduino Agnelli noted in the case
of Heinrich von Srbik. The latter viewed the Hapsburg monarchy as a
synthesis between the universal idea, the imperial idea, and the Central
European idea, which in his opinion exalted German universalism, the
age-old Germanic historical mission in the Danube area, and awareness of that mission. Srbik opposes the *kleindeutsch* or "little German"
ideal, meaning the identification of Germanism with Prussianism, and
also the *grossdeutsch* principle which exalts the Viennese tradition. In
fact he opposes every form of "being Austrian" in the name of an
"all-German" outlook. According to this view of things the idea of
Austria – and all Central Europe, to which Srbik devoted a famous
essay in 1937 – appears as "an essentially German idea"; Austria "is part
of the German soul, of German glory and of German toil," and the
mission of the Hapsburg Empire was to assert the superior Germanic
idea in Central and Eastern Europe, to create in that area a universal
civilization, one that would be Holy, Roman, Imperial and Germanic.

As one descends the Danube, does one then pass through some
Carolingian macrocosm? Srbik was not a racist: German civilization
for him meant the Christian universality of the Holy Roman Empire,
which was supposed to transcend all states and impose its higher
ethical values on all policies based on naked power. More than once he

speaks of the German people living peaceably side by side with the
other peoples of Central Europe, of the recognition of the full rights of
life to every nation. But for him the German people is indisputably the
fittest for the guidance of Central Europe, the only one which can be
spokesman for civilization and universality: the Holy Roman Empire
is of German nationality.

Srbik was not interested in a racial-biological element. On the
contrary, he favoured mixed marriages and ethnic mixtures; he did not
forget that his own family, though Germanized for generations, was of
Czech origin. But for him only German blood was the cement of
civilization, of *Kulturnation* in Central Europe. Members of other
nations could rise to the heights of culture, but only by becoming
Germanized, becoming German in fact, as had happened to his own
family. The alternative was to stay at the level of their own nationality,
that is, at a lower level, respected but subordinate. The Slavs could
become Germans, just as barbarians could become Roman citizens, but
higher culture, *Kultur* itself, could only be German, as it had once been
Graeco-Roman.

To this German universalism – "desperately German" said Thomas
Mann, to indicate the tangle of frequently contorted spiritual values,
passion for order and a secret leaning towards chaos – there is linked a
great phase of European civilization, the intensity of a *Kultur* which
combined in itself the tension between life and value, between existence and order. The parabola described by Srbik certainly demonstrates how when German supremacy is threatened, this universalism
can get twisted into the most chauvinistic barbarities. The "German
destiny", gloomy with pathos and silent spirituality, has above all been
a way of living out the clash between Germans and Slavs in the vast
territory and throughout the centuries during which they have been
face to face. Nazism is the unforgettable lesson of the perversion of the
German presence in Central Europe. Yet this very German presence
there was a great chapter in history, and its eclipse a great tragedy,
which Nazism cannot make us forget. Today, questioning oneself
about Europe means asking oneself how one relates to Germany.

We have all been brought up to see the *Weltgeist* in terms of the big
battalions, and we ought to learn from Herder to understand it even
where it is – or seems – still asleep or barely in its infancy. Maybe we
shall never be really safe until we learn to feel, in an almost physical
sense, that every nation is destined to have its day, and that there are
not, in any absolute sense, greater or lesser civilizations, but rather a

succession of flowerings. Living and reading mean thinking about that "history of the human spirit" at all times and in all countries which Herder wanted to trace through the events of world literature, without sacrificing to any one single model the idea of the perennial universality of this spirit, but also without sacrificing any of the varied forms which have embodied it. He loved the perfection of Greek form, but this did not make him underestimate the song of the Latvian folk-festival.

Like all the writers of the *Sturm und Drang*, Herder loved rivers, the youthful, impetuous torrents rushing downwards with their fecund vitality. Looking now at this slender, newborn Danube I wonder whether, as I follow it all the way to the delta, among different peoples and nations, I shall pass through an arena of bloody battles or else among the chorus of a human race united, despite everything, in the variety of its languages and its cultures. I wonder if what I have to expect is a string of battlefields, past, present, and future, or that "Danubian confederation" in the firm unity of which the great Hungarian aristocrat Count Károlyi never for one moment ceased to believe – not even when his faith in it forced him, as an exile in London, to sell his raincoat to pay his grocer's bill.

6. NOTEENTIENDO

Perhaps the promise of this innocent water is deceitful, and such a universe does not exist. A visit to a concentration camp seems to ridicule all faith in the great tree of humanity imagined by Herder as one harmonious whole. Most likely that image, and the sense of fulfilment that we derive from it, is merely a requirement of our own, superimposed upon the insensate chaos of events. In any case, the "Danubial" journey of a meticulous traveller, as Griselini put it in the eighteenth century, ought to come to an end very soon. Tomorrow evening, here on the Breg, we are expecting the others; but, impatient to check on the hypothesis of this premature ending, we make a rapid excursion to Immendingen, where the Danube, as we have said, sinks into fissures in the rocks to re-emerge mingled with the waters of the Aach, and to flow with them into Lake Constance. A kind gentleman walking along the bank tells us that at that point, in summertime, the river-bed is completely dry. But at Ulm, only a few kilometres further, the river – called the Danube – is broad and navigable even in the summer. In summer, therefore, the Danube rises much further down, at Tuttlingen, beyond the point we are at this evening; it comes from trickles and tributaries from the hills around, which have heard nothing of Donaueschingen or of Furtwangen.

The Danube too, like all of us, is a *Noteentiendo*, a Don't-understand-you, like the figure portrayed in one of the sixteen pictures on a panel called "Las Castas", a kind of Snakes-and-Ladders of love and progeny that I remember having seen on a wall in the Museum of Mexico City. Each of the sixteen squares of the panel shows three figures: the man and the woman whose different blood cries out imperiously to mingle, and a tranquil child born of their union. In the next picture the child is grown up, and the protagonist of the next marriage, from which is born another son destined to continue the chain of mixtures: the Mestizo, son of the Spaniard and the Indian woman, the Castizo his son, the Mulatto to whom a Spanish woman presents a smartly got-up Morisco, and so on and so forth until we get to the Chino, the Lobo, the Gibaro son of the Lobo and the China, to the Albarazado son of the Mulatta woman and the Gibaro and father of a Cambujo, who is father in turn to a Sanbaigo ... The panel sets out to make a rigorous classification and distinction – even in modes of dress – between the social and racial castes, but it ends up by involuntarily singing the praises of the capricious and rebellious game of love, the great wrecker of all closed social hierarchies, the scatterer, the shuffler of every perfectly ordered pack of cards, that muddles up diamonds with clubs or spades so as to make the game enjoyable, or even playable.

In the next-to-last square, the fruit of the love between the Tente En El Aire and the Mulatta baffles the nomenclaturial talents of our anonymous classifier, who proceeds to define him as "Noteentiendo". The Danube that both is and is not, that is born in several places of several parents, reminds us that, thanks to the complex, hidden fabric to which we owe our existence, each of us is a Noteentiendo, as are the Praguese with German names or the Viennese with Czech ones. But on this evening, along the river which they tell us sometimes disappears in summer, the step which treads with mine is as unmistakable as that watercourse, and in the flow of it, as I follow the curve of the banks, perhaps I know who I am.

More subjective and less inclined to private historiography, the mild-mannered, curly-haired Sigmund von Birken saw the curves of the Danube – which whimsically twists first to the east, then south, and after that northwards – as a stratagem on the part of Divine Providence to check the advance of the Turks. This baroque poet's work on the Danube, published in 1684, deals with the banks, the provinces, and the ancient and modern names of the towns on the river banks, from the sources to the sea. Having with the greatest diligence collected a vast mass of erudite material, the author writes that our earthly homeland is an abode of imperfection, and the names which he has been unable to reconstruct with any certainty he therefore leaves blank, inviting the reader to fill in the spaces from his own experience and with due feeling for his own precariousness.

Perhaps writing is really filling in the blank spaces in existence, that nullity which suddenly yawns wide open in the hours and the days, and appears between the objects in the room, engulfing them in unending desolation and insignificance. Fear, as Canetti has written, invents names so as to distract itself. The traveller reads and takes note of the names, of stations his train passes through, at the corners of the streets where his footsteps lead him; and he goes on his way with a breath of relief, satisfied with that rhythmic order of nothingness.

Sigmund von Birken sought for the real names of things and set off on his travels, as he tells us, to observe for himself the source of the Danube, which so many had written about but so few had taken the trouble to go and see. He was not entirely convinced by the *Cosmographia* of Sebastian Münster, which ascribed the origin of the Danube to the Flood (XI, 11), and he wished to find out whether the name of the river could in truth be attributed to the sound, the roar of the waters at the sources, as was asserted by a number of etymologies. His baroque taste for witticisms and extravagances could not, however, induce him to be satisfied with the image of the great river left dry-bedded by the turning off of a tap.

7. HOMUNCULUS

This jest, says Gigi, seated before a bottle of Gutedel at the inn near the Breg – the inn where the *disjecta membra* of the company are if only for the moment reunited – could only occur to a son of our own century, to someone who doubts whether Nature still exists, whether she is the enigmatic mistress of the universe or has not perhaps been ousted by

Artifice. Not for nothing, he continues, is the Danube being threatened at this very moment by plans for the great hydro-electric plant between Vienna and Hainburg, a plant which – according to the protests of the Green Party – would destroy the ecological balance of the "Donauauen", the flourishing lands which flank the river, with their tropical exuberance of flora, of fauna, of life. Gigi, an essayist of full-blooded, melancholy classicism, but above all an obstinate gourmet always ready to pick a bone with someone, is amongst other things a little out of patience, partly because Maria Giuditta, in an attempt to defend, albeit approximately, the results of last year's reconnaissance on the hillside, came out point-blank with the old cliché "to see the light at the end of the tunnel", which is always enough to make him fly off the handle.

For Goethe, Gigi goes on to say, the unnatural probably did not exist. Goethe's Nature embraces and enfolds all things, and it is she who with elusive irony causes and creates all forms, even those which apparently contradict her and which to men appear "unnatural". Even the most deprived, sterile individual, who thinks of himself as banished from her bosom, belongs to her without knowing it, and plays the part which she has assigned to him in the everlasting pageant: the tap and the gutter are vassals of the river-god.

But, around the table at the inn near the Breg, someone is inclined to be doubtful. That *second* nature which surrounds us – the jungle of symbols, of intermediaries, of constructions – arouses the suspicion that there is no longer any primal nature behind it, and that artifice and various kinds of bio-engineering have counterfeited and supplanted her supposedly eternal laws. Austrian culture, in fact, born in the homespace of the Danube, has with disillusioned clarity denounced the falsity of post-modernism, discarding it as stupid nonsense while accepting it as inevitable.

Indeed even Goethe in his late, more enigmatical work, did not overlook that fear: in the Second Part of *Faust* he not only tells the story of Homunculus, the man created in a laboratory, but he conjures up the vision of a total triumph of the unnatural and the defeat and disappearance of the ancient Mother, mimicked and replaced by fashion, artificial products, and false appearances. In the transition to the modern and post-modern, that is the Second Part of *Faust*, the taps are already more living and tangible than are the rivers, and their system of pipes can at any moment cut off the supply of the waters of life, as threatened in the Book of Revelation. The anguished protests against the power-station planned near Hainburg speak of desiccation both of land and of life, of a maternal *amnion* drained and sterilized, of the muddy, primordial jungle of the *Auen* that would vanish for ever.

The loafers who sit splitting hairs in that inn on the Breg are, in their heart of hearts, afraid of having been engendered like Homunculus, and of being liable, in the humus of their hearts, to be desiccated like the bed of the bone-dry river which they delight in dwelling upon. All the same, in secret, they put some hopes in the smile that Goethe kept in reserve even when faced by the Carnival of Artifice so pitilessly portrayed in *Faust*. For us there at the inn, as for everyone else, the dilemma is the one posed by Goethe in his old age, but in Mephistophelean fashion not resolved: is great, creative Nature a limitless horizon embracing even those epochal events in which men lose sight of her, or has she also ended up on the carnival-float of all things spurious beyond which there is nothing whatever? Is the atomic bomb a heinous invention of humanity endangering an eternal harmony, or is it a minute phenomenon imitating, on an absurdly reduced scale, the fissions and explosions taking place all along on God's life-giving sun?

This antithesis, it must be said, leaves us feeling a trifle chilly there at the inn, for even if the much-trumpeted end of time were to be nothing but the cloudburst that puts a rather early end to summer, it would still be the end of our own sweet season. The legs of the waitress who serves us, with the clogs going back and forth over the wooden floor to the greater glory of God and to the edification of those present, are more than sufficient reason to stay in this world a little longer – or even simply in this inn, listening to Gigi holding the floor, and watching the faces around him. Maria Giuditta is busying herself with sausages and mustard, Francesca is listening in silence, insignificant and fascinating like Fontane's Effi Briest: the allurement of water, seeming to run soft and clear as the stream just there beyond, concealing nothing, a bright clear surface like that of a calm sea barely ruffled to froth by wind, more unfathomable than the depths that display their cavernous obscurities, and evoking a gentle, a reticent infinity.

In mountain torrents the young Goethe envisaged fresh, impetuous youthfulness rampaging towards the plains to make them fertile. In the period of the *Sturm und Drang*, with its pre-revolutionary hopes, the river was the symbol of genius, of the vital, creative force of progress. In the fifth volume of the *Encyclopédie* "l'enthousiasme" is likened to a narrow stream that flows, and grows, and winds, and becomes ever greater and more powerful until at last it thrusts its way into the ocean, "having brought richness and fertility to the fortunate lands which it has bathed." But a few decades later, Grillparzer, the great nineteenth-century poet of Austria, in lines of a quite different tone dreamt of stemming the flow of a stream, for he saw it not only growing but losing its way in history, losing the tiny but harmonious peace of its clear, untroubled infancy, becoming restless and confused, dissolving finally in the nullity of the sea.

The Danube is an Austrian river and Austrian also is a distrust in history, which resolves contradictions by simply eliminating them; distrust in the synthesis which surpasses and annuls the limits of the future, which brings death closer. It may be that to us today old Austria often seems a congenial country because it was the country of men who doubted that their world could have a future. They did not wish to resolve the contradictions of the old empire, but rather to postpone their solution, because they were aware that any solution would have meant the destruction of a number of elements essential to the multifariousness of the empire, and hence the end of the empire itself.

To reach the dell of the Breg one has to go down the short slope, albeit only for a yard or two. There begins the river, and its descent. As we follow it, we shall do well to look for places to pause, and detours, and delays; for, as Rilke knew, there is no point in thinking about victories: the only thing that matters is survival.

8. THE RAILWAY-LINES OF TIME

The German Clock Museum, the pride of Furtwangen, is a jungle of instruments of every shape and kind – precious, domestic, automatic, musical – all made to measure time. Outstanding, of course, are the cuckoo-clocks of the Black Forest, the father of which is said to have been a craftsman in Bohemia or, according to others, a certain Franz Anton Ketterer, working in about 1730, or else his father, also called Franz. Here we find pendulum clocks, astronomical clocks, orreries and quartz clocks. We cannot help wondering whether time goes by independently of these instruments, which compute it by means of such different movements, or whether it is not merely the aggregate of these measurements and observations.

Standing among these countless pendulums one does not think of the inquiries of Aristotle or of St Augustine, of those metaphysical speculations about time, but of more modest chronological incongruities. A few months ago, for example, posters were put up by the Italian Neo-Fascist Party (M.S.I.) to celebrate the fortieth anniversary of the *Repubblica di Salò*. Those pictures of arms raised in the Fascist salute, elongated by the daggers held in those fists, were also an allegory of the elastic measure to which time is liable, whether individual or historical. In 1948, during that famous electoral campaign, the year 1918 – with the end of the First World War and the union of Trieste with Italy – belonged to a past already distant and placated, no longer capable of arousing ferocious passions: the thirty years between 1918 and 1948 had found a safe haven for these events, all passion spent. But the forty years that have passed between the *Repubblica di Salò* and its recent celebration are a short time, too short to have put passions to rest: the assembly announced on those posters could well have caused disorders, fighting in the streets, casualties.

Events which occurred many years or decades ago we feel to be contemporary, while facts and feelings a month old seem infinitely distant and erased for ever. Time thins out, lengthens, contracts, forms all but tangible clots or dissolves like fog-banks into nothing. It is as if it were composed of a great number of railway-lines, intersecting and diverging, carrying it in various and contrary directions. For some years now 1918 has come closer to us, for the end of the Hapsburg empire, formerly obliterated in the past, has returned into the present as the object of passionate disputes.

Time is not a single train, moving in one direction at a constant speed. Every so often it meets another train coming in the opposite direction, from the past, and for a short while that past is with us, by our side, in our present. Units of time – those known, for example, in history books as the Quaternary period or the Augustan age, or in the chronicles of our own existence as our schooldays or the time when we loved a certain person – are mysterious and difficult to measure. The forty years since the *Repubblica di Salò* seem short, while the forty-three of the *Belle Époque* seem like an endless stretch of time. Napoleon's empire seems vastly longer than that of the Christian Democrat Party in Italy, though the latter has been far more prolonged.

The great historians, such as Braudel, have dwelt above all upon this mysterious aspect of duration, along with the ambiguity of what we term "contemporary". This word takes on different meanings, as in tales of science-fiction, according to its movements in space. For example, the Emperor Francis Joseph is a contemporary of someone living in Gorizia, who constantly finds traces of his presence in the world around him, while he belongs to a distant epoch for anyone living at Vignale Monferrato. For Hamsun, who was already born at the time of the Battle of Sédan and still alive at the beginning of the Korean War, the two events are in some way encompassed by the same horizon, while for Weininger, who died very young in 1903, they belong respectively to a pre-natal past and an infinitely distant future, to a world which he would have been unable even to conceive of.

As Bloch has written, the non-contemporaneousness which divides the feelings and habits of individuals and of social classes is one of the keys to history and politics. It seems to us impossible that what for us is still an arduous present is for our children already an irrevocable, unknown past. Everyone, looked at in this way, is both victim and culprit in the matter of lack of understanding. Anyone ten or fifteen years younger than I am cannot understand that the Istrian exodus after the Second World War is for me part of the present, just as I cannot really and truly understand that for him the dates 1968, 1977 and 1981 are milestones marking off different and distinct epochs; periods that for me are superimposed in spite of their considerable differences, like the swaying grasses on a plain.

History comes into existence a little later, when it is already past, and the general connections, determined and written down years after-wards in the annals, confer on an event its role and its importance. Speaking of the capitulation of Bulgaria, an event decisive to the outcome of the First World War and therefore to the end of a civilization, Count Károlyi writes that while he was living through it he did not realize its importance, because "at that moment, 'that moment' had not yet become 'that moment'". The same is true in fiction for Fabrizio del Dongo, concerning the battle of Waterloo: while he is fighting it, it does not exist. In the pure present, the only dimension, however, in which we live, there is no history. At no single instant is there such a thing as the Fascist period or the October Revolution, because in that fraction of a second there is only the mouth swallowing saliva, the movement of a hand, a glance at the window. As Zeno denied the movement of an arrow shot from a bow, because at each single instant it was stationary at some point in space, and a succession of immobile instants cannot constitute motion, so we might say that it is not the succession of these moments-without-history which creates history, but rather the correlations and additions brought to them by the writing of history. Life, said Kierkegaard, can be understood only by looking backwards, even if it has to be lived looking forwards – that is, towards something that does not exist.

9. BISSULA

The statue near the source at Donaueschingen shows the Danube as a tender babe in the lap of a female figure representing the Baar, the gentle, hilly region which surrounds it. This image of an infant is unusual in the iconography of the great river, which is generally portrayed in effigies of powerful and majestic maturity, as in the statue on the fountain adorning the façade of the Albertine Gallery in Vienna. In Budapest also, the Danubius fountain, designed by Miklós Ybl and standing in Engels Square, is dominated by an upright, vigorous old man, resembling Michelangelo's Moses even to the hair of his head, leaning upon a staff-cum-sceptre and bearing a shell in his left hand, while from beneath his cloak peeps out a fish's tail. Among the statues on the fountain it is his faithful tributaries – the Tisza, the Drave and the Sava – which are portrayed in soft, feminine forms.

The same is true of the illustrations which embellish the great book of Marshal Luigi Ferdinando Marsili, *Danubius Pannonico-Mysicus, Observationibus Geographicis, Astronomicis, Hydrographicis, Physicis Perlustratus et in sex Tomos digestus* (1726). These personify the river as a virile, dynamic old man, a kind of regal, benevolent Saturn, a Titan not yet threatened by hydro-electric plants, canalization and all the other tricks of those invincible dwarfs who have made themselves masters of the earth. It is true that in German *Donau* is feminine in gender, and that in the Vienna Museum of Crime there is a picture by O. Friedrich, dating from 1938, depicting a drowned body, and entitled *Mother Danube*. It is a picture of modest worth, I was told by the kindly criminal counsellor who showed me round on a private visit, because the police could offer only meagre fees, and therefore had to apply to artists of few or no pretensions. But also a male adult is the Danube symbolizing Europe in Bernini's "Fountain of the Four Rivers" in Piazza Navona in Rome.

One thousand six hundred years ago that spring at Donaueschingen was well known to a girl with fair hair and blue eyes, similar to those

beings who later were destined to entrance Thomas Mann. This at
least is what we are told in the poems of Decimus Magnus Ausonius,
teacher of rhetoric and tutor to young Gratian, son of the Emperor
Valentinian I. In 368 A.D. Ausonius went with the Roman army on the
campaign against the Swabians; the Roman camp was situated near the
confluence of the Breg and the Brigach. The predictable victory of
the Roman legions, which avenged the earlier defeat at Châlons-
sur-Saône, earned the man-of-letters a slave-girl whom he named
Bissula, perhaps from an Alemannian word which referred to the
agility of this young barbarian, or, according to others, to the bifur-
cation of the river's sources.

Ausonius was then fifty-eight years old, and he fell in love with his
Bissula, who went back with him to Rome after he had almost
immediately restored her to the dignity of free woman. In the epistles
he wrote to his friend Paulus we read of the intense and as it were
astonished passion of this old scholar-poet, of his respect for his loved
one, and his reverent gratitude for this unexpected gift of destiny that
had become the centre of his life.

Ausonius knew how to compose poems and teach grammar, and like
the worthy rhetor he was, he left the enigmatical fabric of the universe
to look after itself. It is unlikely that he asked himself why on earth it
had needed so many long marches beyond the Alps, and a war, and all
the art of Roman arms, just so that he might find happiness with a
woman. A hand that we love to clasp and to kiss can also arouse us
because it comes from so far off, and because a contribution to the form
and the seductiveness of those fingers was once made, in a humble way,
by that "Big Bang", the Quaternary age, with the migration of the
Huns from the steppes of Asia.

Ausonius wrote poems for Bissula. They are not great poems
because the professor from Bordeaux – then called Burdigala, where he
was born – was a scrupulous craftsman in hexameters and pentameters,
but certainly not a born poet, as we see from his long, boring
composition about the Moselle. Love is not sufficient to create a poem,
even if sometimes it may be necessary to it; anyone who writes couplets
about his own passion is sometimes inclined to pay more attention to
the former than to the latter. The couplets of Ausonius, however, are
perfectly dignified, and they sing of the twofold nature of Bissula: in
the gold of her hair and the blue of her eyes she was a German, and in
her manners and her attire a Roman; a daughter of the Rhine who near
the source of the Danube became a citizen of Latium. Much as he loves

to see her in Roman dress, Ausonius does not ask the beloved woman who has followed him to Rome to renounce her origins, the woods and rivers of Germany. To acquire a new identity does not mean betraying the first one, but enriching one's own self with a new soul.

Admittedly it was Bissula who went with Ausonius to Rome, not he who remained in Swabia. In every meeting of cultures – in harmony or in conflict, between different individuals or in the experience of one person only – there is always, unavoidably, a moment of choice in which one sees oneself, if only by a hairsbreadth, belonging to the one culture rather than to the other. There are no such things as *a priori* choices. Borges, in one of his tales, shows how the Lombard warrior – who leaves his people to become a defender of Ravenna and her basilicas – and the English lady who abandons her own world to join an Indian tribe are two sides of the same coin, equal in the sight of God.

Maybe Bissula discovered herself in the Latin world, like the barbarians – Aetius, Stilicho – who became the last great defenders of the Empire, more Roman than the Romans and their flabby emperors; or like the English gentlewoman in the Borges story, who found her true self among a tribe of Indians. Identity is a quest that is always open, while the obsessive defence of one's origins can at times be as much a form of regressive slavery as, in other circumstances, is willing submission to displacement. You have not felt your destiny to be a sorrowful one, or that of your people either, Ausonius might have said to his Bissula; adding that, compared with herself, her still-Germanic person, the Roman women seemed to him wraiths and puppets.

10. THE SOURCE OF THE BRIGACH

In the Battle of the Sources, the Brigach has very few supporters, in spite of the deviation at Donaueschingen which turned the brief course of the Danube into its tributary. Only M. F. Breuninger, in his treatise on the sources of the Danube published in 1718, opts for the Brigach; but the reasons he puts forward come down in the end to one only, and that not very convincing: the coolness of its waters. The plaque, very modest and unassuming, does not speak of the Danube; the place is quiet, among broad meadows and the breath of peace. There is no inn, but only a bench, erected (we read) by the *Landesbausparkasse*, the Regional Building Society.

The tiny spring bubbles out of the earth and flows into a still pool, at the bottom of which a metal pipe collects it, takes it back underground and pours it out again a few yards further on, forming a streamlet heading for the valley. In this case also, some trifling damage to that rudimentary metal pipe would change the physiognomy of the Danube . . .

The silence is deep, and the wind comes fresh and gentle, as if to remind us of what life could be, a taut sail leaving a foamy wake behind it. With a wind like this, anyone who succumbs to aridity feels guilty at once, as he shields himself behind a ritual of small phobias, like a bachelor out of Kafka. There is a sort of veil over things, that dims them and prevents us from desiring them. In these moments of inner desiccation we are afraid of open fields; we need a stuffy, closed room in which to entrench ourselves and organize our scant defences. But a pair of Pannonian cheekbones, once again, loosens this congestion, sweeps out the stale air stagnating in a corner, and everything begins to flow again, smooth and free, like the water that so delighted old Herr Breuninger. A little while later, as we follow the course of the Brigach to rejoin the others, I am reminded of the words of the Talmud, and those of Bertoldo – the first laconic, the second torrential, but both unanimous – about what a man is without a woman.

II. THE SACRISTANS OF MESSKIRCH

At Number 3 of the Kirchplatz, opposite the church of St Martin at Messkirch, there is a plaque announcing that this house, in this little town on the banks of the youthful Danube, was the boyhood home of the philosopher Heidegger. It is a low-built, beige house. In the street, in front of the shabby window-sills embellished with beaten copper, there is a stunted old tree; for some reason, someone has driven nails into its trunk.

Number 3 is now inhabited by the Kaufmann family, and the lady who opens the door, when I enquire about Heidegger, asks me whether I mean the son or the nephew of the sacristan. It would certainly have pleased Heidegger to have been identified not as the famous philosopher but as the son of the local sacristan, not as a celebrity who gives lustre to his family name, but rather as a person who receives his own identity and dignity, his place in the world, from the honoured name of his family and the modest decorum of his father's profession. He would probably have felt himself welcomed and sheltered by the tradition, admitted into the landscape, the groove of the generations: a humble yet authentic way of finding himself in Being.

But Heidegger, who more than once repeated his claim to be a Black Forest peasant, in fact profaned this very feeling of loyalty and humility. In that over-emphatic identification with a familiar and immediate community – its woods, its hearth, its dialect – there was an implicit claim to a monopoly of authenticity, almost to an exclusive, patented trademark, as if his sincere attachment to his own soil allowed no room for the loyalties of other men towards other soils and other lands – to their log cabins, or their blocked-rent tenements, or their skyscrapers. Although in a brotherly spirit bound to his own people, Heidegger, in his famous hut in the Black Forest where as an old man he loved to retire into a solitude lacking in all "mod. cons.", may not really have known the humility proper to the Pastor of Being; humility denied him by his stubborn though unwitting assumption of the title of Pastor-in-Chief, the Managing Director of Being.

When Heidegger stressed his own links with the Black Forest and its woodsmen he was perfectly aware of the worldwide process threatening to uproot every individual from his own world and from his fundamental ties. But the inspired asperity with which he affirmed his loyalty led him to accept only the wood outside his own door as authentic, only those peasants whom he knew by name, only that gesture of raising an axe above a chopping-block, only that particular word in Alemannic dialect. Other peasants, woods or words, customs beyond the mountains or the seas, things he could not see or touch, but of which he could gain only second-hand knowledge, struck him as abstract, and unreal, as if they existed only in dry statistics and were the inventions of propaganda. These abstractions were not alive and tangible, made of flesh and blood like the pastor of Being himself; he was unable to perceive them with his senses, as he could perceive the odour of the Black Forest.

Heidegger's unfortunate flirtation with Fascism was not a random episode, because Fascism, in the aspect of it which is least ignoble but for all that no less destructive, is also this attitude of someone who knows himself to be a good friend to his next-door neighbour, but fails to realize that other people can be equally good friends to their next-door neighbours. Eichmann was sincere when, as a prisoner in Jerusalem, he expressed horror at discovering that the father of Captain Less, the Israeli officer who had been interrogating him for months, and for whom he felt profound respect, had died in Auschwitz. He was horrified because his lack of imagination had prevented him from seeing the faces, the features, the expressions of real people behind the statistical lists of victims.

The claim to individual authenticity becomes a pose in one who attacks the masses and forgets that he is one of their number. That rhetoric of authenticity, of "taking root", does however express a real need, though in a perverted form: the need for a political and social life that is not alienated. It reveals the inadequacy of mere positive law, of the purely formal legality that may well sanction injustice, and which is countered by legitimacy, which is to say a value on which a genuine authority may be founded.

But to set up legitimacy against legality, making an appeal to "warm" values (the community, immediacy of emotion, etc.) as against Weber's Disenchantment with the World and the coldness of the democracies, means destroying those rules of the political game which enable men to fight for the values which they hold as sacred; that is, it means establishing a tyrannical legality which denies all legitimacy. To invoke love against law is the profanation of love; it is using love as a weapon to deprive other men of freedom and of love itself.

In any case, it is Heidegger himself who successfully contradicts the cult of putting down roots. In his greatest work he has taught us that "displacement is a fundamental way of being-in-the-world", that without loss and disorientation, without wandering along paths that peter out in the woods, there is no call, there is no possibility of hearing the authentic word of Being.

The son of the sacristan of Messkirch, brought up in the old religious spirit of Swabia, he knew very well that to start out towards truth and love it is necessary to tear up our roots, to leave home far behind, to free ourselves from every immediate link connected with our origins, as in that tough passage in the Gospel in which Christ asks his mother, "What have I to do with thee?" If on the one hand Heidegger is in some respects close to the myth of blood-ties and the soil, on the other he comes near to Kafka's perception of truth, which prompts a man to venture out into the desert, further and further from the Promised

Land. Perhaps this explains why a Jewish poet such as Celan, lacerated by the Nazi exterminations and by the resulting desert of the world, was able to set his foot on the path that led to Heidegger's cabin, to climb to that cabin and to have a genuine dialogue with the ex-Rector of Freiburg University, who in 1934 had put his philosophy at the service of the newly-fledged Reich.

The Black Forest surrounding that cabin has become a transcendental, universal landscape of philosophy. In the luminous clearing in the wood in which, as in the open spaces around my own Mount Snežnik, there is nothing that can be grasped, but only a horizon within which things appear, Heidegger symbolized the greater humility of thought as the "place" in which one listens to Being.

Heidegger discerns that the process leading to the triumph of technology and, as he says, to the oblivion of Being is objective and necessary. In this vision of his he makes what is relative into an absolute; he considers technology to be a calamity peculiar to the modern age; he forgets that the plough which cleaves the earth is already domination and artifice, and that an intellectual of the Roman Empire might with no less intensity have felt the absence of nature and the alienation of man, and have heard the spurious verb "to exist" conjugated in the impersonal.

Heidegger was not an innocent soul; he was not convinced (as Weichert was) that an appeal to good feeling and the simple life was all that it took to restore harmony. His diagnosis of the global thrust towards technology was free of any moralizing, as is proper in a philosopher, whose task is to grasp his own times in the fist of thought, and to understand their laws, not to denounce the iniquities of the age. But this does not mean, though it is often said, that he was a champion of that triumph. Seismologists measure the severity of an earthquake on the Richter Scale without lamenting over the victims, but this does not mean they approve of the earthquake. Talking in the doorway with Frau Kaufmann, who seems unwilling to let me in, I catch a glimpse of a dark, narrow corridor which does not suggest a happy childhood spent in that house. The neighbouring front door bears the name-plate of a tax-consultant, an important functionary of the Spirit in an Age in which the Spirit has become the mathematical mind.

Within the walls of this castle on the banks of the Danube another leading actor on the bloodstained stage of this century lived, suffered and enacted the nightmare of total war. He would watch the river dashing itself furiously against the arches, and imagine it, ferocious and destructive, overwhelming towers and halls and best china and dragging it all down as far as the estuary, crumbling and burying history deep in the muddy detritus of millennia. That phantom of final annihilation brought him a certain sour comfort, leading him to confuse his own hunted flight with the cruel, insensate disintegration of all that is.

The day is a pale blue day, and the smell of snow and the quiet flow of the Danube, with its ducks and its reeds, do not suggest images of destruction to the German scholar on his travels forty years later. There are no R.A.F. bombs raining down on his head, and he is not pursued by the Senegalese of Leclerc's army, brandishing their short swords. These places along the way invite all things to rest: the traveller has no incentive to hurry on, but would rather pause, carry the people and scenery along with him – even the room in Tuttlingen, left only a few hours ago, and the hours spent in that room, the waters of sleep and the amphora that surfaced from that sea. Travelling is the constancy of the sedentary man, who everywhere asserts his habits and his roots, attempting by means of mobility in space to deceive the erosion of time by repeating the familiar things and gestures over and over again: sitting down at table, chatting, loving, sleeping. Among the Latin mottoes which adorn the halls of the Castle of Sigmaringen with all the authority of a dead language, there is one which celebrates love of one's native place, the residing spirit, settled in its own dwelling and free from the craving to leave it: "Domi manere convenit felicibus", the happy do best to stay at home.

The Castle of Sigmaringen, which rises on the banks of the youthful Danube, has not been a place of harmony and fulfilment, but rather of departures, of flights, of exile. Even its lords, the princes of Hohenzollern-Sigmaringen, are chiefly remembered for those of them who went off to become rulers of foreign countries (such as Carol I of Rumania in the last century), and those expelled one night in 1944 to make room for the collaborationist French Vichy government, which was following the German retreat, with the unreal and utterly powerless "court" of Marshal Pétain and his Prime Minister, Pierre Laval. That castle witnessed one of the scenes in the tragedy that depicted the degeneration of Germany and, as a result, the decline of the German element in Danubian Europe.

A young girl acts as guide to visitors to the castle. In a mechanical sing-song she rattles off its History and its Art, the seventeenth-century tapestries, the cannons presented by Napoleon III. When I ask her where Marshal Pétain had his quarters she shrugs her shoulders, as if it were the first she had heard of him. Shortly afterwards, she points out a number of rooms as being Laval's apartment. The words "Vichy" and "Laval" trigger off her memory, and she begins to pour out dates and details; and yet she has never heard the name of Pétain.

This tour-guide's ill-prepared, patchy knowledge would have pleased Céline, who would have discovered in it that tragic-comic schizophrenia of history which he lived through right here at Sigmaringen, where he arrived along with the Vichy government at the time of catastrophe. In *Castle to Castle*, which depicts and dwells upon that period at Sigmaringen, Céline writes, "If I blabber on I talk rubbish; at bottom I resemble many guides." In fact his book is, in its way, a kind of Baedeker, a compendium of history or else, for Céline, of his raving delirium. He himself, in *North*, prophesied that in ten years' time people would no longer know who Pétain was, or else would take it for the name of some grocer.

When he was at Sigmaringen with his wife Lucette, his friend La Vigue and his cat Bébert, among the collaborators and other fugitives, in a chaos of refugees of every nationality, Céline had already been described by the B.B.C. as "an enemy of man". In the opinion of the entire free world he was no longer the great voice of the people as he had been in his early books, in which he had denounced the brutalization of existence and society. Now he was an iniquitous traitor, an anti-semite hunted down and reduced to the scum of the earth on a level with the Nazi butchers. In that papier-mâché palace, among the sneering masks of the old feudal portraits, Céline did his best to alleviate the sufferings of the sick, giving morphine to those in pain and cyanide to those who knew that the time had come to render their accounts. Down below, the Danube, with its bow-bends formed over the centuries and its imperial tradition, seemed to him the putrid river of history, in other words of universal filth and violence. In the lapping of the Seine and the breath of the sea, Céline had heard the voice of a life not corrupted by history, a voice of pure lyricism without a trace of falsehood; but the Danube, heavy with history, struck terror into him, and all the great protagonists of his century were to him "Danubian gangsters", like the princes of Hohenzollern-Sigmaringen.

Céline despised the new masters of the Castle of Sigmaringen, though by choosing Fascism he had hitched his destiny to theirs. He despised them because they stood aloof, because they did not share the abject squalor, the blocked latrines, of their followers; because – like Pétain – they believed that they "embodied" something superior, and therefore lived on falsehood, set apart from the mud and dung of genuine living. Céline, on the other hand, speaks from the seething depths of brute, immediate suffering. He cries out with the broken voice of mangled creatures, he proclaims the contemptibility and the folly of evil. His single-mindedness eventually becomes a distortion, and he ends by putting on the same plane all the actors in any way relevant to the story: Hitler and Léon Blum, for example, insofar as they all appear equally to be expressions of the will to power, beneficiaries of the favour of the masses and therefore possessors of power. Like a grieving, guilty Messiah, he identifies himself with the Nazi butchers, because he sees them losing.

In the fetid, blood-soaked Carnival of Sigmaringen, everything appears as senseless and interchangeable: the powerless Pétain, the madman Corpechet who proclaims himself Admiral of the Danube, Laval who at that time of total collapse appoints Céline Governor of the islands of Saint-Pierre and Miquelon, the French collaborators, the American bombs and the Nazi concentration camps all intermingle in a single atrocious witches' sabbath. Céline to the nth degree suffers this chaos, this "thread of history that passes through me from side to side and from top to bottom, from the clouds to my head and down to my arsehole".

Céline has looked Medusa in the face, seen the void behind the seething and the sewage of life, as in houses gutted by bombs, their façades left free-standing by chance. He has also emphatically reiterated this epiphany of nothingness, which – like any experience of the absolute – can be the object of a sudden thunderbolt, but not of an incessant sermon. Gigi, who has a great love for Céline, is equally capable of looking Medusa in the face, but the sanguine benevolence with which he conceals the fact, coolly taking all the best tricks or handing round the wine, perhaps does more justice to the everything-and-nothing of life.

Grandeur and decline live cheek by jowl throughout the work of

Céline. In the most monstrous of his books, *Bagatelles pour un massacre* – one of the few genuine acts of transgression in literature, culpable and punishable, among so much innocuous licence taken by writers who wish to transgress, but with guarantees of immunity and health insurance – there is the wordy, wearisome passage in which a lower-middle-class shopkeeper gives vent to all the prejudices of his impoverished and disorientated class, but there is also a brilliant, troubled snap-shot of the twentieth century which we would not willingly be without. Céline's outlook, obscured but on some occasions even sharpened by hatred, unmasks the frenetic activity of the culture industry, and in its sterile, frigid excitation, in its invariable and laborious premature ejaculation, discloses an undercurrent of violence. That feverish mobilization, imperiously recruiting the individual into the military manoeuvres of symposiums, debates and interviews, is the hysteria of an overcrowded room, of a world in which every door bears the sign, "No vacancies".

The collective consciousness, which does not wish to overcome violence but at the same time dares not look it in the face, sublimates egoism and oppression in a vacuous cult of sentiment and passion, of the culture which Céline has witheringly described as a "lyrical bidet". The latter, unaware of the elementary truth of sex and the comprehensive truth of love, is the kingdom of the great intermediate falsehoods, the pulsations of *amour-passion* raked up to justify deceit and self-deception. The poet of sex and of the nostalgia of love, Céline implacably unmasked the falsification of feeling, the absence of true sex and true love, that inflow of blood to the lower abdomen that needs must ennoble itself by aspiring upwards and exhaling a sigh of emotion; he unmasked the inability to love and the cowardice – when one does not in fact love – of forcing sex onto emotional crutches which end by tripping someone else up and breaking a leg. The lyrical bidet, unlike the great religions, always feels the need to sugar the pill.

Céline, the reactionary, harried by the obsession of a forthcoming war of total extermination, gives harsh and powerful voice to a real sense of hardship, even of the cures which he suggests are in their turn devastating symptoms and effects of that disease, prescriptions for living that sound like unintentional parodies of the great pages of *Journey to the End of the Night* which lie open over the abyss of death.

And so the great rebel, who in *Journey to the End of the Night* wrote unforgettable pages on the horror of war and the inability of men to imagine it as it really is even when they are living through it, ends by celebrating the firing-line as the moment of truth; the poet of a brutally abused childhood persuades himself to regret the passing of that healthy upbringing, with its ready thrashings and absence of any indulgence. The pamphleteer himself adopts the ghastly anti-Semitic banalities which as a narrator he had put in the mouth of the father in *Death on the Instalment Plan*, representing them as block-headed prejudices; the anarchist who once spoke in the name of the obscure and voiceless deplores the fact that the Christian churches have corroded the supremacy of the white races. His trilogy about the Second World War lumps together in one single global tissue of lies all ideologies of Right or Left, Democracy, Fascism and even anti-Semitism, in a total rejection of society, a rejection that no longer points to a world-wide conspiracy of the Jews, but rather the worldwide conspiracy of all the conquerors and all the powerful, the Jews included, and the banking cartels and the Viet-cong and the space stations.

Céline let himself be dazzled by the revelation of evil. He listened to the voice of degradation, said Bernanos, like a confessor in a slum quarter; but he did not have the ability, unlike some of the old father-confessors, to take a nap between one penitent and the next, weary of the reiteration of predictable sins: he failed to see the stereotyped banality of evil. Like other French writers of his generation, who thought that they could echo Gide in saying "J'ai vécu", he sought for "life" without suspecting the megalomania of such a pretension. By bawling at the top of his voice, as he himself wrote, he thought he was defending a virginal, unsophisticated innocence of the ego. He prided himself contemptuously on not being a clerk, as if that ought to guarantee him some sort of special authenticity, and as if all Hemingway's brawling ought, *a priori*, to be more poetic than Kafka's office routine.

To use the term "clerk" as an insult is simply a banal vulgarity; Pessoa and Svevo, however, would have welcomed it as a just attribute of the poet. The latter does not resemble Achilles or Diomedes, ranting on their war-chariots, but is more like Ulysses, who knows that he is no one. He manifests himself in this revelation of impersonality that conceals him in the prolixity of things, as travelling erases the traveller in the confused murmur of the street. Kafka and Pessoa journey not to the end of a dark night, but of a night of a colourless mediocrity that is even more disturbing, and in which one becomes aware of being only a peg to hang life on, and that at the very bottom of that life, thanks to this awareness, there may be sought some last-ditch residue of truth.

The Messiah will come to aid the nameless and the humble, not the muscle-men of life; the "povareto" Virgilio Giotti, whose poetry shines forth modest and incorruptible from his love of his wife and children and his job in the Town Hall, not the pompous Pablo Neruda, who originally entitled his memoirs *I Confess That I Have Lived*. In one of his flashes of greatness, however, Céline too recognizes the futility of any display of personal vitalism: "My life is over, Lucie. I'm not beginning; I'm ending in literature." He is able to feel the most lacerating pity towards single individuals, as towards the Mongoloid children he looked after during the flight across Germany, in whose eyes he read a dignity capable of transcending the slaughterhouse of history, but he was unable to admit his own mistakes. He never expressed a word of genuine repentance after the extermination of the Jews, incapable of feeling the tangible humanity of people he had not known directly.

At the Castle of Sigmaringen there is a church, and also a museum. In one of the three fragments of the legend of St Ursula painted in 1530 by the Master of the Thalheim Altar, our attention is held by the malevolent eye of an archer, while Crucifixions and Coronations with Thorns depict bestial mobs, cruel snouts, obscene noses, repulsive tongues. In all that lacerating violence, plebeian and rudimentary, Céline might well have recognized himself, for he knew that he too belonged to the anonymous crowd of the people, such as that painted by the Master of Messkirch in his scenes of the Annunciation and the Birth of Jesus. This is the reason for his greatness: only experience of the deprivations of the very poor has enabled certain reactionaries to be true poets, despite their aberrant political choices. Hamsun and Céline are such, thanks to their odysseys of hunger and obscurity, the lack of which makes Jünger's aristocratic veneer perfectly sterile.

Anarchic and self-destructive, Céline suffered the poetic and intellectual consequences of the contempt he fed on. Such contempt is easy enough: any phrase or attitude or human affirmation appears imbecile to someone listening with a prejudicial metaphysical system ready to place against that vague, impalpable background of life. From this vantage point any moral principle whatever stands out as inadequate and presumptuous. The declaration of the rights of man sounds as ridiculous as a volley of blunderbusses, because it is mercilessly unequal to the abyss of existence. But anyone who receives it with the sneer of the all-knowing, considering himself the inspired, brilliant interpreter of that abyss, is at least equally ridiculous, and falls just as short of the mystery. Céline may have poured derision on those who spoke of democracy, but on the basis of the purely mechanical laws of mockery, the last windbag to empty could with equal right laugh every word of his to scorn. Céline is really also a Tartuffe, although he is careful to put this harmful definition of himself into the mouth of Professor Y. "My accusers are all on a pay-roll; I'm not." That is certainly a Tartuffian expression. Kafka, who was in fact a clerk, was certainly no more philistine than was Céline. But then, Kafka was a Jew . . .

TWO

The Universal Danube
of Engineer Neweklowsky

1. BELIEVING IN ULM

Do you believe in Ulm? asked Céline in the course of his flight across a devastated Germany. He was wondering (in a tone of caustic banter) whether Ulm still existed, whether the bombings had not obliterated it. When tangible fact is being erased by violence, then to imagine it becomes an act of faith. But all that is real is being erased each instant, even if luckily not always in the bloodstained theatre of phosphorous bombs. Little by little, however, things are imperceptibly erased, and one cannot do otherwise than believe that they nonetheless exist. A faith lived and forged into the very gestures of the body confers that unruffled confidence in life which enables one to go through the world without turbulence of heart. Count Helmuth James von Moltke, great-grandson of the Prussian field marshal, victor at Sédan, and philosopher of the battlefield, firmly believed in Jesus Christ; and when in 1945 the People's Tribunal of the Third Reich put him to death for his opposition to Hitler, he went to his execution with the air of someone accepting a disagreeable, but unavoidable, invitation to dinner.

One does not need a faith in God. Sufficient is a faith in created things, that enables one to move among objects in the conviction that they exist, persuaded of the irrefutable reality of this chair, this umbrella, this cigarette, this friendship. He who doubts himself is lost, just as someone scared of failure in love-making fails indeed. We are happy in the company of people who make us feel the unquestionable presence of the world, just as the body of the beloved gives us the certainty of those shoulders, that bosom, that curve of the hips, the surge of these as incontestable as the sea. And one who is in despair, we are taught by Singer, can act as though he believed: faith will come afterwards.

I therefore believe in Ulm, while the train is to all appearances taking me there, and in the appointment with my friends, just as at school I believed in the existence of Cherrapunji, a town in India whose existence is attested by the geography book, which added that it was the rainiest place in the world, with 13 metres of rain per annum.

Except, it mentioned elsewhere, that Honolulu got 14 metres. My friend Schultz protested, saying that if this was how things stood then Honolulu, not Cherrapunji, deserved the world record for rainfall. Others, on the other hand, raised in a less severe philosophy, managed to wriggle free by maintaining a rigorous distinction between the two propositions which, deprived of any link, were therefore immune to being contradiction, as the assertion "it was a fine sunset" contained in one novel does not contradict the assertion "it was a stormy sunset" contained in another.

Here the Danube is young, and Austria is still far off, but clearly the river is already a sinuous master of irony, of that irony which created the greatness of Central European culture, the art of outflanking one's own barrenness and checkmating one's own weakness; the sense of the duplicity of things, and at the same time the truth of them, hidden but single. Irony taught respect for the misunderstandings and contradictions of life, the disjunction between the recto and the verso of a page that never meet even though they are the selfsame thing between time and eternity, between language and reality, between the rainfall at Cherrapunji and that at Honolulu, and all the other rainfall statistics mentioned in the geography book. Tolerance of the imbalances and deformities of the world, of its parallel lines that never meet, does not diminish our faith that those parallels meet at infinity, but it does not force them into meeting any earlier.

I therefore expect that Ulm will not be merely the sign saying "Ulm" on the railway station of a flattened city, as it was for Céline when he finally got there. Behind me I have already left Riedling, the little town that was the first Hapsburg outpost on the Danube and is a favourite haunt of storks. On this train I am not threatened by the bombs that threatened Céline, nor by the wolves, ghosts and will-o'-the-wisps, instructions for the avoidance of which are contained in *Fidus Achates or the Faithful Travelling Companion*, a vademecum written in the mid-seventeenth century by one Martin Zeiller, by choice a citizen of Ulm. Maybe all the same it would be prudent to follow another of Zeiller's counsels: make a will before setting out. Having made all one's testamentary arrangements, legacies, bequests and codicils, one would travel as a free man, discharged from life, released from all obligations and functions, in that mysterious, happy, anarchic territory in which one sets foot only when one is already off stage, whatever stage it may be.

2. TWO THOUSAND ONE HUNDRED AND SIXTY-FOUR PAGES AND FIVE KILOS NINE HUNDRED GRAMMES OF UPPER DANUBE

There is no doubt that Ulm lies on the Upper Danube. But, strictly speaking, how far down does this go? Where is its beginning and where its end? What is its extent and identity? What is the concept of it? Engineer Neweklowsky spent a lifetime marking out the confines of the "Obere Donau", the Upper Danube, and – once he had staked his claim – in sifting, classifying and cataloguing it inch by inch in space and in time, the colours of its waters and its customs changes, its landscape as we see it now and as it has been over the centuries that have gone into creating it. Like Flaubert or Proust, Neweklowsky devoted his entire existence to the work, to writing, to The Book. The result is a work in three volumes, a total of 2,164 pages (including illustrations), which weighs 5.9 kilos and which, as stated in the title, deals not with the Danube as such, but more modestly with *Navigation and Rafting on the Upper Danube* (1952–1964).

In his preface, Ernst Neweklowsky specifies that his treatise is concerned with the 659 km between the mouth of the Iller, which flows into the Danube just above Ulm, and Vienna; including, of course, all the tributaries and subtributaries in the area. In the introduction to the third volume he nevertheless admits, with the impartiality of one serving a cause superior to all personal interests, that the concept – and the space – of the Upper Danube varies according to the standpoint from which it is considered. From the strictly geographical point of view it includes the 1,110 km between the source and the Gönyü waterfall, from the hydrographic standpoint the 1,010 km from the source to the confluence of the March, while for international law it extends for 2,050 km all the way to the Iron Gates; that is, to the old Turkish frontier. The Bavarians, with a more narrowly regional outlook, have it end at the Regensburg bridge, after which they even name a hydro-electric company, and consider the short stretch between Regensburg and Passau as Lower Danube. In the military vocabulary prevailing in the First World War, with regard to transporting war supplies, the name "Upper Danube" was understood to include the stretch between Regensburg and Gönyü.

Aware of the chaotic excess of facts, Engineer Neweklowsky sifts, examines, compares, connects and generalizes all these hypotheses of classification, even though his own point of view, which is that of nautical science, induces him to consider the Upper Danube to be the 659 km between the confluence of the Iller and Vienna. Between 1910 and 1963, the year of his death, Neweklowsky, Director of River Works at Linz from 1908 onwards and "Chief of the Danube" between Puchenau and Mauthausen until 1925, wrote on this subject more than a hundred and fifty articles for specialized magazines, along with lectures, exhibitions, scattered articles and a thesis for a doctorate. Between 1952 and 1964, when he was dead, the three volumes appeared – the monument to his life.

In those three volumes you find everything: the history of navigation from the pre-Roman era to the present day, the routes used and the types of vessel, pirogues and steamships, the propellers and the floor plates, the parts and the gear of the vessels and their names that varied with the course of the centuries and from region to region, the characteristics and differences of the various tributaries, the whirlpools and the shallows, the innumerable types of raft and barge, the pros and cons of the kinds of wood employed, the convoys, the fords and crossing-places, the rafting of timber, the composition and customs of the boatmen, the sagas and superstitions of the river, the levying rights, the voyages of sovereigns and ambassadors, the poems, the songs, the plays and the novels born of the river waters.

The "Obere Donau" for Neweklowsky is a universal Danube: it is the world, but at the same time his own map, the *All* that contains even itself. Since, if we are to travel through life feeling truly secure, it is best to take Entirety in our pockets, the Engineer, with an eye to the practical needs of the hasty wayfarer, also took the trouble to prepare a slender, highly condensed portable volume of 59 pages. He arranges, classifies, schematizes and subdivides his encyclopaedia into chapters and paragraphs, and equips the text with appendices, indices, illustrations and maps. Born in 1882, the Engineer has a passion for Totality, the daemon of systematization which inspired the great nineteenth-century philosophies. He is a not unworthy disciple of Hegel or Clausewitz: he knows that the world exists to be put in order, and so that its scattered details may be bound together by thought. In giving his "general presentation" to the press he says that he sees this as "the accomplishment of a task assigned to him by destiny".

Every totality – even that of Hegel, as Kierkegaard said with factious acumen – is an offering made to the derision of the gods. There are centuries, or rather cultures, in which even the genius for speculative thought is by destiny exposed to laughter, because of its claim to pigeon-hole each fleeting detail of existence. Certain passages in St Thomas or Hegel are by no means immune from ridicule, any more than Heidegger is. This comic side of things does nothing to diminish the greatness of Hegel or of St Thomas or of Heidegger: every really great thought must aspire to totality, and this tension invariably brings with it, in its very greatness, an element of caricature, a suggestion of self-parody.

His doctoral thesis, and later on his three volumes, constitute Neweklowsky's triumph, his achievement of totality, which is attained only when the disorder of the world is assembled in a book and arranged in categories. Neweklowsky sets up as many categories as possible, he tames phenomena and makes them stand in line, but he devotes animated attention also to sensitive, ephemeral details, to unique occurrences. His work also deals with changes of weather, the wind, unpredictable mishaps, a list of accidents (mortal or otherwise) taking place on board, the suicides and the murders, the divinities of the river, the busts of 132 boat-masters of Ulm and the little verses devoted to each of them. He describes the heads of the patron saints of the bridges, records the penalty laid down for the ship's cook who puts too much salt in the soup, and lists the names of the boatmen who were also innkeepers on the side, together with the sites of their inns.

Like a good systematist, he mentions all the variants of pronunciation and spelling of the word *Zille*, which means a flat-bottomed boat (*Zilln, Cillen, Zielen, Zülln, Züllen, Züln, Zullen, Zull, Czullen, Ziln, Zuin*), and of countless other technical terms. As a scrupulous engineer he records the dimensions of all the different types of vessel, their respective burdens and tonnages. The comprehensive scientist also becomes a meticulous historian, for his yearning for totality embraces the world, actual and potential. He knows that the past is ever-present, because journeying and surviving in some part of the universe are the images of everything that once was, transmitted by the light. The encyclopaedist's task is to make a complete picture: his Danube is the simultaneousness of all events, the synchronic knowledge of All. He therefore mentions, for example, that in 1552 eleven troops of Duke Maurice of Saxony's soldiers came down from Bavaria on 70 rafts, and that at the end of the last century there were 130–140 pirogues in the Salzburg area, 60 on the Wolfgangsee, 25 on the Attersee, 5 on the Altaussersee, 2 or 3 on the Grundlsee, the Hallstätter See and the Gmundersee.

Tortured by lack of "completeness", to which he frankly admits, Neweklowsky is beset by a gentle obsession with entirety. Reporting on the voyage made from Linz to Vienna by the Empress Maria, wife of Ferdinand III, on March 13th–14th 1645, he lists all 52 vessels in the procession, and for each one specifies whom it was assigned to: to the First Chamberlain Count von Khevenhüller, to three Spanish maids-in-waiting and Countess Villerual, to the Empress's father-confessor, to the father-confessor of the prince himself, to the sedan chairs and their carriers . . . When dealing with literary works which describe navigation on the river, he stresses their inconsistencies and technical inexactitudes, the things that don't ring true, and "poetical" notions incompatible with nautical science. The sheet of paper, and therefore literature, has to fit snugly with the real world, like the map of the Empire imagined by Borges. Neweklowsky's book on the Upper Danube has to fit the river as a hand fits in a glove. Inflexible in his exposure of the falsehoods of the poets, he is happy when among the Muses he encounters not Aristotelian "likelihood", which he despises, but the truth itself. Commenting on a radio-drama by C. H. Watzinger transmitted by the Linz studios on September 8th 1952 (*From the Watermen to the Steamers*), he solemnly declares that the radio-play "breathes the air of the Danube."

From time to time in Neweklowsky's systematic edifice we come across a chink of incompleteness, and sense the presence of some detail that has gone astray. The Engineer sadly laments the fact that a milestone set up by Caracalla three miles beyond Passau has disappeared without trace; while in the judiciously selected list of historic voyages on the river, among imperial fleets or ships bearing ambassadors of the Sublime Porte, a sudden mention is made of the passage of "someone called Stefan Zerer", who in 1528 travelled a short way down the Danube after boarding at Regensburg.

Even for Neweklowsky, it must be admitted, the building sometimes rocks a little: the unexpected gust of some unique, passing freak messes up the papers and the paperclips on the desk and in comes life, immediate and instantaneous. For example, when dealing with the slang and jargon of the watermen, he naturally pores over the existing dictionaries on the subject, expounds them and comments on them, but he is dumbfounded, or rather bewitched, by an anarchical declaration found in a work by J. A. Schultes, *Travels on the Danube* (1819).

In Volume One, on page 12, Schultes writes that he had begun to compile a lexicon of watermen's language, but that he had dropped the scheme because, as he says, you only have to watch the boatmen shouting at each other to learn their language, without having to turn to a dictionary at every moment. Neweklowsky was embarrassed to realize for an instant that only by seeing those gestures and those faces, and harkening to those sounds on the river-banks, could one really and truly grasp a single word, its unique flavour and colour. This language exists in its fullness only in its own immediate surroundings, among that rabble of ruffians as they sling insults at one another. Their reputation as strapping fellows and ferocious drinkers is attested to by many anxious imperial decrees and sealed by the hand of the great baroque preacher Abraham at Sancta Clara. But those scurrilities, those other-than-orthodox gestures, those faces, that jargon, all have vanished now; they have been carried off by the waters of the river, by the flood of time, and there's no dictionary can hold them back, as Schultes knew; and that is why he saved himself the trouble of writing one. It may be that Neweklowsky at this point understands that the current of the Danube will carry off and swallow up also his five kilos nine hundred grammes of paper about the Upper Danube, but he pulls himself together at once, drives back that nihilistic shudder into the undiscovered waters of his heart, and censures Schultes for not having completed his dictionary.

Neweklowsky is in fact sheltered from these sudden gusts from nowhere. His thoroughly meritorious existence is entirely involved in and protected by those 2,164 pages. It has grown within them as in the courtyard of a castle; that black cover and that hefty volume are an impregnable bulwark, a faith that does not disappoint or betray.

Impossible to deny the advantage that he has over the believers in other cults. One who believes in God may feel himself to have been suddenly abandoned, as happened even to Jesus on the Cross; and he can see the real world vanish around him and beneath his feet. That pious man Chaim Cohen, afterwards a magistrate in Israel, went to Auschwitz with the orthodox faith of his fathers, but when he returned from Auschwitz even his God had been exterminated, reduced to ashes in a gas oven. The Revolution also, Communism, the messianic redemption of history, can turn out to be a god that failed, or that does not exist, as for Koestler and so many others. Swann lives entirely within his passion for Odette, and realizes in the end that he has worn himself out for a woman who wasn't worth the trouble. Even the blind, irrational love of the life of hot passions, that for some men is such a powerful charge of appeal and desire, can flop in a moment, so that the erotic spell of vitality can end up like Falstaff in a basket of foul linen, while the banner flying in the wind is just an old washrag.

But the Danube on the other hand, the Danube, even only the Upper Danube, is there before your eyes; it does not vanish, nor does it make any promises it cannot keep; it does not let you down, but flows on loyally and open to scrutiny. It knows nothing of the hazards of theology, the perversions of ideology, the pangs of despised love. It is simply there, tangible and truth-telling, and the votary who gives his life to it feels life flowing in harmonious and indissoluble union with the flowing river. This ceaseless consonance conceals the fact that both of them, the river-god and the votary, flow down towards the river-mouth. It is as if Neweklowsky, like Quine, were constantly pointing his finger and saying "Danube!", and as if this constant gesture beat time for his life, with a passion that was unfailingly requited.

3. THE ENGINEER CAUGHT BETWEEN CONVICTION AND RHETORIC

Was Neweklowsky a man of conviction, then? The death that came to him "benignant and swift" shortly after his eightieth birthday, in the words of his biographer, and made his passing easy and harmonious, would seem to vouch for it. Conviction, as Michelstaedter wrote, is the present possession of one's own life and one's own person, the ability to live each moment to the full, not goading oneself madly into burning it up fast and using it with a view to an all too imminent future, thus destroying it in the hope that life – the whole of life – may pass swiftly. One who is not convinced is consumed in the expectation of a result that is always still to come, that is never in existence. It is life as an insufficiency ceaselessly annihilated in the hope that the difficult present moment is already past, or will be when we are over our 'flu, have passed our exam, got married, filed our divorce papers, finished a job, started our holidays or received the doctor's verdict.

On the other hand "rhetoric", in other words the organization of knowledge, is the vast great cogwheel of culture, the febrile mechanism of activity with which men incapable of living manage to deceive themselves, to hold at bay the annihilating awareness of their lack of life and worth, to turn a blind eye to their nullity. As I leave the library and set off towards the fishermen's quarter, I wonder whether Neweklowsky's 2,164 pages are themselves a bastion in the great wall of rhetoric, blocking his view and awareness of his own emptiness.

I do not know whether Neweklowsky was a man convinced or a rhetorician, whether in his thousands of pages he listened serenely to the voice of his daemon, or whether he was trying to escape from his demons. His mercifully sudden death seems to suggest a life that also flowed by without anguish. Every life is decided by the greater or lesser ability to be persuaded, as every journey is played out between standstill and flight. With charming insistence Neweklowsky, throughout his book, keeps coming back to the "Moidle-Schiff", the merry vessel bearing the 150 Swabian and Bavarian girls whom Duke Karl Alexander of Württemberg sent in 1719, following the Peace of Passarowitz, to the non-commissioned officers who had stayed behind as German colonists in the Banat, so that they could marry and thereby establish that Swabian presence in the Banat which did indeed become one of the central elements in the history and culture of south-eastern Europe. That vessel of the 150 girls, whose free-and-easy merits have been praised in song and story, would be the ideal craft in which to undertake this journey, and moreover to undertake it as a man convinced, without haste, and maybe wishing never to arrive.

4. THE LITTLE BLACK GIRL OF THE DANUBE

In his survey of the *belles-lettres* devoted to the Upper Danube, Neweklowsky mentions a forgotten but graceful tale by Hermann Schmid, *Franzel the Negress*. The story takes place in about 1813, and is set among the actors in the theatre of the watermen of Laufen, which the Engineer has already described in exhaustive detail. The heroine, Franzel, is a daughter of the Napoleonic Wars, and to be precise of a negro – trumpeter in the Emperor's armies – and a German girl. The story tells of her difficulties and humiliations because of her colour, her vocation for the theatre – which has no time for her – of her love for Hanney (an actor who writes her a play, *The Queen of Sheba*, in which she triumphs just because she is black). Intrigues separate the lovers, Hanney betrays her but repents, sends her away and then follows her all the way down to the Lower Danube near the Turkish frontier, where she is playing at the Fair in a company of black actors. He marries her and returns with her to Laufen.

This little "theatre romance" of the Danube evokes the cruelty of racism, unmasks the prejudice of it and dissolves it like a scenic illusion, behind which there is the human truth of the individual, transcending the fact of colour as it does the role in the play. The story has few pretensions, but the intuition of that Swabian actor who, out of love for his black belovèd, invents the tale of the black but comely Queen of Sheba, exposes the whole savage shallowness of racism. The wind bloweth where it listeth, and no one can be forever certain of their own gifts or their own shortcomings. The apocalyptic tone in which the great Céline speaks of the "little idyll between your white maid and your black postman" is, intellectually speaking, a step lower than this story by Hermann Schmid, who otherwise has been justifiably forgotten.

5. THE GERMAN IDYLL

Ulm is a city of the German idyll, of the old Germany of the Holy Roman Empire. The Antiquarius hails it as the "first capital on the banks of the Danube" and as "Decus Sueviae", the adornment of Swabia. The old chronicles praise it for its bourgeois-patrician decorum, the ancient rights of its corporations, its flourishing finances which, according to an old rhyme, could compete with the power of Venice, Augsburg, Nuremberg and Strasbourg.

In quoting these lines the Antiquarius observes in a footnote that they are already a warning of decay, because those cities have lost their pride and are languishing in decline, but he too recalls the ancient wealth of Ulm and above all the independence of its corporations, the privileges of self-government which safeguarded it with respect to the authority of the Empire, the *Jus de non appellando* and the thicket of rights, liberties, powers and exemptions obtained over the centuries by this imperial city at the expense of the Empire itself. When the Emperor Charles IV laid siege to Ulm in 1376, preventing the population from reaching the church, which was outside the walls, the citizens decided to build themselves one in the city itself, and in 1377 laid the first stone of the great cathedral which in 1890 was to become the tallest cathedral in the world. The chronicles relate that the burgomaster Ludwig Krafft, keen to show off the wealth of Ulm, covered the foundation stone with a hundred gold florins from his own purse, and was imitated by the other aristocrats, who also threw handfuls of gold and silver coins on the stone, followed by the "honoured citizens" and finally by the "common people".

Ulm is the heart of German Holy Roman Empire nationalism, that of the old Germany based on the law of custom, which sanctioned historical traditions and differences, opposing any central power, all forms of state interference and even any kind of codified unity. The universalism of the Empire, which, in spite of the great efforts of the Saon or Swabian sovereigns, did not succeed in becoming a compact, unified state, fell into a fragmented dispersal of any kind of political unity or else broke up into a archipelago of local governments and corporate privileges. The *Schwabenspiegel*, the collection of thirteenth-century laws, codifies these liberties pertaining to the various social classes and their separateness, from which arises the tortuous, lacerating German idyll, the particularism, the social segmentation, the conflict between ethics and politics, the tangled skein of "deutsch Misère", German wretchedness, as Heine was to call it.

Common law sanctioned this mosaic of authorities and prerogatives, defended the organic variety of institutions which had come into being over the course of centuries, and opposed every unitary code, every form of unifying legislation. When Thibaut, the jurist influenced by the ideas of the Enlightenment, proposed a code of laws which would abolish differences and privileges in the name of equality and the universality of Reason, Savigny opposed him by appealing to common law, the defence of the differences between men, and the laws which safeguarded these differences, as being the outcome of an organic historical evolution, not of some "abstract" rationalism.

So it comes about that, in Germany, freedom in the modern, democratic sense of the word is countered by the liberties of the classes and corporations, their ancient rights which defend the social inequalities stratified over the centuries. It is not universal human nature that decided on the values and the rights of man, but the concrete historical facts: for Möser, the patriarch of Osnabrück, defending the ancient liberties of Germany from totalitarian tyranny meant defending serfdom and the independence of the free yeoman. Thus the German idyll is ultra-conservative in essence, and heeds the advice of St Paul and of

Luther, not to abandon one's own social position, but to respect the "natural" class structure.

The class pride which animates the protagonists of this idyll is not just a matter of keeping one's distance from the lower classes, but also a pride which jealously guards its own boundaries with respect to those above. In one of Hoffmann's *Tales*, Meister Martin the cooper is unwilling to allow his daughter to marry a young aristocrat because he wants to give her as a bride to a solid representative of the Guild of Coopers. When Faust accosts Margaret, and calls her a beautiful young lady, she replies modestly, but also proudly, that she is not a young lady but a young woman of the people.

At certain times the "free imperial city", such as Ulm, is the incarnation of cast-iron privilege against egalitarian justice, while at other times it vindicates the freedom of the individual against total-itarian levelling-down – as, for example, against Nazi centralism. In general the German idyll – which confines the individual in a con-stricted dimension, and in a society split into separate, stagnant compartments – tends to make the individual (according to Lukács) into a *Bürger*, a bourgeois, rather than a *citoyen*. The result is that pathetic, retrograde inner isolation, "a-political" and "desperately German", of which Thomas Mann was the great interpreter and, at least in part, the representative. This situation is personified in a figure recurring time and time again in German literature, that of the *Sonderling*, the eccentric solitary, whom Giuseppe Bevilacqua has defined as "the expression of a profound uneasiness between a particu-larly sensitive nature and a society incapable of giving free rein to the application of his particular gifts".

Many of the heroes of Hoffmann and Jean Paul Richter are *Sonder-linge*: clerks in Chancellery, assessors, provincial pedagogues or pedan-tic scholars, all inspired by lacerating nostalgia and methodical rigour. Their intense inner passion, swathed in the suffocating weeds of narrow-minded social convention, very often becomes distorted into grotesque extravagance.

Charles Nodier traced the efflorescence of the fantastic genre in German literature to the multitude of local restrictions and special customs. Particularism, sanctioned by common law, is the seedbed of the literature of fantasy, because in view of the diversity of laws and customs it is at the city gates themselves that one begins to venture into the disquieting world of the unknown. This survival of the past gives reality a special aura, anguished and at the same time spectral. Even the lyrical and satirical work of Heine, who is moreover a pupil of the great masters of the historical school of law, is a child of the legal particularism of the German idyll. The *Sonderling* is above all a personification of German inwardness, of the cleavage in it between ethics and politics. This, for example, enabled many individual consciences to put up moral resistance to Nazism, but may perhaps have contributed to obstructing organized political resistance. The idyll of Ulm ended with the bombings of the Second World War, which ultimately spared only 2,633 of the town's 12,795 buildings.

6. THE CAPTURE OF ULM

There is something narrow and diminished about the German idyll, as is suggested by the etymology of the word "idyll", the small image or dainty little picture of rustic life in Greek poetry. German history, which every so often reaches towards universal empires of vast duration, is often born in a provincial context, from horizons no broader than a municipality. For example, one historian gives us the secret plan prepared for the capture of Ulm, in 1701, by Bavarian troops allied to Louis XIV. Some of these had succeeded in infiltrating the city dressed as peasant men and women, with the task (in which they succeeded) of opening the gates of the fortress to their own troops: "Lieutenant Baertelmann will carry a lamb in his arms, Sergeant Kerbler some chickens, while Lieutenant Habbach, dressed as a woman, will carry a basket of eggs . . ."

The Bavarian troops who thanks to this *coup de main* became masters of Ulm – the city today is on the border between Baden-Württemberg and Bavaria – were allies of Louis XIV, but the Sun-King's policy, with its centralistic and imperialistic modernization breaking down local feudal powers, is part of quite another history: it belongs to a chapter which includes Robespierre, Napoleon and Stalin, while the German allies of that French autocrat belong to the medieval, narrow, "idyllic" particularism which modern history, and especially that of France, simply sweeps away.

7. WITH THEIR BARE HANDS AGAINST THE THIRD REICH

At Ulm there bloomed a great flower of German inwardness. Hans and Sophie Scholl, the brother and sister arrested, condemned and executed in 1943 for their activities against Hitler's régime, were from Ulm, and today a university there bears their names. Their story is an example of the absolute resistance which Ethos opposes to Kratos; they succeeded in rebelling against what almost everybody regarded as an obvious and inevitable acceptance of evil. As Golo Mann wrote, they fought with their bare hands against the vast power of the Third Reich, and confronted the political and military apparatus of the Nazi state armed with nothing but their cyclostyle, from which they distributed manifestos against Hitler. They were young, they didn't want to die, and it was painful to them to forgo the enticements of such a glorious day, as Sophie said calmly on the day of their execution; but they knew that life is not the supreme value, and that it becomes lovable and enjoyable only when put at the service of something more than itself, which lights and warms it like a sun. Therefore they went serenely to their deaths, without a tremor, knowing that the prince of this world is judged.

8. A FUNERAL

Another scene in the allegorical theatre of German inwardness took place in Ulm, in the square before the Town Hall. On October 18th 1944, in the presence of von Rundstedt, they celebrated the state funeral of Field Marshal Rommel. The uninformed crowd paid him their last respects in the belief that he had died of wounds received in the service of the Reich, whereas in fact he had been implicated in the conspiracy of July 20th. Given a choice between standing trial and suicide, he had taken poison. This too is a paradox of German inwardness. Rommel was certainly not afraid of execution, and did not lack the sort of courage with which, for example, Helmuth James von Moltke openly faced the Nazi People's Tribunal and consequent hanging. The letters Rommel wrote to his wife, along with the intensity of his love for her, reveal the sense of responsibility of an entirely upright man. He probably believed, at that moment, that he was doing a service to his already tottering country, but avoided the bewilderment and insecurity that would have spread through Germany on seeing a great soldier suddenly transformed into an enemy of the fatherland.

With cool self-mastery and supreme, though paradoxical, sacrifice, he silenced the voice of conscience and brought an indirect but considerable advantage to the Hitler régime which he had tried to defeat, and to Hitler himself whom he had wished to kill. His whole upbringing and education prevented him, even at that moment, from distinguishing clearly between his country and the régime that was perverting and betraying it, while declaring itself to be its very embodiment. It must also be said that the Allies, with their obtuse distrust of proposals for bringing down Nazism put forward by various members of the German High Command, must bear no small measure of responsibility – ever since the "Carthaginian" Treaty of Versailles – in creating this lethal identification between country and régime. In Rommel's decision a pre-eminent role was certainly played by that German upbringing which instils respect and loyalty, in themselves great values: loyalty towards those who are by one's side in any circumstances, and towards one's own words of honour; but it is an upbringing which puts down roots too deep to budge even when one's native soil has become a stinking quagmire. Such loyalty is so strong that it sometimes prevents a man from recognizing the trap he has fallen into, from seeing that he has bestowed his faith not on his own gods but on monstrous idols; and that, in the name of true faith, it is his duty to rebel against those who make spurious and unlawful demands on it.

Von Stauffenberg, the man who actually placed the bomb that was to kill Hitler, was also torn between loyalty to one's country and loyalty to humanity; and this may help us to understand the difficulty of any armed, organized resistance in Germany. But it was certainly not only in the Third Reich that there arose the basic dilemma, cloaked in many guises, between universal loyalty and loyalty towards the task one has in hand – between the ethics of conviction and the ethics of responsibility to follow Max Weber, the unsurpassed diagnostician of the contradictions between systems and values within which our culture moves. Amongst the crimes of Nazism we must mention also the perversion of German inwardness. In the sham of that funeral before the Ulm Town Hall, the tragedy of a man of honour is stage-managed to become a lie.

9. A POUND OF BREAD

In the Bread Museum in Ulm there is a great list of the prices of a pound of bread over the course of a decade (1914–24). In 1914 your pound loaf cost 0.15 gold marks; in 1918, 0.25 *paper* marks; in 1919, 0.28 (still paper); in 1922, 10.57 paper marks . . . and in 1923, 220,000,000 paper marks. By 1924 the price had come down to more or less the same as 1914, 0.14 gold marks, but in a totally different context, and with a different purchasing power.

I have no hopes whatever of grasping the laws of economics and monetary science, of giving intelligent scrutiny to those tangled skeins in which the mathematical curves of financial processes meet and play leapfrog with the unpredictable irregularities of life, the chance occurrence of events, with all the passions and inventions which may hap. A layman reading the paper often thinks that finance is suffering from meningitis, as was suggested by Lafitte, banker to Louis Philippe.

Led by his German studies to conceal his ignorance behind a screen of literary metaphors, the layman does not really think so much of a case of meningitis as of a kind of psychosis, a frenzy of pretence, like that of raving madmen capable of putting on a show of calm and self-control, or that of clinical idiots who – according to a luminary of Viennese psychiatry at the beginning of the century – are able to give a pretence of great intelligence. The statistics of finance appear reassuring but unworthy of belief, the programme for a play that will never be performed.

The dizzying unreality of those 220,000,000 marks for a pound of bread is a true fact of the "grandiose twentieth century", as in 1932 wrote that otherwise negligible author Rudolf Brunngraber in his masterpiece, *Karl and the Twentieth Century*. This is one of the few novels which succeeds in depicting the automatic mechanism of history and world economics, which incorporates individual lives and turns them into mere statistical data, crushing and recycling the individual in the maw of collection processes while degrading the idea of the universal into the law of numerical vastness. The novel deals with the great inflation, not so much in Germany as in Austria. Taylor, the rationalizer of production, comes to occupy the place of Destiny, which makes the individual superfluous. Global laws and objective economic data – production, unemployment, devaluation, prices and wages – become characters in the book, phantoms, maybe, but still solidly threatening and as much the arbiters of human fate as were the tyrants in an ancient tragedy.

Karl's life – with its dreams, its hopes, and his own inability to understand what is happening to him – is composed and dismantled by all pervasive mechanisms, as the meeting of currents and winds forms and dissolves the crest of a wave; but even here – as every life, even the most ephemeral, cries out to be eternal – the drop of water protests, in an agony of torment, at being dissolved into the sea of the social sum-total to which it belongs. This novel about Karl, who never manages to discern the net which ensnares him, is the novel of our own lives, the irregular series of instalments published in a paper whose owner and editor we cannot identify; from time to time the instalments are filled with gory topicalities, news of this swindle or that beneath sensational headlines. Brunngraber's book gives us a genuine, physical fear of a Third World War which the reader is unexpectedly terrified to find inevitable – and shows us that those 220,000,000 marks for a small loaf of bread are ominously real, however unimaginable; they are an immense figure of flesh and blood, the giant in some monstrous epic poem.

10. AT THE PIG MARKET

The *Fischerviertel*, the fishermen's quarter in Ulm, is enchanting indeed with its friendly, beckoning little alleyways, the inns so liberal with trout and asparagus, the open-air beer-houses, the promenade along the Danube, the old houses and the wisteria reflected in the Blau, the little "home" stream that makes it modest contribution to the great river.

Sweet and fresh is the air, and Amedeo has taken Maddalena by the arm, while Gigi is busy weighing up the merits of the various hostelries. Francesca's face is reflected in an old window-pane overlooking the canal, and life seems to be flowing on quietly and gently, as do these waters through the mystery of evening. The town is charming, the 548 beer-houses mentioned in the 1875 statistics seem in an ideal sense to reconcile Christian Friedrich Daniel Schubart, the rebel poet, with Albrecht Ludwig Berblinger, the famous tailor who was determined to fly and who fell like a stone into the Danube; also with the New German Cinema, which to a great degree originated in Ulm, and with the celebrated College of Design. Further proof of this courteous *genius loci* was furnished by the most illustrious of all the sons of Ulm, Albert Einstein, when in a polite little rhymed quatrain he writes that the stars – heedless of the Theory of Relativity – proceed to all eternity upon the paths laid down for them by Newton.

On the Town Hall there is a plaque to commemorate the fact that it was in Ulm that Kepler published the *Rudolphine Tables* and invented a weight-scale which was publicly adopted by the city. In the pig-market square there is another plaque. This one, in a tone of some arrogance, celebrates the German victories of 1870 and the foundation of Wilhelm's Reich, and adds:

> "Auch auf dem Markt der Säue
> wohnt echte deutsche Treue"

—even in the pig-market beats a loyal German heart.

The rhyme between *Säue* (sows) and *Treue* (loyalty) is already, though unwittingly, a malignant caricature of what in a few years' time was to become the vulgarity of the wealthy, powerful Second Reich. How different and more gentle a spirit it was who in 1717, on the Fishermen's House in the square of the same name, painted a view of another city: Weissenburg, which is to say Belgrade. It was the aim of the painter, Guildmaster Johann Matthäus Scheiffele, to immortalize the ferries carrying troops from Ulm down the Danube to fight against the Turks. Belgrade, already captured and lost, was a strategic point in that war. Others who set off from Ulm, on the old longboats known as "crates from Ulm", were the German settlers on their way to populate the Banat, those "Donauschwaben", Swabians of the Danube, who for two centuries, from the time of Maria Theresa until the Second World War, were to make a basic and important contribution, now erased, to the culture and life of the Danube basin. My own journey down the Danube is first and foremost a journey towards the Banat, in the wake of an expansion now vanished, and in fact reversed; for ever since the end of the Second World War there has been a withdrawal, and indeed an exodus, of Germans from the south-east of Europe.

On the main square of the Ulm rises the cathedral, with the world's tallest spire and a heterogeneous construction begun in 1377 and finished – apart from later restorations – in 1890. There is something discordant about the cathedral, that touch of ill-grace that is often found in record-breaking achievements. Maddalena's nose, as she gazes in perplexity up at the spire and tries to persuade herself that all is well, describes an intrepid, restless curve through the air, in contrast to which the holy pile reveals all the dullness of stone.

Outstanding among the numerous guides to the cathedral is the accurate, fussy one by Ferdinand Thrän, who not only mentions but describes every detail, from the friezes on the columns to the earnings from the sale of a pair of trousers offered by a pious member of the congregation, the miller Wammes, towards the fund for church works (6 schillings and 2 centimes). Apart from being the writer of the guide, Thrän was also a neo-Gothic architect, and came very near to wrecking the cathedral by his obstinate belief in a "law" about arches, which he was convinced he had discovered. On the cover of his learned work (*The Cathedral of Ulm, an Exact Description of the Same*, 1857) the printer, in a moment of distraction which seems to obey the remorseless destiny of Ferdinand Thrän, has forgotten to print the author's name, which the librarian of the National Library in Vienna has added in pencil, at least in the copy housed in the Albertine palace.

This example of forgetfulness was one of the many wrongs suffered by Thrän, architect and restorer of the cathedral during the last century and a hypochondriac specializing in discourtesies, as is shown by the scrupulous *File of Rudenesses Received* which he kept for years and which lies, unpublished and unknown, in a box put away in a cupboard in the cathedral. A pig-headed Jonah and the leather-skinned target of continual abuses, Thrän seems, with bitter gratification, to stress the fact that life is an affront and a dirty trick, so there is nothing for it but to keep a rigorous inventory of its outrages. If genuine writing is born from the desire to account for the copious inconvenience of living, then Thrän is a real writer. Literature here is accountancy, the ledger of profit and loss, the balance sheet of an inevitable deficit. But the orderliness of the register, the precision and completeness of the records, may give a pleasure that compensates for the repulsiveness of what is actually noted. When Sartre says that in his view the

consummation of the sexual act is mediocre compared to the fore-
play, we notice the satisfaction he takes in recording the unsatisfy-
ing final pleasure.

The archivist of affronts makes order among them, keeps them
under control, becomes master of the disgraceful world and of humiliations undergone. When he tells us about the exam in architecture
which he took as a private candidate at Stuttgart in 1835, Thrän makes a
fleeting mention of the good marks he received, but dwells on the
ghastly need to get up at dawn, on the discomforts of the journey and
the discourtesy of the customs men, on the execrable quality of the beer
and resulting sickness, and on how much it all cost: 77 florins and 47
kreutzer. When he became inspector of road-works he was forced, in
ceremonies and servile homage, to visit influential persons, counsellors
of finance and departmental directors; but one of his uncles always
insisted on going with him, considering him too clumsy and thick-
headed to make such visits alone.

While working on the restoration of the cathedral he came up
against his superiors and the city authorities, who accused him of
spending too much money, and he gives minutely detailed reports of
the wrangles, the criticisms, the quarrels with his opponents in the
newspapers, the legal disputes over clauses in his contracts, the fines,
the appeals, the slanders on his account, the contempt and tyranny of
the notables, the squabbles about the introduction of gas lighting, the
intrigues of his rivals, who were unable to prevent the King of
Württemberg from giving him a gold medal for artistic and scientific
merit, but did hold up the official publication of this honour.

Thrän felt like "hunted game", but his rancour is not limited to the
enemies who persecute him, because he rises above mere shabby
personal motives. It is not the single envious and ill-intentioned
individual that is at fault: the whole of life inflicts wrongs and insults,
the whole thing is an affront. Thrän impartially records the knavish
pettiness of men and of things, the intrigues of building-inspector
Rupp-Reutlingen and the malevolence of the storm which ruined the
central nave for him, filling the cathedral with flakes of plaster,
the decision which assigned him a salary with no pension attached and
the nervous fevers with which he is afflicted, his eleven falls from
horseback – imputed to the poor quality of his old nag, which was,
however, the only sort of horse he could afford on his income – and the
death of four of his children, the frequent accidents which cause him to
fall off the scaffolding or end up in the Danube, the inconvenience and

risk of being impaled while being fished out with a boat-hook. Tragedies and mere vexations are all put on the same level, because the real tragedy of life is that it is, solely and entirely, a nuisance.

Central European literature has examples of this self-wounding figure on a grand scale; of the type of man who triumphs over the stupidity and injustice of life thanks to the completeness with which he keeps the record of his misfortunes. Thrän is an infant brother of Grillparzer and of Kafka; he is a sort of cartographer of his own calamities. In his inventory, life reveals all its meanness and spite. One who undergoes and records such things can flaunt this summary of life's impudence in her face and thereby master her, glaring down at her from above like the headmaster handing the class dunce his school report.

Thrän takes a pride in recording the affronts suffered at the hands of the authorities and private individuals, of his superiors and his neighbours, because in the contempt shown him by others he sees the proof of his own dignity, of the ineptitude which renders him worthy of derision, the inadequacy in life which is the mark of true uprightness of character. In the article he wrote for the centenary of his birth, Prof. Dieferlen recalls Thrän, with his long hair and bushy great beard, busy restoring the ruined cathedral overrun by weeds, infested with barn-owls and bats nesting in the Gothic traceries, with icy winds blasting in through the broken windows and the chirping of sparrows above the pulpit during the sermon. Thrän probably loved that desolation and neglect. He notes with satisfaction, for example, that the statue of the sparrow – the symbol of Ulm – has crumbled to pieces, unable to hold out against "the transience of all things", and adds that the new sparrow fashioned in clay, stored away in the cellar waiting for the authorities to decide on whether or not to put it in the place of the old one, is patiently awaiting the end of their squabbles but meanwhile gradually cracking and deteriorating – luckily, however, less swiftly than the councillors disputing on its destiny are themselves falling into decay.

The archivist of affronts takes pleasure in noting the wearing away of life, which will erase him from the world as well, but will also and above all erase those affronts. The universality of death corrects the universality of stupidity and nastiness. But every book written against life, wrote Thomas Mann, seduces us into living it; behind Thrän's obstinate rejection with which he counters the malevolence of things there is also a reticent love of reality, of those rivers and those roads which he measured with persevering exactitude. Perhaps the true friend of life is not the wooer who courts her with sentimental flatteries, but rather the clumsy, rejected lover who feels that she has cast him out from her good graces, as Thrän put it, like a piece of old furniture.

12. GRILLPARZER AND NAPOLEON

Near the abbey of Elchingen, a few kilometres from the city, is the site of the *Capitulation of Ulm* on October 19th 1805; in other words of the surrender of the Austrian General Mack – the "unlucky Mack" mentioned by Tolstoy in *War and Peace* – to Napoleon. A stone commemorates the Napoleonic dead, soldiers from France and the various German states at that time allied to the Emperor: "A la mémoire des soldats de la Grand Armée de 1805 Bavarois, Wurtembergeois, Badois et Français". The landscape, with its misty woods beside the river, could be a print of a battle-scene; a gap indicates the spot at which Marshal Ney broke through the Austrian defences.

This stretch of the Danube has been the scene of great battles, such as that of Höchstädt (or Blindheim), in which, in 1704 during the War of the Spanish Succession, Prince Eugène and the Duke of Marlborough overwhelmed the French army of Louis XIV. But these battles along the Danube are battles of the old Europe, pre-revolutionary and pre-modern, which, with alternate victories and defeats, prolong the balance between the absolute monarchies until 1789. The Danubian empire is the embodiment of that traditional world par excellence, whereas Napoleon, who defeated the Austrians at Ulm and entered Vienna, is the embodiment of the modernity that pressed hard on the heels of the old Hapsburg-Danubian order, in a pursuit which ended only in 1918.

Grillparzer's observations on Napoleon are an exemplary expression of this Austrian spirit, both pre- and post-modern, which sees modernity sweeping away the symbolic defences of tradition, represented by the Danube. A shrewd thinker, and factiously one-sided, Grillparzer – who witnessed Napoleon's triumphant entry into Vienna in 1809 – denounces in him the predominance of an unbridled imagination, of a subjective *hubris* with regard to reality which he is aware of even in himself, and which he considers a danger to his moral peace of mind and even to his work as a poet. Grillparzer, an imitator and a precursor at one and the same time, and the classic of the nineteenth-century Austrian theatre, is in Hapsburg literature the first "man without qualities" and creator of men without qualities. He is a divided, ambivalent individual, but imbued with a profound sense of reverence for that unity of personality which eludes him, and which he judges to be a higher quality. Tortuous and hypochondriac, the pedantic organizer and administrator of his own inhibitions, captiously averse to joy and split between frenzied passions and self-destructive sterility, Grillparzer – no wonder that Kafka read him avidly – is the writer who falsifies his own self-portrait, bringing out all its negative aspects, as he does in his own diaries by adopting the disagreeable *alter ego* Fixlmüllner.

When life is privation, inadequacy, then defence consists in stubbornly keeping to the sidelines, refusing to take part. Danubian culture, so extremely sensitive to the hidden side of life, has been masterly in working out this defensive strategy. But this culture pledged to discovery of the vacuum of Parallel Actions and, like Karl Kraus, to the praise of the world back to front, did not overlook the totality whose eradication it was witnessing, that ordered, harmonious baroque cosmos that it watched being turned upside down. Grillparzer experienced his idiosyncrasies not as psychological contingencies but as a dictate of the times, an imbalance between self and the world at large; like Kafka after him, he did not permit these idiosyncrasies to cloud his objective sense of the Law, of the world which, in the Viennese tradition, is still a world created by God.

Grillparzer is certainly incapable of seeing in Napoleon, as Hegel did, the Weltgeist on horseback; he considers him rather to be a social climber exercising power not in the name of a lofty ideal but of unbridled egocentricity. The effects of Napoleon's career were in fact the source of Grillparzer's play *King Ottocar: His Rise and Fall* (1825), in which he contrasts Rudolph of Hapsburg, founder of the dynasty and the embodiment of power exercised humbly, with Ottocar of Bohemia, whose aim was to use power for his own individual ambitions. For him therefore Napoleon is the symbol of an age in which subjectivity (national, revolutionary, popular) broke away from the *religio* of tradition and brought to an end the rationalistic, tolerant cosmopolitanism of the eighteenth century by imbuing the masses with nationalism.

Napoleon represents the "fever of a sick era", but, like fever, he also represents a violent reaction which can "eliminate the sickness" and lead to recovery. Grillparzer calls him a "son of destiny", and endows him with the nimbus of one who, like Hamlet, is summoned to set right a time that is "out of joint"; but the Corsican lacks the humility of Hamlet, whose awareness of his tremendous mission makes him conscious of his own personal inadequacy. Napoleon on the other hand is small, because he claims to be great, but will only really become so at his fall, in religious expiation, in the recognition of his own vanity, as Ottocar in the play rises to true regality when he is defeated and humiliated in battle and in love, hounded by old age, reduced to the condition of beggary, that is, of a real man.

For Grillparzer, Napoleon, with his assertion that in the modern age politics have replaced destiny, represents totalitarianism, life seen as totally political, the irruption of history and the state into the existence of the individual, engulfed as this is by social mechanisms. The general mobilization typical of modern society and of Napoleonism – Grillparzer grasps its Big Chief element but disregards its impulse to democracy and emancipation – is countered by Joseph II's ethos of the loyal servitor of the state, who does his duty with self-abnegation, but who also defines the limits of political interference, defending the distinction between the public and the private spheres.

Grillparzer calls Napoleon's unilateralism "terrifying": Napoleon "everywhere sees nothing but his own ideas and sacrifices everything to them." Against ideological totalitarianism the Austrian tradition defends the tangible detail, the unique particular, that side of life which cannot be reduced to a system. A religious vision such as that of Rudolph II – the silent Emperor in the great, late play *Family Strife in Hapsburg* – also respects the individuality that is unpredictable and out of shape, in that the sense of religious transcendence forbids us to make idols of earthly hierarchies, and refers us to a higher plane on which even that anomaly finds its place in the designs of God. A purely worldly, historical perspective is dogmatically brutal with regard to what appears minor and secondary: Grillparzer accuses Napoleon of aiming straight for the "Hauptsache", the main point, while ignoring the "Nebensache", the outwardly marginal and secondary but which nonetheless, in the eyes of the Austrian poet who is the defender of "minute particulars", has its independent dignity and must not be sacrificed to a tyrannical overall scheme of things.

Austrian culture is inspired by a baroque oneness which transcends history, or else by a scattered post-historical fragmentation which follows the torrent of modern history. In both cases it rejects the criteria of a purely historical evaluation, the yardsticks according to which we bestow importance on phenomena and arrange them in order of greatness. Austrian culture defends what is marginal, transient, secondary, the pause and respite from that mechanism which aims at burning up such things so as to attain more important results.

Napoleon, on the contrary, personifies the modern frenzy that annihilates the otiose and the ephemeral, stamping the life out of the moment in its impatience to get ahead. In his novel *The Ballad of the Hundred Days*, Joseph Roth later took up the old gossip about the Emperor's premature ejaculation, and made it a symbol of his frantic haste, that had to dispatch all business right away, that always had something else to do, and at each moment was thinking of the next one, without being able to dally even in love or in pleasure; because the man who is not convinced does not wish to act, but to have already acted.

The Austrian viewpoint is discordant, with respect to the Napoleonic myth in the rest of Europe, which is set in quite different keys, ranging from the glamour of a great life emerging out of nothing, which is present in Stendhal and Dostoyevsky, to the apocalyptic passion of Léon Bloy. Grillparzer does have a grasp of certain aspects of the modernity of Napoleon, but he contrasts them with Joseph's enlightened, bureaucratic ethos, which had in its day been radically innovative, but which in the Napoleonic era was becoming a frozen, ultra-conservative apparatus, in spite of the tenacious resistance of its great, progressive ethical and political tradition. In any case Grillparzer's aim was to extol the "grandiose poise" of Rudolph I, "a man entirely silent and tranquil", but in the drama the latter comes out pale and insignificant, while over him looms the giant figure of Ottocar, the defeated Titan. And then again it is Rudolph, theoretician of patience, who acts wisely, because his prudence is a political art, whereas Ottocar dreams of greatness, but deludes himself passively in this giddying but a-political dream.

In his play *King Ottocar: His Rise and Fall*, Grillparzer celebrates the beginning of the eastern policy of the Hapsburgs, their success as the House of Austria, their fateful turning towards the East and their mission on the Danube. Ottocar personifies Bohemia vanquished in Central Europe by the Holy Roman Empire of the German Nation, of which Rudolph wears the crown. But in the play Ottocar also appears as the modernizer, that is, the Germanizer of Bohemia, the sovereign who favours and introduces the German element into his country so as to render his kingdom more efficient and highly evolved; he despises those of his subjects who are reluctant to be torn from their archaic, primitive rhythms of life, from the agrarian world of those Slav nations which in the nineteenth century were called "nations without history".

Ottocar sets out to lead them into history, and he perishes; the Bohemian monarch sets out to Germanize his people to enable them to triumph over the Germans, but in so doing he destroys his power and independence, according to the pessimistic view of Grillparzer and the Hapsburgs, who see this "entry into history" as a fall. In any case Bohemian is – and was to remain for at least a century – an ambiguous term, which can refer to the Czechs, but also to the Germans of Bohemia, so that above all it indicates an identity that is hard to define, like all those borderline cases lacerated by contention. Worst of all, it is a touchy identity, never satisfied with the attitude taken towards it by others, whatever this might be. This play stayed for a long time in quarantine, for fear of giving offence to the Bohemians, and Grillparzer himself tells how he went to visit the tomb of Ottocar, to ask his forgiveness, and that he saw around him, in Prague, many long faces.

13. DEAMBULATORY THERAPY

According to tradition it was at Ulm, during the seventeenth century, that they preserved the shoe of Ahasverus, the Wandering Jew. With those soles which had lasted for centuries one could undertake any journey, and doctors at one time considered walking as very good for preserving mental balance. A footnote in the Italian edition of the complete *Tales of Hoffmann*, concerning a real character used by the writer as a model, informs us: "F. Wilhelm C. L. von Grotthus (1747–1801) attempted to combat the mental disease hereditary to his family by making very long journeys on foot. He died insane at Bayreuth."

The ancient town founded by the Alemanni has a wealth of towers, prominent among which is the slender, soaring tower of the White Horse, the legendary steed, fifteen feet in length, which cleared the Danube in one leap. Like nearby Dillingen, Lauingen has a tradition of theological studies, colleges and seminaries, an atmosphere of silent, meditative Swabian religious feeling, that absorbed and humbly joyous spirituality that, in spite of the din of ferocious sectarian struggles, characterizes the German country parish, particularly in Swabia – even though Lauingen has since 1269 officially been part of Bavaria. The little town is a hive of colleges, such as the Illustrious Gymnasium built in 1561 by Wolfgang, Count of the Palatinate, and now erased from history. It is a place of parish priests, pastors and teachers, such as Deigele, known as the Mendelssohn of Swabia and author of hymns which even today, in certain village churches, give voice to a subdued familiarity with God and a feeling that might be called almost happy, even if we also discern in them the shadow, the brevity, the nullity of living. Lauingen was the birthplace of Albertus Magnus, master of St Thomas Aquinas, and his statue now stands opposite the Town Hall. In his *De animalibus* this encyclopaedic saint even mentions the fish he says he had occasion to observe in his native Danube.

In the eighteenth-century German provinces, in Swabia and Bavaria, the writer Jean Paul's schoolmasters and parish priests move about on their small peregrinations. He follows them along the country lanes, and along the roads of their lives, with that sinuous, uneven, exasperatingly convoluted turn of phrase in which Ladislao Mittner perceived an attempt to reproduce in syntax the mobile nexus of the One-All.

That syntax was also the mirror-image of the Empire, that Holy Roman Empire which, in Goethe's *Faust*, is the cause of wonder as to how on earth it still managed to hang together. Jean Paul's sentences appear to be all subsidiary clauses with no main clause, either projecting out into space or at best sustained by a centre that is extremely hard to find; they reflect a political and social assemblage overcrowded with the marginal, the particular, with exceptions, special statutes and separate bodies lacking any solid central structure, as was the German Empire, already approaching its end.

Even from that world, a real storehouse of material for satire, Jean Paul learnt to feel life as dissolution, as insufficiency. Man's journey on earth seemed to him a continual fall, like that of a falling body. He is the poet of existence interpreted as want of conviction, that is, of real life, but he is also a subtle, insidious strategist who, thanks to poetry, wrenches territories of conviction, moments of the most absolute significance, from the desert of absence and worldliness. A contemporary of Goethe and Schiller, anti-classical as a writer, Jean Paul was held at a certain distance by the great figures of the classical school, and he in turn kept them at arm's length. He satirized the particularism of the Holy Roman Empire, but to some extent remained a prisoner of its provincial horizons. Drawing the chairs up to the stove and pulling on his nightcap before telling the story of his little schoolmaster Maria Wuz, he ridicules the naïvety of those who think that the *grand monde* begins on the other side of the alleyway, but for his own part he had nothing to do with that "great world" of politics in which, during those very years, classical literature was setting foot, like Faust, to keep step with the march of human history.

But Jean Paul gives voice to divisions which were to emerge with violence later in European literature, and which German classicism tended to thrust aside or to exorcize. He grasps the vacuum concealed behind words, the eclipse of values and their very basis, the nihilism which engulfs all things, turning Nature into a corpse and annulling the present. The gentle poet of domestic pleasures and religious simplicity is also the poet who (though transposing it into the indirectness of a dream) imagined the blood-chilling fable of the dead Christ who announces that there is no God. Jean Paul gives expression to the nihilism – the destruction of values and finite reality – which the classical culture of the time thought it could overcome. He is aware of a person's lack of identification with himself, and ventures into the intricacies of dreams and the unconscious, into those dark corridors where his characters are aghast to meet their own doubles. Only humour can heal this anguish of dissociation, for though it cuts the finite down to size, and even shatters it, it does so with good grace and sympathy, opening it towards that infinite which transcends it but at the same time invests it with universal meaning.

It is understandable that Hegel did not like Jean Paul, because he refused to see reality – and modern reality at that – as the complete, perfected self-realization of the Spirit. For Jean Paul the world is covered with holes and fissures from which come whispers and gusts of transcendence, reflections of the infinite. In fact he writes in the *Siebenkäs* that in this world one must always paint a little of the other, in order to complete it. Reality for him depends on an "elsewhere", on the red roads that seem to come into view behind the sunset, or on the summer which the inhabitant of Arctic regions awaits throughout the darkness of his long night. Jean Paul is not a "modern", if modernity is forceful thought systematically bringing everything together, but he could be said to be a contemporary, if by this we mean someone who above all feels the incompleteness and fragmentary nature of reality, of its quality of stalemate.

Whatever the opinion held or faith professed by men, what chiefly distinguishes them is the presence or the absence, in their thought or in their persons, of this "beyond", their sense of living in a world perfect and complete in itself or else incomplete and open towards a beyond. Travelling is perhaps always a journey towards those distances that glow red and purple in the evening sky, beyond the line of the sea or the mountains, to the countries where the sun is rising when it sets with us. The traveller journeys onwards in the evening, each step taking him further into the sunset and leading him beyond the fiery line that fades. A traveller, writes Jean Paul, is like an invalid, poised between two worlds. The way is long, even if we move only from the kitchen to the room facing west, its window-panes catching the blaze of the horizon, because the house is a vast, unknown kingdom and one lifetime is not enough for the odyssey from nursery to bedroom, for the corridor where the children chase each other, for the dining-table where the corks pop in salvos like a guard of honour, and the desk with its few books and papers; one lifetime will not accommodate the attempt to say something about this coming-and-going between kitchen and dining-room, between Troy and Ithaca.

But now it is really evening, between Lauingen and Dillingen, and the red sky is not only an image with pretensions to symbolic value, but also an undeniable meteorological fact. In Lauingen, in front of the bell-founders' house, we met Amedeo, according to plan. And now he is suddenly silent, the prisoner of some reticence lodged in his pineal gland. The pinkness of Maddalena's cheek is even more pronounced than usual, the transparency of evening and of her heart intermingle their tints in her face, and the student of things German, acquainted perforce with the *Theory of Colours* with which Goethe vainly opposed Newton, thinks that perhaps Goethe was not entirely wrong: that the light is propagated as Newton said, but that we, by good fortune, do not see the length of the light-waves, but rather green, blue, and the flush of this evening and of Maddalena's cheeks.

O let this evening last for ever, and let us never arrive at Dillingen, just as we never cross the horizon. The river of life flows in our veins, as it did for Maria Wuz the schoolteacher, and at every heartbeat it deposits in us, as in him, a little of the silt of time which one day will rise as high as the heart, and cover us; but now, at this moment, that torrent does not overwhelm, but cradles us. The sunset glows also on the face of Francesca, as light and enigmatic as a banner in the wind. For an hour of pleasure the senses favour the rotundity of what is classic and perfected, femininity in full bloom that has nothing more to become, the curved, salacious lines of the mature woman, the unimpeachable finish of the *fin de siècle* adulteress. Mere pleasure has need of what is tangible and finite, and does not love the beyond. But if into pleasure there creeps even the most fleeting prelude or glimmer of perdition, it arises only at the call of the beyond, it loves the enigma of what is still in the act of becoming, this reluctant incompleteness by our side, the airy onrush and the straight line, the young girl, the tree rising tall in the evening.

Now Francesca is in front with the others. We – and the language in which I write is deficient, its grammar does not contain the dual number needed to conjugate and decline, without misunderstandings, the continuous substance of life – we have been left a little way behind. But even those figures just ahead, those third parties, are one with us. Our walk through the bare, dim plain will soon be over, Dillingen is already close by, and even the communion of this evening that attunes us all will come to an end. Disintegration is the imperfection of existence, the lack of it; life crumbles into minimal fragments of time, in which – and therefore also in the sum of them – there is nothing whatever.

As was later the case for the old men in Svevo's books, for Jean Paul's gentle characters the light of life is often clouded over by the dread of living, of the fortuitous cares which dog it. In our existence there is too much and too little, a breathless accumulation of inessential inconveniences that leaves us short-winded, and a lack of essential things. Those timid schoolteachers are expert strategists in the guerrilla war to avoid absence, to elude its heart-wringing grip. They try to enjoy life by freeing it from the organization that absorbs it all and leaves it not a moment of conviction, as the plans for a journey which Rector Florian Fäbel, another of Jean Paul's heroes, makes with his graduating class to the Fichtelberg absorb him entirely and utterly. The attention he pays to the map prevents him from looking at the places they are passing through, while as he reads the description of a building aloud from Büsching's guidebook he has no time to look at the building itself.

Jean Paul's mild-mannered wandering pedagogues combat insufficiency by means of a radical homeopathic therapy, by a process of continual withdrawal. They seek for an empty space, a pure suspension in which flashes the light of what is essential, or at least a reflection of it; and to do this they empty reality of all impediments, of all its cumbersome furniture. Maria Wuz closes his eyes as wind and snow bedim the windows, and he sprinkles the frosted fields with images of spring. As a grown-up he spends the evening hours recalling his childhood, and especially those moments at which, in a transport of happiness, he would close his eyes while his mother was preparing supper. Withdrawal is raised to the mathematical square, light blazes in a memory at the second power, when he recollects moments in which he remembered or dreamt of happiness, which retires into a space outside time, the dark cupboard under the stairs that contains the toys and mementos of his childhood, while the verdure of that childhood, for Maria Wuz, still shines beneath the snow that for so many years has covered it.

Jean Paul loves the present – awaited or lamented when it is still the future or already the past, but scorned and squandered when it is the present. This pure present does not exist in time, which destroys it at every instant; it exists outside time, which is to say life, as it is rarefied in the memory or in writing. Smoke, he says in his novel *Life of Quintus Fixlein*, rises from our tortuous existence and crystallizes, like the vapours of antimony, into new flowers of joy, and these are nothing but the flowers of poetry or the images which writing draws forth from the life which wastes away. The family idyll, as sung by Jean Paul, takes on cosmic dimensions, and the world of domesticity – love in marriage, the little household tasks, a happy day, the cradle and the coffin – are grafted onto and woven into the fabric of infinity. As he observes the netting-away of time, the biographer of Maria Wuz feels "the nothingness of our existence" and vows "to disdain, deserve and enjoy a life so insignificant".

Every journey, such as the one we are now making to Dillingen, is an act of resistance to privation, because we do not travel to arrive but simply to travel, and in our lingerings sparkles the pure present. Who is it who is really setting out? In telling the story of the introduction to the life of Quintus Fixlein, Jean Paul says that once on his travels he met a Superintendent of Fine Arts, and that in talking to him he passed himself off as Fixlein, that is, as the character he had invented. But maybe not only Jean Paul, but anyone who writes, is a forger of himself, thrusting the pronoun "I" onto another person, one who is really travelling along his road. Who is it on this peerless evening, walking towards Dillingen, following not the groove of the path but the route being traced this moment by the pen across the paper? Anyone who entrusts his own destiny to paper is a pathetic shadow of Kafka: when he has already grasped the doorhandle and is about to go into the room of the belovèd woman, like Kafka into Milena's room, he relaxes his grip and turns back: back to the science of cartography.

The characters in Singer do not turn back; they calmly enter that room, because they are not afraid of facing life and the risk of not being equal to it. They accept the hour of triumph without pride and the hour of failure without distress, because in the assurance of their bodies there is a deep-seated conviction that both are obedient to a necessary law, like high tide and low tide. Those who fear setbacks, like Zeno Cosini and Josef K., and are unable to accept them, withdraw into literature, between the folds of the paper, where they are able to play with the phantom of defeat, sidling around it, holding it at bay by flirting with it, courting it and putting it off. Literature offers shelter to failure, thanks to what it transfers to paper by stealing it from life, but at the same time leaving the latter still emptier and more arid. Jean Paul says that a writer preserves all his perceptions and ideas exclusively in what he has written, and if someone burns his papers he is bereft of those things and no longer knows about them. When he wanders around without his note-books he is completely stupid and ignorant, the "pallid silhouette and copy of his own self, his representative and *curator absentis*".

But paper is kindly, because it teaches this humility and opens one's eyes to the vacuity of the ego. Someone who writes a page and, half an hour later while waiting for a bus, realizes that he understands nothing, not even what he has just written, learns to recognize his own inconsequence, and as he dwells upon the fatuity of his own page realizes that each person takes his own lucubrations to be the centre of the universe. And there you have it in a nutshell – everybody does. And perhaps the writer has a fraternal feeling towards that myriad of everybodies who, like him, fancy they are souls elect as they trundle their whims towards the grave; perhaps he realizes how stupid it is, in our common, jostling rush towards nothingness, to do each other injury. Writers constitute a universal secret order, a freemasonry, a Grand Lodge of stupidity. It is no coincidence that they themselves, from Jean Paul to Musil, have been the ones to compose essays and eulogies on Stupidity.

But this inadequacy of writing helps us to discover the paltriness and relativity of intelligence, and can thus prepare the way for a fraternal, reciprocal forbearance. The sheet of paper teaches us not to take it too seriously: even one who is more like Kafka than like Singer learns from *The Castle* and the *Letters to Milena* that he must turn that doorhandle, open that door, enter that room. Some time later he will be delighted to see his children creating havoc with his papers and using them to make boats or darts. When Buffetto II, my highly esteemed guinea-pig, gnaws at the cover of the *Genealogy of Morals*, raising his dusty, decorous whiskers to the height of the bottom shelf, loyalty to Nietzsche teaches me to let him be, and in fact to rejoice in his tranquil familiarity with the world beyond good and evil.

Let the man of letters who, as such, is aware of being a fool, in virtue of this self-awareness which knows it cannot fulfil itself, therefore be allowed to cultivate his passion for the written word, which helps him to keep going, to feed, like one of Jean Paul's characters, on old prefaces, programmes, playbills, obituaries and posters; and to write what comes, catching at images and sentences as best he may. When the note-book is covered with scribbles the spirit is calmer; it whistles nonchalantly at passing time. It is nearly night, we are at Dillingen, and the melancholy of evening has been put to flight. It is possible, without dismay, to accept the decree that commands the enchantment of these last few hours to come to an end. The Königstrasse, with its medieval gateway and baroque buildings, welcomes us into its meditative quiet, with the relaxed, discreet German familiarity of its ancient streets that seem merely to prolong the absorbed tranquillity of a square in space and time.

The inn is cosy, with its dark wood, the tankards of beer and the igloo of eiderdowns on the beds. We say our goodnights and scatter to our rooms until tomorrow. What a stupid word tomorrow is! The dream of life, said Jean Paul, is dreamt on too hard a mattress, but to sleep together makes up the grammatical deficiencies: it is conviction.

At Günzburg, this small town known as Little Vienna in the days of the Hapsburgs, on April 28th 1770 the citizens turned out to pay homage to Marie Antoinette, on her way – with her nuptial procession of 370 horses and 57 coaches – to her wedding with Louis XVI and, somewhat later, to her appointment with the guillotine.

But it is not of Marie Antoinette that we are induced to think by these charming houses, these tidy, hospitable streets, and the inn-sign of the *Goldene Traube* with its golden bunch of grapes. This is the birthplace of Josef Mengele, the jailer-doctor of Auschwitz, perhaps the most atrocious murderer in all the death-camps. Here he remained in hiding – in a monastery – until 1949, and here he made a furtive return in 1959 for his father's funeral. In Auschwitz, always smiling and unruffled, Mengele used to hurl babies into the fire, tear infants from their mother's breast and dash their brains out, extract foetuses from the womb, make experiments on twins (with a particular relish for gypsy twins), gouge out eyes, which he kept threaded on strings and hung on the walls of his room, and then sent to Prof. Otran van Verschuer (Director of the Berlin Institute of Anthropology, and a professor at Münster University even after 1953), inject people with viruses and burn their genitals. He has eluded capture for forty years, and may be still alive. It must be said that even someone who can kill another man for fun, and force the man's son to watch, is capable of loving his own father.

Infamy invites complicity: Mengele was discharged from prison by the Americans, perhaps helped to escape by the British, hidden by the monks, and protected by the dictator of Paraguay. Nazism is certainly not the only barbarity to have existed in the world, and the condemnation of Nazi violence, which is no longer a threat, is today used by many to cover up other violence, inflicted on other victims of other races and colours, and to make peace with their consciences thanks to this profession of "anti-Fascist" faith. But it is also true that Nazism was a summit, an unsurpassed climax of infamy, the closest link that has ever existed between a social order and atrocity. In the case of this smiling, sadistic doctor, it is wrong-headed to fall back on pathological explanations, as if he were a patient in the grip of an uncontrollable impulse. In the monastery at Günzburg where he was in hiding he did not gouge out eyes or disembowel people, and I do not imagine that he suffered from withdrawal symptoms. He will have behaved well, a quiet, discreet gentleman who may have watered the flowers and respectfully attended Vespers. He did not kill because he couldn't, because circumstances forbade him to, and he resigned himself to this sacrifice without making a fuss, accepting the limitations placed on his aspirations by real circumstances, just as one learns to live with not being able to become a millionaire or go to bed with Hollywood stars. The fear of the Lord is the beginning of wisdom: if there is no law, no fear, no barrier to prevent one doing what in Auschwitz could be done with impunity, not just Dr Mengele, but perhaps anyone at all could become a Mengele.

Mengele's crimes comprise one of the most horrific chapters in the history of the extermination camps. Like every criminal passion, even his enjoyment of torture reveals a vast banality, as vacuous as his stupid smile during the execution of a crime. A Jewish doctor, forced to assist him in his experiments, once asked him how much longer the business of extermination was going to last. Smiling, in sweet tones, Mengele replied: "Mein Freund, es geht immer weiter, immer weiter," for ever, my friend, for ever. That ecstatic, feeble-minded phrase contains all the obtuseness of evil: the mechanical, moonstruck repetition of a kind of ritual formula, somewhere between the refrain of a psychedelic pop-song and a religious litany; it is the babbling of a weak mind drugged with cruelty.

Mengele, at that time, was bewitched by the act of transgression, which he practised as a kind of cult, thinking that it illuminated everyday life with a "higher" light. The acts he carried out, apart from being atrocious, were of an extreme degree of stupidity, things that anyone could do and that he, in his ignorance dazzled by kitsch, thought of as deeds reserved for the chosen few.

The rhetoric of transgression presents crime, maybe on account of the unhappiness which is assumed to accompany it, as carrying its own redemption, without the need for any further catharsis. Violence thereby appears as one and the same as redemption, and gives the impression of installing some kind of innocence among the psychic drives. The mystique of transgression, a word invested with edifying claptrap, deludes itself in exalting evil for evil's sake, in contempt of all morality. The murky but spell-binding technicolor of evil is more be-witching than the sober black-and-white of good; an evil deed excites admiration, almost as if it were enough to shoot a friend, as Verlaine shot at Rimbaud, to enable one to write the poems of Verlaine.

The fascination of transgression has ancient origins. The Jewish tradition speaks of the Messiah who will arrive when evil has reached its zenith, and, according to certain extremist sects, to hasten the triumph of evil by collaborating with it means hastening its end, and therefore the coming of redemption. Faced with the obscure violence latent in the hidden depths of our being, we would all, like the ancient Gnostics, wish to convince ourselves that our actions, even if smeared with filth and cruelty, cannot tarnish the gold concealed in our souls; we should like to be permitted, or better, commanded, to give free rein to that violence under the impression that it confers innocence.

As long as transgression is applied to codes of sexual behaviour things are easy, because infractions of erotic taboos do not constitute evil if performed by responsible persons and inflicting no harm on others; and the zeal of the orgiastic is just ridiculously innocuous. Things are a bit different when Mengele rips the genitals off people who have not given their consent to the game; when our desire which, like every desire, is understandably reluctant to be repressed, can be satisfied only at the cost of the suffering of others. The crimes of Raskolnikov, and that of M., the child-murderer in Fritz Lang's famous film, are not born of mere whims, but from real, lacerating passions, which must be respected on account of their own sufferings, but not justified in the suffering they inflict on others. The arts are particularly fond of these extreme, abnormal examples, but even our small everyday lives are studded with clashes between our own pleasure and the rights of others, and vice versa.

The mystique of transgression aims at loving not so much the sinner as the sin itself, and in the belief that the only prohibited thing is sex, it reverses every impulse on the grounds that it is a sexual impulse, maintaining that this authorizes or demands its satisfaction. It is probable that Mengele's sexual urges had to do with his predilections, and that at Auschwitz his sexual life was satisfied, but it is questionable whether this justified his actions, and that he should be seen as an uninhibited man who, without any moralistic restraints, lived his own life, as the saying is.

Art strongly influenced by redemptive transgression is in fact only able to glory third-rate offenders, the mere menials of evil. The redeemer-delinquents whom this art – Genet's fictional work, for instance – offers us as models are thieves, rapists, murderers: cruel, unhappy criminals on the retail side of wickedness. No one dares to perceive the Messiah of Sin in the head of state who orders the dropping of the atom bomb or orders a city to be razed to the ground, the corrupt governor who embezzles the money intended for the hospitals, the manufacturer of weapons who pushes a country into war to increase his profits, or the boss who humiliates an underling. It is right to have more sympathy for the cut-throat in the street than for the office-bound exterminator, when one considers that he has more extenuating circumstances of need or unhappiness; but anyone who argues in this way is making an appeal to values, and is an upright man who seeks for good, even if for the sake of sheer caprice he does not wish to admit it.

If, on the other hand, the redeemer is the one who takes evil as far as it will go, then the leader who orders the dropping of the atom bomb, the war profiteer, the Mafia boss who crushes strikes and the crooked governor are much more genuine Messiahs than Jack the Ripper. The naïve artist who praises the latter is fascinated by his erotic perversion, by the sexual excitement which he presumes to accompany such an act; but it may be that the man who presses the atomic button or defrauds others of their sustenance experiences, in his satisfaction, who knows what kind of perverse orgasm, one supposed to raise him in the esteem of those who hold that sexual excitement ennobles every act. The honeyed sweetness of Mengele, of his words and of his smile, which he hoped would endow him with some resemblance to the Angel of Death, is the genuine, imbecile expression of every kind of fascination with evil; it is the expression featured in every demi-culture that expects the shoddy junk of the shadows to make amends for its own paltriness. The prohibited act, often as trite as throwing rubbish out of the window, is no less obtuse just because it torments or tortures. The Gorgon, said Joseph Roth about Nazism, is banal. Mengele's victims are characters in a tragedy, but Mengele himself is a figure in a farrago of gibberish.

16. AN EMPTY TOMB

"The map of the Danube," writes Trost, shortly after discussing the Battle of Blindheim and the siege of Donauwörth by Gustavus Adolphus in 1632, "is similar, even later on, to a military atlas." In the fields and woods of Oberhausen, a little before Neuburg, there is a small piece of land belonging to France, bought because it contains the sarcophagus of Théophile Malo Corret de Latour d'Auvergne, first grenadier of the republican army. Formerly an officer in the King's army, then a participant in the American Revolution, and subsequently in the French Revolution, he finally enlisted as a private soldier in the armies of Napoleon and died in battle on the Danube.

The sarcophagus is empty, for his bones have been moved to Paris. In the solitude of the fields it is watched over, like a guard of honour, by a square of trees. The burial-place is also reserved for de Forty, commander of the sixth semi-brigade of infantry, who died the same day, but the real protagonist is the private soldier, "Premier Grenadier de France, tué le 8ième Messidor, an 8 de l'ère républicaine." Straight after seeing this tomb, how mincing and glossy appears the Renaissance scenery of Neuburg! Churches, palaces, aristocratic mansions and noble courtyards seem like a period stage-set, with stylized, artificial wings to recreate the grace of Italian art on the banks of the Danube. That deserted tomb, on the other hand, speaks of glory, *la gloire*, and at the same time the futility of it; it embodies the meaning of a life that takes up arms out of faith in a new banner, rather than putting them at the service of the wars between local princes, of family feuds; and it also stands for the great void that looms behind every glorious cavalcade and streaming banner; or else for the infinite, mindless background of the sky, outlined against which, in the film of universal history, rides the army of men who are summoned to die.

The monuments of the German princes are museum pieces, while the sarcophagus of the republican and Napoleonic grenadier is, like the Revolution itself, a modest monument to grand dreams of freedom. On the other hand the barracks, now named after Tilly, are a reminder of other wars, of great swords hired by a dynasty rather than pledged to a cause. Of course, Latour was also taken in, because Napoleon sacrificed him to his ambitions, along with the hundreds of thousands of men whom – as he cynically put it to Metternich – he was prepared to send to their deaths for his success. But the subjective meanness of Napoleon did not prevent the gathering under his banner of a great and genuine – though swiftly corrupted – revolution.

Gigi and Amedeo, who love the aura of *la gloire* but also analytical precision, are attracted by the Descartes Junior School, not because of its box-like architecture, but on account of its name. It was in this little town, in 1619, that Descartes spent the winter days in his comfortable, heated room, and here he had his famous conceptual illumination.

Maria Giuditta has vanished; Maddalena is outside the school, waiting for the two of them to finish confabulating with the caretaker. Her clear-cut, upright figure, her flowing hair, seem to be there to demonstrate that there is no contradiction between clear and distinct ideas and the true glory that comes from the luminosity of a person, from those whom the evangelist calls the salt of the earth and the light of the world.

The heart requires the *esprit de géométrie*, as does the demonstration of a theorem. The kingdom of the visible should be measured with set-square and compasses, the curve of a destiny is revealed thanks to the system of abscissae and ordinates in which it is placed. Only the precise identification of what is visible enables us to reach its confines and direct our gaze beyond, to the source of the light that is in Maddalena, or of Francesca's silence. Even that light and that silence from a hidden source, even the beyond and the invisible, are clear and geometrical, abhorring a blur. The geometry of that light can give order and passionate clarity to a whole life, and not just to a series of equations. It is time Gigi and Amedeo packed it in with the caretaker and stopped keeping Maddalena waiting.

17. MARIELUISE FLEISSER OF INGOLSTADT

Like the names of medieval chroniclers, the name of this forceful authoress is always recited with the addition of her native town, almost as if it were a single word. Marieluisefleisserofingolstadt is most certainly bound by profound polemical roots to the Bavarian town which traditionally boasts of its military pride, the virginity of its fortress, many times besieged but never taken. Today Ingolstadt is the start of the famous oil pipeline leading to Trieste.

Ingolstadt is a town of military traditions, from the siege by Gustavus Adolphus in 1632 to the death of Tilly, the great general of the Empire during the Thirty Years' War; from the celebrated fortress in which, during the First World War, De Gaulle and Marshal Tukachevsky were prisoners, to the present-day (and celebrated) School of Pioneers. *Pioneers of Ingolstadt* is the title of a play written by Marieluise Fleisser in 1928–9 – revised in the 1968 draft – which created a great scandal and, as happens to many authors who do not mince their words in describing their provincial world, caused her to be rejected and reviled by public opinion in town.

Like another and even more noteworthy play, *Purgatory at Ingolstadt* – and like her work in general – *Pioneers at Ingolstadt* with laconic intensity depicts the suffocating violence of the provinces and the sufferings of individuals, and above all of women: their cries of pain and protest are a constant voice in the author's writings, at times as grating as the gulls screeching above the river this evening in the darkness.

Marieluise Fleisser, whom Bruno Frank defined as "the finest bosom in Central Europe", both experienced and portrayed the suffocating, outraged situation of women; she endured that condition of violence, in her own muddled, maybe pathetic way she rebelled against it, and she overcame it in the epic quality of her poetic work. She so far identified with female subjugation in its visceral immediacy that she risked being crushed by it, but at the same time she rose above it, and gave a firm, objective picture of it in her writing. Her work, especially her dramas, has a dry, realistic precision to it, along with full-blooded working-class naturalism and visionary power. It was Brecht who introduced her into the tumultuous world of Berlin and made her famous. It rightly saw her as an example of that literature of the people, abounding in reality, immune from "realistic" commonplaces and local colour, which seemed to him the only literature equal to the situation in Germany – hence the rediscovery of Marieluise Fleisser in recent years after a long period of neglect.

Her meeting with Brecht was intellectually a stroke of luck for the authoress, but probably an existential misfortune. In her emotional relationship with Brecht, from which she felt the burning need to break away, she experienced the very masculine dishonesty and feminine subjection which she denounces in her art, that coercive mixture of collaboration and submission, culture and sexuality, surrender and revolt, that precludes equality and accepts, under protest, that the male will inevitably dominate the female by violence. Brecht, she writes, used to consume people, and she herself did not escape the role of an item of consumer goods.

Marieluise Fleisser was like Berta, a character in her *Pioneers of Ingolstadt*, a victim who collaborates in her own unhappy destiny because she takes her subordinate role for granted, embedding it in feeling and above all sanctioning it by her own behaviour. In her relationship with Brecht or with other men she was a passionate creature, both gentle and rebellious, protected and ill-treated, but defenceless in any case; she never managed to be a partner on equal terms and with equal rights, probably because she herself – in this sense rooted at the very extreme of traditional femininity – did not feel herself to be so. With Lou Andreas Salomé – but also with some of the girls I knew at school! – Brecht would not have lorded it like that, simply because from the very first instant, with his whole being even sooner than with his intelligence, he would have realized that it would not be possible to act that way, and it would never have even crossed his mind to do so.

Victims sometimes smooth the way for men who treat them shabbily, though this certainly makes men no less guilty. In her work, which is strictly devoid of muddled feelings, Marieluise Fleisser also demonstrates what happens to women like her.

18. THE ROMAN LIMES

Local folklore, recorded what is more by Johann Alexander Döderlein, rector of the Lycée in Weissenburg, in a learned monograph with an enormously long and digressive title, attributes the construction of these walls, this now crumbling stone boundary, to the devil. For the late medieval peasant, who could see no further than the field he was ploughing, the very idea of the *Limes*, the rampart intended to mark the frontiers of the Roman Empire all the way to the Black Sea, was unthinkable and superhuman, something that as pure Idea transcended tangible everyday immediacy and must have appeared to be the work of mysterious forces. It was not the devil but the Roman Emperors, from Augustus to Vespasian, from Hadrian to Marcus Aurelius and Commodus, who marked out the stone line of that frontier. On this side of the line was the Empire, the idea and the universal dominion of Rome; on the other were the barbarians, whom the Empire was beginning to fear, and no longer aimed to conquer and assimilate, but merely to keep at bay.

Like the peasants of *Raetia secunda* and *Germania superior* when these provinces had already been abandoned by Rome, even contemporaries find it hard to understand the vastness of these stones, and see them as the work of the devil, perhaps the devil of imperialism.

Certainly Rome meant also – and above all – dominion, and the universality to which she laid claim was a mask for dominion, and as such destined to perish in spite of all her pretences to eternity. For every power which claims to represent universality and civilization there comes the time to pay the price, to deliver up its arms to those who a moment before were thought of as uncouth inferiors. The despised barbarians became the artificers of the new Europe; later on the Slavs, for centuries considered an obscure race of serfs without a history, heard their hour strike, while the Chinese, who used to wheel white men around in rickshaws, are now a world power.

To each his hour, and his mission in history. That rampart, the ruins of which emerge from fields and hedgerows, speaks of the great hour of the Roman Empire, its foundation and unification of the world of those days. Our history, our culture, our Europe, are the daughters of that *Limes*. Those stones tell of the urge to frontiers, of the need and ability to give oneself limits and form. The *imperium* is a barrier, a defence, a rampart against the uncouthness of the indistinct and individualistic. Even this mouth I am looking at now is line, is form, is the exact frontier of a realm in which the indefinite – and therefore unreal – potentiality of sexual love becomes reality. We kiss and we love a mouth, a form, a *Limes*. Though, of course, before a mysterious face and a sidelong glance even the confines of imperial Rome appear an antiquarian curiosity, precious but marginal, like Rector Döderlein's learned monograph.

19. A WALHALLA AND A ROSE

The monument raised by Ludwig I of Bavaria to the German wars of liberation from the dominion of Napoleon, called the "Befreiung-shalle", towers above the Danube and the little town of Kehlheim from the hundred-metre eminence of Michelsberg Hill. The romantic Bavarian King conceived the idea during a trip to Greece in 1836. The foundation stone was laid in 1842, and by 1862, when the building was completed at last and officially consecrated, the sovereign had for many years been missing from the political scene, overwhelmed by the events of 1848 and by his passion for the beautiful Lola Montez, in whose arms – said Grillparzer – a king had become a man.

The round building erected to the glory of Germany in the wars of 1813–15 looks like a gasometer – a monument to human achievements no less arduous or long-lasting. The circular façade is adorned with eighteen limestone statues, six metres high and supported on gigantic pilasters, each personifying one of the eighteen Germanic races (a figure which includes Bohemians and Moravians) which took part in the campaigns against Napoleon. Inside, eighteen white goddesses of victory in Carrara marble, 3.3 metres in height, bear bronze shields on which are engraved the names of the battles, while plaques above their heads bear the names of the great generals.

This chalky, clumsy Pantheon looks a pallid thing in comparison with the fields surrounding the gasometer: it lacks the glory that there is among the tattered banners in the Invalides in Paris, that dazzle of wind, gunpowder and vanity that makes a battle resemble life. The German wars of 1813, with their unified national uprising and the reforming spirit spread abroad by the enlightened Prussian politicians and generals – Stein, Scharnhorst, Gneisenau, Yorck, Clausewitz – have little in common with the nationalistic bombast suggested by this monument. The Germany which reawoke during those years – Prussia in particular, but it was not alone – experienced a brief period of progress, reform and hope of civil liberties, whereas the Germany which a few decades later erected this monument was already stagnating in reaction and the Restoration. It had already created a schism between love of country and love of freedom, and the latter frightened it; so it set out to achieve national unity at the expense of liberalism. The Germany of Bismarck and Wilhelm was at least in part the negation of that of Stein and Humboldt. Admittedly Ludwig I reigned in Bavaria, over a state – reactionary and liberal by turns – that represented the most noteworthy alternative to German unification under the leadership of Prussia and to German nationalism as later dominated by Prussia. But this funeral "glory" is already an ossification or a parody of the liberal patriotism of 1813.

Romantically in love with Hellas and its struggles for independence, to the point of forcing his son Otto onto the throne of Greece as soon as the country was liberated from the Turks, Ludwig I was the sponsor of another monument to German glory, the Walhalla, a "Doric" temple overlooking the Danube a few kilometres below Regensburg. This white Hellenic temple with the mythical nordic name symbolized the hoped-for symbiosis between Greece and Germany. The Germans, descendants of the ancient Dorians, were to be the Greeks of the new

Europe, and to bestow on this Europe a new, universally human culture, such as Hellas had given to the ancient world. For Hölderlin this had been an anarchic, revolutionary dream, a Utopia of freedom and redemption open to the entire world.

The Walhalla partakes of this dream as those films on the labours of Hercules, starring Steve Reeves and Sylvia Koscina, partake of Greek myth itself. The place contains the busts of 161 great Germans; some are identified only by name (Goethe), others with their professional qualification (Mozart, composer), others again by solemn definitions (Klopstock, sacred bard). Admission to this Pantheon continued beyond Ludwig's time, and even today, those who crave immortality stand at least some chance of admission after a complex bureaucratic process. But right was on the side of Metternich, who did not like the place, and Hebbel, who wouldn't be seen dead in it.

The Walhalla is a waxworks. It is easy enough to see the futility of it in comparison with the wind-ruffled grass, the shining waters of the Danube a hundred metres below, the shade of the trees. It is easy to side with poetry against literature, or the genuine against the artificial, or life against mere objects and the museum of objects. But as is suggested to us by a hard-hitting fable in the cyclostyled news-sheet of a certain elementary school, it may be that taking sides with a flower against a column can also be a kind of rhetoric, an offence against that life which longs to love, and against its secret sorrow.

The story was written by a little girl for the *Giostrino*, or *Gazette of San Vito* for May 1973. The author, Monica Favaretto, was in the first grade of the de Amicis School in Trieste. The story is called *The Rose*. "The Rose was happy. She got on well with all the other flowers. One day the Rose felt that she was wilting and about to die. She saw a paper flower and said to it 'What a lovely rose you are!' – 'But I am a paper flower!' – 'But don't you realize that I am dying?' – The Rose was already dead and spoke no more."

This tiny tale, which says almost all there is to say about the tenderness of living and the impenetrable grief of dying, reminds us that things do last a little longer than life, but that they too are destined to fade; and that faced with the sorrow of death, there is little sense in extolling the genuine at the expense of the artificial. We are loyal to the tears of living things if we listen to their weeping, their yearning to last a little longer, even if as counterfeit things, such as are the Doric columns of this false Walhalla.

I don't know where this unknown first-grade schoolchild is or what she is doing, whether she has vowed to become a great writer or whether that flash of genius is fated to remain a unique, unrepeatable revelation, and she is now a girl like any other. Poetry is impersonal, it bloweth where it listeth as the wind does, and does not belong to the name written at the foot of the page. At times it is born from the hand, like certain doodles traced idly on the page, which then turn out to be enchanting; or certain gestures in which, without realizing it, a person reveals a grace she never knew she had, and perhaps will never have again.

20. REGENSBURG

Even the *Volksbuch*, the popular version of the Faust legend, celebrates the fame of Regensburg and its stone bridge, wonder of the centuries and of the world. The chroniclers write of its magnificence as an imperial city and bishop's see, while in 1517 Maximilian I, the knightly Emperor, called it "once upon a time the most flourishing of the rich and famous cities of our German nation". Eulogy and nostalgia surround the splendid Gothic and Romanesque city of the hundred towers, with its squares and alleyways in which layers of history are condensed in each carved stone.

Eulogies of the city fill whole libraries; but these are always directed at the magnificence of a bygone age – *einst*, once upon a time, as the Emperor Maximilian said as long ago as 1517. The churches, the towers, the noble houses, the carved figures, all speak to us of the majesty of the past, of a glory that can only be remembered and never possessed, which has always been and never will be.

The nostalgia of the inheritors guards the vestiges of a past which in turn cultivated the relics and memories of an even earlier age. "The city is antiquated," wrote Johann Andreas Schmeller in 1802, "and the Senate speaks in the manner of the fifteenth century." But even in the fifteenth century they lamented their lost splendours. Maybe for this reason, and not just on account of its towers, Regensburg has been compared to Prague, the golden city which also seems to exist only and always in the memory of a vanished magnificence.

Regensburg is a place of people devoted to their city-state, students of the memories preserved on every portal and every capital. Enthusiastic and serene as local sages always are – even if among their treasures they do not come across mere antiquarian curios, but vast pages of history, with Frederick Barbarossa himself riding across the stone bridge – these learned scholars discover and meet other learned scholars of the past, also intent at their time on the guardianship of the vanished centuries. In 665 dense pages of microscopic print, Karl Bauer reconstructs the map of the city stone by stone, with the history and significance of every house and important building, the ghosts of those who hundreds of years ago peopled the alleys, the archways, the gates, the wonderful intimate little squares. In his book published in 1980 he dwells upon the house at 19 Kreuzgasse, and gives us a description of Christian Gottlieb Gumpelzhaimer, the historian of Regensburg who died in those rooms in 1841. The past of his city was Gumpelzhaimer's consuming passion; in the first volume of his *History, Legends and Wonders of Regensburg* (1830–38) he speaks at length of his love for the antiquities of his native town.

Seat of the permanent imperial Diet from 1663 on, Regensburg is one of the "hearts" of the Holy Roman Empire. This may be another reason why it was born under the sign of nostalgia, since the Holy Roman Empire from its very beginnings was essentially the reflection of a sun that had set, the dream of its rising once more in splendour; an echo of the universal idea of Rome, an empire whose political structure had disintegrated. To be sure, as the more lucid and restrained historians have clearly seen, the Holy Roman Empire was not the universal empire as conceived of by ecclesiastical thinkers; it did not identify itself with the *res publica christiana* or coincide with Western Christianity (Julius Ficker); it did not imply, as Barraclough writes, any claim to universal dominion. From Otto the Great to Henry IV and Frederick Barbarossa, from the Saxon to the Salian and thence to the Swabian dynasty, the outstanding Germanic sovereigns had in mind a strong German monarchy, a firmly unified state, which in part they succeeded in creating, indulging in fanciful dreams of world dominion.

Not only man, though, is vicissitude, as Herodotus says; so are ideas – in this case the concept of empire. In the course of the centuries, with the changing of historical situations, the content of the imperial idea changed also. The more the Empire was drained of real political importance (whether crippled by the independent power of the princes or subordinated to dynastic interests, as happened with the Hapsburgs), the stronger the growth, almost by way of compensation, of a universalistic feeling about the imperial theme that covered a power vacuum. Thus, during the period when the Germanic political situation was uncertain, and threatened by foreign interventions, Alexander von Roes warned that if the Empire was destroyed, world order would crumble.

The fervour of empire is one of absence, of the lack of balance between the grandeur of an idea and the poverty of reality which D'Annunzio represented in the destiny of Sigismund of the flowing hair, "the tempestuous imperial spirit/ who had a handful of castles and not the world". The imperial concept reaches out to a Utopian future, but it feeds off a mythical past, draws on a splendour vanished and remote. Its glory is always of once upon a time, as the Emperor Maximilian said of the glories of Regensburg.

The Danube, which beneath the Stone Bridge flows broad and dark in the evening, streaked with the crests of ripples, seems to evoke the experience of all that is missing, the water that has vanished or will vanish, but that never is. The air and the dark waters are rich with breezes, with reflections and colours, with sounds, with the wings of birds, with grasses slightly bending and immersed in shadow; but as I enter the towered city I have the impression of slipping in between two pages of a book, old Gumpelzhaimer's book as he re-evokes the bygone centuries, and Karl Bauer's book as he re-evokes Gumpelzhaimer. In the infinitesimal space between the two pages – or perhaps they are not two pages, but the two sides of the same leaf – I feel at my ease, sheltered from the inclemencies of events. Heinrich Laube, in 1834, dreamt the idyll of old Regensburg, with sweet-lipped girls who lowered their eyes as they let themselves be kissed, songs as melancholy and fleeting as the waves of the Danube, and not a policeman or literary critic in sight. The idyll does not relish mobilization, and steers clear of police regulations and the bluebottles of the culture industry.

To tell the truth, I have not come in search of things absent, although the past does in a way have to do with this stop-over in Regensburg. The Marshal is going to meet me at one end of the celebrated old Stone Bridge, even though I have arrived in the city from the opposite side. This is no unexpected whim: the Marshal is a woman who has always loved bridges, and the arches which join their banks together – ever since those days in the Lycée, when her laugh seemed to render things palpable and to transform the Roman candle hung from the chandelier into a comet blazing in the night sky.

I can't remember which of us gave her that Flaubertian nickname. For years she has been living far away, first in Vienna, then in Linz and now in Regensburg, with her husband and two daughters whose perfect resemblance to herself is even today the most valid guarantee to us her schoolmates of the continuity of life and the loyalty of things. Time, whose power is sometimes open to question, has in these years only added to her splendour, has been a vassal who has brought her tribute, has enriched her rapacity with maternal tenderness, and endowed her vitality with the profound enchantment of awareness. The Marshal still has claws, and still throws back her head and offers her laughter to the evening winds with imperious, reckless magnanimity. Even at school this made her seem like a nomad queen, and induced the head of the class, when congratulating her on an essay or translation, to remind her of the pre-eminence of virtue over literary proficiency: "Remember, though," he would say, "qui proficit litteris sed deficit moribus magis deficit quam proficit . . ."

The Marshal loved Latin, a subject in which she got excellent marks thanks to which her occasional brainstorm in other areas was forgiven. In the indomitable lucidity with which she rode through life there was a classical sharpness of distinction, the syntax which orders the chaotic dust of the world and puts things in their right places, the subject in the nominative and the object in the accusative. Anyone who has seen her emerge laughing from the sea on one of those late October days she so loved is not likely to be taken in by false mentors.

Regensburg suits the Marshal, with its inexhaustible store of memories, styles and images that nevertheless compose one basic tonal unity. On the façade of the superb cathedral a whole forest of figures emerges from the stone, animals, faces, fabulous or even monstrous creatures, a proliferating jungle of life which reveals a higher consonance, the oneness of creation. The leering faces rising from the abyss are tamed, mellowed by a kind of Christian courage which says yes to the multiplicity of existence, to each one of its innumerable creatures, for the simple reason that it recognizes them as God's creatures, figures in a universal design in which there are no such things as monsters.

The Marshal also is a creature of that wild but Christian forest; she comes forth from the stone to launch herself on one of her reckless flights, but she knows herself to be part of that whole. Life has not been and is not easy on her, as it never is on the strong, or rather towards those who try to conceal their weaknesses so as not to lean on others, but to give sustenance and comfort. Life is hard towards those who live consciously, aware of their own precariousness, but it is indulgent towards the weak, or rather towards those who flaunt their weakness in order to throw all the weight of it on others, and who are petted, pitied and mollycoddled as beautiful, noble souls. Even Jesus was hard on Martha, and found it perfectly natural that she should busy herself with getting lunch on the table while Mary sat entranced and at ease listening to his words. But it was Martha who uttered the most profound profession of faith in Christ, perhaps more intense than that of Peter.

How difficult it is to be a Marshal! The world demands that she should play this role unceasingly; it does not allow her to suffer from toothache or the blues, and heaps everything on those superb shoulders which seem so strong. But even that heart knows weakness, and sometimes trembles and feels the phantoms of its own dark places rising from the depths. However, as in the allegories on the portal of Sankt Jacob in Regensburg, it drives them back into Chaos, chains them to their murky nullity and disarms them. A peaceful night and life everlasting, in the words of the evening prayer. If I had been the Marshal's schoolfellow any longer, my conversion would have been a certainty.

21. IN THE CHAMBER OF THE REICH

This chamber in the Town Hall was the meeting-place of the permanent Diet of the Holy Roman Empire; on this empty chair sat the Emperor, rendered increasingly ineffective by the princes and the guilds, or else himself neglectful of the *Reich*, often more *administrator* than *dominus*. Around it are the halls set aside for the Electors, the princes, the College of the imperial cities. When Regensburg became the seat of the permanent Diet, in 1663, the Empire was already ossified and divested of power. In this room, supposed to rule the world, the world itself is missing; the void of it reminds one of that "nothing defined only by its own confines", to quote from *The Hole*, a play by Achim von Arnim, the nineteenth-century Romantic poet fascinated by the German past. That feeble conjuction, the *und* in the formula "Kaiser und Reich", also seems a nothing, a disjunction, a mere nullity that does nothing but separate. The Empire is an ellipse, wrote Werner Näf, the foci of which are the princes and the guilds, while the centre – the Emperor – appears as a pure abstraction.

This lack of centre, this shortage of cohesive strength and political unity, does not call to mind the clear, penetrating gaze of Frederick II of Swabia, who saw things as they appear to the naked eye, without a trace of recondite significance; what it calls to mind rather is the oblique glance of the Spanish Hapsburgs, focused upon the hidden, twisted side of things, upon darkness and obscurity: the glance which tradition attributes to Don John of Austria, victor of the Battle of Lepanto, born in a house in the Tändlergasse, illegitimate son of Charles V and a beautiful daughter of middle-class Regensburg, Barbara Blomberg. Barbara Blomberg was eighteen years old, while the Emperor, seven years a widower, was forty-six and marked by a precocious, melancholy weariness, by that sense of the vanity of vanities which caused him to decline – according to a line of Planten's – like the old Empire itself, even if that waning of the medieval heritage entailed the rise of a modern world power under his crown.

Mindful of this passion, and of this woman whom he never saw again, Charles V remembered her on the eve of his death, indeed a matter of hours before he died, and secretly left her the considerable bequest of six hundred golden ducats. Heedlessly do we make love, says a line of Brecht's. Don John of Austria grew up for the triumph of Lepanto, but not for happiness; he was destined for the murky obliquities of life, not for life's clarity.

The two-headed eagle on the wall of this imperial chamber sets the seal on a shadowy, melancholy scene. This pathos of decline does not seem to have affected the secretary, or the scrivener, to whom we owe the end of the tradition of the *Konfekttischlein*. On this little table for the display of confectionery the city was wont to offer the delegates to the Diet refreshments, wines and sweetmeats, on which chiefly the secretaries and scriveners made a practice of gorging themselves. During a Diet one of their number had partaken rather too generously of the wine, so that in the course of a session, in which he was supposed to draw up the minutes, he fell asleep and started to snore sonorously, disturbing the discussions on which depended the Holy Roman Empire, and therefore the world at large. The city senate thereupon abolished the traditional refreshments.

22. THE SIX POINTS OF NOTHING

"I know that you like Nothing, not because of its minimal value, but because one can play with it in a light, witty way, like a garrulous sparrow, and I therefore think that a gift will be more welcome to you and more appreciated the more it approaches to zero." The gift which Kepler sent to his friend and protector Johannes Matthäus Wackher von Wackenfels for New Year's Day of 1611 was the little treatise *Strena seu De Nive Sexangula*, which opens with the words quoted above; it goes on to wonder why falling snow condenses into tiny six-pointed stars, and throughout this rigorous, light-hearted inquiry plays around in the ironical space which twinkles between the minimal and nothing at all. The pamphlet dates from the scientist's years in Prague, and is now on sale at the entrance to the house in Regensburg where he died in 1630 – now the Kepler Museum. Among the instruments and apparatus which he made for his experiments, the museum preserves even his beloved barrel with the gadget he invented to calculate exactly how much wine was at any time left inside.

Baroque literature is full of Eulogies of Nothing, of intellectual and poetical conceits bewitched by the inconceivability of their subject, Nothingness, more difficult to grasp than the eternity of God, and by the determination to challenge or to outwit that conceptual impossibility. Kepler sets out to explain the formation of the six-pointed snow-crystal, and in his review of the various hypotheses, all painstakingly sifted and rejected by means of a series of subtractions and negations, he slips into the most minute interstices between imperceptible dimensions, so that the gift he is offering his friend runs the risk of being lost like the water of the Choaspes, which the Persians offered to their king by bringing it to him in the hollows of their hands.

The playful tone of the thing reduces the treatise to a mere nothing, but behind the veil of jesting speaks the scientist who believes in truth and exactitude, who sees geometry as the divine proportion of created things and studies it with rigorous precision, aware that knowledge enriches the sense of mystery, and that genuine mystery is not of the kind before which the mind slumps willingly into superstition, but the kind which reason ceaselessly investigates with all the instruments at her command. It is the geometrician who approaches closest to the design of the Deity. In 1620 Sir Henry Wotton wrote to Bacon that in Kepler's study in Linz he had seen one of the latter's paintings, a landscape; and he adds that Kepler said, "I paint landscapes as a mathematician."

Colours, lights, shadows, trees, thickets of bushes, the variety of nature that appears so profuse and disorderly, these are all obedient to laws, proportions and ratios; they are an interplay of lines and angles, and it is the mathematician who discerns their true face. But a mathematician, writes Kepler to his aristocratic patron, has nothing and obtains nothing. Perhaps because his pocket is empty and his pencil plays with abstractions, he circumscribes nothing with the round sign of the zero; he knows only signs, not things. It is therefore fitting that he should turn his thoughts to the snow, which melts to nothing and which in Latin (*nix*) sounds so like the word for nothing, *Nichts*.

Kepler adhered to the notion that the solar system was in some way the centre of the cosmos; he abhorred the infinite, which for him was chaos, and he gave up his soul to his Maker attended by the Evangelical pastor of Regensburg, Sigismund Christoph Donauer, who comforted him "in manly fashion, as befits a servant of God". But in his amiable treatise on the nothingness of snow he discards, eliminates, negates and proceeds by one exclusion after another, almost as if he were mimicking the dissolving of a snowflake. This "Mathematicus, Philosophus et Historicus", as he considered himself, lived joyously in a cosmos created by God, but our own precision has come to be less commendable, and it may not be advisable to depict the landscapes of our lives as mathematicians. The operation might turn out to be an inexorable and very simple subtraction, the result of which – a round zero – would resemble that snow, a formless erasure of the entire landscape along with its inhabitant.

23. THE PALM SUNDAY ASS

In Regensburg for a long time they kept alive the tradition of the *Palmesel*, the "Palm Sunday Ass", a procession carrying round the streets an image of Jesus mounted on a wooden ass, in memory of his joyful entry into Jerusalem before Passion Week. In this tradition the protagonist appears to be the ass, and that much scorned and maltreated animal deserves this moment of glory. Our conventions humiliate the ass, inflicting on him beatings in real life and insults in our daily vocabulary. The ass pulls the cart, bears the burden, carries the weight of life; and life, we well know, is ungrateful and unjust towards those who come to its aid. Life allows itself to be carried away by rose-tinted novelettes and technicolor movies, and prefers radiant destinies to the plain prose of reality, so it is more taken with racehorses at Ascot than with humble donkeys on country roads.

But poetry is of loftier genius than life, and can celebrate the majesty of the ass. It was an ass, not a thoroughbred, that kept Jesus warm in the stable. Homer compares Ajax, who saves the Achaean ships by resisting the Trojan onslaught single-handed, to an ass whose back beneath its burden and the blows becomes as great as the shield of Telamon. The ass, in its patient sufferings, has also been compared to Christ, scourged for wanting to help mankind.

The strength of the ass possesses the attributes of the heroes of antiquity: patience, the calm, humble, indomitable constancy which does not shrink from its path, that rises above the nervous fits and starts of the noble steed as Ulysses overtops Paris. For this reason, ever since Apuleius, the ass has been honoured for its sexual potency. This potency, on which even Buffon dwelt, is not the arrogance of the bull, all very fine for purposes of *machismo*, nor the disagreeable satyriasis of the cockerel, but is part and parcel of its humble patience, the unruffled strength of the way it faces life. The admiration of the beautiful and very demanding Corinthian lady in Apuleius' *Golden Ass* does much to make up for the offences of our common speech. In Elias Canetti's *Voices of Marrakesh* the author describes the sudden erection of an ass that had been beaten to the point of collapse: a display of riotous vitality that seems to vindicate all those who are humiliated and insulted.

24. THE GREAT WHEEL

In the graveyard of Sankt Peter, on the outskirts of Straubing, the stones scattered around the church, as in a garden, bear witness to tranquil lives now resting in peace in their pride of class: here lies Adam Mohr, brewer, alderman and lieutenant in the Bavarian National Guard, †1826. Class pride sets its seal on a pious harmony between the

individual and the community, but it turns to savagery the moment
other laws or other counsels of the heart throw the individual into
conflict with the social order and induce him, even without wishing it,
to disrupt this order. In one of the three chapels is the tomb of Agnes
Bernauer, the lovely daughter of an Augsburg barber; on October the
12th 1435 Duke Ernest of Bavaria gave orders for her to be drowned in
the Danube, on a charge of witchcraft, because she had married his son
Albert and with this misalliance threatened the policies of the dynasty
and even the law and order of the state.

The tomb shows Agnes Bernauer with a rosary in her hands and two
little dogs at her feet, a symbol of the conjugal fidelity which united this
young woman of the people to her princely spouse. It was erected by
Duke Ernest, her killer. The tradition, taken up by Hebbel in his play
on the subject, is a fable of the Reason of State. Duke Ernest profoundly admired the virtue and personality of Agnes and the pure love which
bound her to his son; but he decided, firmly though unwillingly, to
eliminate her in a brutal manner in view of the political consequences
provoked by the marriage and later complications stemming from it –
disorders, wars, uprisings, the division and collapse of the state,
fratricidal strife and general suffering. Having performed this sacrifice,
or committed this crime, in the name of the state, the duke paid
homage to the victim's moral constancy and innocence, now that she
was no longer a danger, by building her a sepulchre to keep her
memory alive through the centuries, and by himself retiring to a
monastery. His son Albert, who had taken up arms against him, first to
defend and then to avenge his wife, soon fell into line for political and
dynastic purposes, and became reconciled for reasons of state with the
father who had made him a widower. He assumed the ducal sceptre,
and later went on to contract a second marriage more appropriate to
his position.

Agnes was drowned in the Danube, refusing to the last to save her
life by renouncing her husband. Because she floated on the surface, the
duke's hired thugs were forced to bind her legendary tresses round a
long pole and hold her head under water until she was dead. The
formal charge was witchcraft. In mentioning the episode the Antiquarius, writing at the end of the century of the Enlightenment, can no
longer consider her a witch, but like a good middle-class citizen he
drags the superstition onto secular ground and scoffs about her
"shameful" seduction of Duke Albert; he, however, was no babe in
arms, but a knight in the prime of life who had met her and courted her

during a tournament in Augsburg. There is a thread connecting Emmeram Rusperger, the jurist who formulated the charge of witch-craft against Agnes, the Antiquarius, who considers her a brazen hussy, and the opinion still very commonly held today, according to which if the father of a family abandons wife and children for a twenty-year-old, then only the girl is a guilty party and he an innocent victim.

What a pity it is that Marieluise Fleisser didn't write the drama about Agnes Bernauer, because she would have written it from Agnes Bernauer's point of view. The tragedy was in fact written in 1851 by Friedrich Hebbel, admittedly with considerable poetic force. Hebbel is full of admiration for this limpid, lovely woman, who knew the articles of the Christian faith like Margaret in *Faust*, and in whose throat, when she drank, the wine glowed through as though in a crystal vessel. Agnes has to die "solely because she is beautiful and virtuous", and because when the order of the world is disrupted and the Lord intervenes not with a little hoe but with a scythe, which mows down the just and the unjust without distinction, then "it is no longer a question of guilt or innocence, but only of cause and effect": that is, it is purely a matter of eliminating the cause of the disruption. Hebbel goes into raptures about this passion for the reason of state: the nobility and purity of the individual serve only to augment the solemn holiness of those, like Duke Ernest and the poet himself, who place themselves on the side of the whole. The whole is invariably in the right, and the more subjec-tively innocent and admirable is the individual who is sacrificed to it, the more righteous it appears.

Poetry is called upon to celebrate this sacrifice, which is also a self-immolation, because it is the repression of that loving sympathy which poetry, by its very nature, feels for the individual, for the victim, for Agnes Bernauer. "The great wheel has passed over her," says Duke Ernest after he has had her killed. "Now she is by the side of him who turns it." Like all concern with the object, which exults in the annihila-tion and self-annihilation of the subject, this too is suspect, for every example of the magniloquence of the whole is also raising the philistine vulgarity of the Antiquarius into something sublime. There is a rhetoric of objectivity which in its ranting brutality seems to parody the relationship between a society's collective needs and the personal needs of its components. The exultant tone in which so many uninvited advocates of the All repeat Hegel's saying "When you plane wood, shavings fall" is a caricature of Hegel's thought, and indeed of any view that takes account of social and political facts responsibly but without over-emphasis.

Hebbel is sure that such "violence" is "lawful violence". The advocate of the Whole is indeed always sure of something that in fact remains to be proved: that he represents history and the general interest. The very opposite might be true: it is stated in the tragedy that the marriage of Albert and Agnes threatens to undermine the Duchy of Bavaria, and it is added that this undermining might assist the Emperor in his efforts to reimpose the power of the central authority over the princes, like the eagle who seizes the prey while the bears are fighting over it. But history and the Whole might desire such a victory of the Empire over the particularism of the princes, in which case Duke Ernest would be the representative of a subjective ambition, and the marriage of Agnes Bernauer would be not the infraction, but the expression of the will of the Whole. It might have been Agnes who at that moment embodied the *Weltgeist*, the world-spirit.

There exists no register of the *Weltgeist*'s attorneys-at-law, and the indecent hubbub of those who lay claim to the title is interminable. The desire to march with the times, to be swept along in their procession, is the regressive yearning to rid oneself of all choice and all conflict, in short of freedom, and to find innocence in the conviction that it is impossible to be guilty because it is impossible to choose and act independently. In Hebbel's tragedy poetry is the Siren of this illusion, this abdication: not only is Agnes innocent in the play, but above all so is her murderer. "There are things", says Duke Ernest of the crime, "which have to be done in a dream: this, for example."

Grillparzer is also the author of a play about Reasons of State, *The Jewess of Toledo*, in which the Grandees of Spain resolve to kill Rahel, the lovely, daemonic mistress of the King of Castile, who keeps the latter in a state of inert amorous bondage, paralysing the kingdom, which is thus exposed to enemy aggression, war, massacre and ruin. But (to apply Max Weber's distinction) Grillparzer contrasts the ethics of conviction with those of responsibility, showing the reasons of both and not sacrificing the one to the other, though at the same time avoiding any reconciliation of their conflict, which is shown as irremediable, and therefore tragic. The Grandees of Spain who have killed Rahel have pursued "good, but not justice"; they think they have done their duty towards the state, but do not imagine that this outcome renders their action less criminal and justifies their violation of a universal commandment. They admit to being guilty murderers, and only ask pardon from a God who is distant and mysterious.

The necessity of an event – for such they consider their action to be – does not imply its justification or its innocence; universal history for the Austrian Grillparzer is not the same as universal judgment, as it is for the German Hebbel. Moral judgment of the world is not to be identified with the mere happening of the world; facts do not coincide with values, or what is with what ought to be. Against Hegel's identification of reality with rationality Austrian culture proposes a deviation, things that might always take a different turn, history conjugated in the subjunctive, an ironic absence. In Grillparzer's plays the sovereign is always either absent or inadequate; strictly speaking he is not there, and can only be represented, and that imperfectly.

This is a typically Austrian interpretation. Straubing was the birth-place of Schikaneder, librettist of *The Magic Flute*, poet of the fairy-tale folk-drama of Vienna, which capriciously does away with all reality in order to invent another possible, ulterior one, in order to oppose the great wheel which passes over Agnes Bernauer, with the frills and trills of Papageno and Papagena, whom not even Sarastro could ask to relinquish their inner selves, their love and their capers.

25. EICHMANN IN THE MONASTERY

On the Bogenberg a procession takes place each year at Pentecost. The peasants go on foot for 75 km, from Holzkirchen to Bogen, carrying two candles 13 metres in height, and passing them from shoulder to shoulder. The pilgrims pass through the Bavarian woodlands, which only a little further on become the Bohemian Forest – Stifter's woods, age-old quiet, generations who have lived and passed like the seasons, ancient religious piety. When they cut down a tree the Bavarian woodsmen once upon a time used to doff their caps and pray God to grant them peace at the last. There is a religious feeling about wood: its flourishing and aging make us feel towards a tree as a brother. No living creature can be excluded from redemption or deleted from eternity. Like Singer's characters, we ought to recite the *Kaddish*, the funeral prayer, for the butterfly that dies or the leaf that falls.

The woods of Bavaria had their prophets, the *Waldpropheten*, such as the "Mühlhiasl", who worked at the monastery of Windberg in about 1800, and preached apocalypses and the birth of a new world. In 1934, on the other hand, Adolf Eichmann spent a week in the monastery of Windberg, on a kind of spiritual retreat. Trost tells us that the Guest Book still contains his thanks for the hospitality he received, written in his own hand, the expression of an intense experience and a deeply-felt bond. "Treue um Treue", faith for faith, wrote Eichmann in the monastery book on May 7th 1934. The technocrat of massacre loved meditation, inner absorption, the peace of the woods, maybe even prayer.

26. THE DOUBLE CHINS OF VILSHOFEN

The photographs of the meeting show the napes of bulging necks, double chins shaking with laughter, bellies swollen like wineskins, porcine faces sweating from beer and guffawing. One sees why Dionysus, god of drunkenness, had to be the god of wine, not of beer. It is the Ash Wednesday gathering at Vilshofen in Lower Bavaria, a traditional political assembly that dates back to the fairs and cattle markets of past centuries. This folk-festival, formerly a manifestation of the peasant world, and recently transferred in part to the *Niebelungenhalle* in Passau, exhibits the triumph of the Christlich-Sozial Union and, on behalf of the party, of Franz Josef Strauss: his physiognomy gives him all the right qualifications to emerge with his vigorous, superabundant blend of sweatiness, outstanding flair for politics (which makes him a leader of international views), vulgarity, energy and demagogy of a plebeian and reactionary nature. Until 1957 Vilshofen was the platform not so much for Strauss and the C.S.U. as for the *Bayernpartei*, the Bavarian Party, and its bellowing leader Joseph Baumgartner. The Bavarian Party, writes Carl Amery, was still genuinely rooted in that populist, rural and religious tradition which for more than a century had represented an alternative to the enlightened liberal forces brought to power at the beginning of the nineteenth century by the great minister Montgelas.

Montgelas had created an enlightened, authoritarian state guided by an apparatus of bureaucrats, a political machine that in the name of progress and reason had also imposed a strait-jacket on society. As happens according to the logic of enlightenment, the Bavarian state machine had proceeded along the road to modernization, carrying out reforms and achieving notable conquests in terms of civil rights, but its perfect running had ended by constricting society and forcibly integrating it into the cogwheels of the administration. Its opponents – the "blacks", whether peasantry or clergy – represented the tradition, and also reaction and regressive populism; but at times they really did represent the people's genuine needs, liberties and modes of independence, historic particularities which they were legitimately unwilling to see abolished by Jacobin, absolutist despotism.

It is the ceaseless old conflict between Reason, progressive and tyrannical, and the various divergencies which may be conservative at one moment and liberal at the next. Carl Amery, who sees his beloved Bavarian people as on the brink of disappearance, discerns in the history of Bavaria a slow but inexorable fusion of these two forces whose antagonism once ensured some measure of debate and the possibility of alternatives to the political group in power. Little by little the machine gobbles up even those populist elements which had opposed it, transforms them into cogs in its own mechanism, includes among its equipment even that plebeian conservative vehemence against which it had often brandished the sceptre of enlightened Reason, while on their side the popular political forces form no longer a protest from below but the very centres of power.

The C.S.U. has achieved this perfect totalitarianism, this symbiosis of bureaucratic machine and the innermost will of the people, and it therefore holds unrivalled sway in Bavaria. Baumgartner's Bavarian Party, which governed for three years with a coalition which excluded the C.S.U., was still the voice of traditional Bavarian particularism and of its genuinely working-class strata, with all the archaic virtues and the vices of the same. The coalition dissolved in 1957, and shortly afterwards a dubious trial eliminated Baumgartner from the political scene. Ever since then the C.S.U. has been the sole power in Bavaria, compared to which even the Church appears ineffectual. It has inherited two hostile traditions and fused them into one, and it now represents the whole. Vilshofen thus becomes a tiny mirror reflecting the levelling of the world, that overall integration which in Western societies unites in one dominant mechanism such polar entities as Enlightenment and popular romanticism, rationalization and irrationality, inexorable programming and random disorganization, mass-production and the increase in transgressions.

27. IN THE CITY OF PASSAU

In der stat ze Pazzouwe / saz ein bischof, in the city of Passau there reigned a bishop: this we are told in the twenty-first adventure of the *Song of the Niebelungs.* In the great medieval epic poem this bishop is Pilgrim, who appears as the uncle of the House of Burgundy and of Kriemhild, but in fact the whole history of Passau is enveloped in rotund episcopal majesty. Ever since the sixth century innumerable eulogies have extolled the glory and beauty of the "splendid, flourishing" city with three names and three rivers, the Venice of Bavaria, *schön und herrlich,* lovely and magnificent; its diocese at one time extended as far as Austria and Hungary, and its bishops lorded it over Pannonia and the patriarchate of Aquileia. Passau was a free imperial city, and above all the residence of a prince-bishop until 1803. From the hilltop the Oberhaus – the bishops' fortress – kept a wary eye and cannons trained on the burghers and their Town Hall, safeguarding an order in which there was a place for religious devotion, clerical authoritarianism, baroque splendour, sound classical studies and the gentle pleasures of the senses.

The ancient Bojodurum or Batavis of the Celts, the Romans and the Bavarians is one of the hearts of Bavaria, but in 1803 its incorporation into the Bavarian state was felt to be a subjection to foreign occupation. The thousand-year-old, much stratified history of Passau, which at certain times made it one of the capital cities of Europe, was apt to contract into a proud local patriotism such as led Enea Silvio Piccolomini, later Pius II, to say that it was harder to become a canon in Passau than pope in Rome.

Notwithstanding their links with the tragic, heroic cosmos of the Niebelungs, the prince-bishop's three companies of soldiers do not seem to have created a great tradition of warriors. In 1703, when the Austrian general commanding the garrison ordered the citizens to fight against the besieging Bavarians, they excused themselves on the grounds that a nasty fever had put them temporarily out of action, while in 1741 Count Minucci communicated to the Prince Elector of

Bavaria that the city had been conquered without a blow struck. Travellers and chroniclers alike testify to the joyous life of the clergy – their music, liturgical functions, hot chocolate, bonbons and flirtations – the large number of beer-houses and the compliant nature of the girls. When in his philhellenic enthusiasm Ludwig I of Bavaria placed his son Otto on the throne of newly-liberated Greece, along with a Bavarian Bureaucracy, Minister Rudhard, a true son of Passau, embarked in his native city en route for Athens, drinking from a barrel of beer he had brought with him and singing the most Bavarian of songs in which a certain Hans Jörgl ran after his Lieserl. The Bavarocracy installed in Greece immediately saw to opening a large brewery and beer-houses which, in the words of von Wastlhuber, the secret chronicler of the ministerial chancellery, "transformed Athens into a suburb of Munich."

The beer of Passau has always played a leading role. The withdrawn and melancholy Adalbert Stifter, bard of renunciation and destined to a tragic suicide, repeatedly praises it and begs his friend Franz X. Rosenberger to procure him fifty litres of it, twenty-five for him and twenty-five for his wife. Ernst von Salomon and Herbert Achtern-busch, whose sarcasm was respectively of a Fascist-anarchist and of an impulsive revolutionary brand, have given sardonic accounts of how this Catholic-Epicurean society lived through the Third Reich and its disintegration.

Passau stands at the confluence of three rivers – the Danube, the blue waters of the Inn, and the Ilz with its black waters and its pearls. It seems to be nothing but river-banks, a city that floats on the water and flows with the water. The sky is cornflower blue, the glorious, happy light of the rivers and the hill blends with the gold and flesh-coloured marble of the palaces and churches, while the whiteness of the snow, the scent of the woods and the cool of the waters impart a delicate, nostalgic gentleness to the episcopal and aristocratic magnificence of the buildings; the rotund, closed lines of the domes and the streets winding beneath arches and colonnades are set off by an aura of distance.

In Passau there is a prevalence of rotundities, of curves, of spheres; it is a cosmos as closed and finite as a ball, well protected and covered by a bishop's hat. Its beauty is that of a matron, the warm, conciliating seductiveness of the finite. But the curve of the dome fades into the maternal curve of the river-bank, passes into that of the ripples slipping away and dissolving. The elusiveness and lightness of the water give an airy levity to the palaces and the churches, which appear far off and mysterious, as unreal as a castle in the evening air.

Passau is a city of waters, and the baroque majesty of its domes looks out onto that fleeting scene, that flow, that flux of colour in the waters and in all things else, which is the secret source of all authentic baroque. The confluence of those three rivers has the freedom of the sea and a breath of the warm south, inviting us to give ourselves to the flow of life and of our desires. The clear-cut outline of the forms, the friezes over doorways or the statues in the squares, conjure up those Aphrodites and those Naiads who seem to rise from the spray spontaneously, and is all one with the water, like the figures in fountains spurting forth their jets.

At Passau the traveller feels that the flowing of the river is a yearning for the sea. That sense of life-to-the-full, that gift of the blood pressure, or of some acid benevolently secreted by the brain, was something I really felt in the alleys and on the river-banks of Passau; or do I just think I felt it because I am now trying to describe it at a table at the Caffè San Marco? On paper one probably pretends, one invents every kind of happiness. Writing may not really be able to give a voice to utter desolation, to the nullity of life, to those moments when it is simply a void, privation and horror. The mere fact of writing in some way fills that void, gives it form, makes the horror of it communicable and therefore, even if minimally, triumphs over it. There are in existence many sublimely tragic pages, but for someone who is dying or wants to die even those wondrous pages of sorrow would sound trumped up, terrifyingly inadequate to the sorrow of the instant.

Absolute privation cannot speak. Literature speaks of it and to some extent exorcizes it, overcomes it, transforms it into something else, converts its unyielding, unapproachable otherness into current coinage. The hesitant traveller, who in his travels does not know what line to pursue, on re-reading his own notes discovers with some surprise that he was a little happier and more at ease, and above all more resolute and decisive, than he thought he was while actually on the road. He finds that he has given clean, clear answers to the questions that pester him, in the hope of one day being able to believe in those answers himself.

Therefore we enter reassuring literature. In literature everything becomes more gracious, as cheering as the doorways and squares of Passau. And the traveller, distracting his attention from the monotonous thumping that measures the time in his veins, comes to resemble that young apprentice merchant from Nuremberg who wrote some joyful epistles from Passau in 1842, singing the praises of the wines, the libraries, the warehouses, the business dealings, and of a certain beautiful Therese; though he lamented the fact that he had not been able to sit next to the latter at a luncheon, and ended up instead beside her aunt, an imposing matron sporting a plume and talking from hors d'oeuvre to dessert, of nothing but her ailments, disturbances and sicknesses and the medicines suggested by the family physician, Dr Gerhardinger.

28. KRIEMHILD AND GUDHRUN, OR THE TWO FAMILIES

In the great chamber in the Town Hall is a colossal painting by Ferdinand Wagner, an artist of the late nineteenth-century Munich school with a penchant for historical scenes. It shows Kriemhild entering Passau through the Paulustor, accompanied by her uncle, Bishop Pilgrim, and welcomed by the townspeople who offer her homage and gifts. The picture does not call to mind the sombre starkness of the *Song of the Niebelungs*, but rather the grandiose stage settings with which the late nineteenth century accompanied the rebirth of the myth, or the spectacular sets of Fritz Lang's film *The Niebelungs*. In the scene depicted by Ferdinand Wagner, Kriemhild is on her way to Pannonia and her wedding to Attila, the first step in her plan of revenge.

This revenge, narrated with such grandeur in the poem, bears witness to a certain ethos of the family, an ethos to which the traditional nordic version of the myth provides an alternative. In the *Song of the Niebelungs* Siegfried, the solar hero treacherously killed in the forest, is in fact avenged by his wife Kriemhild, who proceeds to marry Attila, the mighty King of the Huns, so as to be able to use his vast army to destroy her own brothers, the Burgundian princes who murdered Siegfried. Also in the nordic versions of the story included in the Icelandic *Edda* (composed probably in the eleventh and twelfth centuries), it is Attila's hordes who annihilate the killers of the hero, here called Sigurdhr, and also in the *Edda* Attila has married his widow, who is called Gudhrun and is the sister of the killer-princes. In both cases the extolling of the mythical hero, who has slain the dragon and embodies the forces of light and the spring, is followed by the adulation of his murderers and of the valour with which they face the sea of invading Huns and ineluctable end. The author (or authors) celebrates the warrior virtues of the Germanic races, who challenge destiny although they know they will be defeated. It is in this way that poems transfigure the fall of the Burgundian kingdom, which was overwhelmed by the Huns at the time of the barbarian migrations.

However, there is one profound difference between the two versions. In the *Song of the Niebelungs* Kriemhild aims to avenge the man she loves and therefore to have her brothers killed, and she cannot rest until they have all fallen, one by one. But in the *Edda* Gudhrun, though she tenderly loved Sigurdhr and laments his death, attempts to foil the trap laid by Attila for her brothers, rather than planning it herself, as she does in the German poem. She does not wreak her revenge upon the brothers who killed her husband, but on Attila and the Huns who slaughtered her brothers.

Dominant in the *Song of the Niebelungs* is love, the conjugal bond founded on free choice, the inclinations of the heart and loyalty deliberately chosen. The story in the *Edda* is dominated by the ethos of the family, the destined loyalty to a tie of blood that one cannot choose, because it transcends all personal feeling and binds by the necessity of nature. Love can come and go, and marriages can be dissolved, but being brothers and sisters is a given fact, as epic and objective as the features or the colour of the hair.

In cultural history, as well as in individual lives, there is often tension and opposition between the family from which one comes, in which one is a son or a brother, and the family which one founds, in which one is a spouse or a parent. It is only natural that in the *Edda* the prevalent one is the first: that iron language has the passion of necessity, not of freedom. In the world of the *Edda* there are only inevitable things and events, a warrior who surpasses another in the battle as an ash-tree towers above the brambles, horses under a leaden sky, the red gold of barbarian jewellery. It is the world of unalterable things as they are, which was so fascinating to Borges, the world in which judgment is entrusted to the sword, or else to the way things happen; a world in which dying means realizing that the span allotted by fate has run out.

Literature is usually more inclined to dwell on the epic totality of the family of origin, in which the individual plays his part as in a chorus:

the Rostovs of *War and Peace*, with the harmony and unity of tone of their household; the Buddenbrooks, for whom collective loyalty to the honoured emblem of the firm is stronger than the charms of the mysterious eyes of Gerda, the foreign wife, and than the beautiful Toni's love for young Morten; or the Buendìas of *A Hundred Years of Solitude*, the members of which are like the stones of the Great Wall of China.

The social transformations which have broken the bonds of patriarchy, and are tending to slacken family unity, have not eliminated our nostalgia for the solidarity of the saga. Poetry has often denounced the stifling repressions of the epic family, but it has also many times paid homage to the appeal of it, as if seduced by a unity that seems unquestionable, like life itself.

The other family, the family which one brings into being, is an arduous and unpredictable odyssey full of pitfalls and temptations, sunsets and new dawns. The hazardous plenitude of conscious, deeply-felt family life has not often been adequately represented in poetry, maybe because of the fear that awareness brings disenchantment, so that taking refuge in childhood is preferable.

In the pages of world literature we find many families such as the Buddenbrooks or the Buendìas, but precious few images such as those in which Homer portrays Hector, Andromache and Astyanax, a life which rises to heights of greatness and which revolves around conjugal and paternal love, around Astyanax playing with his father's helmet, and the father's hopes that the boy will surpass even himself.

Great poetry is capable of dealing with erotic passion, but it has to be the very greatest to represent that deeper and more tortuous love – more rooted, more absolute – which we devote to our children, and which it is so hard to talk about.

The emotional maturity celebrated by Homer is the opposite of the shabby household idyll, unaware of the world and closed up in its paltry intimacy. Hector's love for Andromache and Astyanax makes him a hero who lays himself open to everyone, a man capable of friendship and brotherly love, of filial piety, of human loving kindness towards others. Today it is Singer who depicts the marriage-mystery as the theatre of the world, following in the tradition of Hebrew literature, which has done especial justice to the family unit. In his vagrant, comical stories Sholem Aleichem, a classic of Yiddish literature, gives us all the humour and depth of characters such as Tevye the Milkman, who are fathers first and foremost, and experience fatherhood as the strongest and most intense of all emotions.

The greatest contemporary poet of marriage and family life is perhaps Kafka, who did not feel equal to that adventure and was not unaware of its burdens and hardships. Nevertheless he profoundly felt the grandeur of that state from which he was debarred; though he envied it, he wished to avoid it for fear of all bonds and every encroachment of power. Kafka and his solitude are reflected in many of his characters, those shabby, disagreeable bachelors in some of his stories, who live in rented rooms and cross their dimly-lit landings as nomads traverse the desert. That empty territory, in which they travel without stepping over the line, is also the space which Kafka would have had to break out of in order to leave his father's house, that "single organism" of the family and that "shapeless pap of our origins" that kept him guiltily bewitched, as he himself wrote to Félice, the fiancée destined never to become his wife.

29. THE "BLUE INN" WALTZ

Three rivers meet at Passau, where the little Ilz and the great Inn pour their waters into the Danube. But why should the river formed by their confluence, which flows on towards the Black Sea, be called – and in fact be – the Danube? Two centuries ago Jacob Scheuchzer, on page 30 of his *Hidrographia Helvetiae*, observed that the Inn at Passau is broader and deeper than the Danube, and has a greater volume of water as well as having a longer course to its credit. Dr Metzger and Dr Preusmann, who have measured the breadth and depth of the two rivers, support him. Is the Danube therefore a tributary of the Inn, and should Johann Strauss have composed his waltz to *The Blue Inn*, which apart from all else can lay better claims to that colour? Plainly, since I have decided to write a book about the Danube, I cannot possibly accept this theory, any more than a professor of theology at a Catholic university can deny the existence of God, the very object of his science.

Luckily I am rescued from my quandary by a branch of science, that of perceptology, according to which if two rivers mingle their waters the one to be considered the main stream is the one which, at the point of confluence, forms the larger angle with the subsequent course. The eye perceives (establishes?) the continuity and unity of that river and perceives the other to be its tributary. Let us therefore put ourselves in the hands of science and for the sake of prudence avoid looking too long at the confluence of the three rivers at Passau, or checking for too long on the width of that angle; because the eye, when it has stared too much at a certain point, grows hazy and sees double, throws clarity of perception to the winds and runs the risk of bringing about some nasty surprises for the traveller on the Danube.

What is certain is that the river goes downhill, like him who follows it. It is of small importance to ascertain the origin of all the waters it bears along, and which mingle with its ripples. No family tree guarantees a hundred per cent of blue blood. The motley crowd pushing and shoving in our skulls cannot show an incontrovertible birth certificate, does not know whence it comes or what is its true name, Inn or Danube or any other at all; but it knows where it is going and how it will end.

THREE

In the Wachau

The windows give onto the Danube, look out over the great river and to the hills above it, a landscape marked by woods and the onion-shaped domes of churches. In winter, with the cold sky and patches of snow, the gentle curves of the hills and the river seem to lose weight and consistency, become the feather-light lines of a drawing, an elegantly heraldic kind of melancholy. Linz, the capital of Upper Austria, was the city Hitler loved more than any other, and wanted to transform into the most grandiose metropolis on the Danube. Speer, architect to the Third Reich, has described those unrealized plans for vast, pharaonic buildings in which Hitler, as Canetti has written, gave proof of his feverish need to surpass the dimensions ever achieved by any other builder, his competitive obsession with beating all records.

Linz, the tranquil city which in so many snatches of verse is made to rhyme with "Provinz", a province, is today the industrial capital of Austria, has a moderate rate of nervous diseases amongst the young and, according to an inquiry carried out a few years ago, a population particularly suspicious of the system of justice obtaining in the country. The religious devotion of the people, which struck English travellers during the eighteenth century, does not seem to have died out: in the main square, before the Column of the Trinity – one of those columns which rise in squares throughout Central Europe, to commemorate plagues survived and glorify the majesty of creation – a group of people is praying out loud on this freezing, snowy evening. A pugnacious diocesan newspaper demands solidarity with the workmen sacked from factories in Styria, takes up arms against the managements, incites people to boycott the South African government on account of its racist policies and to bombard its embassy with demands for the liberation of Smangaliso Mkhatshwa, an arrested black priest.

In the Führer's dreams, the cyclopean Linz he wanted to build was to have been the refuge of his old age, the place he yearned to retire to after finally consolidating the Reich that was to last a thousand years and handing it over to some worthy successor. Like many pitiless tyrants, the murderer of millions and would-be exterminator of entire peoples, Hitler was a sentimentalist, whose emotions were touched by thoughts about himself and who cradled himself in idyllic fantasies. From time to time he confided to his intimates that in Linz he would live quite divorced from power but, like a benevolent grandfather, prepared to dispense advice to his heirs when they came to visit him. But perhaps, he would say – flirting with the possibility of his being dethroned, something he was resolved not to permit at any price – perhaps no one would come and visit him at all.

In Linz, where he had spent happy years, this bloody-handed despot had daydreams of rediscovering a kind of childhood, a season free from projects and ambitions. He probably thought nostalgically about that empty future, in which he would enjoy all the security of one who has already lived his life, who has already fought for the dominion of the world and won, who has already realized his dreams, which shall never more be frustrated. When he imagined that future, maybe he felt tormented by the craving to reach his objectives soon, and gnawed by the fear of not being able to achieve them. He wanted the time to pass quickly, so as quickly to be sure of having won; in other words, he desired death, and in Linz he dreamt of living in a sweet security similar to death, sheltered from the surprises and setbacks of life.

The windows of that house overlooking the Danube, and which now has the address 6 Untere Donaulände, could have shown him another way to live, a sense of moderation and a style which he, however, would never have been able to learn. The house belonged, and still belongs, to the Danube Steam Navigation Company, and it witnessed twenty years of the silent life, and also the tragic death, of Adalbert Stifter, one of the most elusive Austrian writers of the nineteenth century, a retiring person who aspired to stem the chaos of life by the modest, impersonal repetition of simple everyday gestures.

From 1848 to 1868, that is, until his death, Stifter looked down from his windows at the Danube, the much-loved Austrian landscape which seemed to him to contain centuries of history transformed into nature, empires and traditions absorbed by the soil like crumbled leaves and trees. That well-known landscape, devoid of strong colours or glaring effects, taught him respect for the things that are, reverent attention to those small events in which life reveals its essence more than in vast upheavals and garish prodigies; it taught him the subjugation of paltry ambitions and personal passions to the great objective law of nature, of the generations, of history.

In his novels, and even more in his short stories, many of which were written in these rooms, Stifter with restless mastery inquires into the secret of moderation, of that acceptance of limits which enables the individual to subordinate his own vanity to a value above the merely personal, to open himself to sociability and to dialogue with others – an affectionate neighbourliness based above all on discretion, on respect for the independence of other people and their need to keep their distance.

This defensive feeling is not without its consequences in Stifter's art. His novel *The Late Summer* describes the difficult maturing of his protagonist, Heinrich, whose developing personality is threatened by a prosaic world, by the objective barriers which modern life throws up in the path of the harmonious, complete and "classical" evolution of the individual. The price which Heinrich pays for his development is a partial renunciation of the world, an aristocratic solitude rejecting the prosaic disorder of things as they are. Schorske has pointed out that for Flaubert's heroes the prose of the world has already entered their souls; it does not rear up before them as an enemy, but has already, far more insidiously, become a structure of their personalities, a part of their natures. Hence it is that in *Education sentimentale* the disappointment of Frédéric Moreau, immersed as he is in the present moment of life and history, and undermined by these, is far more bitter and intense than the ceremonial by which Heinrich, hero of *The Late Summer*, keeps modern vulgarity at arm's length, deluding himself that his inner self can remain immune to it. Flaubert depicts us as we are, while Stifter seems to insist on rubbing off the sharp edges and framing the break-up within a feudal idyll, even if his oleograph is animated by an impassioned effort to avoid the abysses of reality.

Stifter was not unaware of these abysses, the confusion and irrationality of fate, or its sudden, insensate blows, as for example is shown by his tragic tale about the destiny of the Jews, *Abdias*. He did not shut his eyes in the face of tragedy, but he refused to be enraptured by it, and he rejected that cult of the tragic, the passional and the abnormal which he saw spreading throughout European culture, especially by way of late Romanticism. In his stories we find melancholy, renunciation, solitude, but above all a fierce condemnation of all cults of solitude and unhappiness. In *The Recluse* an old woman tells a young man, who has declared his inability to take delight in things, that such words are totally mistaken, and that it is absolutely impermissible to say that nothing gives us pleasure any longer.

Stifter seeks for this joy in apparent monotony, in day by day repetition. At home he would write, look after his plants (especially cacti), restore and polish furniture, including the desk still to be seen in his room today. He would paint, and go for methodical walks; he would praise the succession of days and of weeks, he would listen to the murmur of the river and feel its peaceful rhythm flowing in the cadence of his style and of his life. That gentle scansion, rich in ever-fresh nuances, seemed to him to be happiness, and he longed for that present moment not to pass.

As for happiness, he had precious little of it: in those Danube waters his adopted daughter drowned herself, while he himself, in a crisis of hypochondria and physical pain, hastened his end with a slash from a razor. But for this very reason, his unhappiness, he had understood that what is exceptional, abnormal, dramatic, the cynosure of those who crave a heroic destiny, brings with it all the misery of suffering and nothing else. His characters are nearly always engrossed in cleaning up, stacking the clean linen, tidying drawers, pruning roses; their aims in life are conversation, marriage, the family. Against the bombast of transgression, which loves flashy, blood-curdling effects, Stifter sets up the epic quality of the family, the hard-won originality of orderliness and continuity, the ability to keep one's sufferings to oneself.

In this sense he is rooted in the conservative Austrian tradition, in loyalty to an age-old spiritual harmony, to a long period of time that takes little account of short-term changes and the sensational effects of the stop-press news. The protagonist of another great Austrian writer, Stifter's contemporary Grillparzer, is the "poor street-musician" who is amazed when they ask him to tell his story, because he doesn't think he has a story; he can't believe that the sequence of his days – however abundant in hidden meanings – is anything special. These characters love life, the simple present of their humble but satisfying hours, and therefore have no wish to play a leading part in grand, spectacular events, either personal or historical. If possible, indeed, they fight shy of important happenings. As Musil later wrote, when the rest of the world thought that it had experienced something staggering, in Old Austria they preferred to say nonchalantly, "well, it so happened that . . ." When Stifter died the choir at his funeral was conducted by a man who was in a sense "without a history", as he was. This was Anton Bruckner, a great modern musician who was organist in the cathedral of Linz and did not think so much about being an Artist as (and above all) doing a decent job and performing a religious duty.

Stifter's domestic order is a far more mysterious thing than the monumental buildings dreamt of by Hitler. In Stifter's rooms, which now house a literary institute called after him, I look for traces of that order, the key to that spick-and-span mystery. Meanwhile, on the telephone, a number of functionaries of the institute are having an animated discussion about the obituary for an influential person who has died the previous day. The question is, whether to use the adjective "unforgotten" or the adjective "unforgettable". The debate becomes heated, several dictionaries are consulted and read aloud, someone makes an appeal to precedents . . . When I have to leave, the debate is still in progress. This conscientiousness about keeping to the most precise rules of rhetoric and propriety are not inappropriate to death, to its formal demands. Moreover the comic side, arising from that pedantic search for an adequate expression of solemnity, cuts even death down to size, makes it step down from the pedestal and take its place among good, solid everyday things. "Only when you can laugh again," says a poster on the door of Linz cathedral, "have you really forgiven. Don't drag anything behind you!"

2. SULEIKA

At 4 Pfarrplatz, now the Linz parish office, a plaque informs us that according to tradition there stood on that site the birthplace of "Marianne Willemer née Jung – Goethe's Suleika". This passionate relationship does not wholly befit a presbytery, even though in Goethe's life, from the time of his youthful love for Friederike Brion, there is an undoubted liaison between his heart and the parish church.

Marianne Jung, born "into the theatre" probably on November 20th 1784, was of unknown origins. She played bit parts, danced, sang in the chorus. Or, dressed as Harlequin, emerged into a dance number from a large egg which circled the stage. Willemer, banker, senator, financial agent for the Prussian government and author of political and peda-gogical pamphlets, was also a lover of the theatre and dinners after the show. He saw her at the age of sixteen at one of these performances in Frankfurt and took her home with him, paying her mother two hundred gold florins and an annual pension. In his country house, near an old mill between Frankfurt and Offenbach, Marianne learnt polite behaviour, French, Latin, Italian, drawing and singing. After fourteen years of living together Willemer thought it a good thing to marry her, as he was concerned at the appearance of Goethe over their tranquil horizon.

Goethe at sixty-five was traversing one of his most inspired creative periods, writing the poems of the *West-östlicher Divan*, a brilliant reworking of the Persian lyrics of Hafiz, which he read in the translation by Joseph von Hammer Purgstall, the idea being to derive vitality from the eternal dawn of the Orient and to escape from the tempestuous present of Napoleon's last campaigns.

Goethe is pleased to don Persian costume and enter a tradition in which the whole of tangible reality, in each and every detail, becomes a symbol in which the divine oneness of life becomes apparent. His existence, written in the dust and gladdened by wine, opens out towards infinity and changes colour, ephemeral and eternal at one and the same time, like poppies which resemble Viziers' pavilions. Now he no longer delights in the clear outline of a Greek statue, but in the flowing of water. But even that water is form, is outline, is the mobile but clear-cut figure designed by the play of a fountain. The great classical poet still loves form, and what is finite and distinct, but now he seeks for a form which, like that of water in a fountain or a belovèd body, is not rigid immobility but flowing, becoming and, in a word, Life.

In one lyric in the *Divan* the beautiful Suleika says that everything is eternal in the sight of God and that, for an instant, one can love this life divine in her own person, in her tender, fleeting beauty. Suleika knows that she is only a passing moment, the crest of a wave or the hem of a cloud, but she is soberly content to be, for an instant, the embodiment of that flow. She is neither bewitched nor anguished by unceasing change; she feels so completely at home in the protean, ever-changing life that she has no need to hasten or force along her own metamorphosis, just as Goethe does not need to break the metre and the rhyme of his quatrains to grasp hold of the open, potential melody of becoming and to identify his song with it.

Goethe gets to know Marianne and Marianne, in the *Divan*, becomes Suleika. This gives birth to some of the greatest love poetry of all times, but also to something greater still. The *Divan*, and the superb love-dialogue which it contains, bears the name of Goethe. But Marianne is not only the woman loved and sung in the poems; she is also the author of a number of the most truly sublime lyrics in the entire *Divan*. Goethe incorporated them and published them in the collection under his own name. It was only in 1869, many years after the death of the poet and nine after that of Suleika, that the philologist Hermann Grimm made public the fact that this woman had written those few sublime lyrics in the *Divan*, for to him Marianne had confided the secret and shown the correspondence with Goethe, which she had preserved in faithful secrecy.

Set to music by Schubert, those poems had by then gone round the world as the work of Goethe, and they continue to do so, to bear his name in books and in the memories of those who love those *Lieder* they have to consult the notes each time in Erich Trunz's critical editions of Goethe's works to find out which are the lines written by the Privy Councillor and which, on the other hand, are those of the little ballerina who used to step out of an egg, dressed as Harlequin, and who cost her banker-friend two hundred gold florins.

What strikes us is not only the mimicry, that union of voices merging in an impassioned dialogue, like bodies in the act of love or feelings and values in a life that is truly shared. There is certainly also malpractice, a typical and perhaps extreme case of a man appropriating the work of a woman; the work which bears the name of a man is often, as with this book of Goethe's, also an act of expropriation of a woman's toil. But there is also something more. In the *Divan* Marianne wrote a mere handful of poems, which are among the masterpieces of lyric poetry the world over, and then wrote nothing else ever again. When we read her odes to the East and West Winds, love songs which become the very breath of existence, it seems utterly impossible that Marianne wrote nothing more. Like the tiny fable of the dying rose, by a girl in her first term at school, Marianne's lyrics bear witness to the supra-personal quality of poetry, that mysterious conjunction and coincidence of elements which produce it, as a certain degree of condensation of watery vapour caused by a random or at least rather unpredictable combination of factors produces rain, a boom in the sale of umbrellas and a demand for taxis that outstrips the supply.

When thinking of how her masterpieces came into being, Marianne, born in Austria, might well have quoted the Austrian phrase dear to the heart of Musil, "es ist passiert," it just happened like that, some unexpected perfect contact made between the spirit and the world, a hand that writes words as another might absently draw in the sand or on a sheet of paper, all without wishing to take out a patent or assure himself of exclusive rights to the sketch. Marianne let those lyrics pass as Goethe's; in her devotion she well knew how immaterial it is to distinguish between mine and thine in the union of true love. But those poems of hers that appeared under the name of another person also speak of the futility of every name printed at the foot of a page or on the cover of a book of poems: for poetry, like the air and the passing seasons, belongs to no one, not even to its author.

It may be that Marianne Willemer felt that poetry made sense only if it sprang from a total experience such as the one she had undergone, and that once that moment was past then poetry also was over and done with. "Once in my life," she said many years later, "I was aware of feeling something noble, of being able to say things which were both sweet and heartfelt, but time has not so much destroyed them as blotted them out." She was being unfair on herself, because the awareness and the style with which she underwent the deliquescence of that fullness and the withering of that nobility in turn showed great nobility of soul and intensity of feeling; they were a kind of poetry no inferior to that experienced in those far-off months of passion. Marianne had been far grander and more magnanimous than Goethe, who had filed her away in the archives, using that slippery strategy of his which combined rude good health with the anxieties of insecurity. Willemer, unflaggingly affectionate and respectful, also behaved with more generosity than did the poet.

There is no doubt that even without the enkindled emotion of 1814–15, with her intelligence and the refined literary culture she had acquired, Marianne could have written volumes of fine poetry worthy of a place in literary history. Anyone who frequents literary society is capable of being a fairly decent writer, and often in fact is. Really rotten books are rare and a spectacular literary failure is an exception with regard to the average level of stylistic acculturation, as is a glaring spelling mistake compared with the general standard of literacy. Marianne Willemer could certainly have produced five or ten of those books in verse or prose which the literary culture of any one country turns out by the thousand, with the regular and automatic rhythm of a physiological secretion.

She preferred silence. Her few verses are among the greatest in the entire body of lyric poetry, but this does not suffice for Marianne Willemer to find a place in the history of literature, despite the attention focused on her by astute scholars. Literature is a maintenance system: it is not content with a few sublime lines, but needs a production mechanism – it matters little whether of great pages or banal ones – with which to construct its distribution network, its cycle of editions, reviews, theses, debates, prizes, schoolbooks, lectures. In this mechanism there is simply nothing to be done with Marianne Willemer's poems. And so it comes about that Marianne, who wrote some of the greatest poems in the *Divan*, remains in literary history as a woman loved and sung by Goethe, but she is not inscribed in the register of poets.

3. A.E.I.O.U.

The evening is cold and silent. A group of children pulling sledges do not alleviate the silence and emptiness of the streets, their heavy continental melancholy. On the Friedrichstor in Linz the eye catches the famous, enigmatic initials which the Emperor Frederick III – who probably died not far away, at No. 10 in the Old City with its silent palaces and severe coats of arms – used to have printed on his belongings and his buildings: A.E.I.O.U., standing perhaps for *Austriae est imperare orbi universo* (Command of the universe falls to Austria), or else for *Austria erit in orbe ultima* (Austria will be in the world to the end). Even to Frederick himself this Empire stretching out to the confines of the world and of time seemed threatened by decline and bowed beneath defeat. So much so that in his diary he lamented the fact that the banners of Austria were not victorious, and he attempted to hold his difficulties at bay by means of a strategy of elusiveness and immobility that over the centuries was to become the grandiose Hapsburg stasis extolled by Grillparzer and Werfel. His was the reluctance to act, the defensive posture of those who do not aim to win but to survive, who dislike wars because, like Francis Joseph, they know that wars are always lost.

Adam Wandruszka has pointed out that Frederick III, who died in 1493, already showed the typical traits later canonized by the Hapsburg myth: the symbiosis of inadequacy and wisdom, the inability to act translated into shrewd prudence and far-seeing strategy, hesitation and contradiction elevated to the level of normal conduct, the yearning for peace and quiet mingled with the strength to accept interminable, insoluble conflicts.

The initials A.E.I.O.U., of which there are also some later, less respectful interpretations, has become a code-word in post-modernism, an emblem of the inadequacy and oblique defensiveness which mark our warped and shabby ego. Those grand, agonizing tactics of survival, which have so often seemed to me an unostentatious shield, but one no less protective than that of Ajax, appear to me this evening also in their leathery sterility. I find in them a kind of dignified, sardonic wisdom which, however, barely misses capturing the revelation of ultimate things, of that love which creates and redeems and which is invoked in *Veni Creator Spiritus*.

This Danubian evening, of which the A.E.I.O.U. is the emblem laden with glory and decline, has about it an inland desolation, the dullness of plains and of tax-offices which corroborates some vast monotony of life and summons up nostalgia for the sea, for its ceaseless variations, for its wind that puts wings on things. Beneath the inland sky there is nothing but time, the repetition that ticks it by like morning drill in the courtyard of a barracks, its prison. In the window of a second-hand bookseller's a copy of *Danube et Adriatique*, by the honorary prefect G. Demorgny (1934), offers us a documented treatment of the diplomatic questions connected with the freedom of navigation on the Danube and with the policies of the Central European and Balkan states. But the blue title on the white cover enchants, at this moment, not on account of the analysis of the Danubian question but because of that other blue which it brings to mind, the call of the sea. The ochre and orange-yellow of the Danubian buildings, with their reassuring, melancholy symmetry, are the colours of my own life, the colours of the frontier, of the confines, of time. But that blue, which the culture of the Danube has no knowledge of, is the sea, the swelling sail, the voyage to the New Indies, and not just in the library of the Institute of Geography and Cartography.

From the inland prison of time one yearns, understandably, for the maritime freedom of the eternal, as Slataper, while reading and studying the grand severity of Ibsen, every so often yearned for the wide open spaces of Shakespeare. At this moment it would not be displeasing if some sudden confirmation were discovered to prove the ancient and unfounded hypothesis referred to by Dr Gugliemo Menis, Counsellor to His Majesty's Government, chief medical examiner and health officer for Dalmatia on page 250 of his book *The Adriatic Sea Described and Illustrated* (Zara, 1848): "It was claimed by trustworthy writers, according to Pliny, that the river Quieto is the Ister, a branch of the Danube, down which the ship Argus, on its way back from Colchis, made its way to the Adriatic."

The Quieto flows into the Adriatic on the Istrian coast, near Cittanova. If the renowned authors were still to be trusted, instead of following the route towards the Banat, like the Swabian colonists aboard their "crates from Ulm", I would be going down to the sea, to the islands of the Adriatic, to places where, at certain times, it has seemed to me that the serial novel which began with the big bang does not belong to the literature of trite stories, and that being born and dying are both acceptable. If one is Svevo's Zeno or the man without qualities one knows perfectly well that the game, however much fun are many of its moves, is not worth the candle. It is not worth making a fuss about, and in fact it is incumbent on us to pretend not to notice, but the Hapsburg-ochre colour of time suggests, albeit discreetly, that perhaps it would have been better if the uncouth molecules of hydro-carbons had not, with their incautious libertinism, set the whole business in motion.

Men without qualities, those landlocked armchair explorers, have their contraceptives always in their pockets, and Mitteleuropean culture taken as a whole is also a large-scale process of intellectual contraception. Whereas on the epic sea is Aphrodite born, and there – as Conrad writes – we conquer forgiveness for our sins and the salvation of our immortal souls; we remember that once we were gods.

4. BY CUT AND THRUST

In Linz, in the *Zum schwarzen Adler* (At the Black Eagle) Palace, where Beethoven spent some time, in the year 1680 died Raimondo Monte-cuccoli, the great field marshal, theorist of the art of war and Prince of the Empire. There is an epitaph in the Capuchin church exhorting the wayfarer to pause before the tomb – where his innards are preserved with macabre baroque taste, while his body is buried in Vienna. Montecuccoli fought against Gustavus Adolphus and Louis XIV, was wounded at Lützen and taken prisoner at Stettin. In 1646 he forced the Swedes to fall back into Pomerania and in 1673 compelled the legendary Turenne to withdraw beyond the Rhine. In 1663–4, in the famous battle on the river Raba, he routed the Turks, who had invaded Hungary.

The Capuchin church is dark, and though the Latin inscription on the tomb is in large letters, it is barely visible. One has to search for it assiduously, as if this scant afternoon light were aiming to stage a baroque allegory on the vanity of fame. Montecuccoli is one of those old imperial blades who defended the balance of Central Europe – in the Thirty Years' War and the wars against the Turk – and postponed its end for several centuries: postponed the dissolution of that omnium gatherum held together by prudence, conservative scepticism, the art of compromise and also the art of living. The protective shadow of his sword, like that of Prince Eugène, continued to stretch over Central Europe until 1914, and even then was only shattered by different wars conducted with different means and intentions. For total war no longer mobilizes and annihilates professional armies manipulated by the interests of courts or dynasties, but entire peoples, masses called upon to kill or die for ideals such as fatherland, nation, liberty, justice – ideals which demand complete sacrifice and the complete destruction of the enemy. The enemy, too, is the embodiment no longer of contrasting interests, but of evil (tyranny, barbarity, a race accursed).

Montecuccoli fights on the stage of large-scale world politics, but his strategy and perspective are those of the Cabinet room, in which the troops confront each other as in a tournament, less concerned with winning than with not losing, eager to snatch a victory that gains even a modest advantage and to draw up a diplomatic treaty which confirms that advantage. The great commander can certainly move fast and strike like lightning, but his art of war consists first and foremost in moderation, measured geometric order, carefully weighed-up knowledge of circumstances and rules, a tranquil "thinking things over"; without this there is little use in being acquainted with that "infinity of situations" in which a soldier finds himself.

There is not and could not be in Montecuccoli the headiness, the enthusiasm, the mystic, sacral feeling that was often to imbue the pages of war writers from the nineteenth century on, when war came to be seen, experienced and preached as a destiny, a mission, and even as an education for individuals and peoples. For the imperial field marshal, the art of war is simply a branch of understanding rendered necessary by the malice of history and, more generally, of life; and as the intellect believes it must recognize such a necessity, it has to learn its grammar and logic.

In prison at Stettin, or during the pause after the Thirty Years' War or the campaigns against the Turks, Montecuccoli wrote this grammar: the *Treatise on War*, the *Aphorisms of the Martial Art*, *Of the War with the Turk in Hungary* and other works. The meticulous attention he pays to instruments and apparatus, to tangible details, to the pike, "queen of battles", and the tactics of defence in depth (deployed in at least three lines), does not prevent him from grasping the connections between war and politics. The great commander knows that in order to win one needs to know the remote and also the immediate reasons for the war, the capacities of the soldiers, which is to say the social and political make-up of the states, determining the variety, the quality and the character of the men. Three centuries later, in his works on the strategy of revolutionary and partisan warfare, Mao Tse-tung was to show with incomparable brilliance how even the least act of war has to be part of an overall political and social, as well as military, knowledge of the whole. Only in this way can each particular phenomenon be integrated in the whole and take on its true meaning. Thus the commander may succeed in asserting logical dominion over the factor of immediacy (which threatens to overwhelm the intelligence), subordinating it to the general law of which each particular case is only an example, and so avoid "drowning in the ocean of war", in the hectic chaos of the moment.

Montecuccoli naturally could not know Hegel's dialectics, which enabled Mao to see each particular case in all its fortuity, and to overcome its dazzling, distorting violence. He was a master of more modest arts, of a logic and a rhetoric that permitted him to face the facts – the raging, unpredictable facts of war – by organizing, dividing and subdividing the sea of data. Referring to the custom of mathematicians, he says in the *Treatise* that he is starting from those "principles and major propositions on which, as on a stable foundation, the syllogizing intellect securely rests", to proceed thereafter to concrete examples of practical applications. Behind his geometrical strictness, his passionate involvement with cartography and topography, there is the melancholy pessimism of his much-admired Machiavelli, the conviction that the structures created by a civilization "to live in the fear of the law and of God, would be useless, if their defences were not prepared," and that to defend all that is dear to us we must love peace and know how to make war.

Brilliant, but conservative and attached to the past, Montecuccoli extols the squares of pikemen and the old-fashioned lance, man enveloped in iron on a horse equally heavily armoured, at a time when the fusiliers were already putting those pillars of tactical warfare off-side. But even this attachment of his to classic rules already well on their way out reveals a strenuous love of order, awareness that it keeps fear at bay and that at any moment, in the chaos of the fray and of existence, we need to grab hold of something familiar, find ourselves in something familiar; for in familiar things, as his Machiavelli taught, men do not suffer, or at least suffer less.

The old art of war was a defensive strategy set up against the cruel imponderability of life, a passion for exactitude fated to be comic and painful because of the disparity which there always is between the measures taken to ward off death and their ultimate futility. Gerhard Ritter points out that when Heinrich Dietrich von Bülow thought that he had discovered the secret of success in war in the operating angle of military action, which had to be at least sixty degrees and if possible more than ninety, he was entrusting life to mathematics, which is an exact science simply because it is abstract and independent of the world. Von der Goltz smiled at these Utopias of precision, according to which a patrol could not cross a brook without consulting its log. tables. But in this subordination of the brook to logarithms there is a defensive (and self-destructive) yearning, the impossible wish to put up a barrier against the nastiness of destiny, to dominate it by forcing it into the schemata of classification. Kafka and Canetti have written grandly about this nostalgic delirium of the intelligence which barricades itself in against the world and perishes from asphyxiation for fear of the hurricane.

Gigi has lagged a bit behind, not coming to the church where it is now almost dark. He is with Francesca and Maria Giuditta outside a dingy pastry-shop. All three are standing in the doorway, cakes in hand, outlined against the faint glimmer coming from inside, and for a moment it seems as though some secret uneasiness has stopped them and frozen them on that threshold.

Farther, farther flows the Danube, and a scrap of paper thrown absent-mindedly into the water has already vanished, lost in the future, where we have not yet reached. The edge of the current cuts the water like a sword and ruffles it, the spray glitters in the setting sun and a glory ignites in the heart of the river; and the river proceeds with purpose in its calm, tranquil rhythm. To choose, subdivide, reject, eliminate, exclude; to fight, cut and thrust, to inflict wounds and to clean them, to cut away the tangle which prevents free flow . . .

We must continue our journey and receive, like Marshal Marsili in his great *Opus Danubiale*, the living sense of the regality of the river from the lucid purposefulness of its course, with all its tributaries both major and minor. We must entrust ourselves to the current and its decisiveness, rinse our thoughts of those superfluities that obstruct them and make them afraid to face decisiveness of any kind. If a journey, said Embser, is a war that cancels boundaries and widens horizons, then it is best to travel *more geometrico*, drawn up like Montecuccoli's platoons, or like the regiments in the museum of tin soldiers housed not far ahead of us, in Trauttmansdorf Castle at Pottenbrunn. The little soldiers are on the march; symmetry wipes out all differences, and you can tell a battalion only by the colour of it, which aligns and equalizes its men and advances in a body, fearlessly.

This strict order of the military parade can in any case be a way to avoid coming to blows, to side-step battles, like Francis Joseph when he held manoeuvres and parades in the belief that they helped to exorcize wars. A great general, said Frederick II, never finds himself in a situation where he is forced to fight, because his calculations and his genius have set things up in such a way as to render an encounter useless, and therefore absurd. Like every true science, even that of war, at the height of its perfection, ought to nullify itself, take the ground from under its own feet.

In this way, by a process of elimination, only peace would be left, complete peace. The fields stolen from the battles of the *Aeneid* would be restored to the meek industriousness of the *Georgics*. Unfortunately reality often throws a spanner into the works of these geometric Utopias, scatters the tin soldiers all over the room, and they end up under the wardrobe or in the rubbish. And it would certainly not be wise to leave the search for peace, and the preservation of it, to the strategic plans of the various General Staffs. After two world wars, wrote Stefano Jacomuzzi, not even literature can love parades. Next-door to the building where Montecuccoli died, the plaque of the "Lidea" private investigations agency promises discreet and efficient inquiries on the marriage front. Other geometries, calculations, operational angles; other wars.

5. A PUFF OF SMOKE

In the castle museum in Linz is a nineteenth-century print showing a view of Mauthausen. Peaceful hills, friendly houses, boats on the Danube full of people waving gaily, the idyllic atmosphere of a country outing. From the steamers on the river there rises, cheerfully, a puff of smoke.

6. MAUTHAUSEN

In this Lager, not one of the worst, more than a hundred and ten thousand people died. The most terrible sight, perhaps more so even than the gas chamber, is the large square on which the prisoners were assembled and lined up for roll-call. The square is empty, sun-drenched and sweltering. There is nothing better than this empty space to give some idea of the unimaginableness of what happened among these stones. Like the face of the deity for those religions which forbid the representation of his image, extermination and total abasement do not allow of description, do not lend themselves to art and imagination, unlike the lovely forms of the Greek gods. Literature and poetry have never succeeded in giving an adequate portrayal of this horror; even the most lofty pages pale before the naked account of these facts, which exceeds anything that can be imagined. No writer, however great, can sit at his desk and compete with the evidence, the faithful and material transcription of what occurred in the huts and in the gas chambers. Only someone who was at Mauthausen or at Auschwitz can attempt to tell of that unfathomable horror. Thomas Mann and Berthold Brecht are indeed great writers, but if they had tried to invent a story of Auschwitz their pages would have been edifying pulp compared with Primo Levi's *If This Is a Man*.

Perhaps the most adequate accounts of those events have not been written by the victims at all, but by the butchers themselves, Eichmann or Rudolph Höss, the Kommandant of Auschwitz; probably because, if one is to portray what that inferno really was, one can only quote it to the letter, with no comment and no humanity. A man who tells that story in anger or with compassion unwittingly embellishes it, transmits to the page some spiritual charge which attenuates the reader's shock at that monstrosity. This is perhaps why it is almost embarrassing to have a chance encounter, at an inoffensive and friendly luncheon, with a survivor of the concentration camps; to discover, on the arm of our charming (or unpleasant) neighbour at table, his camp registration number. There is always a paralysing discrepancy between his un-imaginable experience and the insufficiency of the words or gestures with which he alludes to them, making them appear almost a matter of routine.

The greatest book on the concentration camps was written by Rudolph Höss, in the weeks between his death sentence and the day they hanged him. His autobiography, *Kommandant at Auschwitz*, is the objective, impartial and faithful account of atrocities that hurl all human criteria into confusion, make life and reality unbearable, and which ought by right to derange and therefore prevent their depiction, the very possibility of recounting them. In Höss's pages the process of extermination seems to be narrated by Spinoza's God, by a nature indifferent to suffering, tragedy and infamy. The pen imperturbably records what happens, the ignominy and the cowardice, the episodes of baseness and of heroism among the victims, the appalling dimen-sions of the massacre, the grotesque automatic solidarity created for a moment, when the bombs began to fall, between butchers and victims.

Höss is not the usual bureaucrat, ready according to his orders to save or to murder with equal efficiency; he is not a torturer like Mengele, and he is not even Eichmann, who recounted and revised his own experience because he was being interrogated by the Israelis, and was trying to avoid paying the price of his crimes. Höss wrote after he had been condemned to death, without being asked to do it. It is not known what induced him to write, nor can it be explained by a wish to put himself in a noble light, because the self-portrait that emerges is certainly that of a criminal. The book seems to obey an imperious demand for truth, a need to confirm his own life, after having lived it, to register it exactly and to file it, quite impersonally, in the archives. For this reason the book is a monument, the record of a barbarity, and an invaluable answer to the repeated, abject attempts that have been made to deny it, or at least to take the edge off it, to water it down. The Kommandant of Auschwitz, the murderer of hundreds and hundreds of thousands of innocent people, is no more abnormal than Prof. Faurisson, who has denied that Auschwitz really happened.

I go down the Steps of Death, which led to the Mauthausen stone quarry. Up these 186 steep steps the slaves carried rocks, they collapsed with exhaustion or because the SS troopers tripped them and made them stumble and fall beneath the weight of stone, they were struck down by beatings or bullets. The steps themselves are irregular, barely negotiable blocks, and the sun is scorching. The massacre is still close by us, we think of archaic deities thirsty for human sacrifice, the pyramids of Teotihuacán and Aztec idols, even though more moderate and civilized gods did not prevent the torturers from torturing. Höss's book is terrible – terribly instructive – because its epic concatenation of facts shows how in the mechanical wheel of things we can get to the point, one step after another, of becoming not just policemen or cooks in the army of the Third Reich, mere "extras" in the scenes of horror, but even leading actors and directors of extermination – Kommandants of Auschwitz.

The steps are high, I am tired and sweaty even without carrying rocks, and I haven't got the SS breathing down my neck. Adorno has said that after the extermination camps it is impossible to write poetry. This judgment is false – and in fact it has been given the lie by poetry itself, for example by Saba, who knew what it meant to write "After Maidenek", another terrible Lager, but who indeed did write "After Maidenek". It is false also because there has not only been National Socialism, but also the Conquistadores, the slave trade, the Gulags and Hiroshima – and after each, the rhyme "dove-love" was (and is) equally problematical.

All the same, paradoxically, the judgment is true, because the concentration camp is an extreme example of the nullification of the individual, of that individuality without which there is no poetry. On these steps at Mauthausen one feels, *physically* one feels, the superfluousness of the individual, his annihilation, his disappearance, as if he were a dinosaur or an okapi, an animal extinct or on the way to extinction.

Not only the swastika, but the whole of history and processes in general conspire towards this dismissal of the individual. The records of Eichmann's interrogation comprise an extreme documentation of a parcelling out of existence which abolishes both responsibility and creativity. Eichmann does not kill; he arranges the trains and the transport for those who are to be killed. Responsibility appears to involve no one, because everyone, even at the top level, is only a link in the chain of the transmission of orders; or else it involves everyone, for example even the Jewish organizations forced by the Nazis to collaborate, and to select the Jews to be deported. On these steps a single person feels one of the vast numbers crushed by the World Spirit which evidently shows signs of mental instability, just one of those numbers which the appropriate office in the Lager tattooed on the arms of the prisoners.

But on these steps the individual has also succeeded in rendering himself unique and ineffaceable, greater than Hector beneath the walls of Troy. On the threshold of the gas chamber at Auschwitz a young woman turned to Höss and told him contemptuously – as he himself writes – that she had not wished to get herself selected for survival, as she could have done, but chose to stay with the children who had been put in her care, and then went in with them to death, her head held high; she is proof of the incredible resistance that the individual is capable of opposing to what threatens to wipe out his dignity, his meaning. In the various camps, as well as on these steps at Mauthausen, there were many such heroic deeds, these Thermopylaes that stem the tide of abasement.

While still on the steps, I see a photograph in my mind's eye. It is one of the many seen a short while before, in the Lager. It shows a nameless man, who from his appearance is probably of Balkan race, a south-eastern European. His face is disfigured by beatings, his eyes are two swollen, bloody lumps, his expression is one of patience, of humble yet solid resistance. He is wearing a patched jacket, and we see that his trousers have been mended with carefully sewn patches, with love of decorum and cleanliness. That respect for his own person and dignity, preserved in the midst of that hell and applied even to his tattered trousers, makes the uniforms of the SS, or of the Nazi authorities on a visit to the Lager, appear in all their paltry carnival tinsel, costumes hired from the pawnbroker's, but in the conviction that a bloodbath could make them last for a thousand years. Well, they lasted for twelve years all told, less than the old wind-cheater that I usually go hiking around in.

At Sankt Florian, to the greater glory of God and of the Hapsburgs, there triumphs a splendour of late-baroque, imperial staircases, long series of corridors, tapestries, Prince Eugène's room, its bed adorned with the figures of Turks and Hungarian rebels portrayed in vanquished poses. But there is also Bruckner's room, bare and modest, with its brass bedstead, a little table, a chair, a piano, and a couple of pictures of no value. In the church of Sankt Florian is the famous organ on which he played. The ornamental pomp of the great Austrian monasteries – Sankt Florian, Göttweig, Maria Taferl and above all Melk, with its splendour and majesty – does not obliterate their truer nature, that mysterious simplicity that makes their domes and bell-towers an integral part of the centuries-old religious feeling of the landscape, of the curve of the hills, the silence of the woods, the peacefulness of tradition. Bruckner, who dedicated a symphony "to the good Lord", embodies this tranquil inwardness, that lives in religion as in its native air, and understands the dissonance of modernity thanks to its sorrowing, open-hearted feeling of harmony.

The art of Bruckner or of Stifter is born of reverence for the gentle, idyllic Austro-Bohemian landscape, with its forests, the onion-shaped dome of the village church, the tranquillity of the home. Sylvan and domestic peace is an idyll, a reconciliation of conflicts arrived at in a limited and protected sphere. In the woodlands life comes into being and is transformed, but with so slow a rhythm as to seem immobile to the single individual, and to give him a sense of the eternal. The gentle law continues through the centuries, seeing to the organization of life according to a wholesome rule, and transferring it slowly into the depths of time. This morality of time, as Sergio Lupi observed, makes the past appear wholesome, because in it we realize how much good the gentle law has done and how much good it has organized in the world. Stifter loved the past and feared the present; he had a horror of the Faustian instant arrested in all its fullness, thus interrupting the imperceptible flowing on of life.

The two-headed eagle attempted to defend the world of tradition against the rapid, driving rhythms of modernity; and tradition is this long measurement of time, lived as if it were eternal. The generations, writes Stifter in *Village on the Plain*, are a rosary told one bead after another, each one an individual human life, and each, identical to the one before, adding a drop of oblivion to the chain of time, because it becomes part of this chain, and forgets its own self.

Faust's instant, or Stifter's rosary? In front of the church of Sankt Florian Maddalena is buying postcards, bending down to examine them and pouting a little as she always does when she is concentrating on something. The creases which that pout makes in her cheeks are a little deeper, and the gold of her hair is slightly tarnished, as if to remind us that life is not stainless. Even that hair, still blond, is a bead in the rosary, a drop of forgetfulness. Is conviction as according to Faust or as according to Stifter? Is it the ability to arrest the moment, the unalterable gold, or to tell our beads in peace, accepting it calmly as the beads run through our fingers?

All things have a tale to tell, says Stifter, but the man who listens shudders at it, for they speak of the general law, the flowing of the present into the past. Maybe conviction is knowing how to be one with this flowing, with the infinite present of the verb, movement and permanence, time and eternity. For Michelstaedter conviction or persuasion was *peithò*, a Greek word, and Greek nouns have the dual number. Is that figure just ahead of us, about to turn the corner, a drop, a bead, a grain, or is it the whole rosary, the telling of the beads? The span of a shared lifetime is a journey that retraces and, as it goes along, constantly rediscovers the places and the moments of its own odyssey. Make love to a sixty-year-old? my friend Roberto once yelled out in the café. For heaven's sake, no way! However – he added, correcting his rhetorical question – Paola isn't just the sixty-year-old she is today; she's also the forty-, the thirty-, the twenty-five-year-old I've lived my life with. The average, therefore, speaks of youth, and will do so also tomorrow. A face becomes more intense, more marked and aware, more fulfilled and seductive. Around that mouth, beneath that nose, in some slight hint of a wrinkle, in the dark waters of the eyes there move the years, past and present; there time sketches and engraves his mark; the curve of the throat is the womb of time, the bed of its river. The mouth which allures in that river is that of yesterday, of today; perhaps Heraclitus is wrong, and we always bathe in the same river, in the selfsame infinite present of its flowing, and each time the water is deeper and more limpid. To flow on down towards the Black Sea, to accept the current, to play its whirlpools and its ripples, the lines it etches on the waters and on the face.

Stifter loved the vegetable kingdom, and perhaps even more he loved inanimate nature. He used the word "moral" of stone, in which the law has been deposited and reveals its crystalline structure, while to aggrandize the figure of the grandmother in *Village on the Plain* he compares her to a stone from which the sun strikes a dazzle. Objects seem superior to men, because in their obscene motionlessness and objective tranquillity they are in unison with the arcane law of reality. The highest wisdom coincides with the total renunciation of individual *hubris* and even of intelligence itself.

Stifter is masterly when he is telling not positive, edifying stories, but parables of the dark, incidents of a sluggish lethargy in which men seem to sink to the level of objects, to dead, passive things, only to discover, beyond all personal ambitions, a mysterious harmony with the unfathomable flow of life. In his story *Turmalin*, one of his masterpieces, the almost mentally deficient girl, who writes intensely felt pages without realizing what she is writing, embodies an impenetrable obtuseness which draws upon a superior understanding of objects. Her father, the protagonist of the tale, is another figure of darkness and sorrow, who attains to a higher consonance with life – with the flowing of the present into the past – thanks to his total exclusion from the dialectics of history and progress, which deletes him from society.

In order to bow the knee to nature – he seeks for her in her humbler expressions, in the growing of the grass and not in volcanic eruptions – Stifter passes over her function as creator and destroyer and dwells on that of nature the preserver of things. When he is forced to reckon with immensity, with destruction and tragedy, he says that "the strong man submits to it humbly, the weakling rebels and complains, the common run of man is stupefied." Stifter wrote his really great pages when he saw things from the point of view of this dumbfounded stupor in the face of the cruelty of destiny, as in *Abdias* and in *Turmalin*, without any moral homilies or ideological protests. When he chose to put himself in the positive position of the strong man who can take destiny as it comes he wrote pages that were edifying and at times unbearably tedious. The great candid souls, such as Stifter or Bruckner, who reveal far more knowledge of the ways of evil than they think they have, are true poets when, mild but unyielding, they confront the dark and negative side of life, like Professor Andorf in *Turmalin*, who spends his time observing the wilting, the sinking, the crumbling away of things, the birds and other animals little by little taking possession of the ruined dwellings abandoned by men, the moisture dripping down ancient walls.

At Sankt Florian there is another, and more disquieting, connoisseur of evil. On the altar of St Sebastian are some of the most disturbing pictures of Albrecht Altdorfer, scenes of the Passion of Christ and the martyrdom of the saint. Under tragic, flaming skies the two victims are raged against by bestial, mindless violence expressed in sullen, idiot faces which display the whole crassness of evil. Nearby, in a painting by Wolf Huber showing the death of St Sebastian, a woman is brutally beating the martyr with a kind of frying-pan, and even a stupid, malicious child is joining in the lynching. Altdorfer helps us to understand Mauthausen, and his savage colours also cry out against the ferocious folly of the concentration camps.

The Austro-baroque rotundity of the monasteries, the cupolas of Sankt Florian and Melk, shy away from this tragic pitiless facet of reality; they smooth down its rough edges, and in so doing they almost become its accomplices, because they hide it and forget it. The soft baroque curves are suited to a positive and reassuring kind of wisdom, to the gladsomeness of the monks of Melk who in the *Fable of Friendship* by Gütersloh, the Thomist novelist who died a few years ago, play ball, convinced in their innermost being that the roundness and lightness of the ball and the mobile symmetry of the monastery fountain are expressions of the music of the spheres.

That rounded harmony has its own ecumenical grandeur, the wide, embracing gesture that imparts order and assurance to the world in the evening benediction. But the great baroque monasteries, which belong to the history of the most illustrious art, smooth and polish that rotundity too much, while certain suburban parish priests sometimes know how to keep it a little rough and simple, so as to leave room also for anomalies and discrepancies. Beneath the burnished cupolas of those monasteries, on the contrary, there is no place for the senseless agony, the dissymmetry, the barbarous passion and crucifixion, which are at every instant inflicted upon men. It is not the canopies of the church triumphant, but the skies of blood and tragedy in Altdorfer, which do justice to the apocalypse, repeated without ceasing, to the living skeletons of Mauthausen.

8. DUCKS AT GREIN

At Grein there are no longer the whirlpools described by Eichendorff, which terrified travellers and swallowed up boats and ferries. Skilful works, which Maria Theresa nourished hopes of even in her day, but which were completed only in recent times, have turned this into a tranquil stretch of the Danube, this morning engulfed in mists which the sun is just beginning to disperse. The old municipal theatre, next-door to the prison, from which the inmates were able to get a glimpse of the show and thus in true Aristotelian fashion to purge their spirits of criminal passions, is silent now; a few yards below, in the last mist on the river, the ducks bob up and down; they look awkwardly heraldic and familiar, like stormy petrels which have just joined the middle-classes they still have an air of the far north though they stay at their home moorings.

In this vicinity Strindberg lived, with his Austrian wife. Experts tell me that he found inspiration here for *Inferno* and *The Road to Damascus*. Looking around me, it is easy to imagine what this soft landscape might have suggested to the romantic nostalgia of Eichendorff, but it is very hard to understand what message it could have had for the visionary frenzy of the Swedish dramatist.

9. A CAKE FOR THE ARCHDUKE

In 1908 Francis Ferdinand, Archduke of Austria-Este and heir to the throne of the Austro-Hungarian Empire, described the Hapsburg crown as a crown of thorns. That phrase stands out in one of the rooms of the museum devoted to the memory of the Archduke in the castle of Artstetten, about 80 km from Vienna and not far from the Danube, where he is buried beside his much-loved wife Sophie. The pistol shots at Sarajevo prevented Francis Ferdinand from wearing that crown, but even if he had become Emperor, and had reigned as long as Francis Joseph, he would not have been buried in the Crypt of the Capuchins, as were his forefathers. He wished to rest beside his wife, Sophie Chotek von Chotkowa und Wognin, who was merely a countess – belonging to one of the most ancient families of the Czech nobility –

and as such did not have the right of access to the imperial Hapsburg crypt, just as her all-too-modest lineage prevented her from residing in the Hoffburg after her marriage to the heir to the throne, and from making use of the imperial carriages or theatre boxes.

Now they both lie in the crypt of the Artstetten church, adjoining the castle, in two utterly plain white sarcophagi. Of "Franciscus Ferdinandus, Archidux Austriae-Este" the stone records neither his status as heir to the throne nor any other titles or memorials. His existence is summed up, in Latin, by three basic events, together with the respective dates: Natus, Uxorem duxit, obiit. The life-story of Sophie also is expressed and condensed in these three moments. Birth, marriage, death: in this laconic epic is summed up the essence of a life, that of the Archduke or of anyone else. All other attributes, however high-sounding, appear secondary and unworthy of being recorded or engraved in marble. In that tomb rests not only one who happened to be an heir apparent, but someone who is a great deal more: a more universal person, a man who has shared the destiny common to all.

His marriage to Sophie, the deprecated misalliance with a woman who was merely a countess, not only forced him to renounce accession to the throne by his children, but caused him to suffer the most wounding humiliations, the implacable hostility of the court cabal which was later to rejoice, even after Sarajevo, on the occasion of his funeral. Francis Ferdinand had not given up the throne for love, like a romantic philistine, because his life found meaning in dedication to the higher responsibility of the Empire, and only by following this vocation could he really live a full life, worthy of that love which was its crowning feature; but neither had he accepted the equally philistine renunciation of love for the throne.

That marriage had been opposed by everyone, even his brother the Archduke Otto, who liked to appear at the Hotel Sacher naked, wearing nothing but a swordbelt and a sabre, or to dash in on horseback and break up Jewish funeral processions, and to get his henchmen to beat up anyone who criticized him. Like the good, unscrupulous hooligan he was, the Archduke Otto knew how to be slavishly dutiful to the conventions of his rank. The malicious envy of the court aristocracy towards Francis Ferdinand shows the same vulgarity as any other social group which considers itself an élite and thinks it is excluding others, while in fact it is shutting itself off from the world, like the drunkard in the old story who circled round and round a tiny flower-bed convinced that it was the world, and that everything outside its low wall was the prison where everyone else was locked up.

In those rooms in Artstetten Castle which record and illustrate the life of Francis Ferdinand, we get the impression of a contradictory personality, a man who with outmoded conviction felt the authority of the monarch as a power held by divine right, but intended to use it against the privileges of the aristocracy and in favour of the more oppressed peoples of the Empire. Letters, photographs, documents and objects evoke for us the image of an impetuous, obstinate character, unpleasantly aggressive and fanatically authoritarian, but devoted with indefatigable energy to a more than personal mission and capable of intense affection.

Those treasures and mementos are also evidence of happiness in the family and in love, which makes one inclined to envy the destiny of the couple assassinated at Sarajevo. The photographs show Sophie as beautiful and serene, a little like Ingrid Bergman, shrouded in the mystery of a tranquillity full of meaning and of secrets. Sophie's charm is of the kind which emanates from lives fulfilled and fathomless in their clarity; the photographs of the Archduke with his wife speak of the intimacy of tenderness and sensuality, of two bodies happy and satisfied. This harmony extends to the pictures of the children: during a fancy-dress party at Schönbrunn little Sophie, in a pink ribbon, is looking over the heads of her two brothers Maximilian and Ernst, whom Hitler later had deported to Dachau when he annexed Austria in 1938. Francis Ferdinand's postcards to his children are addressed to Their Highnesses, but signed "Papi".

This sweetness turns to vulgarity in the photographs of sporting scenes, which show the heir to the throne as possessed by a mania to accumulate killings, a crude passion for records, such as to shoot 2,763 seagulls in a single day or to bag his six thousandth stag. Triumphantly seated atop a great heap of roe deer the Archduke and his companion sportsmen appear in one photo like uncouth, paunchy workmen in a slaughterhouse.

In that family chronicle there are presents, school reports, parties, toy soldiers, sweetmeats. Who knows if in that year of 1908, when she wore pink at Schönbrunn and her father thought of the crown of thorns, little Sophie tasted the cake mentioned in the letter written by the enterprising pastry-cook Oskar Pischinger, proprietor of the firm which bore his name, to Her Most Serene Highness the consort of the Archduke, elevated by her husband to the rank of Duchess. In this letter, overflowing with obsequiousness and tenacious determination, the most humble writer dares with the utmost respect to take the liberty of fulfilling his most profound and heartfelt desire, which is with all due deference to send Her Most Serene Highness, by way of a sample, a cake of his own invention, trusting in the happy outcome that he might receive her august opinion on the matter. Oskar Pischinger closed his letter with further protestations of homage and gratitude, but repeats his hope of obtaining her yearned-for opinion of his creation.

A reply must have been forthcoming from the archducal household; in fact, according to the indications, an imprudently encouraging one, because in a subsequent letter the pastry-cook expresses his gratitude and untold joy at having obtained permission officially to bestow the name of "Duchess Sophie" on certain cream *Krapfen* of his own manufacture. Of the cake, mysteriously enough, no more is said; perhaps it did not meet with any great favour. But Oskar Pischinger made up for this presumed failure with the *coup* of the *Krapfen*, the name and style of which promised a warm welcome from the public. At this point, however, the Duchess, perhaps regretting that authorization so lightly granted, must have thought it wise to send the insistent pastry-cook some sign of coolness. And indeed the latter communicates that he has promptly executed the commission, and has dispatched to the Belvedere (where the Archduke's family lived when in Vienna) the six *Krapfen* ordered by Her Most Serene Highness. Now six *Krapfen* – six tiny little cakelets, perhaps two a head for the children – were truly few for an archducal household, even given Francis Ferdinand's proverbial parsimony.

Behind these letters one can guess at a small domestic drama: the mysterious silence about the cake, the probable agitation of Oskar Pischinger intent on preparing *Krapfen*, his life's work, the cuffs and buffets which in his nervousness he will doubtless have lavished on his assistants, the chillingly stingy order and the minuscule tray solemnly delivered at the magnificent palace of the Belvedere. A little further on are some photographs of the sequence of events at Sarajevo, so similar to those in Dallas: in those few seconds, between one photo and the next, rang out the pistol shots of the suicide of Europe. It may be that, by the strange twists and turns of logic, those shots which gave us our death-wound also set in motion the liberation of the countries of Asia and Africa, which the old European powers, acting in concert, would have been able to continue to dominate and exploit.

The "Duchess Sophie" *Krapfen* have perhaps survived the crown of thorns, like Pischinger's cake, which today is famous. The world goes on its way, and the epic quality of the family becomes the object of solicitude for sociologists and clergy. Opposite the archducal crypt, the Artstetten parish notice-board announces that next week there will be a "day of reflection for mothers-in-law".

10. KYSELAK

It was perhaps the transience of the river that by way of contrast stimulated Herr Kyselak, assistant in the court registry of Vienna during the nineteenth century, and a tireless walker, to nourish a yearning for eternity, a craving to counter those fleeting waters with something stable. Unluckily nothing better came to mind than his own name, so he began to leave his signature, J. (Josef) Kyselak, in large black letters done in indelible oil paint, throughout his wanderings along the banks of the Danube, especially in the vicinity of Loiben and among the vineyards of the Wachau. He traced it on all sorts of things, for example on rock-faces. Like all those who have to sully Greek columns or the tops of mountains, Kyselak aspired to a little scrap of immortality, and he got it. Gerhard Rühm and Konrad Bayer, two poets of the mythical *Wiener Gruppe*, the literary avant-garde of the post-war years partly invented after it was all over, imagine him as totally in the grip of this consuming passion, intent on limning his signature with ever more demanding perfectionism, with a mania worthy of the divine mania which Plato's follower Ion attributed to poetry.

No doubt about it, the flight of the waters is more magnanimous than that megalomaniac's fixity. It would have been better if Josef Kyselak had daubed the face of the world – or, more modestly, simply the lovely region of the Wachau – with the name of someone else, of some belovèd person, or with one of those meaningless words that one repeats like a magic formula. Certainly he would have been a greater figure if he had gone round rubbing his name out instead of writing it. But the assistant in the registry was an inlander, a solid landlubber, in spite of his excursions in the neighbourhood of the Danube, and to know how to be Nobody, like Ulysses, perhaps one needs the sea. Central Europe is of the earth earthy, *alpenstock* and clothes of heavy green homespun, the meticulous order of Exchequers and Chancelleries; it is a culture that has lost its familiarity with the liquid element, with the maternal *amnion* and the ancient aboriginal waters, and finds it hard to strip off, because without boundaries, a jacket, a rank, a badge and a number in the registry, it feels exposed and ill at ease.

Mitteleuropa is a great civilization of defensiveness, of barriers thrown up against life in the manner of Josef K. or Dr Kien, of trenches and underground passages to protect oneself from outside attack. Danubian culture is a fortress which offers excellent shelter against the threat of the world, the assaults of life and fears of losing oneself in perfidious reality, so that one shuts oneself up at home, or behind documents and papers in the office, in the library, around Stifter's Christmas tree, all wrapped up in rough, snug *loden*. Immured between four walls, one feels a need to see one's name in the registers of bureaucracy, or even to write it on the walls, like Kyselak.

The sea, on the contrary, means abandonment to the new and the unknown, pitting oneself against the wind but also letting oneself go with the breakers. In any little harbour, as we wear an old shirt and the stones scorch the soles of our feet, as we hold out our hands carelessly to receive pleasure and love, which don't have to battle their way through overcoats and the concerns of winter, we are ready to walk aboard the first boat and disappear, like those characters in Conrad who, once free of the harbour office, vanish into the immensity of the Pacific coast, swallowed up by the teeming life of its boundless expanses. The Central European continent is analytic, the sea is epic. Following the sea-routes we learn to rid ourselves of Kyselak's malady, his need constantly to reconfirm his own identity.

Kyselak also, in 1829, wrote two volumes of travel sketches which are worth a lot less than his signatures. In a passenger boat on the Danube this registry-clerk complains about the triviality of the other passengers, the waiters, the housemaids, the travelling salesmen and the boatmen. He displays the vulgarity of those tourists who would like places to be unpolluted and think that only other people pollute them. Kyselak considers himself the only one with noble sentiments, capable of appreciating what is genuine. The rest of them are "semi-men", forming a brutish stupid mass of which he never suspects he is a part.

Kyselak is one of those despisers of the masses, to be found in great numbers even today; when crushed together in a crowded bus or caught in a motorway traffic-jam, they think – each of them – that they are inhabitants of sublime solitudes or of refined drawing-rooms; each one of them despises his neighbour and is unaware of being repaid in the same coin. Or else they wink at their neighbour to make it plain that in all that pushing and shoving they are the only two chosen spirits, and witty along with it, though constrained to share that space with the herd. This "office boss" type of arrogance that asserts "You don't know who I am!" is the clean contrary of true independence of judgment, of that moral pride we find in Don Quixote who mutters, after being thrown from his horse, "I know who I am." It is never seen in company with facile, indiscriminate contempt for one's neighbours.

Standardized haughtiness towards the masses is a typically mass type of behaviour. Anyone who speaks of general stupidity must know that he is not immune, since even Homer occasionally nods; he has to take it on himself as a risk and a fate common to all men, aware of being sometimes more intelligent and sometimes more foolish than his next-door neighbour at home or on the bus, because the wind bloweth where it listeth and no one can be sure that, at any given moment, the breath of the spirit will not forsake him. The great comic writers and comedians, from Cervantes to Sterne or to Buster Keaton, make us laugh at human weakness because they discern it also and above all in themselves, and this implacable laughter implies a loving understanding of our common destiny.

Stupidity is also a question of period; that is, it assumes forms and characteristics according to the particular historical epoch, and therefore undermines and concerns everyone, and not just other people, as Kyselak believed. The disdainful writer who seems to pour scorn indiscriminately on everyone does not actually wound anyone at all, because he addresses each one of his readers in such a way as to lead him to believe that he is the only bright spark in a mob of muttonheads, but in so doing he is in fact addressing the mass of readers. The technique is usually successful, because the reader can easily be titillated by the exception which the disdainer of others makes in his case, without realizing that in fact he does it for each and every one of them. But genuine literature is not of the kind which flatters the reader, by confirming him in his prejudices and certainties, but rather of the kind which presses close on his heels and forces him to make a fresh reckoning with the world and with his own assumptions.

It would not be a bad thing if people inclined to think of their neighbours as "semi-men" were to pick up their pens, like Kyselak, only to write their own signatures. Perhaps by dint of copying those flourishes time and time again they would end by depriving their names of all meaning, like oft repeated words, and forget them completely and lay aside all presumptuousness, and at last become Nobody.

11. THE VINETA OF THE DANUBE

The two neighbouring towns of Krems and Stein, either joined or separated, according to the old quip, solely by that *and*, are famous for wine and the folk-baroque painting of Schmidt (known as "Schmidt of Krems"). At one time bustling centres of trade along the river, they have been completely left out of things by the nineteenth and twentieth centuries, by progress and industrialization. They now form a silent townscape of alleyways climbing emptily upwards, tiny balconies jutting out into small, slumbering squares, hidden flights of steps giving out onto forests of rooftops, shuttered-up hotels and deserted arcades. All is silent, minuscule and dead. All one hears in the court-yards is the rain, discreet and soft.

Krems, which in 1153 the Arab geographer Idris praised for its splendour – in his opinion it exceeded that of Vienna – today resembles Vineta, the city submerged by the waters, along whose sea-bed streets legend speaks of figures walking in ancient costume. When a passer-by is glimpsed among the alleyways or emerging from a doorway, one thinks of those fabled paintings or tapestries from which, in some witching hour, the figures come forth and mingle with the living. At even drowsier Stein, not far from the plaque commemorating Köchel, to whom we owe the catalogue of Mozart's compositions, the pharmacist springs to life at the unwonted arrival of a stranger, shows him round the entire chemist's shop and acclaims the glories of Stein, not without some criticisms directed against Krems, an echo of ancient municipal rivalries.

There is a mortuary stillness here, in which everyone seems chained to an imitation of himself. One feels the charm of abandoning oneself to this lethargic oblivion, but also a desire for flight and an urgent longing for metamorphosis; the wish to be the pilot of the Danube in Jules Verne's book of that name, in which Herr Jaeger, alias Karl Dragoch, a Hungarian policeman, mistakes Ilia Brusch, alias Serge

Ladko, for the chief of a band of river pirates, Ivan Striga (who passes himself off as Ladko), and is in turn mistaken for him.

12. TWENTY PAST TEN

At Tulln time stings, it bites, and life is an arrow loosed towards nothingness, the irreversible process of dissipation spoken of by physicists. In the *Song of the Niebelungs* it is at Tulln that Attila awaits and welcomes his Burgundian bride Kriemhild, and the poem describes the cosmopolitan array of the subject princes and peoples who are with him there, Wallachians and Thuringians, Danes, Pechenegs and warriors from Kiev, whom a little later Kriemhild's vendetta was to thrust into battle and death.

It is cold and rainy, and the woods round the town are of a phosphorescent green, their mosses sodden with water and damp. In the church of St Stephen, a triple-naved eleventh–twelfth-century basilica, there is a tombstone telling us that "Here Lies Maria Sonia", while death points to the spot with an arrow. The clock has stopped at twenty past ten, and its hands are darts like those of death, depicted with a quiver.

The arrow is life, loosed off irretrievably and destined to fall when the force of gravity proves stronger than its impetus; but it is also the death that strikes at life when in full career, it is time which pierces with every passing hour, it is the clock that measures our brief permitted breathing space, and wounds us as it metes it out. Here lies Maria Sonia, our sister in death, and we would like to awaken her with a kiss that is far from brotherly, a kiss on the mouth that would make her body re-emerge from the waters of sleep, breasts and thighs issuing forth from shadow, shoulders to embrace in the night. What cosmic prefectorial decree has ordained that we cannot meet Maria Sonia? What administrative committee of the Universal Performance Authority has arranged for us to play in two different, out-of-phase film studios? If only the montage man or the projectionist were to muddle up our reels, as in *Hellzapoppin'* and send us each by mistake to act in the other film! Maybe heaven is *Hellzapoppin'* and we shall all act together, in a joyous hullabaloo like break-time at school.

The arrow has already caught up with Maria Sonia, but is about to catch up with us too. Perhaps it already has, just a little, for the precision with which death points to the exact spot where she lies is as sharp as a wound. At the main door there is a two-headed eagle holding a Turk's head in its talons, and the tombstone of a gypsy chieftain. The rough, barbarian stone of this church does justice even to the proud nomadic regality of an obscure, neglected people, absent from our consciences as it is generally absent from historical memory.

13. TWO-HEADED EAGLE AND WHITE-TAILED EAGLE

The marshy woods and meadows around Tulln were the country of Konrad Lorenz and of his forays to the Danube and along its tributaries and canals. What animal tracks told his two eyes and the nose of his dog, in the days when he lived at Altenberg, a village between Tulln and Klosterneuburg, is of more interest than what I can gather from ornaments on houses, old books and the odd museum. In my travels I too often meet the heraldic two-headed eagle, and too seldom the golden eagle or white-tailed eagle, both of which circle over the waters of the Danube. Robert Musil, Francis Joseph, the Crescent of Islam and the Café Central elbow out more long-standing and legitimate inhabitants of Mitteleuropa, the elmtrees and the beeches, the wild-boar and the herons.

So it is that in this personal atlas of the Pontic-Pannonian region, as zoologists call it, we register only the most recent arrivals, so rash, as Faulkner might have said, as to consider themselves the masters of the forest. I am aware of how discredited this makes my potamology. In his *Opus Danubiale* of 1726 Marshal Marsili discusses peoples and monuments, cities and crowns, but also metals, and discourses on fish, *de piscibus in aquis Danubii viventibus*; he describes and classifies the *aves vagantes circa aquas Danubii et Tibisci*, the birds which do not eat fish and those of the boggy marshes; he gives examples of their next designs and makes anatomical drawings of the eagle and the sturgeon.

But our Bolognese marshal lived in an age which sought for universal knowledge and based it on the primary, natural foundation both of man and of civilization. A soldier of the Empire, he fought in Transylvania and besieged Belgrade. In Italian he wrote the *Military*

Condition of the Ottoman Empire, the Growth and Decrease of the Same, but was also the author of the *Histoire physique de la mer*, of dissertations on mushrooms, on phosphorus and on the hydraulics of stagnant waters. The strategist and potamologist was also a historian, man-of-letters, mineralogist, limnologist and cartographer. He still possesses an overall, classical concept of life, which does not neglect the material structure of the individual, and grafts the latter's story onto nature.

Great poetry is often permeated by this awareness of the natural history of man: Lucretius and Leopardi, for example, or the Chinese lyric poets who place the individual, and his yearning for a distant friend, in the millenary history of the landscape in which he breathes, in a setting of mountains and of lakes. The great religions, also, take account of the stuff we are made of: "There is one mark of all genuine religions," said Chesterton: "materialism."

A kind of planetary reform has accustomed us to not recognizing animals and not being able to put names to the plants which grow right round the house; the much despised pseudo-sciences of nature have given place, as laid down in ministerial projects, to *humanae litterae*, so that all that is left of the *Systema Naturae* of Linnaeus is the binomial Latin nomenclature, not the living thing which it designates. It has become a catalogue purely of names such as those of the fabulous animals that exist only in the words for them, be it "unicorn" or "phoenix", and all we can do is have fun and games with this mock-Latin in the hope that irony will fill the gap left by reality. If I want to give a name to the birds and flowers I have seen on these banks of the Danube at various times of year, I must have recourse to manuals on Danubian flora and fauna, the works of Bauer and Glatz or of old Mojsisovics.

The split between nature and nurture causes the discomfort of the latter. In German culture there is at least a living awareness of this discomfort and a messianic desire to put things right. The lyric poetry of Eichendorff, the rustling of his woodlands, and the Utopian thinking of Bloch, do in fact remind us of our truncation, while Hölderlin says that we are orphans of the gods and that unless we are conscious of this exile there can be not even the smallest hope of redemption. But our culture does not come from Eichendorff's woods or Melville's ocean; it is more inclined to proceed from the monotonous fantasy of Sade, in which – as Flaubert said – there is neither a real tree nor a real animal. Social frivolity comprises our entire horizon.

This discomfort of civilization, as Freud has revealed in masterly fashion, arises from an incurable contradiction. Civilization and morals are based on a distinction that is necessary and extremely difficult to build on: that between men and animals. It is impossible to live without destroying animal life, even if only those minimal beings which are too small for us to see, and it is impossible to recognize universal and inviolable rights for animals, and in Kantian style consider every animal to be an end rather than a means. Brotherly solidarity can embrace humanity, but there it stops. This impossibility creates an inevitable split between the human world and the natural world, and it forces culture, which struggles against the sufferings inflicted on mankind, to construct its case upon the sufferings of animals, attempting to mitigate it but resigned to not being able to eliminate it. The irredeemable woe of animals, that obscure people who follow our existence like a shadow, throws on us the whole weight of original sin. The work of Elias Canetti, especially *Crowds and Power*, is a discovery of the shadows which accumulate in us with the death of the living beings off whom we feed.

The naturalist who lives with his grey geese in the swamps of the Danube believes that this distinction is based on a case of arbitrary anthropomorphism. Ethology has taught him that the animals do not merely have automatic instinctual mechanisms, as it is comfortable to believe, and he does not incline, as Buffon did, to discern an "infinite distance" between them and man, but rather to follow Linnaeus in including the latter among the mammals. The naturalist tends to view cosmopolitan ideals as a kind of "chauvinism of humanity", a nationalism that has spread from the tribe to the nation and thence to humanity at large, but always excluding non-members of the group from having rights and enjoying respect.

A democrat is a humanist, while a naturalist – even if immune from the leanings towards Nazism traceable in Lorenz's past – is unlikely to believe in the "religion of humanity", because he sees the latter as merely one – even though the most evolved – of the forms of life, and is probably of the opinion (like one of Musil's characters) that if God became man he might or ought to become also a cat or a flower. Observing the ways of rats, or of otters, the naturalist thinks that the struggle for existence is inevitable, and on the other hand he does not believe that man is the protagonist or the purpose of the cosmos, and that they can on such grounds escape from the destiny of fighting each other. He therefore tries to spare every being, human or animal, as much suffering as possible, but is prepared to justify the law which inevitably sets one pack against the other – and, according to the historical situation, such a "pack" can be the city, the party, the class, the tribe, the nation, the race, the West or worldwide revolution. At the moment of battle general principles count for nothing; what rules is the instinctive sense of belonging to the group, in the name of which it is lawful and necessary to strike, whether other men or other animals, since in both cases it is a tragedy, but in both cases a necessary tragedy.

The naturalist, convinced that all types of chauvinism are relative, refuses to consider the human species to be sacred and absolute. In this way he justifies and exalts all kinds of chauvinism, the elementary law of the bond of the group which, in the heat of the struggle, clouds all judgments and values. Thus in the end one can accept any sort of violence committed under stress for the solidarity of the group, and the extermination put into effect by the Third Reich ends up by appearing not all that dissimilar or qualitatively different from the immense slaughter of black rats carried out by the brown rats when they invaded Europe in the eighteenth century.

Not even the colours of these waters and these trees of the "Donauauen", or the calls of these birds, can induce us to disavow the chauvinism of humanity, without which we would surely do nothing to alleviate the suffering of animals, but would fall into obtuse barbarousness and add further agonies to those which are inevitable. But even were the trumpet in *Fidelio* to sound, liberated humanity on the top floor of the skyscraper in which it lived would have to be mindful of all the humiliated, sorrowing storeys beneath, which (as Horkheimer wrote) support that top storey. The lowest cellar – the foundation of the entire building where on the topmost storey we may hear a Mozart concerto or view a picture by Rembrandt – is the dwelling of animal suffering, where flows the blood of the slaughterhouses.

14. KIERLING, HAUPTSTRASSE 187

In one of these rooms, on June 3rd 1924, Kafka died. This little two-storeyed house, today divided into modest lodgings, was Dr Hoffmann's sanatorium in this small town in the neighbourhood of Klosterneuburg. Here Kafka hoped to get well, and here he spent his last weeks. The floor in the entrance bears the Latin word "Salve".

Kafka's room looked onto the garden and was probably on the second floor; the present owner is Herr Bacher. At the main door a number of notices announce that the chimney-sweep comes every third Monday in the month, and that it is forbidden to chop wood indoors and to carry heavy crates up the stairs without written permission.

I ring the bell of the second floor flat, and a kindly, elderly Frau Dunay lets me in and shows me onto the balcony. The balustrade is made of wood, there is washing hung up to dry, a stuffed teddy-bear lying about. On the balcony below, where Frau Hascher is busying herself, a lot of stags' antlers and hunting trophies do not fit in very well with those last hours in which Kafka, in terrible pain, was correcting the proofs of *The Hunger Artist*, the volume which contained the short story of that name, the parable of a perfection which sterilizes life.

From here Kafka, stretched in his deck-chair, looked out on the garden beneath, where there now stands a wooden shed crammed with wheelbarrows, sickles and other tools. He saw the greenness which eluded him, or rather the flowering, the springtime, the sap, everything that was sucked out of his body by paper and ink, desiccating him into a feeling of pure, impotent barrenness. Faced with that utterly feminine verdure, Kafka even in his greatness may have felt himself to be an almost grotesque exacerbation of male insecurity, of his stubborn efforts at self-defence, of his ceaseless need for corroboration. Faced with that epic green, Kafka at last had the company of a woman, Dora Dyment; a woman to whom he had no fear of giving himself, whom he wanted to marry, whom he wanted to live with. It is never too late, not even on the brink of death, to attain to the truth of these words: "What would I be without her?" So said Kafka, referring to Dora. This strength to bring himself to accept help raises him above his characters, in whom he had portrayed his own tormented inability to recognize himself as inadequate and to live with his own shortcomings.

It may be that sickness, by depriving him of the dogged will to write which had alienated him from life, helped him to find this strength, with a humility which writing would not have permitted him. Maybe salvation is the fruit of weakness, of the physical impossibility of being self-sufficient and of writing – but it is still salvation. In his diaries Kafka records the fact that his Hebrew name was Amshel – a name which expressed the human identity which was denied him, the warmth of life, and love, and the family. He had put aside all this so as to exist "solely as Franz Kafka", to be a writer. What happened to him in the last extremity of his life, when his love for Dora reconciled him to

Judaism and the adventure of a shared life, is no part of the story of Kafka the writer, but as Giuliano Baioni says, "concerns only the man whose Hebrew name is Amshel."

Amshel can take the step which Kafka is incapable of, can accept his own weaknesses, give himself to love, admit that without Dora he would be nothing. If a man without a woman, as it says in a passage in the *Talmud* dear to the heart of Kafka, is not a man, then it is Amshel who became a man, even though on the point of death, but it is Franz who narrates this odyssey and teaches us how to become Amshel, how to become a man.

In another room Alberto Cavallari is bending over to read the temperature chart: on April 12th Kafka had 38.5°. Alberto's Shakespearean face grows intense as he scans the register and reads the names of people admitted to the Wienerwald sanatorium on the same day as Kafka: Kraus Olga, Kovaks Bianca, Kisfaludi Etelka. On those predatory yet magnanimous features I read a great but disenchanted friendship for the world, a *pietas* which dwells upon those unknown, lost names in the desire to pay homage to their destiny, to preserve their memory, and to nose out their story with the instinct of a veteran journalist. Our eyes meet for an instant over that register. This instant also, like the three unknown names, is preserved in the eternity of these rooms. Here truly, as in the old medieval morality plays, died Everyman.

FOUR

Café Central

I. THE POET'S DUMMY

Vienna. At one of the first tables on the left as you enter the Café Central sits a dummy of Peter Altenberg, with his deep-set, melancholy eyes and his famous walrus moustache. Among the crowded tables Altenberg's dummy sits quietly reading the newspaper. Seated close by, I sometimes lose sight of the fact that this motionless moustachioed gentleman, with his old-fashioned clothes and vaguely familiar air, is a dummy. As often happens in the café, I steal a glance at my neighbour's newspaper. It could well be today's, the one the rest of us are reading; maybe a waiter slips it between his fingers every morning.

At these café tables in Vienna, in the early years of the century, Peter Altenberg – the homeless poet in love with anonymous hotel rooms and picture postcards – wrote his lightning, impalpable parables, his tiny sketches of minute particulars (a shadow on a face, the lightness of a footstep, the brutality or the desperation of a gesture), in which life reveals its graces, or else its nothingness, while History betrays its still imperceptible cracks, omens of a forthcoming sunset. My artificial neighbour concealed himself in the half-light of that sunset, hid in anonymity and silence, and moreover – reduced to hunger as he was in the slump after the First World War – turned down the offer of a job, on the grounds that he could concern himself with nothing but bringing his own life to a close. At these same tables sat also a certain Bronstein, alias Trotsky; sat to such an extent that one Austrian minister, informed by the secret services of preparations for a revolution in Russia, is said to have replied, "And who on earth is going to make a revolution in Russia? I suppose you're going to tell me it's that Bronstein who sits all day at the Café Central!"

That dummy does not remind us of the real-life Altenberg, for he himself, as he wrote his little fables on those little tables as a shipwrecked sailor scrawls on a floating plank, knew how the true and false in life were muddled together, and would not have regarded himself as being more genuine than a waxwork. One's own life was a theatre in which there were also spectators, and Altenberg himself cautioned us not to take it any more seriously – nor any less – than a play of Shakespeare's, to feel ourselves both inside and out of it at the same time, to sally forth for a walk when we feel like it, at night for a breath of fresh air, and to mingle the real with the unreal.

At the Café Central one is indoors and out at the same time, or at any rate that is the illusion one gets. The glass dome far above, covering a kind of winter-garden, lets in so much light as to make the panes invisible; yet no rain ever enters. The mainstream of Viennese culture had unmasked the increasing abstraction and unreality of life, ever more absorbed by the mechanisms of collective information and transformed into a stage performance of itself. Altenberg, Musil and their great contemporaries realized, in the very depths of their being, how hard it was to distinguish existence, even their own, from the image copied and reproduced in countless imitations: the false rumour of a financial crash as distinguished from the very real crisis caused by such a rumour, which sends all the customers racing to retrieve their savings, or the Mayerling tragedy as distinct from the cliché that makes it a drama. Those who lodged a complaint against the whole idea of making a show of life, though without kidding themselves that they were immune from it, are themselves now on show. That convincing dummy of Altenberg represents this fiction to perfection, and Vienna is the proper setting for this depiction of the depiction of real life.

But the literary strays and tramps who scribbled away at these tables – ironical, disappointed men – were putting up a last-ditch stand for individuality, for the last slivers of bewitchment – something that is itself and only itself, not to be reduced to the assembly line. The hidden, inaccessible truth, for them, was not a non-existent thing, and above all they did not gloat over the death of it, like the wordy theoreticians of insignificance. In Vienna contemporary reality identical to the performance of itself, like that so brilliantly portrayed by Altman in his film *Nashville*, is superimposed on the baroque sense of the world as theatre, in which everyone, even without knowing it, acts out roles and parts of universal significance. Our discreet wooden neighbour, however, suggests that we should not take what is happening too seriously, that things go as they do partly and chiefly by chance, and that they could perfectly well go quite differently.

2. WITTGENSTEIN'S HOUSE

This is to be found in the third district, at 19 Kundmanngasse, as the guide-books conscientiously tell us. It is the famous house built in 1926 by Paul Engelmann for Wittgenstein, who had a share in the design. At first it seems that this house, commissioned by Wittgenstein for his sister, does not exist at all, because the street numbers skip from 13 to 21. The roads are all up, in the throes of "works" which seem to have been abandoned. With a little trouble we discover that the house is on the other side, and that the entrance is in Parkgasse. With its series of cubes jammed one into another and its dirty, yellow-ochre colour, the building looks like an empty box. It is now the seat of the Bulgarian embassy, which occupied and restored it in the 1970s, and of its cultural section. It is six in the evening, the door is open, a few windows are lighted, but no one is to be seen; there is a table on a veranda with four upturned chairs. Prominent in the garden are two large bronze statues of Cyril and Methodius, the two Slav saints, plainly not put there by Wittgenstein.

The geometric rationality of those architectural forms, commissioned by the philosopher who so implacably investigated the possibilities and the limits of thought, at this point appear to reveal a pathetic uselessness. One wonders what Wittgenstein expected from that building: whether he wanted to build a house or prove the impossibility of a real house, or what once was called hearth and home. Who knows what limits its square forms were ideally intended to trace in his mind, what inexpressible spaces and images they were supposed ascetically to leave out.

3. ST STEPHEN

In the square, in front of the cathedral, there is an irregular pentagon marked out on the ground. It is nothing special; it merely marks the spot below which two chapels are located. But it is significant that a guide should mistakenly observe that the pentagon is the spot reserved for a monument which, after many projects of various kinds, was never built. The information is wrong but it reveals an interest in those emptinesses, those absences, those things which are not and to which Austria nonetheless gives expression, like Robert Musil's Parallel Action, consisting of the events which do not happen and initiatives which are not taken. Austrian culture, which has aspired to perfect totality, to the harmonious and complete unity of life, has shed light on those pieces which are always lacking if we are to complete the circle, the empty spaces between things, between facts and feelings, and the cleavages which there are in every individual and society.

Sometimes that empty space can be used to replace something which history had already put away in the cupboard. As Christian Reder mentions in an "alternative guide-book" to Vienna, the monument of the Republic, erected after the First World War, was put back on the Ring after 1945. The Fascists, who had had it removed in 1934, had put it in a warehouse. Never throw anything away, one never knows. In almost every family the menfolk, being more sentimental, cynical and insecure, would like to follow this Austrian caution and constantly put off the moment for getting rid of things. They get a bit flustered when the women of the household start spring-cleaning, throwing away old things, old papers, and bits of presumably unusable junk.

4. THE LITTLE BARONESS WHO DID NOT LIKE WAGNER

The young baroness Maria Vetsera did not like Wagner's music, and in fact stated that she couldn't stomach it. When on December 11th 1888 the Vienna Opera opened a cycle of Wagner's *Ring* with a performance of *Rheingold*, her aversion gave her an excuse not to go to the theatre with her mother and sister but instead, while they were listening to the dwarf Alberich cursing love in his greed for gold, to have a secret meeting with Rudolph of Hapsburg, the heir apparent to the Empire whom she had met a few weeks before. She left the house and at this very corner of the Marokkanergasse, got into the carriage waiting for her on the Archduke's orders, was driven to the imperial *Burg*, where a servant arranged for her to pass the guards and led her to the apartments of the heir to the throne. By nine o'clock she was back home, ready to welcome her mother and sister on their return from the theatre.

The tragedy of Mayerling, the mysterious death of Rudolph of Hapsburg and of Maria Vetsera in the hunting lodge on January 30th 1889, is a sad little tale which for a century has struck the popular imagination, arousing genuine compassion and adding fuel to the heroic-sentimental cult of suicide pacts, suggesting highly coloured novels and hypotheses of dark intrigues guided by Reasons of State. That tragedy is the poor, touching story of one of those misunder-standings which, on account of some banal but ruinous hitch, send life off the rails and hurl it into the melodrama of destruction.

At the time of her death Maria Vetsera was not yet eighteen. The previous summer, before she had met the Archduke in person, she had fallen in love with him from afar, with all the elation of a defenceless spirit in need of some absolute to bow down and sacrifice itself to without reserve; adoring in order to persuade itself that it is living poetically, giving meaning to its still unformed character, which would otherwise wear away in a kind of empty, indefinable melancholy. The Archduke was just over thirty, and was known for his liberal ideas, his arrogantly flaunted loose living, and an imperious impulsiveness which urged him to fits of generosity, tiresome bragging and suspicious irascibility of which the victim was usually his wife, the Archduchess Stephanie.

According to what her mother, Baroness Helene, wrote in her biographical essay *Mayerling*, Maria Vetsera used to go to see the Archduke at the races and at the Prater. She confided in her maid that Rudolph had noticed her, and a short while later that he had greeted her with particular effusion and sworn that he would never love another. In that brief bitter-sweet season between adolescence and young adulthood she was living through the *grands manoeuvres* of the heart and senses, making those first apprentice steps in feeling in which one gropes one's way through the play and enchantment of the first encounters on the road to love.

Those glances exchanged in the avenues of the Prater, and a little later those furtive meetings and subterfuges, ought to have been, for Maria as well, the first, uncertain chords, the orchestral rehearsal of feelings preparing, amidst a still confused hum of instruments, for the grand, united melody of love. A few weeks later, as it turned out, everything had ended in that death at Mayerling, in the outrage which that pistol shot in the temple and *rigor mortis* had inflicted on that tender body, and in the details of the autopsy recorded in documents with a precision that serves only to deepen the so-called mystery of

Mayerling. Looking at portraits of the little baroness, with her delicate but rather inexpressive face, which reveals only the impersonal, superficial grace of her eighteen years, we are led to think of those school tragedies of young lives broken by the first bad mark or mild reproach, crushed by a similar interweaving of absoluteness and chance, brought low by an obstacle that the rest of us, the survivors, simply take in our stride, and which for them was insurmountable.

In her account Helene Vetsera records the most painful details of this story and its ending – or at least her version of its ending, which is destined to remain one of many, contradicted by others even more questionable, such as the reveries of the Empress Zita. The pamphlet, printed in 1891 and confiscated by the Austrian police, is a dry, touching little book, in which the rather slipshod prose is eloquent of motherly love, certainly, but also of another feeling almost as strong: respectability. Baroness Vetsera is eager to free her daughter from the charge of having been actively responsible for that tragedy, and above all she wishes to confute the gossip which accused her of having been in the know about that illicit relationship and of having encouraged it.

The book is a deeply-felt and angry account of those detective-story details which punctuate the story of a forbidden passion, and which the least nuance of tone or style can change from a grand adventure or from a mischievous game into something humiliatingly shabby: the cigarette-case given by the lover and discovered by chance, the elaborate inventions needed to explain its presence, the letters delivered in secret, the little lies, the complicity of the complaisant Countess Larisch. The book grows more tense when it tells of the squalor of the death and its concealment, intended to avoid scandal: Maria's body left for thirty-eight hours without a hand to compose it with proper decency, the body loaded into the carriage in such a way as to hide the fact that it was a corpse, the negotiations between the authorities and the family regarding the disposal of that embarrassing deceased person, the rough coffin, the hurried burial, the grave that for a number of months was unmarked and anonymous, until the remains were transferred elsewhere.

The concern was respectability, which presides over this baroque finale and this allegory of disintegration, is also a passion, and one having all the absoluteness and irrationality of a one-sided passion, in the sense that it does not embrace the whole of a person and of his life but partitions off and over-inflates one single part. The story of Rudolph and Maria, as it is revealed in this book, is that of an abstract, impetuous passion which cannot be identified with love, just as we cannot mistake a psychological or imaginative frenzy for a poetic inspiration.

This *amour-passion* is late Romantic, and Romanticism (writes Broch) is in one respect the substitution of an absolute, which is felt to be lost, by a partial surrogate, whatever it may be, which is supposed to take the place of all values. When this surrogate is sought in love, this becomes a truly-suffered but exaggerated rhetoric, an over-blown sentimental pathos, however genuine the suffering. It is a fantasy-yearning, in which one participant does not love the other, but his or her own yearning. The romantic allurement of love-death hints also at the sterility of this ardour which neither creates nor procreates, either in the flesh or in the spirit.

This passion too is capable of greatness, and so is the poetry which depicts it. Flaubert, in fact, showed once and for all that passion can be true and false at the same time: the unsatisfied cravings and evasions of Emma Bovary are the very opposite of love, but the intensity with which Emma lives out both her unpoetic destiny and the sham poetry with which she herself attempts to disguise it is genuine evidence of the lack of love.

The worldly, libertine eighteenth century had, at least in appearance, broken love down by chemical analysis of the passions and of the behaviour of lovers. It seemed, in the words of a famous phrase, to have put the brain in the place of the heart. But in fact, as in *Les liaisons dangereuses*, it was that dry mathematics which made it possible to sound the depths and the totality of love, its conflicts but also its tenderness, the heart's perdition which appears as all the more over-whelming the more it is filtered through the meshes of proof. It is the *esprit de géométrie* that makes *esprit de finesse* possible. That secularizing, disillusioned culture demystified a great number of over-inflated rap-tures; the sentimental culture which came later was afraid of that rigour and frequently returned to preaching virtue and candour, though sometimes it deceived itself into finding these values in an innocent, spontaneous effusion of the heartbeats of desire, thus mistaking the state of mind for the truth, subjective psychology for moral inquiry and emotional excitement for the poetry of life.

If the heroes of the libertine novels are Machiavellian intelligences, and swear eternal love while lying and knowing that they are lying, the hero of the romanticizing school lies even to himself, dragging the object of his desire into ruin in the name of his own pleasure and caring nothing about his partner and her needs, convinced as he is of obeying a divine voice. The Archduke Rudolph, with his good looks and the slightly turbid expression of the prevaricator – he confuses his own sensuality with a liberating mission – makes Maria the heroine of his drama, with all the impudence of someone who elects himself to be director of other people's lives.

Photographs of Mayerling show a neat, peaceful landscape, the sort of Austrian countryside perfect for family holidays, more suited to the fatherly image of Francis Joseph in shooting costume than to that tempestuous tragedy. The Emperor learnt the fatal news from Katherine Schratt, the lady in whose discreet, tranquil affection he found comfort from the continual agitation of the Empress Elizabeth. There is no saying, of course, that the hours the Emperor spent with Frau Schratt, who made him coffee, were less intense than the passions of the Archduke. It is difficult to know what goes on in someone else's head or heart. Not even scientists today are more ingenuous than Prof. von Hoffmann, a luminary of the Vienna medical faculty, who explained away the Mayerling tragedy to his students as "the premature synostosis of the cranial sutures" brought to light by the autopsy on His Imperial and Royal Highness the Archduke Rudolph.

5. THE STRUDLHOF STEPS

The fluency of its coiling forms and the undulating rhythm of its descent were the inspiration for a long novel by Doderer, the impulse behind which is abandonment to the flow of life which passes down those steps. These flights of stairs form one of the little "hearts" of Vienna, evoking the curves and the motherly embrace of its cupolas, the broad, welcoming spaces of the squares and along the Ring. As we go down those steps we feel ourselves borne upon the flood of a river which is life itself, where we feel at home.

Austria is often a place where one feels at home, in that state of harmony between familiarity and distance that Joseph Roth was so fond of. In the meantime the bookshops are stocking a volume by an old mistress of Doderer's, which lists the mean, shabby, selfish actions, and all those lies and accommodations that can easily make a liaison the most ghastly of all daily chores. That flow of life, so enticing at the head of the steps, can end up in the scum of the laundry in a washing machine. The Danube is not blue, as Karl Isidor Beck calls it in the lines which suggested to Strauss the fetching, mendacious title of his waltz. The Danube is blond, "a szöke Duna", as the Hungarians say, but even that "blond" is a Magyar gallantry, or a French one, since in 1904 Gaston Lavergnolle called it *Le Beau Danube blond*. More down to earth, Jules Verne thought of entitling a novel *Le Beau Danube jaune*. Muddy yellow is the water that grows murky at the bottom of these steps.

Perhaps there is truth only in complete and abiding love, or else in openly animal sensuality, that runs its course in its immediate satisfaction, without kidding itself or others that there is anything else, while the vast range of intermediate gradations in amorous relationships, a typical human invention, is very often just a series of falsehoods and acts of violence tarted up with sentimental kitsch. I'm not sure I'm interested in checking on the veracity of Doderer's revengeful mistress; certainly Vienna, as much as and maybe more than other cities, is a place of such snippets of gossip, of rancorous intrusiveness and indiscretion, because it is a great provincial city. It is the Vienna which Karl Kraus hated, and which – with the vulgarity of whispers on the landing – nourished his satirical ferocity. The great poets of the charms of Vienna – ever since those geniuses of popular comedy during the last century, such as Raimund or Nestroy – have grasped that charm and presented it against a back-drop of the aggressiveness, the brutality masked as bonhomie, that have made Vienna also one of the sewers of history, a "meteorological station of the end of the world", as Kraus put it.

6. DOROTHEUM

This is the public pawnshop, evoked in grotesque forms and under another name in Elias Canetti's *Auto-da-Fé*. Almost opposite is the Café Hawelka, legendarily smoke-filled. Outside the door of the Dorotheum a man is standing beside a car with a parcel – probably a picture – under his arm. He stands stock-still, his face rigid and waxy, far more of a sham than the sham Altenberg in the Café Central.

7. THE LIES OF THE POETS

In a poem written in about the middle of the sixteenth century, Wolfgang Schmeltzl compares Vienna to Babel, because he says he hears people round him speaking Hebrew, Greek, Latin, German, French, Turkish, Spanish, Bohemian, Slovenian, Italian, Hungarian, Dutch, Syrian, Croatian, Serbian, Polish and Chaldean. Certainly the Greek saying warns us that the poets tell us many lies and exaggerate, but all the same . . .

8. THE TURKS BEFORE VIENNA

In Karlsplatz, not far from the Vienna Opera, the imitation entrance to a gigantic tent covers the façade of the *Künstlerhaus*, which at present houses the chief of the many exhibitions devoted to "The Turks Before Vienna", it being the third centenary of the siege and battle of 1683, one of the great frontal encounters between East and West. Visitors momentarily get the impression of entering the vast pavilion of an Ottoman general, the tent which Kara Mustapha, commander-in-chief of the Turkish army, erected in splendour and magnificence in the vicinity of the present church of St Ulrich, in what today is the seventh *arrondissement* of the city.

The immense dimensions of the imaginary tent do in any case call to mind the figure of the Grand Vizier who embodied the Ottoman cult of all that is grandiose and exorbitant. In some of the twenty-five thousand tents of the Turkish army which had since the beginning of July 1683 been surrounding Vienna, Kara Mustapha had also lodged his one thousand five hundred concubines guarded by seven hundred black eunuchs, amid gushing fountains, baths, luxurious quarters set up in haste but with opulence.

The Vizier's head is now preserved at Vienna in the History Museum, which – next-door to the *Künstlerhaus* – also houses one of the exhibitions. Defeated on September 12th 1683 by the imperial troops commanded by Charles of Lorraine, together with the Polish army led by their king, Jan Sobieski, Kara Mustapha was pursued from the field and defeated again at Gran. At Belgrade he was met by the emissary of the sultan, who brought him the silken cord with which the lords of the Crescent who had fallen into disgrace with their sovereign, the "shadow of God on earth", were strangled. Having laid out his prayer-mat, the Grand Vizier offered his neck to the executioners and accepted his fate in the name of Allah. When, decades later, the imperial armies conquered Belgrade, someone dug up his body and brought the head in triumph to Vienna.

When the visitor enters the imitation pavilion, he instantly becomes himself one of the figures in the exhibition, and is uncertain whether he is just daydreaming as he imagines himself a prey – one of the countless prisoners led as slaves to the invader's tent – or else a predator, one of Sobieski's knights who for a whole day after the victory sacked the camp and despoiled even the tent of Kara Mustapha.

The aim of the exhibition is not to set the victors against the vanquished, still less the civilized peoples against the barbarians, but rather to give the feeling of the futility both of victory and of defeat, which follow on each other's heels for every nation, like sickness and health or youth and old age in the case of individuals.

As he walks round these rooms the Western visitor may consider that the victory of September 12th, which saved Vienna and Europe, was a thoroughly good thing; but he does not feel himself to be son and heir only of the swords of Charles of Lorraine and Jan Sobieski, or of the cross brandished by the great preachers who incited people to defend the faith, such as Abraham at Sancta Clara, according to whom the liturgical canon must give place to the cannon of the artillery, or Marco d'Aviano, the Capuchin from Friuli. Walking among those victory trophies, which are also the relics of a shipwreck, the visitor feels himself rather to be the son and heir of a history unified in its fragments, though these are scattered like objects in a pillaged encampment; a history composed of crescents as well as crosses, of Capuchin cords and of turbans.

The exhibition deliberately sets out to differ from previous celebrations of the events of 1683. Fifty years ago Dollfuss, the Christian-Social chancellor, applauded the liberation of Vienna in terms of his corporative, authoritarian Catholicism, with which he opposed both Nazism and Bolshevism. Years later, in a National-Socialist commemorative bronze, the banner of the vanquished Turks bore not the Crescent but the Star of David. The Turks were simply identified with the enemy, which is to say the Jews, by means of a falsification which today, in the xenophobic attitudes towards the seasonal foreign workers, runs the risk of becoming tragically true. We do not want to be the Jews of tomorrow, says a picture by Akbar Behkalam in the Museum of the Twentieth Century, where there is an exhibition by Turkish artists devoted to present-day conditions in their country and among the emigrants.

The shadow of a new, if different, problem looms over relations between Turks and Europeans, especially Germans, and only the clearest awareness of the problem can prevent it taking on ruinous proportions. Repulsed three hundred years ago, the Turks are now returning to Europe not with weapons but as a work-force, with all the tenacity of the *Gastarbeiter* (immigrant workers) who undergo poverty and humiliation but gradually put down roots in a land which they conquer by means of their humble toil. In many cities in Germany the schools are empty of German children and the classrooms are full of Turkish children; the West, which entrusts its decline to the fall in the birth-rate, is reacting with anxious intolerance to the results of a social mechanism of its own making. It may be that the moment is approaching when historical social and cultural differences will reveal, and violently, the difficulties of mutual compatibility. Our future will depend in part on our ability to prevent the priming of this time-bomb of hatred, and the possibility that new Battles of Vienna will transform brothers into foreigners and enemies.

History shows that it is not only senseless and cruel, but also difficult to state who is a foreigner. Alessio Bombaci reminds us that in the eighteenth century the Turks themselves felt the word "Turk" to be an insult, and their history is one of a series of age-old struggles between diverse peoples, originating on the steppes of Central Asia, peoples who began to become aware of their own common identity only when the Ottoman Empire was almost on its deathbed. The first unitary name given to Turkey by the various and often mutually hostile peoples was the name of Rome, *mamālik-i-Rūm*, which indicated the Seljuk kingdom.

But all histories and all identities are composed of these differences, these pluralities, these exchanges and borrowings of diverse ethnic and cultural elements, which make each nation and individual the child of a regiment. The Hapsburg eagle, which halted the advance of the Great Turk, spread its wings over almost as varied a multiplicity of races and cultures, and during the First World War, when the Hapsburg and Ottoman Empires were allied, posters and the press in Austria sung the praises of this brotherhood-in-arms with their age-old enemies.

The meeting between Europe and the Ottoman Empire is the great example of two worlds which, while hacking each other to pieces, end by a gradual understanding, to their mutual enrichment. It is no coincidence that the greatest Western writer to recount the story of that meeting between two worlds, Ivo Andrić, is fascinated by the image of the bridge; it occurs time and time again in his novels and stories, symbolizing a hard-won means of communication thrown across the barriers of raging torrents and deep ravines, of races and religions. It is a place where weapons clash, but where in the end, and little by little, enemies become united in a world that is as variegated yet unified as an epic fresco, as in the Balkan gorges Turkish soldiers and haiduks – the guerrilla-brigands who resisted them – came to resemble each other.

One of the first items in the exhibition is a splendid map of the first (1529) siege of Vienna, undertaken by Suleiman the Magnificent, the great sultan who died at the siege of Szigetvár and whose death was kept secret for several days so as not to discourage his army. Messengers were led into the presence of his embalmed body seated motionless on his throne, listening to them without replying, the majesty of death disguised as regal impassiveness. This map of Vienna is surrounded by areas of blue, as if it were the whole world girdled, as for the ancients, by Ocean. The Turks thought of Vienna as the "city of the golden apple", the almost mythical aspect of the Empire which they had to conquer at all costs; the nomads of the steppes of Asia, the "wild asses" who despised every corrupting urban settlement, seemed to wish to possess, in Vienna, the City par excellence, their very opposite. The sultans who pressed on Vienna perhaps envisaged it as the capital of that universal "Roman-Muslim" Empire which, according to Jorga, the great Rumanian historian, they wished to found, even if Jalal ud-Din Rumi, the Persian mystical poet, said that it was reserved for the Greeks to build and for the Turks to destroy.

A mixture of film and novel, the exhibition puts us right inside the besieged city, with its acts of heroism, cruelty and hysteria, and also on to the battlefield, brought to life for us in a large hall with the help of audio-visual effects. Kara Mustapha's strategic error in leaving the hills without garrisons was fatal to the Ottoman army, which by five in the afternoon was in full flight, thanks largely to a lightning feint by Charles of Lorraine. The Christian army was composed of some 65–80,000 men, the Muslim forces numbering about 170,000. The deaths were respectively 2,000 (with the addition of 4,000 among the besieged) and 10,000 plus vast numbers of wounded and prisoners, as well as casualties from various diseases and men cut down during the retreat and subsequent pursuit, which gave rise to episodes of pitiless ferocity and of magnanimous chivalry. Sobieski, who had served Mass on the Kahlenberg, according to an Italian chronicler, declared to Charles of Lorraine that as far as his person was concerned the King had stayed in Poland and only the Polish soldier had taken the field. All the same, on September 15th the meeting between Sobieski and the Emperor Leopold, who had by then returned to Vienna, was the occasion of diplomatic embarrassments and wounded feelings.

Such episodes taking place behind the scenes of the big show are also part of history – even the untrue legend that it was the siege that led to the founding of the first café in Vienna by an enterprising Galician-Armenian trickster, Koltschitzky. Like all exhibitions, these in Vienna devoted to the Turks give one a slight feeling of unreality, the unreality of our lives and histories, the events we are living through. Often these seem to unwind like a movie, to appear to have happened already, as if like a movie they already had an ending, which we do not know, though it is there on the reel.

As if it were itself an exhibition, the organizers also present the palace and park of the Belvedere, the famous residence of Prince Eugène of Savoy, the victor over the Turks who had his first youthful trial by combat at Vienna in 1683. In that palace, life becomes a symbol of itself. The symmetry of that park – which with its statues, fountains and ornaments rises in allegorical terms from the bounties of the four seasons to the apotheosis of the glory of victory over the Crescent – is the triumph of a civilization which preferred to live within limits over the impetuosity of another which, as has been said, thought in terms of unconfined spaces.

Descendants, tourists and visitors, we now walk among those carefully ordered symmetries, those boundaries and restraints which we love, like extras in some spectacle in the grand manner, some film by Abel Gance. In the grey, dull pictures and photographs shown by present-day Turkish artists in the Museum of the Twentieth Century, other faces and gestures emerge, the obscure, humiliated dignity of the new immigrants, of those who play no part – or not yet, or no longer – in any grand performance. "Our forefathers rode on horseback here," says a caption to one of the photographs, "and we sweep these streets." But the inscription is not looking for consolation, for with absolute honesty it adds "the fault is ours, not of the Austrians."

9. BLOODSTAINS

Blood does not always pale and fade so soon, says a beautiful passage of Lu-Hsün, the great Chinese writer. In the Army Historical Museum the uniform of Francis Ferdinand, the Archduke assassinated at Sarajevo, shows bloodstains on the blue tunic, and ragged holes on the sleeve and one side of the chest – the left. Beside the uniform the hat with its huge green feathers is, on the other hand, unharmed and impressive. The wound inflicted that June 28th 1914 is still open, for the whole of Europe. It may be that it will have to be healed disastrously by a third and final catastrophe, because two world wars have not found a stable substitute for the equilibrium which was shaken at Sarajevo. Francis Ferdinand's menu, that June 28th, comprised Consommé en tasse, Oeufs à la gelée, Fruits au beurre, Boeuf bouillé aux légumes, Poulets à la Villeroy, Riz Compote, Bombe à la Reine, Fromage, Fruits et Dessert.

Those bloodstains remind us that nothing vanishes, that things exist, that no significant moment of our lives is ever shelved. My friends often tease me because in my mind the girls we were at school with are still beautiful and in their first youth, and time has no power over them or over my way of seeing them. I admit that injustice discriminates even between bloodstains: those of the Archduke are preserved under glass, while those of the eighty-five demonstrators killed by the police near the Palace of Justice on July 15th 1927 have been washed away by the rain and rubbed out by passing feet. But even those bloodstains exist, are with us for ever.

10. AMONG THE OTHER VIENNESE

Vienna is also a city of cemeteries, as majestic and friendly as the portraits of Francis Joseph. The *Zentralfriedhof*, the Central Cemetery, is a major march-past in the *grandes manoeuvres* which attempt to postpone the triumph of time. The graves of the great Viennese – the sector devoted to illustrious personages, which starts to the left of the main entrance, Gate No. 2 – comprise the front rank of a Guard which makes a stand against transience but, unlike Napoleon's Guards at

Waterloo, forming square without the least hesitation, this regiment fights according to elastic tactics, seems to wish to defilade itself; it suggests feints, it outflanks death, it jests, it beats about the bush, with a view to frustrating the methodical swish of the scythe. At five in the morning this host of stones, busts and monuments is still almost invisible, opaque and colourless, as it lies hidden in the cloudy night-time drizzle, though here and there a votive lamp punctuates the murk. Herr Baumgartner keeps his shotgun close beside him – a gun he has owned for thirty years, he told me a moment ago – and rests a hand on it with the quiet, affectionate familiarity of long cohabitation, as a musician finds pleasure in touching his violin, which he loves not only for its performance but for its shape, its curves, the texture and colour of its wood.

It is the first time I have ever been in a cemetery next to someone who is handling not flowers, shovels or prayer-books, but guns and cartridges. But today, for an hour or two, before daylight comes, the Central Cemetery in Vienna is a forest, a jungle, Leatherstocking's woods, Turgenev's steppes, the dominion of Diana or St Hubert, a place where one does not bless or bury, but lies in wait, fires, kills ancient relatives for whom no rite prescribes a *Requiem* or a *Kaddish*. This morning, in the Central Cemetery, the order of the day is shooting, even if Herr Baumgartner doesn't want to hear this word, and talks about a necessary, authorized reduction of the number of head: they are harmful, it seems, because of their excessive profusion and for other reasons. He is one of three marksmen employed by the Viennese municipal authorities to maintain a correct balance among the living who unlawfully inhabit this metropolis of the dead (this "city of the *other* Viennese", as the Austrians put it), and prevent them from being too lively by transforming them on the instant into corpses if they reveal themselves too healthy and prosperous in this world. Death is harmless, respectful and discreet; it causes no trouble and doesn't hurt anyone. It is life that is so troublesome, so noisy, so aggressively destructive, and must therefore be kept in check, lest it should get above itself. Hares, for example, have a downright passion – destructive and guilty as are all passions – for the pansies laid on the tombs by pious relatives. They gnaw them, they uproot them, they rip them to shreds, they are not content with satisfying their hunger but they make a massacre of them, like martens in a hen-run. And indeed, the sepulchre in which the presidents of the Republic are laid to rest is littered with torn-up, tattered pansies.

Does this mild irreverence merit the licence to kill? Well anyway, this licence is very restricted and rigidly controlled. Herr Baumgartner's double-barrelled gun only threatens male pheasants, hares and wild rabbits, and even these according to well-established rules. Austria, as they say in my part of the world, both was and is an orderly country, and a gun-licence is subject to strict control. Infractions are severely punished, and there are none of those Sunday hunters who infest Italy, drunken with childish delight in their power to kill, blasting away indiscriminately at wildlife and humans: hunters: more deserving by half of the attentions of Herr Baumgartner than are the hares with a taste for pansies.

The man himself, squatting down beside me in the grass, is beginning to emerge from the darkness in all his massive, paternal bulk; he is not a trigger-happy maniac, he shows no sign of that stupid pleasure in killing and putting a stop to whatever life is seen to move; he does not indulge in threadbare sophisms about the totemistic communion between killer and victim; and indeed he reveals no kind of banal excitation, but rather the good-natured calm of a gardener. He is a good shot and does what he has to do, for Austria is an orderly country, but maybe he is not all that displeased when, through no fault of his own, he goes home empty-handed.

I imagine that, to start with, he was none too keen on the idea of having me under his feet, for no one as a rule is allowed to be present. At the entrance to the cemetery he explained to the night-watchman that I was a professor, a title much honoured here, and that I was allowed in as an exceptional case through the good offices of the department of the burgomaster of Vienna. In this damp dawn, which is already beginning to pale the gloomy clouds, I am experiencing what is not a great hunting adventure, but what may be the zenith of my fame and glory, because it is unlikely that my books on the Mitteleuropa of the Hapsburgs, in virtue of which the municipality of Vienna have given me special permission to be squatting down at this hour of the morning in the grass in the Central Cemetery, will have any greater impact on reality than this, or any further force its limits and prohibitions. It might well be that, in this dawn, I have had my day, as King Lear puts it.

We move towards the edge of the cemetery, passing between the tombs, which are slowly becoming more distinct. The tomb of Castelli, the light-hearted, prolific author of popular comedies, bears an inscription by courtesy of the league for the protection of animals, while from the faint mist rises a tall, simple cross with a phrase that sums up the life of Peter Altenberg, all a toccata and fugue: "He loved and saw." A bare, basic cube is the funeral monument of Adolf Loos, while that of Schönberg, creator of a more disquieting geometry, is also a cube, but a distorted one.

Herr Baumgartner peers around him, lends an ear to every rustle, scrutinizes the foliage, amorphous in the half light. He may fire where he likes, even among the crosses and the still-fresh wreaths, but he is careful to make no mistakes, because that sector of the cemetery – roughly a third, the other parts falling to the competence of his two colleagues – is entirely his responsibility, and he has to answer for where his lead ends up, for any chance bosh-shot that shatters a votive lamp or grazes an angel thoughtfully watching over a tomb. In a couple of hours' time the relatives who find the photograph of their dear departed as riddled as a sombrero in a western movie, or the stone stained with the blood of a rabbit hit at the wrong moment, would know to whom to address their outraged protests. "It shouldn't happen, but it might," he repeats several times, but placidly.

We are on the edge of the last row of graves, set on a slight rise which commands a good view. The bank itself is made of loose earth, debris, and rotten grass and leaves swept up along the avenues and amassed at this point. The soil in this area is particularly well suited to the rapid putrefaction of corpses, as was well known in the last century to the authorities and to the proprietors of plots. During the projection stage for the building of the cemetery the latter used to haggle and stick out for higher prices in relation to the greater or lesser putrefactive vigour of the soil, to the point of exchanging abusive pamphlets such as the one addressed in 1869 by the municipal councillor Dr Mitlacher to Baron Lasky. The area where we are now is unkempt, a large grassy expanse stretching between the wood and a wall surrounding the central workshops of the Vienna tramway company. A few steps away is a tomb bearing the name of the Pabst family, and beneath it the inscription *auf Wiedersehen*. This meadow, extensive as it is, is a small slice of nature hemmed in by society, by the symmetry of the avenues and the funeral industry on one hand and the municipal transport company on the other; but even this minimal space is like the taiga or the savannah, which are also surrounded by civilization but measured by the ancient laws of the animal world, sniffing at scents, crawling, searching for food, coupling, setting and avoiding ambushes; the law, in fact, which rules even in a flower-bed in the garden or in a pot containing a single plant.

The colourless grass now swiftly turns to green, the first birdcall and the first flutterings are heard among the trees, the big crows migrating from Russia rise on the wing, while in the east there rises a pallid lemon-rind sun. Even in that suburban undergrowth the unmistakable smell of morning endows us with a physical sense of happiness, the pleasure of a body at ease in itself, a relish for hearing, touching, seeing things. The untouchable hen-birds which for some minutes have been sporting on the grass are now about to be joined by a cock-pheasant. Still some way off, he approaches cautiously while my neighbour takes aim. Accustomed as I am, on my own Mount Snežnik, to dismantling the traps laid by hunters, I have a vague sense of being a traitor, a man who has gone over to the other side. Is this the way in which each of us goes to meet his fate, with useless even if practised caution? Standing motionless, I ask myself what constellations of possible threats, atomic or microbiological, star-wars, recurrent viruses or overtakings on bends have my life in their sights, as my neighbour's gun now has this pheasant, selected by an infinite concatenation of coincidences.

During this absurd, guilt-stricken wait, I regret the fact that in 1874 the high cost (a million florins) of the operation led to the failure of Felbinger and Hudetz's scheme for funerals by pneumatic post. According to this the dead would be shot off directly to their allotted tombs through miles of tubing activated by compressed air. And I imagine that the air of the cemetery would have rung with the sharp reports made by corpses in continuous arrival, and that this pheasant would have taken wing.

But the interplay of coincidences which holds the universe in its grip, taking on a different guise, though remaining perfectly Austrian and bureaucratic, has decided to grant the pheasant a stay of execution. Just before the target gets within absolutely safe range, at the edge of the wood, near the Pabsts' *auf Wiedersehen*, a lorry comes huffing and puffing along, laden with dead leaves and other debris which the cemetery gardeners – birds almost as early as the gamekeepers – have swept up along the pathways and are about to dump near us. The pheasant takes fright and vanishes, while Herr Baumgartner allows himself a sonorous "Damn!", but greets the spoilsports cordially.

We make for the exit, for the usual visitors will soon be starting to arrive. All in all it has been a dawn in keeping with the Viennese spirit which mocks at death, flatters it but also ridicules it, courts it but at the same time, not being able to leave it in the lurch once and for all, as in the case of a lover who has grown to weary us, at least tries to spite it a little. At the gate we meet one of Herr Baumgartner's colleagues. The hare he has shot is an image of the deficit of the universe and of the original sin of life which feeds on death. In a few hours that hare will be a pleasing trophy, and later still a succulent dish, but right now it is still terror and flight, the suffering of a creature that neither asked to live nor deserved to die, the mystery of life, this strange thing that was in the hare until a short while ago and now is not, the real essence of which is unknown even to the scientists, if in order to define it they must needs have recourse to such tautologies as "the complex of phenomena which oppose death". I don't know exactly why, since – like all those with walk-on parts in the spectacle of the world – I have no central role and therefore no direct, precise responsibilities, but that hare certainly leaves one with a sense of shame.

11. A WORTHWHILE JOB

The present Chamber of Workers and Employees used to be Eichmann's office, and from here he directed the bureaucratic organization of the racial policies of the Third Reich. At his trial Eichmann remembered his period in Vienna as "the happiest and most successful of my life". That work evidently cost him few embarrassments in the city which Grillparzer, the Austrian national poet, defined in the nineteenth century as "the Capua of the spirits" and which has always been mistress of the art of self-mystification. In the (certainly formal) referendum which took place in 1938 after the *Anschluss*, only 1,953 Viennese – according to Christian Reder in the above-mentioned alternative guidebook – voted against annexation to the Third Reich, even if the suicides that year numbered 1,358, as compared with the annual average of 400.

12. GENTZGASSE, 7

One of those suicides, on March 16th 1938, threw himself out of one of these windows. He was Egon Friedell, conservative historian and critic, poet of the ephemeral and of the short comic tale, in which biting irony, reappraising all limitations, gives us a glimpse of infinity, of what eternally transcends our own smallness, making it all the dearer to us. That leap from the window was his last *Witz*, his joke at the expense of the Gestapo who were coming to arrest him. The front of the house is seedy, the stucco is peeling; a few wrought-iron balconies put up a pathetic pretence at being ornamental. Friedell was a Jew, and Nazism forced him to that window in the name of the purity of the Germanic race. The tenants of the building, we are told by the name-plates by the main door, are today called Pokorny, Pekarek, Kriczer and Urbanck. There is an old saying that every true Viennese is a Bohemian.

13. LUKÁCS IN VIENNA

I am at the Café Landtmann, on the Ring near the *Burgtheater*, with Wolfgang Kraus, an essayist and the founder of that Austrian Literary Association which for many cold years after the Second World War formed a real – and rare – bridge between the Western world and the Eastern European countries. He tells me about a lecture which Lukács gave in the cellar of that café. It must have been in about 1952, says Kraus, and remembers the lecture as a drab recital of Soviet propaganda. The audience was small – about thirty people – but at the same time it was transmitted by radio to many Communist countries.

That lecture was of very restricted and yet almost world-wide interest; it does throw light, almost to the point of paradox, on the way Lukács strove for objectivity, and on his ability to put himself at the service of a higher value. He descended from the heights of the grand manner to the humble, almost humdrum level of those microphones, with all the dangerous complicity which every act of service implies, but also with magnanimous transcendence of self.

Lukács is at the antipodes of the Viennese spirit, for which in any case, like a proper Hungarian, he felt no sympathy. Vienna – the

Vienna where he had been in exile – was the city of contemporary *Angst*, which he branded *en bloc* in his *Destruction of Reason*, a book which seems like a parody of his thought. Vienna is a place of failures, though these are masked by irony and scepticism in the face of the universal and of the various systems of values. Over and above that scepticism there might be, possibly, only the reflection of a transcendence, to which dialectic thought is alien. Lukács is the modern thinker par excellence, he reasons in terms of strong categories, sees the world in terms of a system and establishes firm values over and above necessities. Vienna is the city of the post-modern, in which reality yields to the depiction of itself and of appearances, the strong categories weaken, and the universal comes true in the transcendental or dissolves into the ephemeral, while the mechanisms of necessity engulf all values.

As Augusto del Noce has said, *The Destruction of Reason* is tinged with the secret fear that Nietzsche might prevail over Marx. This is precisely what has happened or is happening in Western societies. The interplay of interpretations, the will to power which has succumbed to the automatism of social processes, the capillary, tentacular, widespread organization of needs, and a vague, collective tide of greed seem to have supplanted the kind of thought which determines the laws of reality in order to alter them and calls the world to judgment so as to change it. Culture as a spectacle seems to have defeated the idea of revolution.

The Destruction of Reason, in which Lukács fights against Nietzsche's ghost, which he sees rising again in triumph, is a book written against the avant-garde, against negation, and therefore also against Vienna – even if Vienna also stands for the satirical side of every presumptuous negation, of post-modern arrogance disguised as cheerful and tolerant fatuity. But Lukács had no time for these metaphysical behind-the-scenes acts, for the upside-downness of the Viennese world-theatre. "As long as he was talking," said Thomas Mann, to stress the sheer dialectical power of Lukács, "he was right". Kafka, with whom the spectral events of the world forced the aging Lukács to come to terms, would have been able to teach him that one is sometimes right when one keeps silent. But silence is not dialectical, it is not Hegelian, but mystical or ironical, or both. Silence is not Marx, it is Wittgenstein or Hofmannsthal: it is Viennese.

14. I WAS ONLY ASKING

One of the many photographs in the exhibition in Vienna devoted to Eastern European Jewry shows an old umbrella-mender, with his cap pulled down firmly on his head, a flowing beard and spectacles on his nose; he is doing his best on a rib, using a length of twine. In the dim photograph the craftsman's dark clothes are engulfed in shadow, but the face and hands shine forth as in a picture by Rembrandt, in a holiness pregnant with respect, that no outrage will be able to destroy. It may be that the windows of his shop will be smashed in a pogrom, like the devastated houses we see in neighbouring photographs. Violence may tear the umbrella man's beard, or take his life, but nothing will be able to deprive him of that fullness of meaning, that tranquil self-assurance expressed in those calm movements of his, in his very body.

Behind the glasses perched on his nose his eyes look resignedly at the umbrella-rib with its messy patch, but they also have the roguish gleam, the affectionate irony, of one who knows that the world can be destroyed between nightfall and sunrise, but that its ostentations should not be taken too seriously, or its promises or threats, because the Torah warns us not to make an idol of anything, not even of the word of God.

That old man is the "eternally unharmed" Jew, as Joseph Roth said, the imperturbable, regal beggar who, in his grimy caftan, rises again after each destruction, putting fear into Pharaoh, the camp Kommandant, the petty aristocrat or office boss, with his irrepressible vitality and the strength of his family affections, which feed that vitality with the fuel of religion. Beneath the windows of the West, which was increasingly feeling its own inner laceration, the Jew, rich or poor, has moved like the king of the *Schnorrer* – those dauntless, persistent tramps and scroungers – vagrant, demanding, exposed to ridicule and aggression, but ready to shrug it all off; without a home of his own but rooted in a Book and a Law, entrenched in life like a king and able to feel at home anywhere, as if the whole world were a familiar part of town where he knows every doorway, like the street where he grew up and everyone speaks his native dialect. On one occasion, during a literary conference at the Jewish Museum at Eisenstadt, the capital of the *Burgenland* only a few kilometres from Vienna, a Viennese rabbi taking part in our discussion asked me, in a slightly cautious tone of voice, "But you are not a Jew, are you?" I had scarcely finished telling him that actually I wasn't before he held up his palms, as if to prevent any misunderstanding, or any concern on my part, and said, "I was only asking."

15. THE USUAL, SIR?

Live and let live is the old Viennese attitude, a sort of easy-going tolerance that doesn't take much, as Alfred Polkar said, to become the cynical indifference of "die and let die". The early nineteenth-century (*biedermeier*) cemetery of Sankt Marx is in a state of total neglect. The iron ornaments on the tombs are being eaten away by rust, the inscriptions are becoming blurred: the adjective "unforgettable" applied to those names is being corroded into oblivion. It is a forest of headless angels, of tangled vegetation covering the sepulchres, stelae in the jungle. An angel holding her torch upside down, her hand raised thoughtfully to her brow, indicates the spot where Mozart was buried; the chrysanthemums on this modest cenotaph are fresh.

Here are many Macedonian, Greek, Polish and Rumanian tombs: "Ici est déposé Kloucerou Constantin Lensch fils du Chevalier Philippe Lensch Grand Logothet de Droit." Like Harlequins, or like the Hans Wursts of so many Viennese popular comedies, the visitor to these autumnal avenues, in which oblivion seems to be in full flourish, is drawn by the thought of death to think of love. Not of *perditio* or *affectio*, but of *appetitio*, of bed, in short, and of certain playful, tender moments. This luxuriance of the perishable gives birth to loyalty, to memory, to a guerrilla war with time. I get a sudden urge to slip into the first telephone booth and, with a handful of schillings ready, ring up all those old girl-friends who have so imperiously got ahead in life. Luckily we now have automatic dialling.

The rooms in the Inn at the Cemetery of the Nameless (*Friedhof der Namenlosen*) also bring to mind pleasant pauses in our travels, cosy bedrooms. The inn now belongs to Leopoldine Piwonka: the new wine, *Sturm*, is light and effervescent, while the parlour has a welcoming Austrian friendliness. The Cemetery of the Nameless is the burial place of the corpses found floating in the Danube. There are not many of them, the flowers in their honour are fresh, and some of them, in spite of the title of the cemetery, have names. Here death is elemental, basic, almost fraternal in the anonymity that we all share, all of us sinners and sons of Eve. Only equality, renunciation, deprivation of everything, especially the sloughing-off our vainglorious identity, can do justice to death and therefore to the truth of life. Those who lie here can say, with Don Quixote, "I know who I am."

Compared with these little crosses the circular chapel in the Austro-Fascist style, built at the time of Dollfuss, is drab and irrelevant, a large abandoned dustbin, unworthy of the religious yet irreverent Viennese familiarity with death. My friend Kunz, who embodies that culture even better than Joseph Roth, divides his entertainment expenses between the Aphrodites of the flesh and magnificent funeral wreaths, which he sends to the exequies of even his remotest acquaintances with a munificence that shames even the closest relatives of the deceased. They say that the florist, as soon as he sees Kunz enter the shop, asks solicitously, "The usual, sir?"

16. JOSEPHINUM

This is the institute and museum of the history of medicine, the ancient academy set up by Joseph II for his army surgeons, and the matrix of the great Viennese school of clinical medicine. The Emperor had anatomical models made in wax, life-size or larger, cut in numerous horizontal or vertical sections, so that the visitor can see the viscous, perfect mechanism of the internal organs, the bundles of nerves and the ramifactions branching out from the brain-centres, the labyrinth of the nerves and tendons, of the muscles, the veins, the arteries. A female head with a horizontally cut section reveals, from the front, a soft mouth and a pair of gently half-closed eyes, while from the top we see the convolutions of the brain. In a median sagittal section a beautiful, colourless male profile, endowed with the pure indifference of a neoclassic statue with lips curved in an archaic smile, displays the grey and white matter of a hemiencephalon and the "tree of life" of the cerebellum. A woman with the abdominal walls removed so as to reveal the genital organs lies serenely on her back with false blond hair loose on her shoulders and a necklace round her throat.

That perfect, precarious topography of our bodies, that network of nerve-ends and viscous sheaths that protect our organs, enables us to reflect, to invent or play variations on the sonnet, to become entranced with a face, to imagine a God. This waxworks museum is not a chamber of horrors, because the truth makes us free, and knowledge of the stuff we are made of renders it worthy of our love. Every true word is made flesh, and those dissected figures show us the nature of bodies which, in moments of grace, appear in all their splendour. Even the models of deformed foetuses, of Siamese twins enmeshed together, remind us that it's all about ourselves. In the meanwhile there are university elections in progress. On one wall is a placard of the "Jes" group, which demands the compulsory wearing of ties and the prohibition of left-wing movements. It announces that on June 1st, as part of a cycle concerned with "conservative sexuality", a certain Dr Knax will give a lecture entitled "Wanking: Mass Murder?"

17. A CABARET OF REALITY

Christa Janata takes me to visit the old Jewish cemetery, at 9 Seegasse. In the 1950s Christa was the mascot of the *Wiener Gruppe*, the legendary and now canonized Viennese avant-garde. She was a friend of Artmann, of Bayer, of Rühm, and looked with entranced astonishment on their extravagances, which made fun of everything and everyone except themselves. She probably had more poetry in her than the lot of them, with the exception of Bayer; she certainly has far more today. She is beautiful and disenchanted, and very well knows the way things are, but she has respect and affection for others, unlike the pointless, tightrope-walking tricks of those writers who are so keen on hood-winking the bourgeois that they eventually take themselves in.

It is Sunday and the streets are deserted. We go for a coffee to the *Gasthaus Fuchs*, in the Rogergasse. Vienna – Canetti's Vienna – is also one of the sewers of the world, familiar even in degradation. The three or four customers embody the various stages of alcoholism. There is an old Croat talking to himself, who doesn't even realize that someone has put a glass in his hand. At another table three people are playing cards: one has the completely coarsened, brutish face of a character in Breughel, the body of the second is swollen by beer into a shapeless, effeminate doughiness, while the third – the only woman – has a face as lopsided as an Expressionist portrait. Suddenly in comes a madman with hammer and nails; these he starts hammering in all over the place, into the tables, the benches. It is a typical scene from the Viennese *Kabarett*, but a real-life *Kabarett*, nude and crude, beyond the scope of literature, which becomes fake and scholastic when it tries to mimic such simplicity. The hostess is self-possessed and good-natured, but maybe in a year or two she will have coarsened like her present customers. "You don't look a day over fifty!" one of the drunkards tells her gallantly. Christa gives me a glance, as if to ask me whether she carries her own age (fifty last birthday) as well as she feels she does.

18. REMBRANDTSTRASSE, 35

This is where Joseph Roth lived in 1913, when he had just arrived in Vienna from Galicia and enrolled in the registers of Vienna University under his full name, Moses Joseph Roth. The building is grey, surrounded by the drabness of the suburbs; the stairway is dark, and in the featureless courtyard is a stunted tree. Living in this building it cannot have been difficult to become a specialist in melancholy, the dominant note of Vienna and Mitteleuropa as a whole. Here is the sadness of boarding-school and barracks, the sadness of symmetry, of transience and disenchantment. In Vienna one gets the impression that people live, and have always lived, in the past, the folds of which conceal and protect even joy. It is the *Lied*, the song, of the "lieber Augustin", the vagrant drunkard, who is always living his last day, who dwells in one prolonged epilogue, in the interval between sunset and dark, in a protracted, postponed farewell. This respite is the instant stolen from flight and enjoyed to the full, the art of living on the brink of nothingness as if all were as it should be.

19. ON THE BRINK OF REALITY

Even topnotch economics can become, in Vienna, an art of nothingness. Amongst the papers of Schumpeter, a master of this elusive science, there were also some notes for a novel, which according to

Arthur Smithies in his obituary was to have been called *Ships in the Fog*.
As we learn from the notes for this unwritten novel, the shrewd,
indecisive protagonist, Henry – son of an Englishwoman and a
Triestino of uncertain nationality – was to have gone to America to
plunge into business, attracted not by the profits but by the intellectual
complexity of economic activity, by its interweaving of mathematics
and passion, in which the general laws of economics intersect with the
chance irregularities of life.

In this furtive, fragmentary self-portrait Schumpeter was drawing a
typical Hapsburgian character, the heir and orphan of that many-
nationed crucible the disappearance of which had left behind it a
profound feeling of not belonging to any precise world, but also the
conviction that that elusive identity – composed of mixtures, sup-
pressions and elisions – was not simply the destiny of the children of
the Danube but a general historical condition, the being of each and
every individual.

A contemporary of Hofmannsthal and Musil, Schumpeter grew up
in the great season of the sciences which, like mathematics, reveal their
lack of foundations. Like Wittgenstein, he belongs to that style of life
and thought described by Musil's twin-concept of spirit and precision.
His is an intellect which aims to sound the ambiguous depths of the
spirit with the analytic rigour of science. He shows a modest reticence
which forbids all facile feeling and, out of both honesty and consistency, forces itself to remain in the sphere of what can be rationally
verified, while being aware that beyond the limits of that knowable
territory there loom the great questions of existence, questions concerning the value and meaning of life. Schumpeter's brilliant studies of
the laws of economic development are an example of this mathematics
of thought which looks with impassioned nostalgia, as in Broch's
novels, at sentiments and phenomena which lie outside its dominion.

In the book, Henry was to grow up, like the author himself, swathed
in mother-love and involved in a pure inter-play of lofty, refined social
relations. It may be that in this story Schumpeter wished to hold a
mirror up to the middle-class liberal of *fin de siècle* Vienna who,
according to Schorske's theory, attempted to mask his own economic
rise beneath the forms of the aesthetic culture of the aristocracy.
Henry's life ended by being frittered away into these social forms and
fading into an elegant detachment, an ambiguous interchange of true
and false, a ceaseless evasion of truth of any kind. Henry was to have
discovered that he was alien to every country, to every social class and

human community, and to find it impossible to anchor himself to family, friend, or beloved woman. Our character thus found himself with nothing left but his work, but this was only a piece of flotsam saved from the wreck: "doing efficient work without aim, without hope".

Smithies points out the irony with which Schumpeter provided his opponents with arguments to refute his theories, the irony with which he watched the misunderstandings that accompanied the circulation of his work, uniting the absolute rigour of scientific clarity with a hidden yearning for decline. This errant affinity with the flaws in history, hand-in-hand with unshakeable rational lucidity, is also a legacy of old Austria. Schumpeter's life was punctuated by misunderstandings and cross-purposes: the long delay between his intuitions and the time when they were acknowledged, the worldwide catastrophes that postponed the success of some of his books, which are among the greatest economic works of the century, his failure as minister of finance and as president of a bank, in spite of the fact that he was one of a mere handful of people who could understand the situation and indicate the correct way of dealing with it.

Like Henry, Schumpeter had no place in his heart for any resentment or contempt. He did not blame the world for his disappointments or impute the absurdity of things to others. Austrian culture had taught him the unobtrusive smile which unmasks every certainty, but conceals dismay and appreciates that quota of day-by-day imbecility that the mind needs in order to survive. This genius of economics, who worked out the theory of the dynamism of contracting and free enterprise, thought (like Musil) that the mind is an aged banker, and that mastery of those computations is necessary, but not sufficient, to life. He says in one of his notes that history could be written in terms of lost opportunities, for he knew that, if things go the way they do, they could perfectly well go otherwise.

20. WIENER GRUPPE AND STRIPTEASE

In the short passage leading from the Kärntnerstrasse to the square containing the Capuchins' Crypt, next door to the famous bar designed by Loos, there was once the *Art-Club*, which was also known as the

Strohkoffer, or "straw trunk". It was the headquarters of the *Wiener Gruppe*. In the stagnantly conservative atmosphere of the 1950s and 1960s, this group rediscovered a tradition that was at the same time Surrealist, Dada and popular, attempted to stem the growing alienation which deprived the individual of his immediate sense experience and sought for poetry in the nth degree of experimentation, in montage and wordplay, in phonetic juggling and happenings, in a mixture of advertising and nonsense, in derisive provocation, in projects to conduct a chorus of birds, build a house ten kilometres long and print fake newspapers for a single person to read.

These jugglers brought some life into the sluggish cultural atmosphere of Austria, and among their number was a real poet, Konrad Bayer, who probably died in 1964. But in their flaunted *poetische Acte*, which claimed to transform life, there was some of the arrogant naïvety of those who set out to disobey the laws of the Father by dropping their trousers; there was the pathetic effrontery of programming spontaneity at the push of a button, the arrogance of considering themselves evangelists of a new gospel, clownish, orgiastic, cybernetic, that is actually not novel in the least.

There is now no dearth of scholarly tomes to applaud this "poetry-as-action". These ideological highbrows give us photographs in which the writers display themselves naked before the audience, piss, dipping their cocks into foaming beermugs, or coalesce in poses intended to be obscene – i.e. original and innocent. What is lacking in all this, alas, is invention, genuine nonsense, unpredictable fantasy, and irony. Those nude figures and those gestures are as predictable as the uniforms in a military academy. Now these iconoclasts have turned over a new leaf, like militant students who become notaries, lecture at the university and disparage the events of 1968. On the site of that bar, so I am told by Christa, who used to hang around with the Group in those days, there is now another – closed for the time being – in which the usual fare is striptease, perhaps not all that different from those pretentious stripteases of yore. It is a logical shift from striptease to striptease that would have made Joseph Roth chuckle.

The vast and famous complex of workers' dwellings built by "Red Vienna", the Socialist local government, shortly after the First World War, arose from a desire for reform, a faith in progress, the will to construct a new society open to new classes and destined to be led by the latter. It is easy today to smile at this uniform barracks-like greyness. But the courtyards and the flower-beds have a certain melancholy gaiety, if we are to trust the games of children who before these dwellings were built would have lived in hovels or in nameless ratholes, and also the pride of the families who in these houses, for the first time, had a chance to live with dignity, as human beings.

This monument of the Modern embodies many progressive illusions of the period between the wars – illusions that have collapsed. But it also bears witness to real and considerable progress, which only presumptuous ignorance could underrate. In 1934 these dwellings were the centre of the great workers' uprising in Vienna, which Dollfuss, the Austro-Fascist chancellor, put down with bloody violence. The right wing is patriotic, but it fires more often and more willingly on its own fellow-citizens than on the invaders of the country.

Today we feel ourselves to be orphans of that modern trend and its promises. Vienna, in the years of exile between the two wars, was also a stage which witnessed the downfall of many ideological certainties and great revolutionary hopes.

During the years of Hitler and Stalin, it was above all faith in Communism which collapsed in the hearts and thoughts of many. The deserter from the Party, it is said in a novel by Manès Sperber, set in Vienna, is orphaned by the whole: when the clandestine Communist militant, who has sworn fidelity to the Revolution and is operating in countries dominated by Fascist dictatorships, discovers Stalin's perversion of the Revolution, he finds himself in a no man's land, alien to all societies and exiled from life itself.

Those witnesses and accusers of "the god that failed", who were often to be seen in the streets and cafés of Vienna, in the years between the wars, as in a land of exile, experienced revolutionary militancy as a total vision of the world, with political choices involving questions about ultimate things. Those deserters from Stalinist Communism have taught us a great lesson, because they preserved the Marxist, unified, classic image of man, a faith in that universal-human which is sometimes ingenuously expressed in the narrative forms of the past. They did not see the temporary setbacks to their own dreams as a licence to indulge in irresponsible intellectual liberties, and their very humanity is utterly different from the coquettishness of today's orphans of Marxism, whose disappointment that it has not proved the "Open Sesame" of history gives way to strident mockery at the expense of that which only yesterday seemed to them sacred and infallible.

The wistful though firm resolution of the exiles of yesterday can teach us to live correctly under today's conditions. To be orphaned by ideologies is natural, as it is natural to lose one's own parents. It is a grievous moment, but not one that induces us to profane our lost fathers, because it does not mean abandoning what has been taught us. Political militancy is not a mystic church in which everything stays put; it is a day-by-day effort which does not redeem the earth once and for all, but is exposed to errors and prepared to correct them. Marxism has also undergone this period of liberal secularization, which has no time for idolatries or Vietnam orphans, but tends to form mature personalities capable of withstanding continual disappointments. The time has come when leaving the Communist Party no longer means losing the whole, and this could be a reason for not leaving it. But in their no man's land those nomads of yesterday faced the void with a sense of values thanks to which secularization meant an emancipation from dogmas, not a passive, uncaring subjection to the existing social mechanisms. Those nomads, as Sperber said, were outside the confines of history, living in memories of the past and in the dream of the future, but never in the present. This fate was shared by Austria, and (Sperber adds) in the cafés of exile old Austria died again, this time for ever.

But this death, and this exile, were also a means of resistance to the impoverished pulping process of post-modernity, just as the *Karl-Marx-Hof* was an act of resistance to Dollfuss's guns, and also to the temptation to think that resistance itself was folly. The stark, grey, massive modernity of those tenements impresses by its compactness. It is quite a different thing for someone sixty years later to rediscover and praise it according to the canons of some whimsically progressive taste, and perhaps even attempt – as has occurred in Trieste with disastrous results – to re-instate the tenement dwelling as the model for community living. This daydream of restoring forms now shorn of the historical necessity which in its time produced them is post-modern – it is a pleasure taken in what is fake and gaudy, in ideology shorn of all ideas. In short, it is a culture without any foundations, and has nothing in common with the serious, robust foundations of *Karl-Marx-Hof.*

22. UNCLE OTTO

Mariahilfestrasse. In these rooms lived Uncle Otto, a great-uncle of mine on my mother's side. For decades the waves of history tossed him this way and that, but always ended, quite by chance, in carrying him upwards to safety. During the First World War he was in Trieste as the Austrian official in charge of supplies, an office which he carried out scrupulously, and which enabled him to get through those years of shortage without particular hardship. In 1918 the Italians arrived in Trieste, and he was summoned by General Petitti di Roreto. He got to the appointment slightly late, to find that a small crowd in the street outside had already beaten up his ex-colleague in the same job, yelling "Down with the Austrian starve-master", and its aggressive tendencies were already too thoroughly glutted to give him the same treatment. The general, struck by the neatness of his registers, asked him to be in charge of rations during that difficult transitional period and took him along to a box in the theatre, where they were celebrating the liberation of Trieste, and where the ovations and cries of "Long live Italy!" automatically rained down also on my great-uncle.

On the advent of Fascism he transferred to Vienna, where during the years of the great economic crisis his experience gained him a similar job. He told me that sometimes, before some demonstration, a number of Socialists would come to his office and inform him that the following day they would be demanding that he hand over 200 cwt of flour. He was bidden to say he was prepared to release 100, and in the end they would settle for 150. They then asked which of the rooms in his offices were least used, in case it became strictly necessary to throw stones at a few windows. Having retired from public life, during Nazism he protected a number of persecuted Socialists and Communists, and maybe for this reason in 1945, during the Russian occupation, the Soviet authorities asked him to look after supplies and the distribution of foodstuffs. As an old man he was made a Knight of Malta, and by instinct turned down an important post which a short while later was involved in awkward squabbles. Having been created

Knight Commander, he spent half the year in Rome, in the palace of the Order, along with an extremely ancient manservant whom he, though well into his eighties, helped to move and feed himself. "Come on, Giovanni, let's go to the mountains," he would say to him, and the pair of them would thereupon take deep breaths from an oxygen cylinder. He always glided through the midst of events like an expert dancer who does not brush against other couples on the crowded dance-floor.

23. AT THE CRIME MUSEUM

The kind police official who acts as my guide in the Crime Museum is proud of the crimes and criminals he points out to me, as the Director of the Uffizi might be proud of his Raphaels and Botticellis. Though a faithful guardian of the law, even he takes no pains to conceal a good-natured affection for the king of safe-breakers – Breitwieser. The man was deeply loved by the Viennese, who paid him their last respects in 1919 when he was buried in the Meidling cemetery.

In this museum there are two unforgettable photographs, two women, victim and murderess. The latter is a well-to-do lady, Josefine Luner, hard, fat and conceited-looking, with the square, moralistic jaw of the respectable housewife who betrays the hidden harridan in her. The victim is Anna Augustin, fourteen years old, brown hair in plaits, bright, timid eyes, more of a child than a girl, looking lost and defenceless. Anna Augustin came from the provinces and worked as a housemaid for the Luners. Frau Luner began to torment her by accusing her of non-existent immoral practices and threatening to report her to her family. From that she went on to blows, kicks and beatings; then she locked her up, starved her, subjecting her to horrible ill-treatment and torturing her in the most atrocious ways. After about a year of such torture Anna died. Josefine Luner was condemned to death, but the sentence was commuted to life imprisonment, as it always was in Austria in the case of women until, in 1938, the Nazis abolished this feminine privilege. Her husband, who had known what was going on but had not joined in the torturing, got a few months in prison.

The childhood of Anna, those childlike eyes of hers, tender and harmless, cry out for vengeance. What happened to this creature, and happens in various ways to so many other people, negates the history of the world. All the loftiest works of man, if put in the scales, do not compensate for this horror, or erase this indelible stain from creation. Like Alyosha Karamazov when faced with the general who had ordered his dogs to tear a boy to pieces, one is aware in this case also that God is not omnipotent, that he cannot forgive Josefine Luner, that it is impossible to conceive of a final state of harmony in which this squat butcher-woman is accepted among the blest.

This violence is also social violence. Anna never dared to rebel, or to run away at a time when she was still able to do so, when her mistress, after putting her through agony, sent her to do the shopping, and she obeyed. No one had taught her to think of herself as having equal rights; the social authority of her mistress instilled in her a sense of timid submission, and prepared the way for the other's ferocity. Josefine Luner, on her part, would never have tortured the daughter of a State Counsellor; it would never even have entered her mind. Also, she had never tortured anyone before, and had not suffered on account of this abstinence. When she found herself faced with a girl who was totally defenceless, and certainly not very bright, that lack of resistance and the sheer ease of the crime aroused in her the desire to commit it.

The weak have to learn to frighten the strong, or else to realize – if they wish to, and if they can get rid of their own fear – that they too can be strong and pay back Frau Luner blow for blow. Those who bow down and serve do it because, like the elephant in Kipling, they have forgotten their own strength. When they remember it, and are prepared to give anyone who tries to sting them a good swipe with their trunk, then perhaps there will be peace in the zoo.

24. "HAPPILY LIVED AND LIGHTLY DIED"

For Grillparzer the Augarten, the large park between the Brigettenau and the *Leopoldstadt*, was a place of pleasure and happiness, at least during the popular festival which he describes in *The Poor Street-Musician*, a story written in 1848. The Augarten today, with its dead-straight, almost bare avenues, brings to mind the solitude that lurks in all geometric forms, a garden for pensioners to take walks with their dogs beneath the three peeling, neglected *Flaktürme*, three disused anti-aircraft towers that loom like squat barbaric ruins.

Like Grillparzer's story, a hypochondriac, sad farewell to a familiar harmony that is vanishing, old Vienna is the landscape of a farewell to happiness. Amedeo is organizing a judicious comparison between the *Most* and the *Sturm*, two varieties of Viennese wine drunk very fresh, while Gigi is making the ladies laugh with stories about his uncle, who promised his mother, when she was on her death-bed, that he would marry a certain woman, and naturally he would never have forsworn that sacred oath; but before marriage there is always an engagement, and then there are so very many things to do, that engaged he remained until the age of eighty-three, evidently with the intention of getting married as soon as possible, a wish cut short only by his sudden and unexpected death. Francesca raises her head slightly, in a gesture habitual with her, giving due emphasis to her throat, white in the evening light. The years have not yet finished her portrait, they do not give us a glimpse of what will become of that face that has traversed the seas in silence and let the water run from the cheeks and hair; a beautiful, unostentatious face, seeking for discreet and normal anchorages that will not attract attention.

Even this loafing about will come to an end – we may give ourselves the air of casual strollers, but we are in fact all of us fine upstanding professional people, reliable and on the ball. The mechanism of rhetoric keeps us on the leash and will bring us back to heel; given a tug, we will run back to our kennels and bark out the music laid down for performance by the seriousness of life.

The trunks and leaves of these trees reflect, with a brilliance at odds with the greyness of the sky, the glare of the festival described by Grillparzer, the light of his pages which evoked the trees and foliage of the Augarten a hundred and thirty years ago. The "poor street-musician" is a man who has never had anything and never wanted to, a beggar who loves music with religious fervour but scrapes at his violin most vilely, who with tortuous and meticulous candour has organized his own failure, finding in his existential and social decline a modest, hidden harmony with the flow of life, the fulfilment of each instant, and, in short, "conviction". Kafka, who saw the "poor musician" as one who has renounced everything and can taste life to the full, because that renunciation has left him free of all harassing projects, compared him to Flaubert, to the absence and void of *L'Éducation sentimentale*. Grillparzer's character lives "dans le vrai", as Flaubert puts it, but for him simplicity and truth coincide with art, with his dedication to music, while for Flaubert and Kafka the imperious vocation of art isolates one from that human truth. The art of the poor musician, on the other hand, despite the fact he worships it as harmony, is a hideous squeak. All the same, his failed life is what saves him. It rescues him from the roles dictated by history and society, it allows him to devote himself to insignificant trifles, to waste his time and throw it away, to take pleasure in small, ridiculous things, and in his clumsy way to approach to a kind of Mozartian lightness.

Austrian-ness is the art of flight, of escape, of vagrancy, of the love of sitting back and waiting for a country which, as Schubert's Wanderer puts it, is forever sought and foreseen but never known. This unknown country, in which one lives on a constant overdraft, is Austria; but it is also life, gracious and – on the brink of nothingness – even happy. A gentle poet, a drinker and scavenger of Grillparzer's times, one Ferdinand Sauter, who spent his life in the pubs of Vienna, says in the epitaph he composed for himself,

> "Viel empfunden, nichts erworben,
> froh gelebt und leicht gestorben"

– that he had much experienced, nothing gained, happily lived and lightly died.

25. BERGGASSE, 19

"When he was here he had only a few visitors, but now everyone goes," says the taxi-driver who takes me to Freud's house and surgery. The rooms are famous, and I myself have been here often, but every time they make a deep impression; in the very atmosphere one can feel the respect and paternal melancholy with which this nineteenth-century gentleman descended into the underworld. In the entrance we find his hat and stick, as if Freud had just come in; there is his medical bag, a travelling trunk and a leather-covered bottle, the drinking flask which he used to take with him on his trips into the woods, which he loved with the precise conventionality of a *paterfamilias*.

The photographs and documents that cram what was his actual study, portraits of Freud and of the other founders of the new science, and editions of celebrated works, are simply informative and rather banal: this is no longer Freud's study, but a didactic museum of psychoanalysis, practically reduced to the stereotyped formula that is by now *de rigueur* in every speech or paper.

But in the small waiting-room there are some books from Freud's real library: Heine, Schiller, Ibsen, the classics who taught him the prudence, the precision, the *humanitas* indispensable to any journey to the lower world. That walking-stick and flask tell us everything about the greatness of Freud, his sense of the measure of things and his love of order, his simplicity as a man resolved in himself and free of manias; one who, by plunging into the abysses of human ambivalences, both learns and teaches how to love those family outings in the mountains more, in greater freedom.

Of all this there is little left in the conferences of psychoanalysis: here haphazard salvos, ignorant of syntax, all too often degrade psychoanalysis into an unwitting parody of itself and apply the Oedipus complex to problems of refuse disposal or the monetary spiral. The true heirs of Freud are not the hot-air ideologists who make spectacular use of psychoanalysis as a chewing-gum, but the therapists who with infinite patience help some people to live a little more easily. That modest, reassuring leather bag makes me think of all those to whom I myself owe what little self-confidence I possess, that essential minimum of ability needed to live with the dark places of myself.

At the end of the *Himmelstrasse*, in a spot with a fine view of the Vienna woods, a monument erected in 1977 in the place called Bellevue states, not without rhetoric: "Here, on July 24th 1895, the secret of dreams revealed itself to Dr Sigm. Freud." It is droll to think of that Mr Secret who, like an impostor in a comedy, finally takes off the mask.

One prefers to think of that landscape, and of Freud looking at it, reading the curved outlines of the distant city like a map of man's inner meanderings, never entirely explored. What is touching in that rhetorical inscription is the "Dr", standing as it does for academic dignity, for demanding studies achieved not without some pride.

26. SPACE ODYSSEY

The enormous building at 95 Obere Donaustrasse, on the banks of the Danube canal, is the I.B.M. Centre. A plaque at the main entrance informs us that on that site, in the Diana Baths which now no longer exist, on February 15th 1867 Johann Strauss for the first time performed his *Blue Danube*. The Diana Baths were certainly more attractive than this box-like structure, but the calculators and electronic brains now installed over what was once a temple of transience, in which a civilization asked flirtatiously for the avoidance of a tragedy, do not disturb the whirlings of that waltz which, as Kubrick was clever enough to realize in his *2001: A Space Odyssey*, keeps in time with the rhythm and the breathing of the worlds. If the Japanese are announcing a computer that will soon be capable of attaining the complexity of the human mind, then maybe one day in the distant future it could compose the circular rhythm of this waltz, a joy that forever escapes one and always returns – more distant and tenuous, though.

The calculators and electronic brains, like the space-ship which they control, are part of that music of space in which the ship travels. In the ceaseless iteration of the waltz there is something of the eternal, and not only an echo of the past – of the epoch of Francis Joseph which, according to the old saying, ended with the death of Strauss – but the unending projection of that past into the future, like the images of remote events which journey through space and, for those destined to receive them some time, somewhere, are already the future.

That I.B.M. Centre is also a heart of the business world, but even Strauss, a genuine artist admired by Brahms, was a hive of industry turning out consumer goods for the mass market – goods which however, miraculously, approached the shores of poetry. The plaque on that building makes us feel a little like Hal, the computer in *Space Odyssey* who became so human as to make mistakes, to suffer from emotions and fears. Anyone who loves the waltz should try not to be upset at the idea that in 1982 a computer was nominated "Man of the Year".

27. THE LOOK BEHIND

As the plaque states, on the site of the present building at 15 Schwarzpanierstrasse, now guarded by an intractable concierge who expels me
instantly with sharp words, until 1904 there stood the house in which
Beethoven died. In the same house, on the night of October 3rd–4th
1903, Weininger shot himself through the heart. A few weeks earlier he
had described the feeling of bewilderment one feels on looking back
along the road one has just walked, the indifferent street with its
rectilinear length that speaks of the irreversibility of time. In the end
this is all there is, the backward glance that perceives the nothingness of
it all.

28. WORDS, WORDS, WORDS

The *Hermesvilla*, with its *Art nouveau* ambiguities, set in a park full of
deer and boar on the edge of Vienna, was much beloved of the Empress
Elizabeth, the mythical, unhappy, and practically unbearable wife of
Francis Joseph; that bashful, retiring Sissy dear to the popular imagination. In her bedroom Hans Makart, the official decorator and
illustrator in the Vienna of the time (the villa was built in 1882–6), had
been commissioned to paint scenes based on *A Midsummer Night's
Dream*, and in fact sketched out designs which were executed by his
successors.

The colours are soft and dark, the Empress's bed is a genuine funeral
couch watched over by an allegory of melancholy, while the scenes
from Shakespeare are of a glacial yet ingratiating lasciviousness, present again in the mythological figures adorning the gymnasium; here
Elizabeth subjected her androgynous body to physical exercises which
she practised religiously, as if they had been spiritual exercises. The villa
is a fit dwelling for the Empress's frigid, enervated tenderness, which
made her insensitive to sexuality in the raw and eager for disembodied
raptures, to the point of cultivating the clean, slender lines of her body
with ascetic narcissism, of taking pleasure in being wanted by men
without feeling the need to reciprocate, and of becoming chastely
infatuated with feminine beauty. She went so far as to ask the

Hapsburg ambassadors to procure her portraits of the most beautiful women in the countries where they were posted. There is in Sissy a hermaphrodite purity, which abhors the physical side of sex and is capable of loving only in sublimation and absence.

As often happens, Sissy's frustration sought to be transfigured in poetry, to experience her parching sterility as a sign of being one of the chosen. The Empress wrote lyric poems, and she was not entirely wrong when she thought of entrusting to them – jealously concealed as they were – the essence and the predictable secret of her soul. In the old Hapsburg Empire it was a tricky business even for a high-school student to write verses, so that Hofmannsthal, for example, was forced to publish his brilliant youthful poetry under a pseudonym. Even a sovereign as impatient of protocol as Elizabeth had to keep her poems to herself and a few trusted intimates, and in fact she hid them in a box and left careful instructions to her heirs.

Elizabeth's poems, as stated in their overall title, comprise a poetic diary; that is, they record not daily events but their most recondite meanings, that flash which ought to illuminate them but which the dullness of every day snuffs out, or at least conceals. Sissy's poems are poems of absence, of distress, of what life ought to be and isn't; they are poems opposed to life as she actually lived it. Her story is well known: the Bavarian girl-princess, cousin of Ludwig of Bavaria, who married Francis Joseph; the marriage that at first was happy but then more and more of a grind as the atmosphere in the family and at court grew ever more oppressive; her growing intolerance of her own role as Empress, her inner detachment from her husband and children, her melancholy and restlessness, her increasingly frequent travels and absences; her alienation from everything, even from herself, and her absurd death in Geneva at the hands of the Italian anarchist Luccheni.

Her poems show her longing for a life of her own, her rebellion against that of the court, which reaches the point of actually criticizing the Hapsburg system and professing faith in republicanism. But they speak most of all of lack of fulfilment, of a nostalgia which cannot and does not wish to be defined, which surrenders to this remoteness, this absence of something: what this something is she cannot describe, but its absence is the real and constant stuff of her life, which plunges into this tremulous void and takes root there. The main background of these lyrics is the sea, its ineffable vastness, the murmur of its waves, as ceaseless and untranslatable as that of the soul. Sissy is the sea-gull, the sea-bird without rest or destination, just as Ludwig of Bavaria, the cousin who was so like her, is the eagle, kingly but foreign to the earth, unsuited to it. In the Hermesvilla there is also a portrait of Ludwig by Gräfle. The sovereign who loved beauty, the swan and the eagle, is plump and curly-haired, with a heavy, Levantine vulgarity about him.

In her elation the Empress thought that her verses, however banal and often lame, were dictated to her from "beyond", through the offices of a medium, by Heine. Elizabeth does in fact write in the manner of Heine, using his typical melody and lyric repertoire which found so many imitators during the nineteenth century as to constitute a stereotyped poetic language of its own.

The hackneyed music does not obliterate the agonized individuality of the voice which sings it, just as the uniformity of life does not lessen the intensity with which one person lives it. It is to the impersonal melody of that idiom, which appears to her as a sort of song without words, an empty structure to be filled up at will, that Elizabeth entrusts her genuine, deeply-felt conflicts and passions. Even these passions, such as her maniacal cult of Achilles, were historically dated, part of the climate of the times; but Elizabeth, like Ludwig, experienced them directly as part of her sad, sterile existence, in the throes of a melancholy that bordered on mental disturbance. Eccentric to the point of cruel indifference, which Francis Joseph managed to tolerate with true affection and great style, Elizabeth could also be magnanimous, as on the occasion when she went to meet the Emperor at Vienna station on his return from the smarting defeats he had suffered at the hands of the Prussians, and kissed his hand in front of everyone.

In spite of her four children, she was not made for other kisses. Her restless personality lacked conviction, was ignorant of values and of relaxed sexuality, incapable of dwelling in life itself, in the moment or in the present. For this reason it was to her poems that Elizabeth confided her true nature, that of a wild, migratory bird. Those verses were sometimes melodious, at other times clumsy, and could have been written by anyone; they form a sort of public rhyming dictionary which many could have used, and did, and in which personal sufferings sank as in the sea. Lyrics of rather the same kind had been penned by another noble and unsuitable sovereign, Maximilian of Mexico, born for the sea rather than for the throne, though he, unlike her, was able to face up to his destiny with a sober sense of duty. The poetry in Sissy does not reside in the extremely mediocre writings themselves, but in the tension between her lonely sorrow and the completely superficial quality of its expression. The poems the Empress wrote are the "poetic diary" of anyone or no one, but this fate, which the Empress shares with many writers, some of whom have had success, makes her a small but real personality in the world of literature, in her constantly repeated dialogue between the voice of the heart and "words, words, words".

29. ECKHARTSAU

In this little castle, or hunting-lodge, among these blue firs, the age-old history of the Hapsburgs came to an end; for here the last Emperor, Charles, abdicated. The people of Trieste called him Carlo Piria, "piria" being a funnel, on account of his love of wine, and the current image of him is of a limited but good-natured man. He was not only good-natured, however, but really good; and goodness, in this life, is an imperial virtue. When he visited the front-line, on the Isonzo, and saw the frightful, futile massacre, he exclaimed that he would stop the war at all costs. The courage to put an end to a war, to see the abysmal stupidity of it, is certainly no less than that needed to start one – it is courage worthy of a true emperor.

The little castle has the air of a peaceful domestic dwelling, and on the roof there is a reassuring stork's nest. This pleasant, discreet simplicity is a fit setting for the end of the Hapsburgs, of a dynasty abounding in motherly and fatherly figures, from the great Maria Theresa to the last symbolic Emperor, Francis Joseph, with his grand-fatherly charisma, wise and a trifle absent-minded. In the park there is a huge tree, the branches of which create a mighty hall, grander than the royal chambers within. This tree has never thought of abdicating. In the country round a number of posters announce the cultivation of *Sieglinde*, a Wagnerian-sounding name for a particular variety of potato.

Among the ruins of this Roman city, when it was very far from being ruined, Marcus Aurelius wrote the Second Book of his *Meditations*. "My city and my country is Rome, in so far as I am an Antonine. As a man, it is the universe." Marcus Aurelius was capable of being Roman Emperor, accepting without pride the position and responsibility which had been assigned to him, and also a citizen of the world, the equal of every other man on earth, and indeed a simple creature living in the universe, part of the ceaseless flowing and transmuting of all things, and prepared to accept his own parabola without putting on glum airs. He was "aware of his own natural political essence, as Roman and Emperor, already prepared for his position", and, as a soldier, he knew how to go into the assault against a wall without being ashamed to seek for help if he was unable to scale it alone; but he also recognized the equality between all men in virtue of which the man who defeated the Sarmatae was also a murderer, like anyone who kills.

This Roman Emperor is a great writer and a great teacher. There was piety, respect and cordiality in his attitude towards life, but no idolatry, because he knew that that is only "opinion". When he was fighting the Quadi and the Marcomanni he led his troops to the Hungaric Gate, into the territory between the rivers March and Leitha beyond which wave after wave of barbarian invasions were pressing in, destined to spread further in the centuries that followed. He defended the Empire, but he did not allow himself to be swayed by the emotivity of it, or permit himself to become "caesared", as he put it, because he knew that to defend the Empire was only his duty and not an absolute value: "Asia, Europe," he wrote, "small parts of the universe."

He cultivated the ultimate and essential things, aware that a person is made up of the values in which he believes, and which stamp his features with the imprint of their nobility or vulgarity, as the case may be. The spirit draws upon the images which form in it, he wrote, and the value of every person is in strict proportion to the value of the things to which he has given importance. This is perhaps the most blinding intuition of the essence of a man, the key to his history and his nature: we are what we believe in, the gods whom we house in our minds, and this religion, whether lofty or superstitious, marks us indelibly, prints itself on our features and in our gestures, and becomes our mode of being.

Convinced of the unity of the universe in all its incessant transformations, Marcus Aurelius nevertheless did not allow mental activity to become confused with the principle of life, as if it were a mere physiological secretion of the brain. He demanded that it should rise in judgment over that very universe of which it is a provisional part, even though he was certainly not lacking in grandiose intellectual familiarity with the matter of which life and the animal unions which produce it are made, "the attrition of membranes and the emission of mucus accompanied by a certain tremor".

This pacific Emperor took pleasure in the fact that he had not given proof of his virility before it was due, but at the right time; in contrast to his late Hapsburg successors to the imperial crown – still called Roman – he was not afraid of change, because without change nothing can happen. This philosopher-emperor, mindful of Plato's great distinction between philosophy and rhetoric, thanked his teacher Rusticus for having passed on an aversion to rhetoric and poetry, for polished speech. Marcus Aurelius wanted the truth, and for him poetry was falsehood. As readers of Umberto Saba it is easy for us to refute him and show him the truth which can reach poetry and which eludes not only rhetoric, but even philosophy.

Marcus Aurelius probably did not know that he was a great poet, even when he thanked the gods "for not having put it into his head to be a writer". His poetry is that of the moral being, and is in contrast with another kind of poetry, that of the imaginative dissolution of all bonds, both logical and ethical, as wrought by those pervaded by the divine mania of the muses. He is against the poetry of those who listen to the song of the Sirens or have the Lotus Eaters' longing for oblivion. In this sense the Emperor, although he travels through remote Pannonia and dies so far from Rome – at Vindobona – is what Gadda would call a sedentary, the sort of man who with patient consistency forms his own personality. The nomadic poets, Baudelaire's *vrais voyageurs*, wander without destination, trying every experience and deliberately dispersing their specific personal identity, losing themselves and dissolving into nothingness.

The intrepid journey made by Marcus Aurelius, intent on constructing his own self, does not refute the journey that Rimbaud aimed towards the disintegration, the abolition of himself. But perhaps all the Emperor wanted to say was that sufficient unto philosophy are thought and the world, whereas the art of speech requires manuals of poetics, handbooks, libraries and such things, which it is not easy to carry with one. Almost as if to warn future travellers on the Danube, weighed down with tomes and bibliographies, which they rattle off like little prayers to prop up their vacuity, it was right here in Carnuntum that he wrote, "But get rid of that thirst for books, unless you want to go to your death mumbling . . ."

31. A MINORITY THAT WANTS TO BE ASSIMILATED

Eisenstadt is already beyond the Leitha, which marked the border of the Kingdom of Hungary, to which it belonged. Here begins the lethargy of Pannonia, the low houses in the plains like sleepy eyelids, the storks' nests on the roofs of Illmitz and the reeds in the lake of Neudiedel, roofs made of straw and of mud, and the yellow-ochre of the Esterházy palace, a colour which one comes across throughout the territories of the Hungarian crown. The *Burgenland*, of which Eisen-stadt is the capital, is no longer governed by feudal overlords but by the *Landeshauptmann*, the "captain" of the Region, Theodor Kery, known as the *Landesfürst* or prince of the Region, on account of the manner in which he governs the *Land*, typical of a big Magyar magnate, giving fewer audiences than the nobles of yore, cutting debate short with the statement "I am never wrong," and receiving homage on his birthday like a feudal lord.

Kery, who does nothing to discourage the rumour of his presumed blue blood and has in his time aroused the interest of the state legal advisory office – a road leading to his country house was built with public money – is a Socialist, and said to be very close to Chancellor Sinowatz. Sinowatz also comes from the *Burgenland*, and is of Croat origin. He seems to sum up and exemplify the destiny of his people, of the Croat minority and its imminent assimilation. The Croats have been living in the area for 450 years and are rapidly becoming extinct: Martin Pollack calculates that at the next census there will be 10,000 of them.

While practically all over Europe there is an awakening of small nations and a fierce and often even aggressive assertion of their own identity on the part of national minorities – the Basques, the Corsicans, the Albanians of the Kosovo – the Croats of the *Burgenland* are pressing for their assimilation. As Martin Pollack discovered in the course of his inquiry, they are as eager to collaborate in their extinction as the Slovenes of Carinthia are fierce in their claims to ethnic independence.

Croatian place-names are disappearing little by little, being preserved chiefly in the churches, as in the time-table for Masses in the parish of Hornstein/Vorištan. Josef Vlasits, grammar-school teacher in Eisenstadt and a member of the commission for nomenclature, stresses the Croat minority's lukewarm love for their own language, while Fritz Robak, former burgomaster of the mixed commune of Steinbrunn-Štikapron and member of the Conference of Burgomasters and Vice-Burgomasters of the Croat Communes and Bilingual Communes, asserts that one can change one's language as one changes one's political party or religion, and told Pollack that in the mid-1970s he tried in vain to persuade Tito that the Croat minority was not being forced into assimilation, but actually wished to become assimilated.

Robak is a Socialist, and is perhaps in favour of this process, because as the Croatian peasants become Germanized they abandon their traditional Catholicism. "Look at this," he said to Pollack with satisfaction, as he pointed to a dot on the map. "Here in this village, Tschantschendorf, there used to be lots of Croats, and now there are none . . ."

Some of the young try to react to this, with that yearning for the past which is typical of the third generation – it was also a feature of the rediscovery of Judaism on the part of the young Jews in Kafka's Prague – and to retrieve the Croat tongue of their grandparents. Their parents, on the other hand, wished to abolish Croat in schools, so that their children could learn to speak better German and integrate more readily into Austrian society. Croat, for them, ought to be at most a dialect spoken in the home. Is this sad? Professor Josef Breu, viewing change in the same light as Hegel and Goethe, thinks not. "The world is in continuous movement," he says. "If everything always had to stay the same we would still be speaking Celtic."

32. WHEN HAYDN'S AROUND, NOTHING CAN GO WRONG

Eisenstadt is Haydn's town, the town of his birthplace and of his tomb, of a museum devoted to his life and relics. The *Wienerisches Diarium* of October 18th 1766 defined his music as pure, clear water, even if it went on – thinking that it was paying him the highest compliment – to compare it to the poetry of Gellert, now known almost exclusively to teachers of Germanic studies. Haydn is perhaps one of the last, or simply one of the rarest, expressions of an intact, harmonious whole, of a creation without shadows. There is in the museum a vocal quartet of his, and it is a farewell of the most crystalline tranquillity; like the song of the *lieber Augustin*, or Sauter's epitaph, or the serenity of the poor musician:

> "Hin ist alle meine Kraft,
> Alt und schwach bin ich . . .
>   [. . . .]
> Der Tod klopft an meine Thür
> unerschreckt mach' ich ihm auf,
> Himmel, habe Dank!
> Ein harmonischer Gesang
> war mein Lebenslauf."

(My strength has gone, I am old and weak . . . Death knocks at my door, I open it without fear, Heaven, receive my thanks! One harmonious song my life has been.) This confidence enabled Haydn to remain unmoved by the bombs while the French were besieging Vienna, and with childlike ingenuousness to reassure the others: "When Haydn's around, nothing can go wrong," he said with that assurance of a man totally free and resolved within himself; a man, wrote Freud, who knows in his unconscious that nothing can threaten him.

Another visit to Vienna. Alone, yet feeling at home. "Remember that sense of infinite distance, in the hotel, incognito," wrote D'Annunzio in Vienna on April 10th 1900, on the occasion of the first Austrian performance of *La Gioconda*, with Eleonora Duse in the leading role. This sense of solitary intimacy is the impression one gets on returning home, but to a home altered by years of absence.

Our identity is partly made up of places, of the streets where we have lived and left part of ourselves. A map of Mount Snežnik, bearing the names of its clearings and its paths, is also a portrait of men, the image of what I have experienced and what I am. Sometimes places can also be atavistic, and emerge from some Platonic anamnesis of the soul, which recognizes itself in them. Vienna is one of these places, in which I rediscover the familiar and well known, the enchantment of things which, like friendship and love, become ever fresher with time. This feeling of ease in Vienna may derive from the city's being a crossroads, a place of departures and returns, of people, both celebrated and obscure, whom history gathers together and then disperses, in the vagabond impermanence that is our destiny.

The city is thus one vast café, scene of methodical habits and of casual comings and goings. It also leads us to think of death, of our last exit from the door of the café, and draws all of us, like that character in Roth, towards the Crypt of the Capuchins, in an attempt to understand what death means. But the answer is not even there. While I am looking at the tombs of the Emperors there comes to mind a passage in an unpublished manuscript which I recently read. The author tells how, as a little girl, she was astonished when her religious instructor asked her what death was and, when she said nothing, defined it as "the separation of the soul from the body". The little girl was disappointed, because, without being able to be more precise about it, she was thinking "of something more gloomy and more glorious". The child was certainly thinking of another kind of glory, not that of these majestic tombs, and not even the kind promised by a Hapsburg official to a writer who was complaining about being unknown: "Just wait until you're dead, and then you'll see! You'll be a famous man!"

FIVE

Castles and Huts

1. AT THE RED PRAWN

Bratislava. On the ceiling of the entrance hall of the old pharmacy called *The Red Prawn*, in Michalská Street, there is a fresco which portrays the god of time. The potions and mixtures surrounding him in that atrium like a confident challenge, and the learned tome lying open in front of him, threaten to exorcize his power and hold up his advance. That eighteenth-century shop – now transformed into a Pharmaceutical Museum – gives the impression of a military parade in its rigid symmetry, of an unassuming yet determined art of war displayed against Chronos. The pots on the shelves, in cobalt, emerald green and sky blue, embellished with floral designs and biblical quotations, are like the ranks of tin soldiers in museum reliefs of famous battles; the tinctures, balsams, balms, allopathics, purgatives and emetics are there at their battle stations, ready to intervene according to the requirements of strategy. Even the labels, with their abbreviations, are reminiscent of military contractions: Syr., Tinct., Extr., Bals., Fol., Pulv., Rad.

The art of the herbalist seeks to defeat the wastage of the years, to restore the body and the face as one restores the façade of a Renaissance palace. But it is nice in the little museum; it is quiet and cool in the midst of this torrid summer, as it would be in a church or under the pergola of a country inn. As one stares at the alembics in an alchemist's laboratory, or the bust of Paracelsus erected to commemorate the period when he worked in Bratislava, the jars of aconite and Cinnamomum, the papers on pharmaceutics in the fourteenth to eighteenth centuries, and the wooden statue of St Elizabeth, patron saint of herbalists in the baroque era, one is infused with a neat, modest middle-class sense of intimacy.

This museum of palliatives against the outrages of time is a museum of history, which is the mundane branch of time – the agent of its inception and of its ravages – but also the remedy, the memory and the salvage of what has been. On the shelves the Austrian magazine of the Pharmacists' Union is flanked by *Pharmaceutica Hungariae*, a very hefty volume, *Taxa Pharmaceutica Posoniensis* by Ján Justus Torkos, published in 1745 in four languages: Latin, Slovak, Hungarian and German. Bratislava, capital of Slovakia, is one of the "hearts" of Mitteleuropa, with layer upon layer of centuries forever present, unresolved conflicts and lacerations, unhealed wounds and unreconciled contradictions. The memory, which is in its way a branch of medicine, preserves all this under glass, both the lips of the wounds and the passions which inflicted them.

The Central Europeans are ignorant of the science of forgetting, of filing away events. That manual of pharmacy in four languages, and that adjective "Posoniensis", remind me of how at school, my friends and I used to discuss the city's name, which ones we liked best: Bratislava, the Slovak name, Pressberg, the German one, or Poszony, the Hungarian name derived from Posonium, the ancient Roman outpost on the Danube. The fascination of those three names bestowed a special glamour on a composite, multinational history, and someone's preference for one or the other was, in a childish way, a basic stance taken towards the *Weltgeist*. That is to say, we had to choose between the instinctive celebration of great, powerful cultures such as the German, the ones that make history, or our romantic admiration for the exploits of rebellious, chivalrous and adventurous peoples such as the Magyars, or else our fellow-feeling for what is more subdued and hidden, for the small peoples such as the Slovaks, who remain for a long time a patient, unregarded substratum, a humble, fertile soil waiting centuries for the moment of its flowering.

In Bratislava, a town famous in the past for its excellent watchmakers and collectors of these artefacts, now on show in the museum in Zidovská (Hebrew) Street, one is aware of the imperious presence of ages woven through and through with conflict. The capital of one of the most ancient of Slav peoples was, for two centuries, the capital of the Kingdom of Hungary when practically all the latter, following the Battle of Mohács in 1526, was occupied by the Turks. It was to Bratislava that the Hapsburgs came to don the crown of St Stephen, and that as a young woman, after the death of her father, the Emperor Charles VI, Maria Theresa came to enlist the aid of the Hungarian nobility, bearing her newborn son Joseph in her arms. All that mattered in Bratislava at that time was the dominant Hungarian element, or perhaps to some extent the Austro-German one; the substratum of the Slovak peasantry had no standing or relevance whatsoever.

Until 1918 the Viennese thought of Bratislava as a sort of pleasant suburb, which they could get to in less than an hour and enjoy its white wines, a traditional product already flourishing at the time of the Slav kingdom of Great Moravia, in the ninth century, and watched over by St Urban, the patron saint of vintners. As we wander round the city, through charming baroque squares and small, abandoned byways, we get the impression that history, in passing by, has left many things here and there, things still full of life, that flourish again for us. Ladislav Novomeský, the greatest nineteenth-century Slovak poet, has a poem about a year he lost in a café, just like leaving behind an old umbrella. But things turn up again, and the old umbrellas of our lives, left here and there over the years, one time or another end up in our hands again.

2. WHERE ARE OUR CASTLES?

This is the title of an essay written in 1968 by Vladimir Mináč. The *Hrad*, the castle, soars above Bratislava with its mighty towers and robust symmetry, a massive fortress which combines the rough, indestructible loyalty of a sentinel with a fairy-tale remoteness. Slovakia is strewn with castles, fortresses and lordly dwellings; here, we have impregnable castles on peaks and hilltops, with their turreted Disneyland fantasies (but genuine), and there, manor houses and low-lying out-buildings, usually of an ochre colour, which dwindle little by little into the more familiar dimensions of large farm houses.

But what Mináč seems to say is that these castles are somewhere else, in another history that was not created by the Slovaks. Most of the gentlemen who resided in these mansions were Hungarian. The dwellings of the Slovak peasants were the *drevenice*, wooden huts held together with straw and dried dung. In the castle of Oravský Podzámok, in the Otava valley, there is a picture revealing the white complexion and plump hands of the Celsissimus Princeps Nicolaus Esterházy, while the hands of the peasants in the village beneath the castle even today are the colour of earth, wrinkled and knotty as the roots of trees writhing among the stones. The difference between those hands is a symbol of the history of these peoples. The Slovaks have for centuries been a downtrodden people, the obscure substratum of their country, not unlike the straw and dried dung which hold their huts

together. We have no history, writes Mináč, if this is made up solely of
kings, emperors, dukes, princes, victories, conquests, violence and
pillage. In a poem by Petöfi, the national poet of Hungary, the Slovak is
depicted, though in a good-natured way, as a red-nosed tinker in a
washed-out smock.

But what the nineteenth-century notion labelled "nations without a
history", as if they were mythical communities destined by nature to a
perennially land-bound, subordinate position, were nations which
some political or military defeat had deprived of their ruling classes.
Mináč argues furiously for the role of the Slovaks in this obscure but
patient work of construction, in which destructive violence was never
committed against others, but which has long been a losing game. In
1848, when revolutionary hopes set Europe ablaze, the Slovaks turned
to their Hungarian masters (themselves at that time in revolt against
the Hapsburgs) with the so-called "claims of Liptovský Mikuláš", a
demand for the most basic rights for their people. It was answered by
the Hungarian authorities with arrests and tough repressive measures.
The Austrians, for their part, once they had quelled the 1848 uprisings,
tried to make friends with the Hungarians and abandoned the Slovaks
to their tender mercies. After 1867, with the Double Monarchy, the fate
of the Slovaks was crushing oppression. Particularly on the grounds of
the Hungarian law of 1868, they were considered nothing more than a
sort of folk survival within the Magyar nation, denied their identity and
their language, and impeded in the running of their schools, while their
demands were quashed if need be with bloodshed, their social aspirations smothered, their delegates to parliament obstructed in every way.
The figures given in a monograph by L'udovít Holotík clearly show an
overwhelming Hungarian social and economic predominance, which
confined the Slovaks to a rural way of life, putting them quite out of
reach of cultural development or capitalistic enterprise, which is as
much as to say the formation of a middle class. This was the cause of
widespread emigration, largely to America. More than any other
element it was the Church – Catholic and Evangelical alike – which
safeguarded the nation, set up schools and defended the obscure,
despised Slovak language.

The question of the language created difficulties even within the Slav
brotherhood and its emancipation movement. A number of Czechs,
who were the leaders of the Austro-Slav movement, called for the use
of Czech as a written language even in Slovakia, with a view to giving
unity and efficiency to the movement; but at the same time this

relegated Slovak to the status of a dialect spoken in the home, clearly a subordinate tongue. Even Ján Kollár, the great Slovak intellectual assimilated by the Czechs, upheld these positions; but they were contested by his fellow-countrymen, who saw them as meaning the end of their identity, and demanded the independence of their language.

These tensions, still alive today in the rivalries between Czechs and Slovaks, undermined the unity of the Slav renaissance, and Austro-Slavism in particular. On one hand, in fact, in so far as they were a nation thrust into the sidelines and retaining their primitive character uncontaminated, the Slovaks considered themselves to be one of the original, genuine cradles of Slavia, of its ancient, unitary civilization, and for this reason felt particularly akin to the other peasant Slav nations, such as the Ruthenians and the Slovenians. As early as the eighteenth century Jan Baltazár Magin had words of praise for this flawless, pristine purity in the *Apologia* he wrote – in Latin – to rebut the denigrations of Michal Bencsik, a professor at the university of Trnava. Ján Kollár, who turned to the Czech language and wrote in Czech, but was a Slovak, expressed this exalted Slavophilism in his long poem *The Daughter of Sláva*, which dates from 1824. It was in Slovakia that messianic Slavophilism found its first expression, and not only earlier but more vigorously than among the Czechs.

These ferments were susceptible to different and even conflicting developments. One possible outlet was filo-Russian Panslavism, another was Austro-Slavism, as championed by such a pugnacious leader as Milan Hodža, who was close to the three-pronged ideas and projects of Francis Ferdinand. But if the Austro-Slavism professed by the Czechs could hold out some hopes of securing a position of consequence in the desired structure of the Empire, the Slovaks were in a different situation: under pressure to become Hungarianized and at the same time rather firmly divided from the Czechs, it was hard for them to see any way of escaping their minority situation. Towards the end of his life the revolutionary poet and patriot of 1848, L'dovit Štur, wrote a book called *Slavia and the World of the Future*, in which he prophesied the dissolution of the Hapsburg Empire.

Štanislav Šmatlák, an essayist and member of the Academy of Sciences, tells me that Slovak literature has been the plaintiff in the lawcourt of world history, bearing witness to its "tremendous power of annihilation", as Nietzsche put it. In one of his pieces, written for the conference on peace, which took place in Prague, Šmatlák commemorated these painful yet pacific traditions as the thread which runs through the entire literature of his country, from the *Gentis Slavonicae lacrimae, suspiria et vota* (1645) by Jakub Jacobeus, or the *Desiderium aureae pacis* (1633) by Michal Institoris – two Latin compositions which lament and indict the tragedies of war – down to the *Bloody Sonnets* published in the fateful year of 1914 by Hviezdoslav, one of the fathers of the nation's poetry, and whose statue may be seen in the main square of practically every town, large or small.

These themes emerge in recent literature as well. Mihálik writes a poem about the dreams of serving-maids, while Válek's lines speak of the life of an old grandmother whose days were marked as if by whiplashes or the plain grooved by the carriage-wheels of the gentry – grooves imbued with sweat and blood. In a wonderful story called *The Priest*, that vigorous, fertile storyteller František Švantner describes the humble, uncertain awakening of an ethical-political consciousness during the nationwide uprising against Fascism in 1944, a thing that emerges gradually from centuries of the repetitive life of the peasantry, a life completely ruled by the seasons, the soil, the cycle of agricultural production. In a trilogy of novels Vincent Šikula brings the historical events of the nation back to life, but as seen from below, from the point of view of the obscure, oppressed classes. Even *The Millenial Bee*, the novel by Peter Jaroš which became famous thanks to the film version of it shown at the Venice Festival in 1983, is the saga of a family of bricklayers in the Liptov region.

The history of these peoples has not been an easy one. On a coat of arms in the City Museum of Bratislava the Hapsburg two-headed eagle is glossed by the words "sub umbra alarum tuarum", but the Slovaks did not rest under the shadow of any wings, they were not subject to the tolerant, fair-dealing Austrian administration, often raised by the Slav peoples to the level of myth, but to the markedly nationalistic dominance of the Hungarians. The Pan-Slavic ideology, or the claim to an ancient national identity, is explained by the need of the Slav peoples to defend themselves, by exalting the myth of their own indestructible essence, against power and against culture fascinated by power, which denies dignity and a future to those who have until that time remained in shadow.

The nineteenth-century philosophers who traced out the necessary laws of historical "becoming" were often neither tender nor optimistic with regard to the minor nations, as many of the Slav nations were minor. Those fascinated by the "great world" of politics often forget that even the great powers were once small, that the time of ascendancy and of decline comes for all, and that even for the smallest comes the time to raise their heads.

But a small people which has to shake off the disdain or indifference of the great – of those whose greatness may perhaps have only a little while to run – must also shake off its complex about being small, the feeling of having constantly to rectify or cancel this impression, or else totally reverse it, glorying in it as a sign of election. Those who have long been forced to put all their efforts into the determination and defence of their own identity tend to prolong this attitude even when it is no longer necessary. Turned inward on themselves, absorbed in the assertion of their own identity and intent on making sure that others give it due recognition, they run the risk of devoting all their energies to this defence, thereby shrinking the horizons of their experience, of lacking magnanimity in their dealings with the world.

Kafka, in spite of being so fascinated by the life of the Jewish ghetto and its literature, sadly but sternly proclaimed that a poet must remain detached from the literature of any small people, which does not tolerate a great writer because it is forced to defend itself from outside influences, and is wholly taken up with this struggle for survival. Giuliano Baioni has written that Kafka consciously became that great writer rejected by a minor, oppressed literature, intent on defending its own national identity and culture and eager for positive and consoling voices; rejected because such a writer creates a void around himself, provokes schisms and imperils the compactness of the little community.

A writer is not the father of a family but a son, and he must leave home and find his own way. He is faithful to his harassed little country if he bears witness to the truth of it, or if he suffers its oppression unstintingly and takes it upon himself, and if at the same time he transcends it, with that stern distancing needed by every kind of art and every liberating experience. Even today the relation between Czechs and Slovaks has to free itself of a reciprocal spiral of suspicion and distrust, the shadows of old prejudices on the one side, but also persistent retaliations on the other.

The most lively trends in Slovak culture display this freedom, and simply because it is enamoured of its own green and pleasant land it is able also to reveal its failures and shortcomings. In 1924 Štefan Krčméry complained about how difficult it was to write a Slovak social novel: political conditions were too restricting and views and experience too limited. Today, in spite of the heavy hand of a police state, one

gets the impression of a country in which people have retaken possession of their own history, or are in the process of doing so. It is as if
the styles of the public buildings and the houses of the lords and gentry,
the Austrian and Hungarian styles which tower above the Slav flatlands
with their one-storey peasant houses, were gradually merging with the
latter, and no longer crushing them with their loftiness and grandeur.

The castle of Pezinok, an ancient royal free town surrounded by
vineyards, merges imperceptibly with the ramparts, where there is a
local *vinarna*, which offers fairly rudimentary accommodation but
good fish and good white wine. It may be that Justice – which is
represented on the roof of a public building in Oravský Podzámok by a
statue with the scales and, rather than a sword, a far more frightening
scimitar – has cleanly cut a number of iniquitous Gordian knots, and
has brought that fish and that wine, at one time the privilege of the
overlords, to more accessible tables.

Slovakia, though it made some considerable contributions to the
spring of 1968, was paradoxically spared and even benefited by the
brutal Soviet and pro-Soviet reaction of that August, which suffocated
and extinguished Czech culture. While Prague was, as it were, decapi-
tated, the totalitarian restoration of 1968, while it was certainly savage
in repressing civil liberties and the rights of the individual, nevertheless
increased the political weight of the local population, either as a result
of political calculation or out of faith in the Pan-Slavic (and therefore
pro-Russian) tradition of the country. Slovakia today is therefore at
one and the same time beneath an iron heel and in a phase of historical
regeneration, with an expanding role in affairs. Ever since the events of
1968 the splendid city of Prague has given an impression of being under
the spell of neglect and death, while Bratislava, in spite of everything, is
sanguine and cheerful, a vital world in an expansive phase, looking not
to the melancholy of the past, but to growth and the future.

3. THAT OBSCURE OBJECT OF DESIRE

Even though we are in Slovakia, which is proud of its wines, it seems
perfectly legitimate to want a glass of beer, since Czechoslovakia
produces some of the finest beers in the world. But this wish is almost
impossible to fulfil, like attempts to make love or to eat in a famous film

by Buñuel. Amedeo, though thirsty, is accommodating, but Gigi, whose brow is quick to darken, begins to live up to his fearful reputation. Whether in the most famous places, such as the *Vel'ki Františkani*, or in ordinary bars, the request for a beer seems to the waiter quite bizarre. In one bar we asked in vain for *pivo*, and were told elsewhere that perhaps we should have asked straight out for Pilsen or Budweis, two particularly well-known brands.

The *Kyjev* Hotel is one of those big hotels typical of the eastern European countries, luxurious and yet dreary and a bit disreputable; here foreigners can find anything at all, from the most expensive liqueurs to available female company – certain Arabs from Kuwait spend nights with them which are embarrassingly noisy for their more temperate neighbours. But even at the *Kyjev* beer is a chimera; one evening, from under the counter, the porter furtively produces a lukewarm bottle for us.

The length and breadth of valleys and rivers, through towns, over hills, from the lowlands to the high Tatras, our search becomes nervous and disordered, while the guide-books we consult go on for page after page, lauding the various beers of each single place, telling us about their degree of alcohol, the differing pressures in the barrels, the nuances of colour and the subtly different ways in which the froth froths. Some of us attribute our failure to a sudden seizing up of the mechanisms of distribution, and begin to reflect upon our Socialist convictions, while others see it as a national Slovak Fronde in opposition to the Czech national beverage. When we enter an inn at Podbiel, a small town in the Tatras, there are foaming tankards on the tables, but when it comes to our turn the barrel has run out. At Trenčín, beneath the vast castle, a waiter finally approaches us with a few beers, but a few steps from our table he trips up, the glasses shatter on the ground, and long, methodical labours of gathering up the fragments, sweeping and washing the floor, drying it and putting the rags away, once more postpone the fulfilment of our desire until some other stop in the unknown future.

4. TO EACH HIS HOUR

Gondola Ilica is the seat of the Philosophy Faculty of Bratislava University, which is named after Comenius, the philosopher and teacher whose *Orbis Pictus* is to be found, in old editions in four languages, in the library of the old Slovak towns. The dignity of these buildings reminds me of a singular figure to whom I owe my interest in German culture ever since I was a schoolboy, and my discovery of the world of the Danube. He taught in a secondary school, though in his young days had been reader in Italian at these universities in Mitteleuropa, whose atmosphere he conveyed with effective and intense ham acting. I will call him Trani. He was a little like Napoleon when already fat and a little like Shylock. His marked features, never well shaven or rinsed, formed the impenetrable mask of a great actor, a personage ostensibly destined to play a leading role in the great theatre of the world, to be a great man, but whom fate had consigned to teaching German to schoolboys.

Pupils and teachers had many and justified reasons for complaining about him, for his eager, theatrical, reticent personality was not without shadows, and his open-mindedness could be very far from praiseworthy, but it is to his genius that we are indebted for a number of basic intuitions. He did not consider us an audience unworthy of his gifts, which could and should have given proof of themselves in far loftier places, but he studied the *coups de scène* of his actions for us as if we had been the audience at the *Comédie Française* or the Swedish Royal Academy, which confers imperishable glory.

With us he only spoke in German or Triestino dialect. To make us understand what poetry was, he read us those lines of Dante's about the siren in mid-sea who misleads sailors, and when he wanted to make us understand what poetry, in his opinion, was not, he read those lines of Carducci's about Tittì, who is not clad simply in feathers and has more than just cypress berries to eat. Only the bad taste of an Italian professor, he said, could grudge his daughter the few pennies that he had to fork out for her maintenance. There are certain conventions, he added, that must be respected: if someone should ring the door bell at Professor Carducci's, the door cannot possibly be opened by the professor's daughter in the nude. You ought to have thought first, he said in dialect, because you don't have to have children, but now that you have a daughter, love her, enjoy her, maintain her. But he became most furious when he read the poet's nostalgic invocation immediately corrected for reasons of prudence and opportunism: "Ah with what warm heart would I stay with you . . . with what warm heart! But, little cypress trees, ah let me go . . ." Really and truly scandalous, was his comment. "It's as if I were to say, 'Magris, I'm going to Paris; shall I call in on your grandmother?' – 'Oh, that would be splendid. Poor old dear, she'll be so pleased.' – 'But, you know, I'm only there for two days, and I've a lot to do, and she's out in the suburbs, I'd have to change trains three times and then take a bus . . .' – 'Oh go to hell then, who asked you for anything!'"

He wanted to teach us to despise the soppy mush of feeling, the false generosity that for an instant, and in all good faith, promises the sun, moon and stars, convinced of its own generous impulse, but that for all sorts of sound, valid reasons draws back when it comes to the point. In his way he was really fond of us, and wished to prepare us for the pitilessness of life. "For tomorrow I want 300 lines by heart," he would say. "Anyone who doesn't know them gets a Fail. I know this is unfair, because it's impossible to learn 300 lines in a day, but life's unfair and demands impossible things, and I'm training you to put up with it and not to let it suddenly overwhelm you. So tomorrow it's sink or swim."

To that man, the butt of so many criticisms at the Parents' Meetings, I owe not only my discovery of Central European culture, but also of one of the most important and unusual lessons in morality. If it is true that he trafficked in private lessons, then he was unable to practise strict justice himself, but to us he taught the sense of what is right and contempt for what is wrong. Like so many classes, our class had its victim, a fat, very timorous lad who blushed and sweated at the drop of a hat, who was unable to trade insults and was the object of that unwitting but no less blameworthy cruelty that we all have in us; cruelty which, if not kept at bay by some precise law imposed from within or without, will flare up in spite of ourselves to the detriment of whoever is weak at that moment.

Not one of us was innocent in his regard, and none of us was aware of being guilty. One day, while with theatrical gestures Trani was teaching us the conjugation of the German strong verbs, this boy's next-door neighbour, by the name of Sandrin, suddenly seized his fountain pen and snapped it in half. I can still see the victim's face as it grew red and sweaty, and his eyes filling with tears at the injustice of it, and his awareness that he was incapable of putting up a fight. When the teacher asked him why he had done that, Sandrin answered, "I felt

nervous . . . and when I'm nervous I can't control myself . . . I'm just
made like this, it's my nature." To our astonishment – and to the
delight of the aggressor and greater humiliation of the offended party –
Trani replied: "I understand. You couldn't do anything else, you're just
made that way, it's your nature. We can't blame you, it's just life, that's
all . . ." And he went on with the lesson.

A quarter of an hour later he began to complain about the fug, to
loosen his tie and unbutton his waistcoat, to open the window and
slam it shut again, to tell us that his nerves were on edge until, feigning
a sudden fit of rage, he seized hold of Sandrin's pens, pencils and
note-books, snapped them and ripped them and threw them all over
the place. Then, affecting to grow calm, he said to Sandrin: "I'm so
sorry, dear boy, I had a fit of nerves. I'm made like that, it's my nature.
There's nothing I can do about it, it's just life . . ." And he returned to
the German strong verbs.

Ever since then I have understood that strength, intelligence, stupidity, beauty, cowardice and weakness are situations and roles which
sooner or later happen to everyone. Anyone who dishonestly appeals
to the mischance of life or of his own nature will, whether it be an hour
later or a year, be repaid in the name of those same ineffable reasons.
The same thing happens with peoples, with their virtues, their periods
of decline and of prosperity. It is unlikely that an official of the Third
Reich concerned with the "final solution" could have imagined that
only a few years later the Jews would create a state with enormous
military capacity and efficiency. Bratislava, the bustling capital of a
small people long trodden underfoot, brings to mind memories and
thoughts such as this, including that lesson in justice from the distant
past.

5. A WORKING-CLASS DANUBIAN SUNDAY

Nedel'a (Sunday) is the title of one of the most famous books by
Ladislav Novomeský, published in 1927. From the very start of his
career Novomeský posed himself the question of his nation's identity –
ever since, as a young man, he had heard its very existence denied. An
avant-garde poet and a militant Communist, in both his work and his
political activity, he has fought parallel battles for the national culture

and for the internationalist viewpoint, for the "melancholy of the East" which, as he says in one of his poems, runs in his veins, and also the Marxist revolution. In the struggle for this latter he saw the deliverance of all the oppressed, and therefore of his own people – an almost completely proletarian nation. The precarious frontiers of Slovakia, which have often left the country open to foreign domination, become in his lyric poetry the symbol of a world without frontiers.

But the "melancholy Danubian procession" which the critic Stefan Krčméry sees in *Sunday*, is not just a procession of the humble, sorrowful destinies celebrated by Novomeský; it is also the melancholy of a contradiction which pervades all his poetry, constituting its greatness and making it one of the nerve centres of Slovak culture and politics. In the beginning Novomeský's art is rebel art, *poésie maudite*, a symbiosis of the poetry of revolution and the revolution of poetry. It is that negation of what is, which pervades the avant-garde throughout Europe and which, in socially committed poetry, aims to overturn reality and create a new reality and a new mankind, free from the chains of alienation.

But if at the beginning the melancholy of poetry is its futility in an alienated world, later on – with the advent of real Socialism – it is the feeling of being futile in a world which needs the prose of labour and not the poetry of revolutionary expectancy, which the new system, according to how one looks at it, has either achieved or belied. And it would be sadder still, with the Revolution as an accomplished fact, to have to repeat a phrase written years earlier, in a moment of depression while awaiting the Revolution:

> "This childlike poetry
> Did not change the face of the world."

Novomeský has never been prone to this disillusionment, even when he was arrested in 1951 and condemned as a "bourgeois nationalist", remaining in prison until 1956. Seated at the pleasant table in the *Klastorna* cellars, among barrels from which they draw smooth, fragrant wines, Šmatlák talks to me at length about Novomeský, who represents not merely the poetry he has written but also an exemplar for the whole of recent Slovak history. Here the memory that still smarts is not that of 1968, of events in Prague in the spring of that year, but that of 1951, of the Stalinist trials of the 1950s which mowed down the flower of Communism. In the West, Communists only began in 1956 to become aware of Soviet totalitarianism. The trials and executions which took place in the early 1950s, all the more serious because they were perverse and unmotivated, at that time only shook a handful of militants.

Rehabilitated with full honours in 1963, Novomeský, who died in 1976, did not side with the spring uprising in Prague. To praise him today is, in part, to praise a figure who stands for what is claimed to be the continuity of Communism, a continuity violated by what are officially considered to be the bloody distortions of Stalinism, but not violated, nay restored, by the Soviet intervention of 1968 – so preaches the rigid official ideology. Novomeský is thus the symbol of a poetry rooted in the Slovak, internationalist, anti-Stalinist humus, but foreign to the tumults of 1968. Paradoxically, his dramatic destiny supplies an alibi for the conservatism and authoritarianism of the regime.

One gets the impression – no more than an impression, in view of the reticence which is *de rigueur* on this subject – that people in Bratislava were more easily reconciled to the restoration carried out by the Soviets in 1968. As Enzo Bettiza wrote at the time, until the eve of that spring Bratislava had played the role of an effective opposition, combining a strong thrust towards internal democratization with an emotional and spiritual closeness to Russia. The changes, both real and purely formal, introduced since 1968, have increased the importance of Slovakia within the state and have given the Slovaks some measure of satisfaction and compensation, in comparison with the desert created among the Czechs and in Czech literature.

If Czech literature has been thrown out of office, and now survives only amongst exiles, while those writers who have remained in the country have to choose between being ghosts, parasites or Kafka's animal which digs itself underground tunnels, Slovak literature today has its own effective organic unity, even when it clamours for a new "epic" and a new positivity, a political and social function of collaboration rather than of opposition. There is certainly a measure of opportunism in the criticisms levelled at Mňačko, the writer who emigrated to Israel, and whose *Belated Reportages* were in the 1960s a highly popular indictment of the Stalinist terror; but the story called *Fever*, in which Jozef Kot shows the uprising of 1968 in a critical light, cannot be compared at all with the servile encomiums with which, in the 1950s, certain intellectuals in Czechoslovakia gave their assent to the elimination of friends or Party colleagues.

The assertive epic quality now frequently to be found in Slovak literature is not acceptable to the poetic taste of Western countries, but perhaps it is appropriate to a nation under the weight of an oppressive bureaucratic élite, which nonetheless feels itself to be the subject of its own history to a greater extent than in the past, and is therefore in a phase of initiation, not of imitation. The world has been changed, even though in all probability not by the poetry of Novomeský.

6. ROADSIDE CEMETERIES

One of Novomeský's poems is about a Slovak cemetery. In many mountain villages the cemetery has no wall, or one that you would barely notice. These places are unconfined and spread into the field, or border the roadside as at Matiašovce near the Polish frontier; or else they are simply there at the edge of the village, like a garden in front of a house. This epic familiarity with death, found again, for example, in the Muslim tombs in Bosnia, quietly set in the orchard of the dwelling – things which our own world neurotically tends more and more to set apart – has the measure of how things ought to be, a feeling of the relationships between the individual and the generations, the earth, nature, the elements which compose it and the law which presides over their combination and dispersal.

In the windows of the shacks beside these cemeteries appear broad, good-humoured faces, resembling the good, sound wood of which the houses are made. Those cemeteries which know nothing of sadness tell us how deceitful and superficial is the fear of death. As these cemeteries are located side by side with everyday life, rather than in a place remote from it, maybe we ought to learn to look at death from the other side of it. A poem by Milan Rúfus contains the lines:

"Only before us does death strike fear.
Behind us
it is suddenly all beautiful and innocent.
A carnival mask in which,
after midnight, you collect water
to drink or, if you are sweaty, to wash."

In the violet of an inexpressible sunset the high Tatras are already black outlines, sharing the profound mystery of all great mountains. Amedeo and Gigi are commenting on the play of light, the effects of refraction, the relation between those distant things and the perception which we have of them. At this moment we are all convinced that this blue and violet evening must exist somewhere, and in some way, forever, in the hyper-uranian world or the mind of God, as the incorruptible and everlasting Platonic Idea of Evening. It seems to us that those outlines, that light, that splendour materially contain in themselves these days through which we are passing, and their secret, like a fairy-tale lamp or ring that one only has to rub for a Genie to appear.

As we drive through the dark wood the headlights suddenly flash onto a signpost marked "Matliary, 2 km". In the sanatorium at Matliary Kafka spent the months December 1920 to August 1921. The moment the lights unexpectedly pick this sign out of the darkness I remember a photograph showing Kafka in a group, with a timid, almost happy smile; and in the background are these trees of Matliary. That photograph, with that dark and utterly mysterious foliage, and this same wood which we are passing through this moment, are like walls of infinite thinness that have been blown away. That life which the photograph fixed in one of its instants has vanished for ever. Not even Kafka's work renders up its secret entirely, because it too is paper, though far more real and substantial; but it is still unequal to the vanishing of existence, as even to the shadows of the wood we are passing through.

The holiday resorts in the Tatra Mountains, such as Tatranska Lomnica, sport a *belle époque* luxury tourist décor. Apart from Czechoslovaks, most of the present clientele comes from East Germany. The elegance of these resorts is not without some of the ostentatious unreality of places which only exist in the holiday season, or where the latter has overwhelmed or completely erased the original existence and life of the community. Vulgarity triumphs, showy and sophisticated, when people go to a town not simply to enjoy tranquil or prohibited pleasures, but rather to celebrate a rite which they consider necessary to their own rank and style. A libertine who indulges his own inclinations is not vulgar; but he becomes vulgar if as he does so he is concerned not only with enjoying his pleasures, but also with making a meaningful gesture which raises him a cut above other people.

A specific élite which carries out its historical and political function – an aristocracy still in command or a military caste in power – can even be odious and criminal, but it is neither gross nor snobbish, because it is doing a real, impersonal job which transcends each individual member. The visiting celebrities who created the myth of Capri have very often been stigmatized as vulgar, in so far as they constitute a dreary crowd of eccentrics, not representative of anything at all, but convinced of representing something thanks to their predictable capriciousness and ostentation of elegance. We are therefore not too unwilling to leave the restaurant of a big hotel in the Tatras, even if the meal was decent and at last – thanks to the international atmosphere – we have been able to drink a decent glass of beer.

8. OLD BOOKS, LIFE AND LAW

In the post-war years the second-hand bookshops in Czechoslovakia were a gold-mine for people interested in German studies. Families of German origin, but resident here for centuries, were expelled: a stupid act of injustice which, aimed at avenging the infamy of Nazism, simply deprived the country of one of its essential components. These families left the country, and they sold their books. In the second-hand bookshops one could reach out and touch the liquidation of German culture in Czechoslovakia. Now many years have passed, the traces of that tragic exodus have been all but erased, and few of those books are to be found. On the other hand we come across bound volumes of *Lecture illustrée*, a delightful French magazine published at the end of the last century, and two Latin tomes of *Ethica catholica* (*Generalis* and *Specialis*) by Dr Josepho Kachník, professor in the theological faculty at Olmütz in Moravia, issued at Olomucii (Olmütz) in 1910.

Dr Kachník's work is a treatise without any claim to originality, but presumes only to expound the doctrine of the Church. He embraces the whole range of human actions, the alternatives they offer and the rules to be followed; he studies and classifies the freedom and the necessity to act, the order and nature of human and religious laws, obligations and exceptions, customs and departures, circumstances and passions, distinctions between the various sins and the various virtues. He gives a survey of adultery and of the phenomenology of drunkenness, he deals with moral and social values, with all the impediments, the attenuating and aggravating circumstances, the phantoms which cause bewilderment in the conscience and the insidious self-deceits with which the conscience tries to bamboozle itself.

One chapter, of extraordinary psychological insight and rhetorical expertise, is devoted to the over-scrupulous conscience, to the neurotic disability of those who are obsessed by sin and see it everywhere, who confess themselves with maniacal insistence to one confessor after another without allowing themselves to be convinced by any of them, or cured of their groundless fears; and who lose themselves and wander off into the desert of their own anguish and pride, into moralistic quibbles about what is fair and what not, their opinions vacillating from one moment to the next.

The logical Doctor, who is not without his comic pedantries and naïvely clerical conclusions, sees acutely that these obsessions of the overly rigorous conscience, which the Church considers an evil and a sin, are in fact a disease, a mental disposition which comes "e corporis constitutione", from a melancholic temperament and organic malfunctions. Depression tending towards feelings of remorse is the result of some evil affection of the nerves and brain, "nervorum atque cerebri mala affectio", which corrodes the psychophysical integrity of the individual. The over-rigorous conscience has nothing to do with morality, but with a mixture of stubborn pride, unwilling to allow itself to be persuaded that it has not sinned, and neurotic *Angst*. A person with such a conscience "without any reason fears that he is sinning, both before and after acting, discovers sin in places where it in no way is, tortures himself uselessly over the most insignificant causes and, even when he is assured that a thing is licit, persists in believing that it might be wrong."

Timorous boys and girls, observes the Doctor, might out of ignorance be disturbed by scruples relating to the matter of the Sixth Commandment, but proper instruction can easily free them from this. He urges confessors to be patient with the over-scrupulous, though not to pander to their phobias, but rather to give them the firmness they require, preventing them from indulging in their obsessive, self-satisfied guilt complexes, and during confession going at length into all their fancies, manias and supposed sins, especially "si de turpibus agitur." To the over-scrupulous themselves, among various remedies he exhorts them not to keep company with other neurotics, but above all to overcome that horror of society and love of solitude which are false signs of profundity and spiritual election. He urges them to accept human intercourse and sociability which, as even Goethe's Mephistopheles knew, are the conditions in which each one of us truly finds himself.

In one volume of *Lecture illustrée* a French physiognomist describes the mouth of Cléo de Mérode, the voluptuous actress – "broad, avid, curious" at fifteen, but latterly "shut tight . . . as befits a self-satisfied person with nothing to learn . . ." The French physiognomist and the theologian's high-flown Latin seem to be set in contrast – both full of charm and wisdom – as two ways of understanding and living life. The story which the physiognomist reads from the mouth of the lovely actress is a story which one can sense but not explain, a life which without wishing it or knowing it has tended towards melancholy. It is a life of the dark depth and the fleeting surface, which comes and gives the impression of not being able either to choose or to explain. The moral theologian, on the other hand, does not allow himself to be drawn or dismayed by the indistinct flowing of existence, by the vague shadow or contradictory murmuring of a state of mind. He wants to make things clear, to establish laws, to fix the universal nature of the concept.

It is more fun to side with life than with law, with mobile, spontaneous creativity than with the symmetry of a code of regulations. But poetry dwells more in Dante's triplets than in any vague formlessness. Moral creativity is the ability to find a law and establish it freely. Only the power to put order into the fluctuating contradictions of life can do justice to those contradictions; they are rhetorically falsified when we see in them and their ill-defined vacillations the supreme truths of existence and mistake them for mental activity. Marcus Aurelius warned otherwise.

When we confuse all gestures and actions, putting them all on the same plane in the name of the philosophy of "that's just life" which Professor Trani refused to let my schoolfellow Sandrin get away with, then the face of justice is darkened and vitality itself grows sad, shackled with falsehood. The sense and rigour of law do not suffocate passion, but endow it with strength and reality. If Cléo de Mérode had studied Latin, and Dr Kachník's treatise, maybe the shadow of sadness might not have fallen across her lovely mouth, because the Doctor of Olmütz taught above all that we must not allow ourselves to be overcome by sophisms and the weaknesses of "indoles melancholica . . ."

SIX

Pannonia

1. AT THE GATES OF ASIA?

The yellow of the sunflowers and maize is spread over the fields as if summer had set up camp among these hills. Hungary – which the eighteenth-century Hapsburg chancellor Hörnigk, supporter of a mercantilist economy, wished to turn into the granary of the Empire – is redolent of this warm, vivid colour which extends to the orange-ochre hues of the buildings large and small.

If not the journey itself, at least the pretension to talk about it starts to get a little hazardous, because the most diligent – and diligently consulted – bibliography does not cater for a shaky fund of knowledge; and in a country where they speak an agglutinative language one cannot pretend to move around with the same ease as one moves through the streets and among the people of Vienna. The traveller feels a little more superfluous than usual, a character in one of those "hitch-hiking novels" popular in the 1970s with a generation of Hungarian writers: these were people who had grown up in a climate of internal political *détente*, of liberal wellbeing, and impatiently pawed the ground when faced with what they considered to be the over-cautious progress of Hungarian society. They therefore fell into a state of impotence and emptiness, viewing existence itself as a roving, intermittent thing, like the aimless vagrancy of their protagonists, whose lives depend on the lifts they get.

It may therefore happen that my Danubian note-book, along this stretch of the river, will end by resembling the "prose in jeans" (as J. D. Salinger calls it) of those authors, and the rambling inconsequence of their conversations. Besides, not even far more decorous clothing is a guarantee against reckless judgments. The Iron Curtain, which at the Austro-Hungarian frontier separates the hemispheres of influence of the two world superpowers, prompts one to make large, facile metapolitical definitions, lapidary formulations of universal history such as that of Prince Metternich, who said that immediately across the Rennweg, the street which runs right through Vienna, one is already in the Balkans, and in Asia.

This strong and yet slothful Magyar landscape would already be the

Orient, a still-fresh memory of the Asian steppes, of Huns and Pechenegs and of the Crescent. Cioran celebrates the Danube basin as an amalgam of vital but obscure peoples, ignorant of history, or rather of the ideological periods invented by Western historiography; as the womb and sap of a culture not yet devitalized, in his eyes, by rationalism or progress.

This visceral feeling, which proclaims itself immune from ideology, is an ideological artifice. A moment spent in a Budapest pastry-shop or bookshop will give the lie to anyone who thinks that an indistinct sort of Asiatic womb begins just east of Austria. When we enter the great Hungarian plains we are certainly entering a Europe that is in part "other", a melting-pot composed of elements rather different from those that form the clays of the West. The poetry of Endre Ady, the greatest Hungarian poet of the twentieth century, is darkly oppressed by the age-old burden which, as has been said, weighs on the Hungarians; that is, the necessary and often impossible choice between East and West. In Hungarian history the choice has in fact often been more an imposition, from the Turkish conquest to the link with the Hapsburgs and the Soviet bloc. Or else it has been a forced decision: "The West has rejected us, so we turn to the East," said the Social Democrat leader Garbai in 1919, during the brief Republic of the Councils. In the last century, the novelist Zsigmond Kemény asserted that the function of Hungary was to defend the multi-national nature of the Hapsburg Empire, splitting Germanism and Slavism and preventing either of them becoming supreme.

The nationalistic passion of the Magyars, which runs with heroic and ferocious fury all through Hungarian history, is born from a land in which wave after wave of invasions and immigrations, Huns and Avars, Slavs and Magyars, Tartars and Kumans, Jazigs and Pechenegs, Turks and Germans are superimposed and deposited one upon another in layer after layer. The migrations of peoples bring devastation, but also civilization, like the Turks, who not only brought plunder but also the culture of Islam. They produce mixtures, the secret roots of every nationalism and its obsession with ethnic purity, as in the legend of the Hunnish origin of the Hungarians. Janus Pannonius, the fifteenth-century poet and humanist, was of Croatian origin, as was the aristo-cratic family of the Zríny, which fathered heroes and poets of the Hungarian "epic". The mother of Petöfi, the Magyar national poet, could not speak Hungarian, while Count Szécheny, a great patriot and father of the cultural conscience of the nation, learnt it when he was

thirty-four. The symbol of the irredentist protest against the Hapsburgs, the tulip which Kossuth's followers wore in their buttonholes, is
the flower brought by the Ottoman dominators and celebrated in their
national poetry as an emblem of Turkish civilization. The national
"passion" is the imperious necessity not simply to be, but – as in Mór
Jókai's novel *The New Squire*, written in the mid-nineteenth century –
also to become ardent Hungarian patriots.

Hungary was a whole range of different cultures, a mosaic in which
diverse sovereignties flourished, and occasionally intersected: the
Hapsburg territories, the *villayet* or Turkish districts, the principality of
Transylvania. At the end of the eighteenth century, with the gradual
withdrawal of Ottoman power, Austrian dominion asserted itself
throughout the country. In his book *Hungary in the Year 1677*, Marshal
Montecuccoli, leader of the military party, wrote that the Hungarians
were "proud, restless, voluble, impossible to satisfy. They retain the
nature of the Scythians and the Tartars, from whom they originate.
They yearn for unbridled licence . . . A Proteus every one of them, now
loving and now falling out of love, quick to raise up and quick to bring
low, they demand at one moment and reject the next . . ."

The energetic marshal had no intention of expressing racial prejudices. With his anti-reformist, Germanizing programme, he saw
Magyar particularism as constant, bloody chaos, a total absence of
clear, distinct laws, a riotous, centrifugal multiplicity that had to be
tamed by the schematizing, unifying imperial state, and thus brought
back to orderly conformity, "governed with an iron rod and vigorously
reined in". Making allowances for the inevitable differences between
historical phenomena occurring centuries apart, the absolutist policy
adopted by the Hapsburgs in the years 1849–60 was inspired by an
analogous process of levelling down.

But this modernizing process of levelling and centralizing constitutes an exception in the centuries-old policy of the Hapsburgs, which
is more inclined to rely on flexible prudence, on wary carelessness.
Hapsburg sovereignty is not the levelling, centralist despotism of
Louis XIV, Frederick the Great or Napoleon, but tends more to
administer the resistance which universalism and medieval particularism put up in opposition to the modern state. The Hapsburg art of
government does not stifle dissidence or overcome contradictions, but
covers and composes them in an ever-provisional equilibrium, allowing them substantially to go on as they are and, if anything, playing
them off against one another. The ruler of the Empire is, by definition,

a Proteus himself, changing his mask and his policy with supple mobility, and he therefore has no wish to transform his Protean subjects into a set of identical citizens. On the contrary, he allows them to pass from love to rebellion and vice versa, from depression to euphoria, in a game without end and without progress. He has no wish to impose some rigid unity on the various peoples, but to let them be themselves and live together in all their heterogeneity.

Rather than violating and absorbing society – or rather, the various societies – the state attempts to touch them as little as possible. The Hapsburg bureaucracy is scrupulous and far-seeing, but it seems to confine itself to drawing lovely, orderly maps, like those of the Danube prepared between 1816 and 1820 by the office responsible for the cartographical description of the Danube, mainly under the auspices of Chief Engineer Otto Hieronymi and the Inspector of Navigation Paul Vásárhelyi. Behind and beneath the maps the life of the river flows calmly on, with its boats and its fishing-lines, which require no recourse to cartography.

The state seems to wish to see politics forgotten, or at least to lessen the extent of their interference, to slow up and attenuate change, to convince its subjects that changes occur over long periods of time, and are therefore more noticeable to generations than to individuals; to leave things as they are for as long as possible, things and feelings and passions and memories. In a poem by János Arany, Petőfi's great friend, we find an old man strumming a zither, and drawing forth old Magyar sounds, the national microcosm buried and preserved in the memory of the people, voices that tell of the deeds of ancient times, echoes of the ringing hoofs of the Hun cavalry. The Compromise of 1867, the *Ausgleich* which brought into being the double Austro-Hungarian monarchy, was the greatest attempt on the part of the Hapsburgs to transform a wound in its side – Hungarian separatism – into a medicine; to draw the fangs of that zither and its songs by making room for them beneath its own crown, to survive by allowing the rebel power and the role of Hungary to remain intact, and even to reinforce them.

Historians still argue over whether the Compromise of 1867 was, politically and economically, a victory for the Austrians over the Hungarians or vice versa. That the Austro-Hungarian monarchy was certainly not marked by harmony, but rather by tension between its two elements, is a well-known fact, we only have to take our pick among episodes and anecdotes. Count Károlyi tells us that his great-grandfather had a votive chapel built to thank God for the defeat suffered by the Hapsburg army at Kñiggtätz, and that his mother, whenever she had to go to Vienna, passed through the town in a carriage with her eyes shut, so as not to see it. Tisza, the Hungarian political leader, in 1903 defined the Austrian Prime Minister Koerber as an illustrious foreigner, while for Bánffy, ex-Prime Minister of Hungary, the Hungarians economically damaged by the customs tariffs in Cisleithania should be considered as war deaths, and their families ought to be treated accordingly.

Perhaps some measure of Austro-Hungarian solidarity exists only now, on account of the end of the Empire and the fact of the Eastern bloc, which gives rise to nostalgia for "Mitteleuropa" and inspires projects such as the parallel revision of Austrian and Hungarian schoolbooks and the correction of nationalistic views on either side. Likewise, the foundation of a multi-national "Danubian University" and a knowledge of the common Austro-Hungarian culture serve as a prelude to the formation of a common cultural consciousness. The Rennweg is not the border of Asia.

2. THE KING IN DISGUISE

The melancholy, symmetrical dignity of the Hapsburg buildings of Sopron provides a frame of decorum and stability for that slightly uneasy feeling of being a hitch-hiker in bluejeans. At 11 Templom Utca I go through a gateway embellished with an iron crown, enter a courtyard and climb several flights of steps. There is very little light and the hand-rail is rusty, but in the shadows on every landing there are statues, majestic and banal, with that mystery which envelops the most conventionally imitative and realistic art – the art which creates figures aping the trite transparency of persons in official poses. The arabesques of the Alhambra, or Michelangelo's Prisoners, are there for eternity, while the imposing, melancholy statues on this staircase, insignificant as ourselves, grow old like us, moulder away in this semi-darkness amid the understandable neglect of all and sundry. They exhibit the useless-ness and solitude, the incomprehensibility of old age.

The city is anything but showy. It is solid and inscrutable, as if it were hiding something behind its rather crumbling decorum. Near the Liszt

Museum a man is leaning out of a ground-floor window in his
nightshirt. He is young, with dark, smooth, greasy hair, and a gypsy
face warped by a gentle, vacuous expression. He is gravely handi-
capped: his body droops like an empty sack, his lethargy is shaken only
by an oft-repeated convulsion. As we pass he leans further out and,
with effort, drones a few long-drawn-out sounds, words, or stumps of
words, in Hungarian. Gigi stops, listens, tries to understand him and
to reply with gestures, fuming at himself because he fails, and railing
against the creator of this debatable universe.

Had we understood what this stranger wished to say to us, perhaps
we would have understood everything. Of course, we cannot credit
that emaciated youth, who could not refrain from dribbling, with any
clear, deliberate intention; but in his sudden lunge towards us, in the
ways and the forms proper to his person and to his possibilities, there
was an urgency to say something, and therefore something to say, at
that moment, to us.

It is written, the stone which the builders rejected, the same is
become the head of the corner. Maybe the stranger we left in his own
filth was that royal stone, the king disguised as a beggar, the princely
prisoner. But maybe he is our liberator, for it would be enough to call
him brother to be free of all our fear, our hysterical shudders of disgust,
our impotence. It may be that he is one of the thirty-six just men,
unknown to the world and unaware of it themselves, thanks to whom,
according to the Hebrew legend, the world continues to exist.

The fictions of Danubian civilization, its ironical dissimulations,
help us to elude the intolerable scandal of pain, and to carry on. We
must be grateful to these fictions, then, even if that is all they can do. To
stop in front of that window with the expression I then saw on the face
of Gigi, one needs to have heard other voices, other cries. Musil could
not possibly have written the Gospels; Dostoyevsky nearly did so.
Henceforth, from this morning onwards in Sopron, Kafka's emperor,
whose message never arrives but is always on the way, will be that
sallow youth.

3. KOCSIS

At Sopron, as arranged, we were joined by a colleague whom I shall call Kocsis. Or rather, we joined him, since he was waiting for us. He is a critic of talent, a *grand seigneur* of culture who speaks several languages and whose books are highly thought of, as the phrase goes, among the international community of scholarship. He is a vigorous figure, in spite of his age, with a broad Pannonian face and something unfathomable in his dark eyes, counterpointed by a frank, winning smile. He often holds a cigarette between his fingers, and before lighting it taps it rhythmically on the edge of the table or on a chair; he reaches out with it into the space around him like a shaman tracing magic circles in the air, as if he wished for some moments to postpone something threatening, the smoke that dispels it and abolishes it for ever.

Kocsis is a small power in the Party, and is therefore a valuable companion. With his unlit cigarette he points, like an expert guide, to objects and figures, wrought-iron balconies and drowsy fountains, old books in the windows of second-hand bookshops, and, amongst the crowd, the occasional face which he finds anthropologically of interest. Perhaps all this is a role appropriate to an intellectual with his place on the echelon of the world, and aware of his ancillary position. Among the events of history he moves not like the artist who creates works, nor like the director of a museum who chooses and arranges them, but like a guide who points them out and comments on them.

Within the Party Kocsis is a small power dethroned. He can no longer give orders but he enjoys respect and favours, like the ex-chairman of a company, who has been removed from the levers of power but still has the use of a chauffeur-driven car. His political career is a very parable. Excluded as a young man from an academic career, because he did not agree with the infamous charges levelled against Rajk – the Communist leader accused of Titoism, falsely charged with treason, and executed – he re-emerged in the 1950s as a Stalinist, never personally involved with the tyrannical machine of Rákosi, but a convinced supporter of the absolute primacy of the Party.

Far too cultured and subtle to believe in the Soviet paradise, during those years of Cold War he must have thought that the world was on the brink of a vast and final conflict, which would once and for all decide the victory or defeat of the Revolution all over the world. The

West was the pure mechanism of society, the will to power of economic processes abandoned to the mercies of the strongest, to things as they are, enthralling life, if you like, but wild and brutal. The Communist East had to be the correction of reality in the name of things as they ought to be, the institution of justice and equality, the imposition of meaning on the rush of events.

It was in Hungary that Lukács had confirmed the classic thesis of Marxism, according to which immediate spontaneity is inauthentic, and takes on meaning only from the discipline of a form. The Stalinist ritual seemed to be form, order, assertion of principles over a Nietzschean "anarchy of atoms". Western liberalism appeared as formless spontaneity, immoral vitality, random egoism, a mere process of needs divorced from any ethical criterion. The one thing was the state, the other was society. As late as 1971 Tibor Déry, a committed dissident writer, wrote a novel expressing his disgust for the promiscuous, undefined innocence of the "pop" youth of America, of a society functioning at the zero setting of a libidinous flux.

On the eve of the battle of Gog and Magog, Kocsis considered it perfectly understandable that the state should assume the full control of society, including the limitation or suppression of liberties that takes place in a wartime economy and discipline. Even in 1956, during the few short days in which such a position appeared to have been defeated, and was dangerous to uphold, Kocsis was pro-Soviet, opposed to the Nagy government's decision to withdraw from the Warsaw Pact. At his own personal risk he was a champion of the integrity of the Eastern bloc. At the moment he is practically in a position of dissent with regard to the policies of Kádár, whose liberalism – which has made Hungary the most democratic, prosperous and "Western" of the Communist countries of Europe – seems to him both too cautious and too authoritarian.

Kocsis is one of the countless examples of quick-change artistry which are a feature of Hungarian politics during the last few decades, and which have little or nothing to do with opportunism. Andrá Hegedüs, a confirmed Stalinist and right-hand man to Rákosi, rescued from the people's fury in the 1956 revolution by a Soviet tank which took him over the border, in the course of the 1960s became a liberal intellectual, a symbol of critical independence and revisionism. His periodical, *Valóság*, opened an unbiased social and political debate on the way the country was run, and on the theories of Marxism itself, leaving Hegedüs open to charges of heresy. Others have trodden the same path in reverse, from the uprising of 1956 to a position of new Marxist orthodoxy.

It is Hungarian history itself which produces these "turncoat" situations. There are the outlaws of 1956 who come back and reoccupy important posts; the swing of the pendulum between democratic phases and yet another turn of the authoritarian screw; the virtually preferential treatment which the government reserves – at least in the eyes of many old militants – for those who are without a Party. Kádár himself is a macroscopic example of such transformations, performed, in his case, in the name of dedication to a higher mission. A militant Communist from the word go, tireless in the clandestine struggle during the years of Fascism, tortured by the Stalinist police, who pulled out his nails, the man who supported the Soviet repression of 1956, and the statesman who has brought his country to the greatest possible degree of independence from Russia, of freedom and wellbeing.

Life is a compromise, Kádár once said during the public celebrations for his birthday, and the true short-cut may sometimes be what appears the longest way round. Kocsis today, with his unlit cigarette between his fingers, may be treading that short-cut, attempting to pause every so often, perhaps, to sit down on a bench and look at the landscape. That very revolutionary war economy, in which he believed, turned out to be the weak spot in Socialism as it really was. When power directly assumes the whole yoke of society and its problems, taking on the onus of every detail and the control of every detail, its totalitarianism (as Massimo Salvadori has said) turns against it and undermines it from within, as happens with a human organism subjected to immense strain for enormous stretches of time. The 1956 Revolution was, in part, an apoplexy on the part of this excess of power, the collapse of this titanic effort by the Party-State: the attempt to invade and control every aspect of social life. With its elastic and elusive formula, "whoever is not against us is for us," Kádár's compromise turns that totalitarianism upside down, allowing room for a whole range of components and attitudes, no longer strictly regimented according to a single standard ("with us"), but limited simply in a negative way, according to the liberal viewpoint: it is enough to be "not against us". Kádár's long short-cut, and his compromise, are a typically Hapsburg strategy. Out of the cracks in the system forged according to the Soviet model something is reborn: not only a nostalgia for Mitteleuropa, but even the form appropriate to it, its ethical-political style.

Kocsis has also, in his way, found an allusive Mitteleuropa of his own, a personal short-cut. He tells me that he is at work on a monograph on Babits. And in its way the choice is significant, because it is a secondary choice, but not too much so. The ideology of the régime favours Marxist writers, or else – and even more so – the great national classics, such as Petöfi or Vörösmarty, whose legitimate heirs Communism proclaims itself to be. Or even the "exploded" interpreters and unmaskers of the decadence and crisis of the bourgeoisie, such as Endre Ady. Revolutionary poets such as Attila József are more suspect, because their radicalism is likely to collide with the Party line, even if the monumental work on Attila József by Miklós Szabolcsi does in fact give evidence of the cultural freedom pertaining in Hungary today.

Mihály Babits is a special case. In literary manuals, as in the going cultural debates, he is a poet who receives the homage due to a somewhat marginal classic – he is accorded a sort of respectful oblivion. Babits (1883–1941) was a humanist intrigued by tradition, but also a master of the split with tradition that has in many ways taken place in modern lyric poetry. This split he attempts to restrain, finding a happy medium in well-defined form, much as though he were throwing a lifebelt to the great shipwrecked mariners of modern poetry. Babits protested against the enthusiasms and horrors of war, accepted the Chair of Literature in Béla Kun's Communist republic, but declared himself to be an anti-Marxist, withdrawing thereafter, however, when faced with Horthy's Fascist régime, into a discreet opposition. He opposed all kinds of irrational thinking, and on the exquisitely crafted jewellery of his poems he bestowed an afflatus of human suffering. He was sensitive to the "tears in things", but above all to the sufferings of individuals and the downtrodden classes.

He never praises the victors, and this must be something to recommend him to Kocsis. Perhaps Kocsis sees himself mirrored in the lines in which the poet tells us that he wishes to concentrate the All into his sonnets, but never succeeds in reaching out beyond himself and his own small *impasses*. Poetry dies, says Babits in a poem; and elsewhere he says that it is useless writing with a finger like drawing on sand. The gods die and mankind goes on living. Maybe the gods of Kocsis are dead, but he certainly is going on living, amiable and helpful, and he takes his mind off things by listening to the whispered words of this poet. With equal discretion Babits guided the vagrant letters and words through their paper labyrinths, keeping his own weariness at bay, and harkening to the sounds of the boats and the muffled engine-noises coming up from the Danube; he hoped that some god might offer a bed to the river of words which rose to his lips, so that it might flow between ordered banks to the sea, there to vanish.

The poetry of Babits cannot today become a banner in the ideological debate and the underground clash between left and right, the conservatives and progressives of Hungarian culture and politics. His is a clear voice but a gentle one, an arcadia like the one the poet himself saw around him in his childhood, among the vineyards of Szekszárd – a Pannonian arcadia, and therefore well acquainted with the violence Babits sometimes forced himself to slide over.

4. TANK-TRACKS IN THE SNOW

We have just left Fertoöd, the Versailles of the Esterházy, the feudal lords who in the eighteenth century owned an area of one million jugers – close to two million acres. Together with the other members of the nobility, they composed the entire *natio hungarica* as so recognized.

Our comings and goings over these few kilometres are as scattered and irregular as the wanderings of the hitch-hikers or of Gyula Krúdy's famous red cart which roves the old country roads: we shift in zigzags. But although we throw straight lines to the winds, it is a deliberate intention which leads us, thus, to Mosonmagyaróvár. Here, on the night of November 2nd 1956, Alberto Cavallari, correspondent of the *Corriere della Sera* covering the Hungarian revolt, made headlines himself – a nine-column banner – because word had got around that he had been taken prisoner by the Russians. In fact he had spent the night in a rebel hide-out, after making a vain attempt to reach Vienna to announce – a day in advance – that the revolution had not won the day, as was generally thought, but was petering out . . . that the Soviet suppression was under way. With his typical sharp, laconic edge, Cavallari narrates that night of chaos and snow, the car sunk up to the axles, the roads lost in the mud and dark, gunfire, people injured, unexpected roadblocks thrown up by the patriots, the Russian tanks which he runs into by accident in the dark, while they are spreading like the meshes of a gigantic net between Vienna and Budapest, sealing Hungary off from the world.

Following his route between Budapest and Vienna, we seem to be tracing his footsteps, while some of the articles he wrote during those weeks in October-December 1956, which catch the essence of an epoch-making event in unknown faces that vanish into the marshes or behind the barricades, are a kind of breviary for this Hungarian journey. It is a tragic breviary for a harmless journey, which we none the less take with us as Bérard carried the *Odyssey* when he travelled round the Mediterranean, to identify places and their secrets from that kind of Baedeker which the poem contains. But thirty years have melted that snow and erased the trackmarks of the tanks, even if not the memory of them. The judgment, in those days, was clear: Kádár was an accomplice to the betrayal and the massacre, a Soviet pawn evidently under their control, already used and about to be discarded. Thirty years later it is only fair to recognize that he put his whole person at the service of his country, that he set out along the only road that was realistically possible, and that he has followed it with ability and rectitude for the good of Hungary.

All this does not modify the judgment made then, but it flanks it with other different judgments, which do not negate it but create a counter-point, as if one were to flank a picture of an individual with one showing him decades earlier or later. The positive evaluation which can be made of Kádár today does not mean that the negative one made then was wrong, or that to have resisted him at that time was unnecessary.

The past has a future, something it becomes, and that transforms it. Like the facts themselves, the person, the "I", who experiences it and looks back on it discovers that it is not singular, but plural. Travelling through those places marked down in those epic chronicles of thirty years ago, one gets the impression of slicing through paper-thin, invisible barriers, different levels of reality, still present and with us even though not discernible to the naked eye, infra-red or ultra-violet rays of history, images and instants that at this point cannot print an image on the celluloid, but which nonetheless *are*, and exist in the same way for tangible experience as electrons which elude our grasp.

I don't know if some science-fiction writer has invented a space-time camera able, perhaps in a succession of enlargements, to reproduce everything that has occurred, in the portion of space framed in the lens, in the course of the centuries and the millennia. Like the ruins of Troy with its nine cities one above the other, or a simple calcareous rock-formation, each scrap of reality requires the archaeologist, or the geologist, to decipher it; and it may be that literature is nothing but this archaeology applied to life itself. Of course, any mere three-dimensional traveller – even if the fact of travelling is itself four-dimensional, or multi-dimensional by definition – is rattled when faced with the whims of the fourth dimension, and has a hard time sorting out such a mass of assertions, both contradictory and otherwise. One feels a little like Cardinal Mindszenty, just freed from prison and, after so many years in a cell, confused by the new things that met his eyes. One has to draw breath and look around and, before replying to any question, one would like to give the answer, proposed by the Hungarian Primate to Cavallari's request for a statement: "I will answer you on Friday," said the newly-liberated Cardinal, "when I have understood how the world is made."

5. IN THE MUD OF PANNONIA

The Hungarian television is showing *The Glambayas*, the celebrated, virulent drama written by Miroslav Krleža, directed in this case by János Dömölky. Very few Hungarian writers have given a picture of the world of Pannonia, of the mosaic of peoples and cultures between Zagreb and Budapest, with a power and violence to equal that of Krleža, the grand patriarch of Croatian literature. One dark, obsessive image recurs throughout his writings, and that is the *mud* of Pannonia, the Magyar-Croatian flatlands pasty with soil, with marsh, with sodden leaves, and the blood-filled footprints which have been left in the course of centuries by migrations and the clash of conflicting civilizations which on those plains and in that mud have been stamped one upon the other like the hoofmarks of barbarian horses.

Krleža, who was born in Zagreb in 1893 and died in 1981, has works translated into every language in all sorts of countries. He is a masterful, excessive writer, abounding in earthy vitality. He is the poet of the encounter, and clash, between the Croatians, the Hungarians, the Germans, and all the other peoples of the Danubian universe. He is a writer supercharged with multi-lingual culture and with passion, an expressionist intellectual and poet who loves argument at the level of criticism, but at the same time puts his heart into leaps and breaks and fractures, aggressive sallies and sarcastic invective. The central theme of his work, many-faceted and measureless as it may be, is the dissolution of nineteenth-century civilization, with particular reference to the break-up of the Austro-Hungarian Empire, and the riot of irrational and pathological forces unleashed by the collapse of a social order. From his denunciation of this orgiastic, nihilistic decadence – best shown in *The Glambayas*, a grim and cruel picture of the decline of the Hapsburgs – Krleža draws the sap for his ferocious analysis of totalitarianism, which he views as having been born from that corruption to spread like a cancer throughout the Europe of the 1930s.

A militant in the Jugoslav workers' movement, and arrested by the Ustachi authorities, Krleža did not abandon Communism; but his early and radical anti-Stalinism – in the years of Stalin himself and even during the struggle against Fascism – got him into bad trouble with the Party. Among the accusers who at that time cried out for his head was Djilas, then sectarian and absolutist, though later the standard-bearer of dissent. It was Tito who always defended Krleža, and who understood, far better than the intellectual Djilas, that Krleža and his independence were an invaluable asset to the new, revolutionary Jugoslavia, of which the writer was in fact a father and a patriarch, a "grand old man" on a par with Tito himself.

A Croatian nationalist before the First World War, then a patriot in a Jugoslavia dominated by the Serbs, though soon disgusted by the reactionary regime of the monarchy, Krleža returned to his Croatian roots and the Danubian culture put in terms of the Marxist internationalism for which he was a courageous militant. His Pannonia is a melting-pot of peoples and cultures, in which the individual discovers plurality, and the uncertainty – though also the complexity – of his own identity. Into the Pannonian mud sink the Austro-Hungarian gentry, represented by the Glambayas family; sucked down into the Pannonian mud is the hero of his most remarkable book, *The Return of Filip Latinovicz*. Published in 1932, this book was much admired – perhaps too much – by Sartre, who saw it as a parable of the identity crisis of the individual, a depiction of the alienation of the individual who dissolves in nothingness, aware of the decay of his own class and the crumbling away of his own selfhood.

Krleža wrote an enormous amount, too much: poems, novels, plays, essays, of very uneven quality. His strength resides in the complexity of his thought, in his ability to grasp the connection between everyday social life, historical processes and the laws of nature; it is in the glance which discovers the gnawing of death in the most ordinary gestures, which sees the necessity of the universe, the convergence and dispersal of atoms, the obscure biological rites concealed in the movement of ideas. His grave shortcoming is his miry exuberance, the rhetoric of truculence and abjection, the display of putrescence which occasionally causes him to repeat himself unduly.

Krleža's anti-Hapsburg critique is certainly factious and one-sided – as, in the other direction, are many nostalgic idealizations of the Empire – but poetic and moral truth sometimes needs this sectarian passion if, beyond the fact of exasperated distortion, it is to grasp an essential moment in life and history, an absolute human value which objective precision is not capable of attaining. This fact is well known to the great satirical poets, who are tendentious but, thanks to their visionary obsession, called upon to shed light on some eternal moment in life. Vienna was not as infamous as Karl Kraus described it, any more than ancient Rome was as Juvenal says it was, but without the raging exasperation of Kraus or Juvenal the veil would not have been rent, and we should have had no revelation of all those extreme expressions, those abnormal grimaces, which the face of man is capable of assuming.

Krleža's work, above all the late novel *Banners*, which is intended as a kind of *summa*, constitutes an encyclopaedia of Pannonia and a monumental fresco not only of Croatian life but also, and above all, of Budapest and the Hungary of the early years of the century. Krleža is very hard indeed on the Empire of the Danube, but at the same time his protest is imbued with the culture of that world, as we see from his essay on Karl Kraus, which is the voice of Hapsburg culture contesting its own self.

In a book of memoirs written late in life, a book which evokes the whole Hapsburg mosaic, and not without a certain tenderness, Krleža describes himself as "a man from Agram", using the German name for his hometown of Zagreb. The vast royal and imperial union had taught even him, as it had taught so many others – even his old accuser Djilas, who today feels nostalgia for the old Mitteleuropa – to love it, or at least to understand it by rebelling against it.

6. SADLY MAGYAR

The Danube threads towns together like a string of pearls. Györ, in 1956, was the centre of the most radical demands, imposing an ultimatum on the more moderate Budapest, and the Nagy government itself, which it considered too pro-Communist. It is a beautiful, tranquil town, and the old streets lead like a Sunday morning stroll to the banks of the river, with its *quais* and the green water of the Raba, which here flows into the Danube. On the façade of 5 Dr Kavacs Utca is a medallion on which a pair of proud, noble Magyar moustachios adorn the countenance of Petöfi; in the Jesuit church the windows are framed by green leaves gilded by the sun, and for an instant the faces are seen in that light, a beauty more touching than the glow of stained-glass windows. In Alkotmany Utca Napoleon lived for some time. The balconies exude a tranquil, measured elegance, featuring caryatids and sabre-bearing lions.

Komorn, a large part of which is on the opposite bank of the Danube, in Czechoslovakia, is a sort of small concentrate of symbols of the Magyar spirit. The statue of Klapka, the general of 1848, represents the rebel spirit of the Magyars; the plaque commemorating the birth of Mór Jókai is a reminder of the national illusionism, widely cultivated especially after the Compromise, with which the Hungarian ruling class made itself a mask of vitality and splendour, transforming the Magyar spirit into a cliché of itself. Having grown up in the optimistic atmosphere of liberalism, Jókai gives a glowing picture of that Hungarian aristocracy which Baron József Eötvos describes as oppressive and parasitical. Eötvos was a novelist, as well as being the author (1868) of an enlightened law on the various nationalities which has often been disregarded.

The great literature of Hungary is not the literature which glories in the splendour of a heroic Hungary, but the one which reveals the misery and darkness of the Hungarian destiny. Even Petöfi, the bard of the fatherland and of the God of the Magyars, lashes the inert selfishness of the nobles and the indolence of the nation. Endre Ady writes of the "gloomy Hungarian land", describes himself as "sadly Magyar", and declares that "the Magyar Messiahs are Messiahs a thousand times over," because in their country tears are more salt, and they die having redeemed nothing. One born in Hungary already has a price on his head, because (as he says in another poem) the country is a stinking lake of death; the worn out Hungarians are "the buffoons of the world", and within himself, as he grieves, the poet bears the whole of that melancholy plain.

Magyar literature is an anthology packed with wounds of this sort, with this feeling of abandonment and solitude which leads the Hungarians, as we read in a poem by Attila József, to feel that they are "sitting on the brink of the universe". László Németh, the leader of the school of writers who aim at popular appeal, has said that Hungarian literature is in a situation of "permanent death agony". In Hungary there is one question which has been repeated like a refrain throughout history, from the Battle of Mohács until the rebellion of 1956: Are we always going to be defeated? When will the Hungarians at last arise as victors? It is a question which pupils ask their history teacher when he tells them about the Rakoczi rebellion, which was crushed by the Hapsburgs, and is even talked about in the official Party newspaper; it is a rhetorical question posed also by Tibor Déry, even by Kádár, though according to the latter this destiny of perpetual losers is a thing of the past, not of the present.

The national illusionism, as cultivated by Jókai and many other authors, is therefore counterbalanced by a most desperate disenchantment, by voices speaking from the shadows. We should not say that self-accusation and self-pity are necessarily any more truthful than self-congratulation: pressed upon by the German, Slav and Latin worlds, Hungary has been threatened, but certainly not enslaved by her neighbours. In spite of the long Turkish domination and the failure of so many revolutions, Hungary has also been a nation of dominators, and has imposed its will on its own Slavs or Rumanians. It has not been a province forgotten by the history of the world, but a nation which has made its own contribution to history.

It is therefore not unfair to bring about a partial rehabilitation of the picturesque optimism of Jókai. It has to be said that in his novel of 1872, *A Modern Midas*, Jókai himself displays a sadness far from the stereotyped, "local-colour" melancholy of the Hungarian steppes. In this book a tiny island in the Danube, hidden and unknown, becomes the non-place in which Mihály Timár, the waterman who had made a lot of money and was disappointed with his rise into the middle class, finds his refuge and his happiness. In this novel Jókai wrote a little *Robinson Crusoe* of the Danube, the story of a man who starts from nothing to rebuild an existence that had been demolished by society, and who, unlike Crusoe, has no wish to go back to the world as it is.

His island becomes a paradise, an Eden, a South Sea atoll, even though his melancholy innocence is not protected by the ocean, but only by a stretch of the Danube.

   Another plaque in Komorn, in two languages, informs us that this house was the birthplace of Franz Lehár, master of illusionism to the nth degree, and of two-bit music in which, for all his flair, the nostalgia of the Strauss waltz is corrupted into shameless vulgarity. The sleight of hand of the operetta, which resolves all the problems of life with a "Waiter, champagne!", cannot conceal the fact that it is but a brilliant pretence, the simulation of high spirits. His commercial enterprise of sensual and sentimental cynicism is made of cardboard; it does not assume any airs of importance, but it distracts one from the seriousness of life.

7. AN IMPERIAL BUST UNDER THE STAIRS

Esztergom. Here it was that Geza, prince of the Hungarians who had arrived a century earlier from the Russian steppes, under their leader Arpad, established his residence and court in the year 973. This was the birthplace of his son St Stephen, first King of Hungary. The first Christian king, who converted the country to Christianity, and defeated the pagan Pechenegs, put an end to the dominion of the shamans and vagrant gods of the steppes. The town is today the official see of the Primate of Hungary. The vast neo-classical cathedral which looms above the Danube has all the cold, dead monumentality of a cenotaph, and beams forth a glacial temporal power, or insolence.

   There has been a lot of fighting at Esztergom, what with Mongol invasions and Turkish sieges and conquests. Here, in battle against the Turks in 1594, fell Bálint Balassi, one of the earliest poets in Hungarian literature. The museum dedicated to him is closed: the girl who opens the door knows nothing, and the doorway is full of piles of plaster. Abandoned under the hall stairs is a bust of Sissy, the Empress who loved Hungary so much. The smile on the face, carved by an utterly conventional hand, displays a suitable unreality for that impossible Empress with her dream of being a sea-gull. Even world history is composed of changes of address, often unfinished, with furniture left behind. Sceptres, crowns and robes end up with the rag-and-bone man. In the course of the liquidation of the Hapsburg Empire, who knows by what mistake Sissy ended up pushed aside there under the stairs. Maybe to spare us the possible disappointment of another closed, dilapidated museum, Kocsis avoids taking us to the one bearing the name of his beloved Mihály Babits.

8. THE INNKEEPERS OF VÁC

This little town, also rich in memories of bloodshed, is really beautiful, with its Renaissance and baroque buildings. Even earlier than the Antiquarius, on his way from Vienna to the Tartar Crimea, the noble gentleman Nicolaus Ernst Kleemann complained about Hungarian innkeepers in general, and those of Vác in particular, saying that among them one found "the quintessence of innkeeperish incivility": the food and drink were bad, served in filthy kitchen-ware at exorbitant prices. But Vác has seen worse. In the *Theresianum*, the old academy for the sons of nobles built by order of Maria Theresa and later converted into a prison, the Horthy regime imprisoned and eliminated the militants of the workers' movement.

9. SZENTENDRE

Szentendre is a Montmartre of the Danube. The colours of the houses and the pictures on show in the streets filter off into those of the river, while a light, liquid gaiety enfolds the dawdler and draws him gently along the picturesque alleys which move down towards the river-banks in a tranquil flow. The town has a Serbian air, though this is fading little by little. At the end of the seventeenth century, during the Ottoman reaction to the advance of the imperial army, Szentendre took in a great number of refugees from the Balkans, all fleeing before the Turks. There were Albanians, Greeks, Bosnians, Dalmatians, and above all Serbs, led by their patriarch Arseniji Crnojević. Being enterprising merchants, the Serbs – along with the Greeks – bestowed on the town both prosperity and an opulent elegance, with baroque, rococo and neo-classical churches, the houses of great merchant princes, the harmony of quiet squares and the signs of illustrious business concerns.

Of the eight hundred families who arrived with the patriarch, some sixty or seventy still remain. A journey is always a rescue operation, the documentation and harvesting of something that is becoming extinct and will soon disappear, the last landing on an island that is sinking beneath the waves. Cuvier divided travellers into *voyageurs-naturalistes*, *-géographiques* and *-botanistes*. Things are easier for a botanist: he can carefully pick the last specimen of a plant and preserve it in his herbarium, or even transplant it in a pot and take it with him, weather and climate permitting. Human geography complicates matters a little, since it is more difficult to embalm a landscape which is vanishing beneath the cement of the building speculators, a minority on the decrease, its roads, its customs, its people gesticulating in the market-place. But the decline of the Serbian presence in Szentendre is not in the least melancholy, for it does not consist of a few pathetic survivors isolated like the Last of the Mohicans, but a compact group with its part to play in Hungarian life.

A *voyageur-botaniste* would certainly have a lot of things to collect, with the requisite care, and put into a herbarium that would protect them, even if it is always too late, from being crushed by the wheel of things as they are. However, grief there is, and no reliquary can keep it at bay. There is grief even in the splendid ceramics of Margit Kovács, on permanent display in the eighteenth-century house known as the house of the Serbian merchant Dimšić Vazul. In the figures of Margit Kovács suffering is dumb and inexplicable, the sorrow of a great motherhood, which creates both life and pain. But in that silence there is an unshakable dignity even more mysterious than sorrow, the enigma of existence and even of happiness in spite of tragedy.

A few steps further, before climbing back into the car for Budapest. In a small second-hand bookshop is a volume containing several letters of Ninon de Lenclos, and this reminds Gigi that Maestro Eulambio di Gradisca, who taught music at Leipzig for thirty years, had composed an opera called *Ninon de Lenclos*, performed at the Teatro Verdi in Trieste. A decorous and useless opera, says Gigi, which demonstrates the tragedy of a worthy disciple whose undoubted musical expertise no longer has anything new to say. Verdi's worthy disciples are tragic figures: they emerge at once for what they are, and waste away their lives in work that, however respectable, is dated from the start. The wily followers of Schönberg or of Pound, equally able and useless, succeed in hiding the fact that they are late in the day, to pass themselves off as originals, and to avoid tragedy thanks to their philistinism. Let His Majesty Oblivion, to whom Lichtenberg dedicated his works, issue an immediate decree against Maestro Eulambio, while he tinkles at the keys a little, after dinner, with some trendy colleague of his.

10. AN ICE-CREAM IN BUDAPEST

Budapest is the loveliest city on the Danube. It has a crafty way of being its own stage-set, like Vienna, but also has a robust substance and a vitality unknown to its Austrian rival. Budapest gives one the physical sensation of being a capital, with the urbanity and grandeur of a city that has played its part in history, in spite of Ady's lament that the life of the Magyars is "grey, the colour of dust". Certainly, modern Budapest is a recent creation, very different from the nineteenth-century city which, as Mikszáth wrote, in the 1840s drank Serbian vermouth and spoke German. The metropolitan magnificence of Budapest, based on the solid foundations of political and economic growth, also presents an aspect of intriguing illusionism which the photographic art of György Klösz has captured with magical lucidity. If modern Vienna imitates Baron Haussman's Paris, with its great *boulevards*, Budapest in turn imitates this imported town-planning of Vienna: it is the imitation of an imitation. Perhaps this is the reason why it resembles poetry in the sense in which Plato used the word, and its townscape suggests not so much art as the feeling of art.

It is no coincidence that at the beginning of the century Budapest was the cradle of an extraordinary culture which – with Lukács as a young man, but with others as well – posed itself the question of what relation existed between the soul and form, whether behind the multiplicity of the inessential there was an essence of life, and what relation there might be between the play of things as they are and the truth of having to exist. That stage-set of fictions was taken to extremes by the spectacular and monumental celebrations of the Hungarian millennium of 1896. It encouraged the sense of artifice and experiment, of the search for and construction of new languages, as is shown by the great Hungarian avant-garde in art and music. It encouraged the essayist, because the essayist's craft displays the agonizing, ironical vicissitudes of the intellect which is aware how far immediacy lacks authenticity, and how far life diverges from its meaning; and yet the intellect aims, however obliquely, at that ultimately unattainable transcendence of meaning – whose flickering presence is to be seen in the very awareness of its absence.

The young Lukács lived not far from the castle of Vajdahund, built in the years 1896–1908 in the Varosliget Park, which starts behind the Square of the Heroes, and he could see the Potemkin effect of official culture in the Hungary of the millennium. The castle, which imitates the homonymous one of János Hunyadi, built in Transylvania during the fifteenth century, is the essence of kitsch, a heterogeneous mass of styles jammed one into the other: a Gothic gateway, a few Romanesque blocks, some Renaissance features, baroque façades, and a tower which is a copy of the enchanting tower at Sighişoara (Segesvár, Schässburg), now in Rumania. The friends who in 1915 used to meet at the home of Béla Balász in the so-called "Sunday Circle" (they included Lukács, Hauser and Mannheim) were wont to enquire into the "possibilities of the adequate life", being a life imbued with meaning. They knew they were living in an age of the "weakening of reality", as Lukács put it, in a historical period of instability and crisis, and they opened up new avenues for aesthetics and for sociology by analysing individual possibilities of asserting value in an objective world which denies it; of underlining the tragedy of those who reject an empty reality; and of asserting the essayist's ironical tolerance which inhabits those who, despite all, do not wish to deny themselves tragically to this reality – that is, to die. The fetching kitsch of Budapest was the scene which urged on the search for the real life, and the investigation of the truth, or the falsehood, of form.

The splendour of Budapest is in part the compensation of a city which is losing its character, a mixture of giantism and exuberance, which corresponds to the hybrid alliance between the Hungarian capital and the Hapsburg eagle, and is also betrayed by the eclectic quality of the architecture. The old parliament is an example, as is the Opera House built by Miklós Ybl in the style of the Renaissance, and the new Gothic-baroque parliament by Imre Steidl. The enterprising new middle-class, it has been said, wished to build itself a heraldic past. It wished to disguise the feverish metamorphosis and tumultuous industrial expansion of the city – which led to the Seventh District being called Chicago – behind an appearance of frothy lightness, and to flaunt Magyar culture at all costs, and the more so since capitalist development was tearing its traditions up by the roots. In 1907 Géza Lengyel denounced the empty, theatrical façades, the "plaster Potemkinism" of Budapest which masked a quite different reality, just as Broch denounced the non-style of the Viennese Ringstrasse which conceals a lack of values. In 1900 Lechner designed the Post Office Savings Bank, while the art of Miksa Róth, who conquered the entire world with his opalescent glass, also comes in useful in displaying the "economic power of the Company" in terms of glass windows, as in the Gresham Insurance Building designed by Zsigmond Quittner; but its chief task is to lighten and civilize the brutality of this power.

The "small-scale America" of Budapest between 1867 and 1914 is cloaked with liveliness and light-hearted effervescence. Mór Jókai celebrates the old Budapest of the legendary magnate Moritz Sándor, with his dashing exploits, the vendors of melons, coconuts and glasses of water on the banks of the Danube, and the famous Lawyers' Annual Ball. Like the aristocratic Kleemann a century and a half earlier, he too devotes special attention to bad manners, and goes to the extent of making a classification of mannerless boors, with first place going to the cabman of *fiacre* No. 37 and second to the cashier at the theatre.

Even the giantism afflicting the metropolis takes on this old-time grace, which seems to make room for provincial familiarity and offers itself as a background for *joie de vivre*, with its riverside embankments and long boulevards in which life seems to flow happily and gloriously, with the pulsing of a robust, uncaring health. Balconies, façades, friezes and caryatids mask that tragedy of the modern age which the young Lukács and his friends of the "Sunday Circle" investigated with brilliant, sympathetic acumen. Even the bombs of 1944–5 only just succeeded in revealing, behind the shattered buildings, the majestic, crumbling statues, back-shop of the poverty and darkness which the *belle époque* managed to keep hidden, and which only Fascism, the violent and most extreme disease of the modern age, aggravated and – paradoxically – unmasked.

Even today the stroller becomes immersed in this archaeology of splendour and concealment, this mixture of the robust and the illusory, of agonizing verse and indeed the pompous elevation of the world's prose to the status of poetry. Among the figures surrounding the statue of Szécheny in Roosevelt Square, Neptune correctly symbolizes navigation and Ceres agriculture, Vulcan is called upon to represent industry but Minerva, goddess of thought and of the intelligence, is the allegory for commerce. In Petőfi Square there naturally stands the statue of the national bard of whom the 1984 "Corvina" guide-book (which tempers daring with the caution of someone never sure of the stability of the Stock Exchange) observes that "he is, so far, the greatest Hungarian poet." Anyway, in the monument built in the Square of the Heroes, Hősök Tere, for the Hungarian Millennium in 1896, along with the statues of the mythical Árpád, and other heroes of Hungarian history such as János Hunyadi or Kossuth, we now view those of Work and Welfare, Honour and Glory, displaying the bourgeois spirit of the mythical-heroic in fancy-dress.

The Danube flows broad, and the evening wind passes through the open-air cafés like the breath of an old Europe which may already be at the brink of the world and no longer produces history but only consumes it – as Francesca's lovely mouth now sucks at an ice-cream in the Gerbeaud pâtisserie in Vörösmarty Square. Francesca watches her life slip away through half-closed eyes; her famous eyebrows are slightly knitted, perhaps, at that rustling of time in transit. Europe also means this café, at which we no longer find the Managing Directors of the *Weltgeist*, but at the most the functionaries of one of the lesser branches, who do not make decisions but carry them out, and the occasional beautiful woman who gets herself talked about.

From the shop-windows of photographers the faces in school photographs look out at us: sixth forms on the verge of leaving, boys at the first-cigarette stage, girls in sailor-suits with ties, they all look out towards their future, which is rushing upon them at a speed that perhaps they have realized only at that very moment, at the classroom door, as if they were being bombarded by particles accelerated in a syncrotron. Szendy Marianna has black hair, dark eyes and an imperious nose that at least promises to give tough work to the great grindstone which awaits her, and not to fall into the net of the old fisherman before she has, if only for a moment, played a little havoc with his numerical blocs. Kis Zoltan is the inevitable fat boy of the class, and runs the risk of ending up in the frying pan a little earlier, just as in Gymnastics he brought down the bar of the high jump, but his face – in the photo of the school-leavers each one wears a label with his name on it – is the face of a person who knows how to laugh when the headmaster hands him his report with the satisfied gravity of one who announces a Fail. Perhaps he will be able to laugh in the face of the other messengers of tragedy who are waiting for him in the narrow pass.

The Danube runs verbosely beneath the titanic bridges, as Ady wrote, invoking the flight and even the death of the Seine, in that Paris which Budapest reflects as in a Regency mirror. It may be that Europe is finished, is a negligible province in a history decided elsewhere, in the press-button rooms of other empires. The European spirit feeds on books, like the demons in Singer's stories, gnaws at the volumes of history in the libraries or, like moths, eats into ladies' hats, shawls, and other dainty items of the wardrobe.

We should not take it for granted that Europe is irreparably destined to play this role of operatic confidante. Familiarity with the cast of Mitteleuropa, and its rehearsals, in any case induces us not to believe in irreparable destinies, but rather in the principle of indeterminacy. In Budapest, certainly, one can discern this feeling of a Europe "after the show", but the city is not, as Vienna is, just a setting for the remembrance of past glories. It is also a robust, full-blooded city, which suggests the strength which Europe could and should possess, if it found a way of making use of all its multiple energies, and unified its forces, instead of wearing them away in a perpetual annulment, a state of permanent stalemate. In Budapest one thinks intensely of the decline, or the feared or decreed decline, of Europe, and simply because Europe is still there: its sun is still high above the horizon and gives good warmth, but at the same time it is veiled by clouds and curtains, which imperiously remind us of its declining phase. Thus the great Hungarian cultural avant-garde of the early nineteenth century was a mixture of sunset and new dawn, with the new order in the music of Bartók and the self-afflicting triangle of Endre Ady, Ödön Diósy and their Leda, a *femme fatale* and a victim, as many such women are, with her hair dyed blue and her nostrils tipped with red like the valves of a seashell; she was the protagonist of a *fin de siècle* (and *rétro*) love story, but the poetry of Ady has brought to light and celebrated in it a core of piercing truth.

The buildings of Budapest are eclectic, given to historical posturing, weighty in themselves and often adorned with heavy decorations; their non-style occasionally appears as some bizarre face of the future, the sort of backward-looking yet futuristic townscape of the cities posited in science-fiction films such as *Blade Runner*: a future that is post-historical and without style, peopled by chaotic, composite masses, in national and ethnic qualities indistinguishable, Malay-Redskin Levantines who live in shacks and skyscrapers, twelfth-generation computers and rusty bicycles fished up from the past, rubble from the Fourth

World War and superhuman robots. The architectural townscape of this metropolitan future is archaic-futuristic, with skyscrapers kilometres in height and temples in the *kolossal* style like Milan Station or Grand Central. The eclecticism of Budapest, its mixture of styles, evokes, like every Babel of today, a possible future swarming with the survivors of some catastrophe. Every heir of the Hapsburg era is a true man of the future, because he learnt, earlier than most others, to live without a future, in the absence of any historical continuity; and that is, not to live but to survive. But along these splendid boulevards, in a world as lively and elegant as this, a world which does not display the melancholy of the Eastern Bloc countries, even survival is charming and seductive, magnanimous and maybe, at times, almost happy.

11. THE TOMB AMONG THE ROSES

The tomb of Gül Baba, the sixteenth-century Muslim holy man buried on the hill of roses, is enveloped in peace and watched over by the rose-garden. It looks down upon Budapest not, indeed, with the proud glance of the dominator of yore, but with that serene distance of one who rests in Allah. Before this tomb and amid this tranquillity death has no fears for us. It is rest and repose, an oasis reached after crossing the desert.

12. THE EPIC, THE NOVEL, AND WOMEN

In an antiquarian bookshop I buy a manual of poetics in Latin. It is *Institutiones Poeticae in usum Gymnasiorum Regni Hungariae et adnexarum provinciarum*, published in Buda in 1831. As the title states, it is a textbook for grammar schools. In 1831, therefore, the schoolchildren of wild Pannonia wrote their homework in Latin.

The manual introduces, classifies, subdivides, and proceeds with that geometry of the mind which is the first guarantee of *esprit de finesse*. The chapters which follow are refined and inexorable: *Definitio Poeseos, De Materia, De Forma* . . . One paragraph is devoted to a question which is less than chivalrous: "Potestne esse femina, quae dicitur heroina, materia Epopoeiae?" Can the totality of the Epic, which embraces the world in unity and harmony and rises above each and every mere detail, admit a woman as its protagonist? Is not woman the chance, accidental creature of metaphysical misogynies, matter without form, mere passive sensitivity incapable of transcending itself?

Who knows how the students who used the manual responded to that question in their compositions. It was in those years, or very little later, that János Arany asked himself rather more serious questions regarding the epic. He wondered whether, in his "industrial" age which demanded and produced "enjoyable" art, it was possible to achieve the totality of the epic, for that presupposed a life imbued with meaning, the breath of the All which binds together every minute particular. The society of the time did not allow the least measure of epic innocence, no *Iliad*, no *Song of the Niebelungs*. It was the age of "Ossian", not of Homer, the season of elegiac laments for the passing away of everything. For Arany the modern age is a Virgilian age, which allows for no fresh creativity, but only for cultural recapitulations. The world, he writes in a poem, is an old mantle, second-hand. During that same period Zsigmond Kemény, Transylvanian novelist and critic, urged that the task of the novel is to disenchant.

The great debate over epic and novel, which started in Germany at the time of Goethe and Hegel and culminated a century later in the youthful work of Lukács, involved not only questions of literature, but also the essence of life and history, the possibility of genuine existence and individual fulfilment in the modern age; and in Arany it found an intelligent and perceptive voice. Like Pushkin, he knew that his time "indulges in serious prose." Himself the author of epic poems, he says that his lines evoke the Hunnish horsemen of yore, but they stumble and falter if they try to follow the impetus of their galloping. All the same, he adds, a modern poet may draw some personal comfort from the fact that, though he cannot be Homer, he can at least be Tasso, and reconcile epic innocence with the drift towards middle-class values, thanks to the emotional awareness of his own distance from life, and to the intellectual nostalgia which obliquely outflanks that distance.

In this way Arany hopes that his work might be an "epos", no longer gushing forth from experience, but firmly based on culture; and he mentions the *Saga of Frithjof*, *Childe Harold*, and *Eugene Onegin*. The true poet of the people, he says, today is a learned poet; he imitates the old songs, but in that way he makes songs of his own which have

imbibed the ancient spirit and therefore really and truly get across to
the people, becoming part of the common legacy. For the Magyar poet
and patriot the true entity is the nation, with its uninterrupted
continuity of past and present, which will be projected into the future.
Rather than being the root of poetry, the objective tradition is poetry
itself.

13. MITTELEUROPA AND ANTIPOLITICS

The book by György Konrád, which enjoys the favour of the public but
not that of Gigi, was not published in Hungary for reasons of
censorship, but came out in Germany in translation. Konrád is a
Hungarian writer known, even in Italy, for his novel *The Visit*. His
banned book is called *Antipolitics*, and carries the subtitle *Mitteleuropean Reflections*. Mitteleuropa becomes the cipher for a refusal of
politics, or rather for the intrusion of the state and of reasons of state
into every sphere of existence. The division of Europe between the two
superpowers, sanctioned by Yalta, seems to Konrád a typical and tragic
effect of these falsely grand and spuriously world-wide politics, and
indeed tyrannically dishonest.

   To the ideologies of the two rival blocs Konrád opposes a flexible
intellectual strategy, both liberal and tolerant, inspired by a sense of
proportion and empirical realism. For him too, the Mitteleuropean
sensibility means the defence of the particular against any totalitarian
programme. Mitteleuropa is the name Konrád gives to his concept or
hope of a Europe united and independent of the two blocs; and this in
the conviction that the present disputes between Americans and
Russians, which appear today to be the pivot of world history, will one
day seem as absurd and irresponsible as those between the French and
the Germans of a few decades ago. In Budapest, therefore, Europe does
not exist solely in the cafés along the river embankments, but also in
people's heads. All the same, it may be that Gigi is not entirely wrong:
for Konrád, as for Kundera, Mitteleuropa becomes a word that is
noble, but at the same time vague and generic, an illusory master-key
for each and every political aspiration. Konrád himself observes that
the unity between the intellectuals and the people, which he hopes will
come about, does in fact only happen when power collapses; that is, in

exceptional and tragic situations which he is very far from wishing on the world.

14. TWO TELEGRAMS

May 15th 1919: telegram from Baron Szilassy, a working diplomat, dispatched from Hôtel Salines in Bex, Switzerland, to People's Commissar Béla Kun, Budapest: "Propose requesting American Protectorate of Hungary and if possible declare Hungary a State of the American Union stop." The laconic reply of Béla Kun, two days later: "Nous avons reçu votre dépêche." ("Communication noted.") Politics here seem to be imitating cabaret. Danubian history is not short of unrealized plans for multi-national federations, from the German-Magyar-Slav-Latin confederation or the Danubian federal republic open to all nations dreamt up by Baron Miklos Wesselényi in 1842 and 1849, to István Szechenyi's multi-national programme of 1849; from Kossuth's tardy change of heart (in his fiery years he said he never managed to find Croatia on the map) to the grandiose scheme of the Rumanian Aurel Popovici, dating from 1906 and entitled *The United States of Greater Austria*. None of these schemes was carried out. Baron Szilassy's telegram just seems a joke – or perhaps not so much of a joke, if we think of what happened later as a result of Yalta. However, the notion of a Hungary bordering on Texas or Wyoming shows what incongruity is born, quite objectively, from the concrete and calculated actions of politicians. With their two telegrams, the Baron and the People's Commissar sound like Vladimir and Estragon chatting away while waiting for the Godot of world history.

15. CURVACEOUS ENLIGHTENMENT

Close to the so-called Vienna Gate, Bécsi Kaput, on the Várlegy, Castle Hill, is a statue which metaphorically commemorates Ferenc Kazinczy, a man of the Enlightenment. The female figure holds a lantern, symbol of the light of Reason; her form is slender, the curves of her body are light and soft. This Enlightenment in feminine guise softens the edge of rationality, seems to remove a little of its intellectual dryness, that progressive's self-assertion, and to confer on it a supple and even amorous understanding – something that perhaps might save it from that dialectic of progress and violence which, according to the famous analysis by Adorno and Horkheimer, is forcing our civilization into a fatal spiral.

The day is generous with undulating lines and sensual pleasure. At 9 Fortuna Utca it even offers us the compliant breasts of the goddess Fortuna, carved by the not very famous Ferenc Medgyessy in 1921: they are tender models of the curvature of the earth. At No. 4 in the same street there was once the Fortuna Inn, which now houses the Hungarian Museum of Commerce and Catering. Clearly inspired by this name, Amedeo, who, like Monsieur Teste, goes through life classifying, begins to expound a theory concerning the connection between erotica and the art of travelling. He subdivides it into a number of sections: eros and coaches, eros and post-houses, adventures in trains, licentious cruises, the customs of ports and of inland cities, the differences between capital cities and provincial towns, the aeroplane and sexual inactivity (imputed chiefly, but not solely, to the brevity of air trips and the constant interruption to which one is subjected).

The *Musée de l'Hôtellerie* appeals to gluttony rather than to lasciviousness. It displays posters for historic pastries such as Joseph Naisz's creation which promised maraschino from Zara, Curaçao, Anisette and Tamarind; it shows majestic cakes like towering temples, reproduces sweetmeats of illustrious memory, figures once fashioned of chocolate and cream, Gâteau d'ananas à la Zichy, Fruits entiers à la Duchesse Gisèle. Gluttony ogles other pleasures in the Pain de Framboises à la Leda, a pyramid of temptations, a dish supporting a naked woman in a shell, who appears to be offering herself to a swan: the bird, who looks equally delicious, is stretching out his neck to her. These dainties end up by making one feel slightly sick, like every kind of affectation. But in the reconstruction of an older-days pastry-shop, the knobs on the drawers are exactly the same as those in use in Fiume and Trieste forty years ago: the tiniest indications of a domestic Mitteleuropa, mysterious treasures of childhood, the distant feel of home.

We stop at Margaret Island where, according to the proverb, love begins and ends. This transience of the heart and senses was made much of in the Hungarian novels of the 1930s, that production line of books entitled *The Most Beautiful Woman in Budapest* or *Meeting at Margaret Island*, which seemed to match the caressing, stereotyped aura of these burgeoning flower-beds, parks, hotels and *belle époque* pavilions, with fountains playing among the roses. But even this allurement touches the soul, like some tired old waltz, and is a little promise of happiness; it induces the melancholy associated with any meditation on joy. And that love can end is always a thought that wrings the heart, even if expressed in the banal refrain of a popular song. That evening, at the *Matthias*, a gypsy fiddler plays the *Pácirta*, the skylark. All this is still "décor" of the beginning of the century, the style of the superannuated gentry who liked Hungarian gypsy music, which was really neither Hungarian nor gypsy. But the *Pácirta* is a lovely song, the violinist plays it in masterly style and, at least for this evening, love is not over. Even on an ordinary evening it can happen that one finds real life in something false.

16. THE LIBRARY ON THE DANUBE

One of the last photographs of Lukács shows him at eighty-six years old, standing beside his desk which is covered with books and papers, and in the background the huge library of his home on the fifth floor of 2 Belgràd Rakpart in Budapest. His shoulders are slightly hunched, and in his right hand he is holding his famous cigar, half-hidden against his side: a cigar that makes a fit companion and comforter to a long lifetime spent as a protagonist in the major events of our century; more so and more faithfully than the *Weltgeist* or the core-thread of world history.

The photographs, then of very recent date, show a forceful, battling old man; and the papers cramming his work-table – the lecture he is preparing or the debate – still seem to represent gestures full of significance for him, concrete expressions of something essential, in which he believes. At eighty-six, he was suffering not only from cancer but from a sclerosis which progressively deprived him of his capacity for intellectual concentration; and yet in 1971 he was still the man who declared that he was "no longer competent to judge the *Ontology of Social Being*", the philosophical work to the writing and revision of which he had devoted his last years; he was hoping to complete it while still in full command of his faculties, running a step ahead of the disease. Calmly taking stock of his own physical decline, and of no longer being able to dominate and evaluate his work, he entrusted it to his pupils, in the humble yet self-confident certainty that he was entrusting it to history. He was certain of the fact that history would not be able to ignore the book, to let it fall into oblivion.

Lukács recorded his own biological decline and retired from the scene with a gesture similar to that of the Eskimo who feels that his end is near and his existence is useless to his community: he leaves the igloo and goes away to die. That symbolic gesture with which Lukács handed in his resignation to lucidity and vitality was also a victory over his own incapacity, the extreme intelligence of one able to realize that his logical clarity is occasionally becoming clouded. Lukács's last months were not months of inertia, but of activity, stripped of any sentimental pathos and of the melancholy of those who see their sands running out.

But in that last portrait the face seems changed. The expression is tired, ironic; it looks beyond that order of things which the philosopher had made the principle of his existence and his activity. Lukács gazes in benevolent perplexity at a territory which is no longer his and which he can no longer dominate, almost as if he were watching some insane comedy on stage and were surprised by this revelation and scornful at his own surprise. That expression is one of farewell; it is the expression of one who discovers the mystery, the sorrow and the ridiculous misunderstanding of every farewell, which laughs to scorn our longing for eternity. In that last expression of the aged Lukács, the philosopher who has sought for unity between reality and reason, we seem to glimpse the yearning of the youthful Lukács, who in his early essays – from *Soul and Form* to *The Theory of the Novel* – brilliantly described the gulf between existence and its meaning, between the soul and the word, between essence and phenomena.

But while he was posing for the photograph, that ironical, enigmatic look which Lukács turned towards the photographer took in the opposite wall of the library. There he saw, not the image of Irma Seidler, the woman for whom he had written his youthful essays, but the three portraits of his beloved wife Gertrud, with whom he had lived for more than forty years in the purest of harmony and happiness. Irma had represented his yearning to live, the figure which symbolized the impossibility of reconciling existence with the work of art, genuine living with everyday banality. Above all she had been the symbolic figure for male egoism, which loves not so much the woman but its own fantasies about the woman, and sacrifices the actual person to the literary phantom, so as to give birth to the work of art. In a draft of a letter never sent, and found many years later, Lukács told Irma that he was thinking of committing suicide. But, after breaking with him, and an unhappy marriage, it was Irma who killed herself, in 1911, while he survived her, as healthy as could be, for sixty years.

Those books written by Lukács as a young man are his masterpieces, and speak more clearly to us than the polished orthodoxy of *Studies in European Realism*, or other woodenly didactic books, which betray signs of the compromises he made with Stalinism. But Lukács is great not only because when he was young he put to himself the question as to whether there is not a melody which composes an individual's life into a unity illuminated by a meaning; he also sought the answer to this question, and accepted the limitations implied in any answer given to a vague, indefinable nostalgia, in any concrete social and historical reality, without which life is empty rhetoric.

On the wall opposite the bookshelves, and before the eyes of Lukács in the photograph, were the three portraits of Gertrud; and they are still there today, before the eyes of the visitor. Following his egocentric but lyrical love for Irma, and his short, unsuccessful marriage to Jelena Grabenko (an anarchic revolutionary with Messianic, Dostoyevskian notions similar to those of the young Lukács himself), it was Gertrud Bortstrieber he married, and with her he was to live for forty years, until her death in 1963.

Gertrud represented love and marriage in epic form; she was the woman whose approval Lukács needed at all costs, and with whom he could not bear to be out of harmony. Even with her, he said, there were obviously moments of estrangement, but – unlike what occurred in his previous emotional attachments – now "they were unbearable to me". Perhaps he placed even too much confidence in his Hegelian harmony with the *Weltgeist* and was rather too readily inclined to portray his own most original intuitions in the name of that *Weltgeist* (and maybe for this very reason he was uncertain of his own innermost spiritual substance); but Lukács declared that his highest sense of self came from realizing that for Gertrud, too, their shared life had been formative and plentiful.

Gertrud, with her unspoken stringency, was probably what led Lukács to become a Communist. From that moment on his biography is inextricable from that of Communism: it becomes a history lesson, crammed with facts and lucidly inspired by severe dedication to an objective cause. This on occasion involves an arrogant measure of self-identification with the necessity of events. Remembering his own youthful passion for Dostoyevsky, which he later kept quiet about, Lukács (like a great sinning mystic, as Strada put it) agreed to sacrifice his own soul to the Cause, taking upon himself the blemishes which such an act implied. For Lukács even autobiography takes on an objective and supra-personal value, as evidence of the connections between the history of the individual and the general processes of the world and of society.

Lukács is chiefly concerned with stressing the unity and consistency of his biography, the ordered and organic formation of his personality. "In me, everything is the continuation of something. I believe that there are no inorganic elements in my evolution," he claims, with that peremptory ingenuousness which one forgives in grand old men who come to stand for the great processes of history. Lukács is the great example of a tenacious effort to make sense of life and events, and a forceful confidence in his ability to do so: "I interpreted 1956 as a great spontaneous movement. This movement required a certain ideology. In a number of public lectures I attempted to take this task on myself." His thought is a grandiose attempt to reduce the chaotic many-sidedness of the world to a unity and to rational laws, even if we too clearly perceive the effort and the cost of this operation, marked as it was with Stalinism.

For Lukács, Gertrud was life, and her mystery was no lesser than the unexpressed longing for life. Of those three portraits two show her as an old woman, and the third as a young, luminous girl, with a clear, enchantingly pure face beneath a surge of hair over her brow. The history, and the length of time, which flowed between those portraits is no less moving than the hours which marked the unhappiness of Irma. Even Bloch, as he tells the story of his friendship and disagreement with Lukács, says that something in their story must have been lost.

The greatness of the mature Lukács consists in the force with which he fought against this leaking away of life into indistinct nothingness, wrenching from it with rigorous discipline the moments of meaning – such as the famous daily hour after lunch spent, at all costs, alone with Gertrud – which otherwise, if entrusted to the spontaneity of the minute, disintegrate before the assaults of worries.

In that room Lukács lived his life, devoting himself to meditation and knowing that that does not lose its life. In front of his dark, heavy wooden desk is a bust of Endre Ady, the Hungarian *poète maudit*, reminding him of his youthful, and repudiated, love of the avant-garde. From the window he could see the great Danube, but he probably had little appreciation of it, insensitive as he was to nature, which in his eyes was blemished by not having read Kant or Hegel. Bloch reproved him for his lack of understanding for nature, for the "tears in things"; and certainly to derive comfort from the pages of Lukács we need to be in good health and not afflicted by too much suffering, while in Bloch there is also room for darkness, for the moments when one feels like the refuse and wreckage of the world.

Behind the weary, elusive old man who presents himself, perhaps for the last time, to the photographer, rises the library of the great German *Kultur*, which has not just given a description of the world, but has insisted on it giving an account of itself, and a meaning. From those books I pick out Wittgenstein's *Tractatus*. Some of the propositions have marginal notes by Lukács. We wonder whether that gaze, with so little time left to look upon the world, was considering the possibility that the most profound philosophical problems – as is stated in Proposition No. 4003, which he had underlined – were not really and truly meaningless and bereft of any hope of an answer, other than the recognition of their meaninglessness.

17. A BIT OF STALIN

Csepel, the island in the Danube south of Budapest, is one of the industrial and political centres of Hungary, a working-class district of steelworks and factories. In 1949 and the ensuing years a lot of enthusiastic young Communists arrived there, intent on building the new revolutionary society by Stakhanovite methods. In 1956 Csepel became the Stalingrad of the anti-Bolshevik revolution, the centre for the anti-Communist Soviets. The workers' councils in the factories, set up during those weeks, put up the most strenuous armed resistance to the Russian panzers. While elsewhere the insurgents were laying down their arms, the U.S.S.R. was still besieging a bulwark formed by the industrial proletariat. These are the words of Cavallari on November 9th-10th 1956. The proletariat was making a liberal revolution – the liberal revolution long beyond the capacities of the middle class. In the present age the epic, the total vision which enables men to face death with courage and simplicity, is mainly a feature of the working classes. It is from them, where they still truly exist, in their bare, essential hardness, that the characters of a present-day *Iliad* might emerge.

In the autumn of 1956 the European order as laid down at Yalta began to crumble and go to pieces. The immense effort of power required to hold it together suddenly revealed its staggering cost, and the veins of the weight-lifter swelled to bursting point. In those same days, in Budapest, they dismembered the giant statue of Stalin. The young reporter who covered those events is like a Tacitus faced with the ruin of an empire. "The monument to Stalin", wrote Cavallari, "had already been toppled, but on the pedestal there remained the stubs of his boots, and people were climbing up a long, enormously long ladder, carrying stones, hammers and even metal-saws, and gradually smashing even the dictator's feet to pieces. I remember that we too climbed the long ladder, to get a better view, and we took a 'bit of Stalin' as a souvenir. But we lost it at once, running away from the circling armoured cars, while they, the Hungarians, continued among the flying bullets to climb the ladder, to hammer and crumble and smash. I recall that they did not climb down even when the tanks arrived, and that two workmen were patiently sawing away at a boot as the rattle of the tank-tracks grew louder."

The order which was then shaken to the point of collapse has been re-established, though in a different form. Stalin's statue has not been put together again, or hoisted back into place, but the fragments of it have not yet become souvenirs, they are still functional objects, though put to other uses. Even the Hungarian revolution of 1956, in spite of the radical change which it brought about, seems in part to obey that hidden monarchy which rules over world history, concerned above all with neutralizing or stifling the consequences of great events, and to arrange things so that, as soon as they are over, it is as if they had never happened.

18. KALOCSA

On the gateway to the archbishop's palace, placid and protective, rests a bishop's hat. The late summer is sultry, the box bushes are covered with spiders' webs, the finest and most precarious gossamer the making of which, like all the investments made by nature and individuals, seems quite disproportionate to the modesty of the results. A hot wind wanders the streets like a nomad, the avenues offer a deep dense shade. In the main square, on the base of the inevitable pillar of the Trinity, there is a frieze depicting the whole of the pillar itself, complete with the image of itself, and so on into infinity, like Scheherazade telling the tales of the *Thousand and One Nights* which contain the story of Scheherazade telling the story of . . . But any story is a paradox, an endless play of mirrors. Anyone who tells a story is narrating the world, which contains himself. The bold narrator who describes two dark eyes, an expression profound and almost imperceptibly surprised, in those dark waters discerns all that may be seen in their mirror, even his own face anxiously peering into it.

Kalocsa is famous for its traditional shirts and blouses, with red embroideries surging around the neckline as the foaming undertow swirls its patterns on a beach. Buying a couple of these shirts is not in itself a metaphysical act, but a generous décolletage, happened upon at the right moment, is Newton's apple, Descartes' piece of wax, and the discovery of a bountiful, indisputable reality.

At Kalocsa art does not, however, pander only to feminine vanity, but also to the vanity of funereal matters: statues carved in wood and painted in colours as vivid as the Day of Judgment; stylized, archaic figures, as epic as the earth and as death. Over one tomb rises the head of a woman, black as night, an effigy that might have come from Easter Island and from the ancient of days. Instead it commemorates Kakony Lászlóné, who died in 1969. On the other hand the monument to Apostol Pálné, who died in 1980, is red: warm, dark, brick-red – a colour set in the earth like a wild flower, harsh and unconcerned.

19. EPILOGUE AT BAJA

The ochre light of this afternoon, and the gilded green of the river, are – like the spacious, elegant *Béke Tér* with its yellow buildings – a worthy setting for the epilogue, or rather the postscript, to the history of the Hapsburgs, which occurred on these very banks of the Danube. Charles, last of the Emperors, had in 1921 attempted to regird his head with the Crown of St Stephen. The attempt failed, and caused a rather small battle, too small in fact to interrupt an important football match going on in Budapest. A British gunboat transported him – in company with the Empress Zita – from Baja to Madeira, his place of exile. It was on these shores that the Papal Nuncio gave him his blessing. And with that the last of the Hapsburgs departed down the Danube, the river that was the very image of his crown, on his way to the Black Sea, the Mediterranean, the Pillars of Hercules, and exile.

So the river flows on, flows on. But Hölderlin, the greatest poet to sing of the Danube, celebrated it not only as the mythical voyage of the Germanic forefathers, travelling down its waters towards the days of summer, to the shores of the Black Sea and the children of the sun, but also as the voyage of Heracles from Greece to the Hyperboreans. Hölderlin demanded of poetry that it should heal the terrible schism of modern life, and he too tears himself in half over this burning need to put two parts of life together, and for him the Danube is the journey and the meeting between East and West, the coming-together of the Caucasus and Germany, of the Hellenic springtime that has to reflower in German soil and bring the gods back to life again. That poet has a longing to flow down towards Hellas and the Caucasus, the cradle of everything, and the Danube is the road to this redeeming journey. Nevertheless, in his hymn to the Ister, it seems that the river flows uphill, coming from the East, from Greece to Germany and Europe, bearing morning and rebirth to the land of the evening.

So the river leads back to its source, and those Black Sea Mouths, with their high-sounding names, could they be not the end, but the entrance into life . . . ? Perhaps every journey makes towards its source, seeking for its own face and the *fiat* that called it forth out of nothing. The traveller is fleeing from the restrictions of reality, that trap him in repetition after repetition, and seeks for freedom and the future; or rather, the possibility of a future that is still open, and subject to choice – childhood, the house where he was born, the place where the whole of life is still before him.

Maybe he hopes that there, where the Danube flows, his face will lose the world-weariness that has afflicted it of late, and that his eyes, instead of glancing timidly and eagerly this way and that, in the manner of a man who somewhere along the way has lost his gods, will open again in enchantment like those of a child snapped in a photograph while he was happily looking at a cat in a courtyard. Sweet cheats are these, a long time with us and hard to lose, with the illusion of being able to go back home and drink at the source, and having the poetry of the heart within reach once again. Virgil is a poet because, even though too late, he realized that the *Aeneid* had to be burnt, and the impossibility of it had to be declared. The traveller who dreams of an Odyssey, of the fulfilment and the homecoming, has to be able to stop in time, so as not unwittingly to play a comic role; to sit down on the banks of the Danube and ply a fishing-rod. Maybe, if he does that, he will find some measure of decorous salvation in those waters, even if "What the river does," as Hölderlin says in his *Ister*, "no one knows."

The waters of the Danube, a river "cloudy, wise and great", for Attila József, with their monotonous flowing, meant old age and the contemporaneous presence of many centuries, the confluence of the victors and the vanquished, the impact of races which then became mingled in time and in the waters, as the Cumaean blood of his mother mingled in his veins with the Rumanian Transylvanian blood of his father. His Danube was "past, present and future". József was a great poet, and in his work he succeeded in fusing the anarchic freedom of poetry with rational, human, loving, social solidarity. Personal and political despair thrust him, in 1937, under the wheels of a train. In his poetry of the Danube he has tender memories of his father. According to Miklós Szabolsci, this father simply abandoned his family and never knew that his son was a poet. Several years after his son's death he was amazed when they came and told him that he had sired a writer famed throughout Hungary and the whole of Europe.

It isn't easy to write about the Danube, because the river – as Franz Tumler said a few years ago in his *Propositions on the Danube* – flows on in a continuous and indistinct way, unaware of propositions and of language sewing and severing the fabric of existence. The depths are silent, says József in a poem. If we insist on making them speak we run the risk of putting into their mouths an eloquent, stylized rhetoric, as occurs in the *Carmen saeculare* of two Rumanian poets, Dimítrie Anghel and Stefán Octavián, in which the Danube converses nobly and uselessly with the Doina, the allegorical personification of folk poetry.

20. THE WINE OF PÉCS

Dem Deutschen Bécs, dem Ungarn Pécs, says the proverb: "The Germans have Vienna and the Hungarians have Pécs." Tranquil and withdrawn, the city – which in German is called Fünfkirchen, the Five Churches – is not unworthy of the hyperbolical comparison with Vienna, nor with the long catalogue of encomiums which have celebrated it ever since the Middle Ages. Its climate is applauded, with its mild winters, breeze-cooled summers, long and balmy autumns; its cultural traditions abound in Roman antiquities and are similar to those of Chartres; it boasts chroniclers, scholars, a university founded in 1367, the most ancient in Hungary and the fourth oldest in Central Europe, and the library of Bishop Georg Klimó. Panegyrics are also directed at its wines: those of Mecsek once favoured by the Germans, the Siklós preferred by the Slavonians, the Alfó-Baranyer in which the Serbs of the Bačka indulged to a man.

In terms of the wine the eulogy of the Baranya, the region of Pécs, has indeed for a long time set two factions at odds – the one which awards the palm to the local wine of Pécs, the capital, and the more pugnacious one which extols the wine of Villány. The judgment of Paris is left to Gigi, or at least he is elected foreman of the jury which has met, *motu proprio*, in the Rózsakert restaurant. "Judge not," it has been said, but being a juryman can be a pleasant occupation when one is not weighing up human actions and years in prison, but the books or the wines of the season. The juries of literary prizes meet, discuss, sift, proclaim, assign, banquet; dull old life meanwhile passes by, thank goodness, dim and unobserved; as for the vague feeling of importance that inhabits the one who presents the prize, bending slightly towards the prizewinner who is climbing the steps to the stage, it helps him to forget his own vacuity and the approach of the final epilogue. This evening, at the Rózsakert, there are no authors but only works, bottles from the cellar, and there is not much to discuss. The white wine of Pécs is excellent, fine and slightly sweet, while the red wine of Villány is sour. Thus, on an evening like any other, the tenacious reputation of the latter comes crashing to the ground.

The Baranya, which Alexander Baksay compared to a tapestry inlaid by two rivers, is a border area, composite and stratified. As well as Hungarians and the German minority there were the Serbs and the Schokatzi, the latter being Slav Catholics from the Balkans who made the sign of the cross with the open palm of the hand and amongst whom it was usually only the women who could read and write – perhaps to save the men even this chore, and render the exploitation of women even more complete. They say that at Ormánság, in Baranya, when the examining commission once asked a candidate for the office of magistrate whether he could read and write, the answer they got was, "No, but I can sing."

The German presence was particularly strong; the committee of Baranya was known as "Swabian Turkey". Eighty years ago Adam Müller-Guttenbrunn, the defender of German solidarity against "Magyarization", represented the Swabians of the Banat and the Transylvanian Saxons who were staunchly loyal to Austria and opposed to the Hungarian Revolution in 1848; today, however, the literature of the Germans in Hungary, cultivated chiefly in Pécs and Bonyhád, extols the bond between Swabians and Hungarians in that territory as being anti-Hapsburg and anti-Austrian – still with reference to 1848. In an open letter of November 17th 1967, Wilhelm Knabel, who died in 1972, explicitly theorized the present function of the German writer in Hungary. His own verses, written in German and in Swabian dialect, are worthy and imitative, like the prose pieces of the authors represented by Erika Áts in her anthology *Deep Roots*, who are voices of an ingenuous local clique. The more encouraging critics, such as Béla Szende, speak of their "simplicity that touches the hearts of all". The German community in Hungary – threatened by Magyarization in Hapsburg times, in even worse decline after 1918, and compromised by Germanic chauvinism during Nazi times was oppressed and ignored after 1945. Efforts are now being made, even artificially, after the community's total silence, to restore some vigour and meaning to it. Stress is being laid on its function as a mediator between differing cultures (the key slogan of the whole of Mitteleuropa), similar to the role it played in the last century, when, for example, the German-Hungarian Jew Dóczi Lajos – or Ludwig von Dóczi – translated Goethe's *Faust* into Hungarian and Mandách's *Tragedy of Man* into German.

The persistent Hungarian patriotism of these German writers is an attempt to erase the memory of the fierce Magyar-Germanic clashes during the period of Dualism, and even more the tensions built up during the Third Reich. The situation throughout this last period was extremely complicated. The German-National movement of the German-speaking group in Hungary, led by Jakob Bleyer, did not identify itself with Nazism, in spite of Bleyer's ideology of the *Volkstum*; while Hitler, on his side, watched after the interests of the German minority, but made no attempt to annex the areas in which it lived. At the same time Hitler's ally Horthy, leader of the Fascist (or para-Fascist) regime in Hungary, pursued a nationalistic policy which came down hard on all the minorities in Hungary, including, of course, the German one.

In the years immediately following the Second World War the Hungarian government repressed and expelled the German minority, identifying it with Nazism. But today German-speaking writers in Hungary, encouraged and patronized by Budapest, profess loyalty to the Hungarian nation and to Socialism. It is true that the *Bund*, the Nazi organization, did in its day find most of its adherents in the Baranya, and at Bonyhád in particular. Unless this too is Jewish slander, responsible, as we all know, for every conceivable evil including Nazism itself: Hitler also – according to the anti-Semitic viewpoint – must have been a Jew, because only a Jew would have been capable of his crimes . . . According to Bleyer, the German-Nationalist leader, in Hitler's day the Hungarian correspondent of the Nazi newspaper *Völkischer Beobachter* was of Jewish origin and wrote anti-German articles under a pseudonym for the Hungarian papers, to arouse people's spirits . . .

21. THE FAKE CZAR

Following the example of Captain Speke as he travelled along the Nile, we occasionally indulge ourselves in a zigzag route, leaving the river for a trip in some other direction, to join it later at a point only a mile or two downstream. Amedeo suggests a diversion to Szeged, because he once met a certain Klára, who came from Szeged and wore striped stockings.

The dusty *puszta* is the gloomy Magyar landscape described by Ady: its Hungarian life, he said, as grey as the dust. The road runs along the southern border of the low-lying plain, as endless as the sea, wrote Petőfi, the bard of little Kumania, of its storks and will-o'-the-wisps on the far horizon. In this empty, uncaring landscape, life flows negligently by, moving towards infinite distance like a herd of cattle. The only thing that happens is that time passes. The years, says one of Petőfi's poems, flash by like a flock of birds after a gunshot.

To cross the Tisza, the slothful Hungarian Nile, as Mikszáth calls it, on a dark, dull evening, is slightly unpleasant, like leaving a land where one feels at home and entering a foreign country. Obedient to the authority of the book, I am anxious to seek out Yellow Island, at the meeting of the Tisza and the Maros, and the hostelry in which, according to Kálmán Mikszáth, "one ate the tastiest fish soup in the world," but literature, it seems, does not belong to the falsifiable, which is to say the true, sciences. It is therefore open to question whether, as claimed by the Antiquarius, the Tisza is composed of two thirds water and one third fish, pike and carp, so plentiful as to cost scarce a ducat a thousand.

In his picture of the city written for the monumental work produced under the patronage of the Archduke Rudolph, *The Austro-Hungarian Monarchy Described and Illustrated*, Mikszáth, the amiable narrator, says that "as among nearly all peoples who live in the plains, at Szeged also there is less poetry than in the mountains." It seems that even in love the inhabitant of Szeged has little verve, and would be inclined to select his father one from among the girls with a decent amount of money, or at least with shoulders strong enough to carry heavy sacks.

The town is shabby, with the air of a station yard. Its history, writes its stern bard, "swarms with catastrophes of every sort and kind," both historical and natural. Maybe so many calamities are a punishment for the rebellious spirit of the citizens, and their deep-rooted democratic tradition. Even the wealthy burghers sympathized with Dózsa, the great leader of the peasants' revolt, so that the nobles, having won the struggle, and captured and tortured Dózsa, cut off his head and sent it as a warning gift to Blasius Pálfy, chief magistrate of Szeged. Violence seems at home in these parts. In 1527, from the windows of the noble palace of Ladislaus Szilágy, a volley of musketry struck the false Czar Ivan (or Iova), the "terrible black man" who with his bandits had terrorized the area between the Temes and the Tisza. Ivan, whose real name was Franz Fekete, is one of those false Czars who abound in Slav history. He was one of those bandit-usurpers who are stirred in the first place by a thirst for plunder; thanks to their abilities, but without intending to, they rise to the point of playing a real political role, and in the end are pursued back to their brigandish origins and destroyed like weeds.

Having arbitrarily proclaimed himself a descendant of the family of the Serbian despots, Franz Fekete gathered an army of five – some say ten – thousand men, mostly peasants, with which he proceeded to ravage the country. Six hundred soldiers formed his bodyguard, his "janissaries", as he called them, probably in a delirium of grandeur and to compare himself with the Sultan of Constantinople, Suleiman the Magnificent, who had won the Battle of Mohács and conquered Hungary.

During that period, following the catastrophe of Mohács, the crown

of Hungary was disputed between the Emperor Ferdinand of Hapsburg, who lived in Vienna, and the Voivode of Transylvania, John
Zápolya, who at certain times enjoyed the support of the Turks, then
masters of the country. The rivalry between these two powers enabled
the false Czar, allied now to one and now to the other, to enter the
"great world" and the Machiavellianism of high politics.

Who knows whether the Terrible Black Man realized what was
happening to him, or the part which history was summoning him to
play, or whether he thought to the last only of plunder and pillage.
Without knowing or wanting it, maybe he started on the way to
becoming a double personality, one of those characters gradually
transformed by the mask which they adopt. The learned Stojacskovics
has him down as the seventh Despot of Serbia, whereas Schwicker, the
old historian of the Banat, questions this appraisal and places him
simply among the bandits. Defeated and wounded at Szeged, he
escaped into the woods, but was pursued and annihilated, along with
his last followers. His head was sent to Zápolya, whose residence was
in Ofen, the ancient Buda.

Death evidently suits Szeged. In Dom Tér, the cathedral square, is a
marble pantheon with the busts and effigies of illustrious men along
three sides. The encyclopaedist Apaczai Cseri Janos is depicted by a
skull, with a jacket and collar but missing two teeth, and in skeletal
fingers holding a book, the Magyar Encyclopaedia for the year
MDCLIII. Is learning therefore like death, the lethal stiffening of
existence and of its flow? In the Serbian church, not far from the
cathedral, not even the Virgin bestows liberation, or the womanly,
maternal intercession that melts the ice of the heart. The brow of this
Balkan Madonna is crowned, but the crown pierces her flesh and the
blood runs down onto the head of the Babe at her breast, soiling His
lips. This grim, sorrowing deity scarcely evokes the litanies of May or
the invocation of the morning star.

22. A VIOLIN AT MOHÁCS

Our detour is over, and we are at Mohács. The ancient battlefield, on
which in 1526 the Kingdom of Hungary was overwhelmed by the Turks
and obliterated for centuries, is a host of maize and sunflowers. The
weather is heavy and sultry, and scattered clumps of blue flossflowers

and red-flowering sage remind us, uselessly, that life is not just a war. Mohács, in its way, is a museum – a painful museum, not the display of something, but life itself, its transience and its eternity. Beside the date someone has laid some fresh flowers: that old defeat still smarts and those dead are recent.

A number of wooden statues, planted in the earth like pikes or the poles of overthrown tents, suggest the battle, its order and disorder, its confused symmetry, the instant of gunpowder which disperses and the unalterable fixity of violence and death. Those rash, ingenious carvings hint at the heads of men and of horses, the manes of dying steeds, huge turbans, deadly maces crashing down, faces contorted by agony or ferocity, crosses and crescents, slaves beneath the yoke, heads rolling to the feet of Suleiman the Magnificent. Everything is abstract, essential, the swift allusive hint of a carving sketched out in wood repeated in the swaying of the corn.

The wind tinkles the metal pendants which with barbaric splendour adorn the head of Suleiman the Magnificent, and that subdued sound, mingled with that of other trembling blades, is the echo of that distant clamour, a sound-wave travelling through the centuries, deceptively gentle like any sound of sorrow that reaches us from the past, touching us as musical enchantment and not as suffering.

That host is a chessboard turned topsy-turvy, and the ears of corn wave in the wind like the pendants of the warriors. The arrangement of the figures is circular, but troops of fugitives and their pursuers fall exhausted outside the circle, dispersed or lost in the dust-storm of things. Life seems eternal, and eternal appears each gesture of the battle which for ever carves an image, before God and the void, of violence, of sobbing, of cries, of the breath, the flight, the misting over of the world in the eyes of the dying, of the fall, the end. In these torrid fields a great collective sculptor has raised a monument to the perennial present of every death and to the geometry of the battle, the meticulous order with which it pursues chaos, the dispersal and break-up of the formations, the bodies and molecules beneath the sun.

Mohács, like Kossovo, is an epoch-making moment, a battle which for centuries seals the destinies of a people. On the day of Mohács, according to tradition, the olive-tree planted at Pécs two hundred years earlier by Louis the Great suddenly became barren. The pages which tell the story of that August 29th 1526, such as *De conflictu hungaorum cum turcis ad Mohatz verissima descriptio* (1527) by István Brodarics, constitute a paragraph in the history of Hungarian literature. At the approach of the mighty army of Suleiman the Magnificent, Louis II of Hungary, according to the ancient custom, sent a bloody sabre round from house to house, to persuade everyone to respond to his appeal and take up arms under his banner. The Hungarian nobility, more anxious to weaken the power of the King than to keep the Ottoman menace at bay, remained practically deaf to his call, or else they were involved in squabbles of their own. With his army at reduced strength, Louis tried to postpone the encounter and wait for reinforcements, but in the council of war the nobles present, egged on by Archbishop Tomori, vociferously demanded that they should give battle.

The King, writes the Antiquarius, shrugged his shoulders and, with this gesture of nonchalance, went to meet his fate, of which he was well aware, after giving orders for his hounds to be washed twice a week. Once on the field, we are told by the chronicler, he paled for a moment when his squire placed his helmet on his head, and then hurled himself into the fray. A few hours later, during the rout, he was killed when his horse fell on him and crushed him in the mire of a little stream, the Csele. A song still sung in Baranya a century ago celebrates the briars which cover the King. The booty captured by the Turks, scrupulously recorded by the Antiquarius, is an example of that poetry of catalogues which so abounded in baroque literature, eager as it was to call everything in the world by name.

József Pölškei's great gate, the fountain by Gyula Illyés, the sculpture by Király, Kiss, Szabó Jnr. and Pál Kö – Oceanian or African statues transplanted to Hungary like trees on which are grafted the flowers of an ornamental local or Transylvanian art – give the appearance of being a single monument, as unified and various as nature, as epic and unisonal as war. Everything is motionless, but that stillness has caught the sudden, desperate dash of battle, and the absolute moment of death.

It is hot, and we sit down to rest in the cool of a clump of trees. Amedeo takes out the old fiddle that travels with him, improvises a music stand and starts to play, while in the background the pendants continue to tinkle. He does not, for once, play passages from the classics, but Hungarian gypsy songs, the *Lieder* that wander from courtyard to innyard, like one of the wandering minstrels in Yiddish literature. That music is the answer to the battle, to the ring of metal. In one of the novels of Sholem Aleichem, Jossele Solovej – Jossele the Nightingale – takes violin in hand and plays what is missing to the heart. Solovej, Solovej the solo that tells of pain – in one of his poems

Israel Bercovici plays with this bewitching Yiddish word, Solovej, nightingale; he divides it into syllables and imagines that the nightingale is a solo voice that speaks of *vej*, which is melancholy.

Amedeo's short-sighted eyes look afar off, over his nineteenth-century lenses, onto that plain of dying horses and horsemen. His violin speaks of something that has been lost and will be lost. But heartache for the poetry of the heart which is vanishing is nostalgia that catches fleeting love by the tail, like the invincible pirouette of the Jewish wandering musician. The violin contests the field of battle, the great world, the blood-shedding glare of epoch-making events. Beneath these trees we are at home. Perhaps we pale for a moment, like the luckless monarch, but then we shrug, thank the imaginary audience for the coins which it would doubtless throw into the player's hat, then, bidding each other farewell, we all depart, each on his own road.

SEVEN

Grandma Anka

I. THINKING "WITH THE MIND OF SEVERAL PEOPLES"

This story was told me by Miklós Szabolcsi, at his country house at Göd, on the Danube near Budapest. The river was flowing gently on, that evening, towards its distant mouths, and we were talking about old stories of Temesvár, Timişoara, Temeschburg, the town (Hungarian? Rumanian? German?) that has played a part in so much of the history of Eastern Europe, from the times of the Tartars to those of the Turks and of Prince Eugène, and down to Francis Joseph. Some years ago Szabolcsi made a series of television programmes in an attempt to evoke the fervent cultural scene in Hungary during the first two decades of this century, the great age of the young Lukács, Endre Ady and Béla Bartók, tracking down all the figures, both major and minor, and reconstructing the events of their lives even after that brilliant, passionate epoch – brought to an end in the 1920s with the installation of the para-Fascist regime of Horthy.

After a lot of research, the mosaic put together by Szabolcsi was nearly complete, but one small tessera was missing. He had lost track of a certain Robert Reiter, or rather Reiter Róbert, an avant-garde Hungarian poet who had been a member of the most embattled experimental groups. A true literary critic is a detective, and perhaps the fascination of this debatable activity does not consist in making sophisticated interpretations, but in having the bloodhound scent that leads him to rummage in a certain drawer, or library, and to find the secret of someone's life. In this way Szabolcsi found his man. That is, he learnt that Reiter Róbert was alive, that he lived in Timoşoara in Rumania, that he was now called Franz Liebhard, and that he wrote somewhat traditional poems in German, sonnets and pieces rhyming a b a b . . . He had changed his name, nationality and literary style, and now he was honoured as the patriarch of the German-speaking writers of the Banat; belonging, that is, to the German minority living in Rumania. In August 1984 his eighty-fifth birthday had been celebrated.

Represented in an anthology of Hungarian experimental poetry published by the Budapest Academy of Sciences, famed as a German poet in Rumania, the author (also) of poems in Swabian dialect (i.e.

the dialect of the colonists who came to the Banat at the beginning of the eighteenth century), Reiter Róbert alias Franz Liebhard said in an interview that he had "learnt to think with the mentality of several peoples." His identity is even more complex than his double surname suggests. In the first place, it is not double but triple. "Liebhard" was the name of a friend of his, a miner killed in an accident, and the poet took his name in the early 1940s, as a token of loyalty. Thus Reiter Róbert became first Robert Reiter, the author of the pages which bear this signature, and then Franz Liebhard. But this German surname furthermore reveals the personality of the writer, a Swabian from the Banat who, with his *Swabian Chronicle*, published in German in 1952, gave a voice to his people, the Germans of the Banat, subject first to Vienna, then to Budapest, and now a tottering minority in Rumania.

Why did Reiter Róbert suddenly fall silent? By what route did he return from Hungarian to his mother language of German? Some years ago a critic compared him to Rimbaud, certainly more on the grounds of that mysterious silence and that metamorphosis than for his poetry itself. His first published poem, which appeared in November 1917 in the famous Hungarian avant-garde magazine *Ma* (Today), was called *Wood*, but his linguistic rope-dancing said little about a wood, its shade and its greenness. The "today" which gave its name to the magazine has become yesterday or the day before. Now, in rhymed verses and images that take no risks, Reiter-Liebhard as an old man describes good old familiar woods, with their friendly, restful fragrance.

2. A GREEN HORSE

Is the story of Reiter-Liebhard a step ahead or a step backwards, the epic homecoming of Ulysses or the grovelling return of one who had left home protesting and comes back with his tail between his legs and vowing to turn over a new leaf? Is that "thinking in the manner of many peoples" a unifying synthesis or a heterogeneous jumble? An addition or a subtraction? A way to be more abundant or to be Nobody? Maybe it is partly to find an answer to these questions that I am now in the Banat with Grandma Anka, who, with her eighty years, already constitutes an answer in herself. The starting point for our sorties in Bela Crkva (White Church), her home town. The 1914 railways timetable for the Hapsburg Empire called it Fehértemplom, in accordance with the principle of using the name most common in the place itself, and the town, which is now in Jugoslavia, was then part of the Kingdom of Hungary. Today the official trilingual notices carry Bela Crkva, Fehértemplom and Biserica Albǎ, which is to say the Serbian, Hungarian and Rumanian names. The German name, Weiss-kirchen, has all but disappeared. The churches here are Catholic, Protestant, Russian Orthodox, Greek Orthodox and Rumanian Orthodox. Some, like the church of the Slovaks, are in ruins.

This irregular detour from the correct and linear course of the Danube has, in this case, a historical justification – apart, of course, from the psychological one, which means Grandma Anka's way of swift decision-making. She simply wanted it to be this way, instead of passing first through Apatin, Novi Sad, Zemun and Pančevo, according to that splendid ordering of space and time which lays it down that what comes first precedes what comes later and that four comes between three and five. But here I am with Grandma Anka, and it is she who decides what comes first, with the calm assurance of one who is at peace with herself and has no need for systematic order.

It is therefore from Bela Crkva that we shall move towards the other Danubian places of the Banat and environs, as out along the spokes of a wheel, but with frequent returns to the hub. In any case, even the Antiquarius, who usually follows the river yard by yard with exasperating pedantry, on reaching these parts allowed himself detours and excursions. He even abandons the river altogether and dwells, for example, on Temesvár, which is about a hundred kilometres away. But he, and Grandma Anka along with him, was perfectly right; for the whole of this region is "Danube", for the Danube is its life and its nervous system, its very history, if I may quote Schwicker, the erudite chronicler of the Banat. Without the "universal-historical" river, said Müller-Guttenbrunn, picking up the theme, and without the world history which it has borne upon its waters, these lands would be nothing but marshes and flatlands. The walls of Temesvár are banks of the Danube, and the churches of Bela Crkva are the poplars and willows of these shores.

Grandma Anka shows me the house where she was born, the house of the prosperous merchant, administrator and victualler Milan Vuković who, on account of Hungarian nationalism, wrote his name Vukovics, as in Hungarian. In front of this house, after the First World

War, could be seen the carriage of Dr Jon Gian, deputy to Belgrade of the Rumanian minority, one of the many claimants to the hand of Grandma Anka, and of the few who did not in fact succeed in becoming her husband, seeing that she has so far married, served with impartial solicitude, and buried, four of them. Children she has never had.

Bela Crkva is a small town in the Banat, on the left bank of the Danube, little more than a hundred kilometres from Belgrade, and is one of the centres of Pannonia and of the old Hapsburg Empire. Today the Banat is one of the three zones which make up the autonomous region of the Vojvodina, which is part of Serbia. It forms the north-eastern part of Vojvodina, and has a long border with Rumania. The other two components of Vojvodina are the Srem (Syrmium for the ancient Romans), to the south of the Danube, and the Bačka, to the north-west. But a vast part of the old historic Banat, which for good reason bears the name of the Banat of Temesvár, is now in Rumania; its capital is indeed Temesvár, or Timişoara. Francesco Griselini, a Venetian son of the Enlightenment who travelled in these areas in 1774–6, depicting them in his still valuable *Lettere odeoporiche*, traced its boundaries and wrote that it comprised the territory bordered by the Danube, the Tisza, the Maros and the Transylvanian Alps. The Banat is a mosaic of peoples, a superimposition and stratification of races, powers, jurisdictions. It is a land which has seen the encounter and the clash of the Ottoman Empire, the Hapsburg authorities, the stubborn will to independence – and later the dominion – of the Hungarians, and the rebirth of the Serbs and the Rumanians.

A television documentary on the Vojvodina speaks of twenty-four ethnic groups. More modestly, Griselini talked of ten different nations, which he described minutely: Wallachians (i.e. Rumanians), *Rasciani* (i.e. Serbs), Greeks, Bulgars, Hungarians, German colonists, Frenchmen, Spaniards, Italians and Jews. It is a fact that after the reconquest of Temesvár, which Prince Eugène took from the Turks in 1716, General Mercy, a wise and enterprising governor, drained swamps and repopulated deserted plains by bringing in immigrants from many countries. In 1734 the town of Becskerek was full of Spaniards, who had there founded a New Barcelona.

The largest group of colonists was German, summoned in the eighteenth century by Maria Theresa and Joseph II. Most of them came from Swabia, the Palatinate or the Rhineland, descending the Danube on the Ulm barges. They were tough, hard-working peasants who transformed unhealthy marshlands into fertile soil. Swabia, one of the heartlands of old Germany, was thus transplanted into the Banat; and even today, in the areas now in Rumania, one can in certain villages hear the Swabian or Alemannic dialects, as if one were in the Württemberg or the Black Forest.

The Germans were certainly not the only ones to arrive. There were the Slovaks, most of them Protestants, the Serbs who arrived in a series of waves over the centuries, pressed back by the advance of the Turks, and also many others. Nations emerge and the world trembles before their power, wrote the learned Schwicker, but they too soon pay tribute to the transience of earthly things. Everyone trembles before everyone else, the Turks before the imperial troops who capture Belgrade and the imperial troops before the Turks who capture it back. With the passing of years, of decades, of centuries there is a change in the statutes of cities and the numbers of each nationality or religion – the boiling pot does not cease to boil, to fuse and amalgamate its contents, to burn, to consume . . .

At Pančevo, even at the end of the nineteenth century, there were Székely villages, while Becskerek does not remember that it was once a Spanish town. Until the middle of the last century one cannot think in terms of nationalism or nationalistic movement. When Governor Mercy called in those German farmers, he did not intend to "Germanize" those lands, but simply to populate them with skilful peasants and artisans who would come to the aid of enlightened progress. As Josef Kallbrunner observed, these German immigrants could well be Rumanians or Slavs, just as long as they had learnt, and were therefore in a position to broadcast and diffuse, the industry and diligence which was typically German.

The five principal groups co-existing today in Jugoslavian Vojvodina, living peacefully side by side in the manner sanctioned by the 1974 Constitution, are Serbs, Hungarians, Slovaks, Rumanians and Ruthenians, but there are numerically lesser national groups, such as Germans, Bulgars and gypsies. And there are still a few Bunjewatzi and Schokatzi, who came centuries ago from southern Dalmatia and Bosnia and Herzegovina, and have been claimed (being Serbian Catholics, for some strange reason) both by the Serbs and the Croats, though they have always tended to think of themselves as a group of their own. This idyll is a real thing, even if it is somewhat stressed by magniloquent propaganda; but who knows if people still repeat the old Rumanian proverb that runs as follows: "Who ever saw a green horse or an intelligent Serb?" Grandma Anka, who quotes this to me without resentment, is of ancient Serbian stock. And who knows the respective thoughts of Reiter Róbert about the Germans, and Franz Liebhard about the Hungarians?

3. THE WISE COUNCILLOR TIPOWEILER

In all fraternal official statements, the various ethnic groups are constantly clapping each other on the back and declaiming each other's best qualities. In Grandma Anka, who speaks all the languages, the different nationalities, on the other hand, overlap and clash. On our way to Bela Crkva we pass through the Rumanian village of Straža, and this gives her an opportunity – forgetting her own beloved Rumanian grandmother – to call the Rumanians thieves and ragamuffins, without so much as a sandal between them, among whom her father drove his cart with a flaming torch in one hand and a pistol in the other. As she runs down the Rumanians she pays tribute to the orderly, hardworking Germans; but a little later, devoutly recalling the "Rumanian courtliness" of President Popescu, former Chief Justice of the court in Bela Crkva, she says that the fine conduct of the Germans frequently concealed pig-headedness and dishonest greed, and she calls them "Romany rabble, worse than the gypsies who now swagger around in a Mercedes". Moreover, as a fierce anti-Communist, she recalls the terrors of the Nazi occupation and the epic of the partisans in the snow.

The most fervent Germanophile in Bela Crkva, who bore the rather un-German name of Ben Mates, was at one time raving in a bar about wanting to play bowls with the heads of the Serbs; but Grandma Anka's mother, who happened to be passing at the time, gave him this quiet riposte: "Have it your own way, Mates: you do it to us today, we'll do it to you tomorrow." And in fact, it did end tit for tat. At the end of 1944 and into 1945 came the enforced exodus of the Germans from the Banat and the Bačka, their indiscriminate deportation into work-camps and concentration camps – which even became deathcamps; and all this in the name of a collective responsibility laid to the charge of everyone, and which became a reprisal and racial persecution. Kardelj, the Slovene Communist leader who died before his time, was one of the few to raise objections against this policy of revenge, and to deplore the expulsion of groups who were socially and economically productive.

Grandma Anka has it in for Tito and Communism, even though with imperturbable impartiality she mentions the injustice and social oppression obtaining in her infancy. But her love of order and Slav feelings prompt her to love the Soviet Union, and for this reason she looks down her nose at America and Reagan, "a rotten actor; when he talks on TV, he seems the whole time to be listening to the whispers of his Jewish advisers." In the concentrated essence of historical prejudices and resentments which Grandma Anka embodies, there is naturally – like one of the rings in an ancient tree-trunk – anti-Semitism as well. But this suddenly vanishes when she talks about Herr Loewinger, the lawyer who, in the terms of her description, becomes the personification of age-old Jewish wisdom and dignity.

There is maybe a smattering of truth in these absurd prejudices, since no people, and no culture – just as no individual – is free of blame in the course of history. To keep remorselessly reminding oneself of the defects and dark places of all of us, and of our very selves, could be a promising basis for living together in a civilized and tolerant fashion – more so than the most optimistic claims flaunted by any official political declarations.

In Grandma Anka these conflicts are totally impersonal. Every prejudice recognizes the right, or even better, the necessity of the next person's prejudice. In Bela Crkva, also, we come across those low houses, reddish, or yellow-ochre, and all on the one floor, which we find all over Hungary, and which give Central Europe that snub-nosed look which Musil wrote about. In Partizanka Street were the houses of the Germans, better maintained, decorated with friezes and female heads moulded in plaster above the windows. They are faced with tiles in bright, Rumanian colours and open onto gardens at the back. Tradition has it that the Swabians of the Banat were so well-off that they used gold ducats for buttons on their clothes. Since the exodus of the Germans – in Bela Crkva today there is only one, and he is very old – the Macedonians and Bosnians have moved in, and they are contemptuously called "colonists" by the local people, and even by the Bosnians and Macedonians who arrived a few decades earlier. Weisskirchen, the German Bela Crkva, survives today in the community of exiles which settled in Salzburg, which issues volume upon volume of memories of the past, erudite volumes, touching and rancorous. A recent volume, consisting of 666 densely printed pages, *The Homebook of the City of Weisskirchen in the Banat*, was edited by Alfred Kuhn. "I know him well, that rotten little German," says Grandma Anka.

Old Tipoweiler lived in one of these houses. He was a town-councillor and a frequent visitor at the house of Grandma Anka. A real gentleman, she said. No sooner had the war against Serbia broken out in 1914 than a few of the local German bigwigs got together one night to talk over the chances of eliminating the most eminent local Serbs; the ones, you understand, on whose front-doors hung a wreath of yellow flowers and carnations of St Ivandan. After a calm discussion of the matter, when the proposal seemed to be gaining the approval of the majority, old Tipoweiler, a person of common sense, observed that the notion might be good in itself, but added that Bela Crkva was close to the Serbian frontier, and that if the Serbian army made a swift advance and occupied the place, all the Germans in town would be massacred for revenge. What then? The meeting broke up peaceably.

What happened that night did not diminish Grandma Anka's regard for Herr Tipoweiler, though his list perhaps included her own father's name. But Grandma Anka, in any case, uses the term "gedža" – "Serbians" – for the Serbs on the right bank of the Danube, those who were for centuries under the heel of the Turk, but at the same time she tells me that she would never have married a Serb, even from the left bank. "But what on earth are you?" I ask her. "A Serb," she replied with pride. "Ours is one of the most ancient Serbian families."

4. A POLYGLOT PARROT

There were also gentler international interweavings, at Bela Crkva, as in the case of Schescherko's parrot. This Schescherko was a plutocrat, and his house – beside the ruins of which there now stands a dusty bus station – was close to the main square, the site of the "palace" of President Popescu, impressively turreted, as well as the pavilion of the Hungarian general in command of the garrison, the Officers' Club, and the "Realgymnasium" – one of the best in the Kingdom of Hungary, according to Grandma Anka. In this house, in a cage as big as a room, lived a parrot who could sing. When the kids used to beg him (in German) to give a performance, he would first of all act coy, answering in German with a Swabian accent, but at last he would condescend to sing a passage from *The Princess of the Csarda*, in Hungarian. Asked for an encore (in German of course), he shilly-shallied for a while, but then sang the same passage in Hungarian. But if anyone went on, and demanded another encore, he flew into a passion and replied, in German, with the phrase known in Germany, in a polite periphrasis, as "the *Götz* quotation". The reason for this is that Goethe's *Götz Von Berlichingen* is the earliest illustrious text in which the expression "lick my arse" is raised to literary status.

5. BENEATH THE BUST OF LENAU

Vasko Popa is one of the leading poets of contemporary Jugoslavia, and a voice of these very regions. In one of his poems he has a scene in which kissing is going on in the public gardens in Vršac, beneath the bust of Lenau. Vršac is the administrative centre of the Jugoslavian Banat, only a few kilometres from Bela Crkva and from the Rumanian border. It was to the women of Vršac, his birthplace, that Ferenc Herczeg – the brilliant, superficial Hungarian novelist who entranced a vast audience throughout Europe with the embellished passions of fashionable elegance, the tinsel circus tricks of the gentry – in 1902 dedicated his novel *The Pagans*, a fresco devoted to the struggle between races and religions, between Magyars and Pechenegs, between the Cross and the sacred oak of his ancestors, at the very dawn of Hungarian history. His rhetorical, kaleidoscopic narrative re-evokes the Golden Horde of the Pecheneg nomads, the wind of the "puszta" which prevents the spirit from rising to heaven and drags it down into the flatlands, and the barbarian migrations absorbed and vanished in the Balkan-Pannonian mists.

In a far more forceful way the poems of Vasko Popa – who originally wrote in Rumanian, but has for many years been writing in Serbo-Croat – evoke barbaric winters and the wolves of yesteryear. The literature which is already written is a concave mirror set down on the earth like a dome, as if to shelter our inability to give direct utterance to things and feelings. A well-cultivated literary taste and a measure of cautious modesty prevent a mere follower from speaking of the solitude and the wind of the great plains, of the tracks of migrations printed in the muddy soil of his homeland. But if a second-rate novelist, or indeed an exacting poet, recalls that wind or that age-old asperity, a perfect quotation may permit us to mention them, through the medium of the words of others, without fear of falling into sentimental "local colour". So literature rests upon the world like one hemisphere resting upon another, two mirrors reflecting each other, as at the barber's, exchanging between them the elusiveness of life, or at least our own inability to grasp it.

Lenau's bust used to be in the park, but has now been removed to the museum in Vršac. His birthplace, however, is now over the frontier in Rumania, not far from Timişoara, where the German lycée is called after him. A great Austrian poet, whose origins were also Slav and Hungarian, Lenau, who died a madman in 1850, was an outstanding poet of solitude and suffering. His character was at one and the same time charming and eaten away by nothingness, by a cosmic sadness experienced throughout every fibre in a sensitive nature that was ultra-musical, neurotic and self-destructive. His *Faust*, negative and desperate as it may be, is one of the great *Fausts* written since Goethe, when the classicism of Goethe, loyal despite everything to the notion that human history had some meaning, was subverted throughout European culture by a profound crisis, the conviction of meaninglessness and nullity.

His Faust, who kills himself because he feels that he is no more than a vague dream dreamt by a God, or rather, by an Everything that is as indistinct as it is wicked, is a work of great poetic merit, in which the errant multi-nationality of Lenau overflows into a universality innocent of any Danubian local colour. Lenau has an international literary society which now bears his name, formed in the spirit of the cultural unity of Mitteleuropa. In 1911 Adam Müller-Guttenbrunn, the great champion of German culture in the Banat, resisted the attempts of the Magyar elements to "appropriate" the poet, and opposed their raising a monument to him in his hometown (which is now in Rumania), inscribed "To Lenau Miklós, a Hungarian who wrote in German". Herczeg is sometimes bitterly anti-German; his mother-tongue was German, and he is a Hungarian nationalist who shares to some extent the chauvinistic attitudes of István Tisza. This emerges even in his *Pagans*, while on occasion he even indulges himself in sympathies for the Bunjewatzi. Nonetheless, in his novel *The Seven Swabians*, published in 1916 but set back in the 1848 Revolution, his protagonist remarks that he feels it his duty to side with the Hungarian rebels in the very name of "German loyalty", because he has lived his life side by side with them and now, as a German, which is to say an upright man, he cannot abandon them in their time of peril, even though they are raised in rebellion against the power of Austro-German Vienna.

The plain surrounding Vršac is wreathed in melancholy. Milo Dor, a contemporary Austrian writer born in Budapest of Serbian parents, and now a resident of Vienna, wrote a book called *Nothing Other Than The Memory*, in which he described the slow decline of a prosperous Serbian Banat family, the melancholy torpor which is embodied in a bottle of slivovitz and transforms it, once empty and discarded, into a bottle jettisoned in the Pannonian sea, but containing no message. This melancholy, like Lenau's nihilism, wears a sense of emptiness, which is nonetheless linked with nostalgia and the need for values and meanings. In one of his poems Vasko Popa addresses himself to "our forgetful children, without original sin". With the sometimes facile enthusiasm of the avant-garde poet he celebrates the freedom of this new generation, but also the absence of memory and lack of awareness of moral conflict give those children the appearance of a crowd on this side of good and evil, amorphous and colourless, without sin and without happiness, innocent and vacuous.

6. EVERGREEN VITALITY

"What a great gentleman," says the Magyarophile Grandma Anka as she stands before the tomb of Adam, who was shot by the Hungarians in 1914 as a suspected Serbian spy. This is one of her favourite expressions. Grandma Anka is what Lenau's Faust longed in vain to be: pure vitality, demonic through calm immutability, as epic as nature. She is eighty years old, but with the energy and alertness of a youngster. She looks at life from above, with the round eyes of a hawk, as life can only be looked at by those who have been rooted in land-owning, and who, when they look out from their properties, do not see small personal troubles or the nervous nuances of states of mind, but fields and woods and the passing of the seasons.

It matters little that she now lives extremely modestly in a small apartment in Trieste. She carries with her, in her own person, the ease and confidence of that towering viewpoint. Grandma Anka brings to mind the last pages of Benedetto Croce in which, to the consternation of his faithful disciples, he was bothered and bewitched by finding a moment of pure life which could not be reduced to any moral or spiritual dimension, an untameable "evergreen vitality" totally innocent of values or reflections. Croce also used the term "economic" for this moment, this affirmation and expansion of energy. For Grandma Anka, though very generous towards others with her own money and highly modest in her own personal needs, life is a ledger of credits and debits, while youth and marriage and old age are all bound up with estates, whether increased or lost, woods cut down or fields acquired, as in the veins of Balzac's characters the blood seems to flow like the pulsing of money. She shows me the orange-ochre house that was the home of Lazar Lungu, the biggest pork-merchant in the Lower Banat, and a suitor of hers. "Do you want to live among pigs, Anka?" asked her father. "Money means much, a very great deal, but not everything. Choose a young man you like and I'll buy him for you."

The epic quality of agrarian life imposes an impersonal style which excludes any kind of self-regarding subjectivity. Grandma Anka has had four husbands. Two of them – the second, with whom she lived for twenty years, and the fourth and last, whom she met in old age – she loved very dearly, while the other two she patiently endured. Love and vexation, however, had not the least effect upon her exemplary dedication, because for her marriage was an entirely objective thing, which the uncertain nature of the feelings involved could not so much as scratch.

There is in her life no such thing as complaint, or protest against her troubles or those of others. She has no pity for herself or for others, it never crosses her mind to fear death or to get upset about other people dying, even though she is ready to help anyone in need, disregarding the effort and unaware of the very concept of sacrifice. In her world things simply happen. She shows me the house where an old friend of hers lives, a woman destroyed by sickness and reduced to a practically vegetable existence ruffled only by the occasional spark of fear or tenderness. When she is in Bela Crkva Grandma Anka spends her nights on her feet by the bedside, evidently without feeling any weariness. She talks to her for hours, strokes her hair, wipes away the saliva from her chin, and carries her to the balcony to let her see the passers-by, all that riotous riff-raff, as Grandma Anka puts it. But it does not occur to her that she is performing what might be called a charitable action. Such a concept does not exist for her: this is what is done, and that's all there is to it.

When one is with Grandma Anka one feels that nothing can possibly happen to her, that she could never feel lost or bewildered. She identifies herself with the centuries of Pannonia. At eighty years old, her shapely, imperious body is firm and confident. To love her world of yesterday she has no need to idealize it, and she tells me in detail about the thievish ways of the judges of those times. That house, she remembers, was the home of the lawyer Zimmer – and his wife, she adds, counting thoughtfully on her fingers, was the mistress of Dr Pútnik, Attorney Raikow, Schlosser the pharmacist and Colonel Németh. A few yards off is a house which tells a story not of Hapsburg times but of the years after the Second World War. It was the home of a mill-owner called Maierosch, and it was confiscated by the Tito government. The ex-owner's daughter refused to leave, and when the police threw her furniture out into the courtyard she slept for the next two years in the entrance, wrapped in a blanket, until the Jugoslav authorities gave her back some part of her flat. Works to restore the building are still going on. Building works are always going on everywhere in Eastern European countries, always energetic but never finished. One returns to a place after a year, and there are the bricks, the tools, the rubble, the beams, all the signs of a provisional state of affairs. Time passes more slowly, and this renders those countries more reassuring and familiar to the visitor, giving him the comfort of things already known to him.

Grandma Anka loves the many cemeteries of the various communities, and takes me to the oriental-style mausoleum of President Popescu, to the sumptuous sepulchre of Boboroni, a millionaire murdered by twenty-three stab-wounds, to the chapel where Schmitz the pharmacist went every evening to tell his wife, who was buried there, all the events of his day and to ask her advice. She loves cemeteries because to own a grave is to own land, it marks the boundaries of a property; and in fact she often returns to Bela Crkva, chiefly to quarrel with the council and her neighbours on the subject of burial places. She reminds me of the mother of a friend of mine, terribly proud because her family vault overshadowed that of her envious acquaintances, but also a little sad, because funeral ceremonials also require mourning; as a result of which she would say complainingly: "Think of it! Such a fine family vault, and almost completely empty!"

7. TIMIŞOARA

The Antiquarius says that this city, Temesvár, the capital of the old Banat, "has over the centuries been subject to many fatalities." Lovely in a slightly melancholy way, in spite of its green open spaces, Timişoara in every stone tells of an ancient, troubled history. Griselini described it as abounding in taverns and fever, the latter produced by the mists rising from crow-infested marshes, and he made a note of the widespread use of emetics. The symmetrical style of Maria Theresa's times alternates with heavy Hungarian eclecticism and the more dazzling Rumanian colours of the ornamental features. In the splendid Piaţa Unirii, vast and silent, there rises, as in all the big squares in Mitteleuropa, the Pillar of the Trinity. At the gates of the city, in 1514, the forces of the nobility defeated the great leader of the peasants' revolt, György Dózsa, who was chained naked to a throne of red-hot iron, while the flesh was torn from his bones with pincers.

The stones evoke John Hunyadi, the champion of the struggle against the Turks, Muslim domination, Ali Pasha, and the Austrian siege of 1848. On one tumbledown little red-ochre coloured house, with geraniums on the window-sills, we find a plaque telling us that at that point, on October 13th 1716, Prince Eugène made his entry into Timişoara, liberating it from the Turks. When requested to surrender, the pasha who was defending the place replied that he knew perfectly well that he couldn't win, but that he felt it his duty to contribute to the Renown of Prince Eugène by making his victory more arduous and glorious. The tourist leaflets prefer to stress the fact that the city can boast of having had the first electric tram and of having given birth to Tarzan, alias Johnny Weissmuller.

As well as having minority populations of Hungarians and Serbs, Timişoara is one of the centres for the Germans in Rumania. They number about 300,000, a figure that is diminishing drastically from year to year. The other main centre is in the Siebenbürgen in Transylvania, where the Saxon group has been living for eight centuries. The city is a capital, and an epic centre of the infinite number of stories told by the old Danube. There used to be literary cafés, but the most eminent meeting-place at the beginning of the century was the barber's shop in the Lonovichgasse; its owner, Anton Dénes, was not only the Figaro but the Eckermann of one of the local literary heroes. This was Franz Xaver Kappus, known not so much for what he wrote as for the *Letters to a Young Poet* addressed to him by Rilke. In the chair of that barber's shop Kappus sat like the Turk Nasreddin: this was the witty sage, whose facetious quip, while at the barber's, silenced the terrible, world-conquering Tamburlaine.

Kappus's little tales are witty anecdotes, jokes and scraps of gossip. It is hard to distinguish the pages written by him from what life and the small epic tradition of the Lonovichgasse, which converged on the barber's, recounted of him. Those anecdotes are an age-old sediment, crumbs of an ancient History, the remains of idylls and racial conflicts which the wind for an instant raises like dust, and blows into the barber's shop. Shortly afterwards the barber gets his broom, sweeps the floor and sends them out into the street again, along with the hair of the client he has just finished shearing.

Temesvár was the capital of the Banat, and therefore also of the Swabians, the Germans of the Banat who, unlike the Saxons of Transylvania, were little given to the impetuous defence of their national consciousness. Immediately after the last war the Germans of the Banat were harshly ill-treated: expropriations, collective deportations to Russia, discrimination. In his novel *The Problematical Report of Jakob Bühlmann*, which came out in 1968, Arnold Hauser, a German writer who occupies an eminent place in the cultural and political life of Rumania, narrated and analysed this odyssey of his people and these errors of his Party. In 1972 Ceausescu himself officially condemned the forced transportation of Serbs and Germans and the expropriation of their lands – measures decided on by the Rumanian government years before.

The Rumanian state now encourages an increase in the production of the linguistic minorities. Specialized publishing houses issue magazines and a great number of books in Hungarian, German, Serbian, Slovak, Ukrainian, Yiddish and other languages. This solicitude is, however, accompanied by harsh and oppressive political control: anyone who has asked for a visa to leave the country, as have many Germans, is not allowed to publish. Exaggerated and obsequious homage to the President is compulsory.

The result of this is a difficult but fervent literary life, marked by a mixture of frankness and reticence, hounded by the threat of persecution. The centres of this literature – apart from Bucharest, where the leading publishers and magazines have their headquarters – are the Banat, in the environs of Timişoara, and the Siebenbürgen, which is to say Transylvania, with the three cities of Braşov (Kronstadt), Sibiu

(Hermannstadt) and Cluj (Klausenburg). A very flourishing centre of German culture was the Bucovina, as it was in the time of the Hapsburgs. It was the homeland of Rezzori, of Margul Sperber, and of the great (and extreme) Paul Celan; but the capital of the Bucovina, Czernowitz, now belongs to the Soviet Union.

If in the Vojvodina the German population is now down to four or five thousand, in Rumania – or rather, in the Banat and the Sieben-bürgen – their culture is still very much alive. More than a hundred works of literature were published between 1944 and 1984, and poetry in dialect has taken on a new lease of life. Nikolaus Berwanger – until recently the all-too enterprising leader of German-Rumanian culture, and now living in West Germany – a few years ago announced the need to write in an "esperantosamizdat". True poetry ought to be secret and clandestine, concealed like a prohibited voice of dissent, while at the same time it should speak to everyone. His position as leader inevitably drew him towards the universality of esperanto. On the other hand the stories of Herta Müller, entitled *Lowlands*, are as simple and complex as the passing of the years, and possess the existential truth of the *samizdat*, of the poetic word that is always non-official. Herta Müller writes about the village, like so many earlier writers of the Banat, but her village is the place of absence, in which obscure things, strung out senselessly in sentences lacking in predicates, speak of the oppressive alienation of the world and also of the individual from himself.

Owing much to the new, alienating "village literature" flourishing in Austria with Bernhard, Handke or Innerhofer, Herta Müller explores its dark, sensitive roots in an original manner. When she theorizes about it she occasionally falls (like her models) into a stereotyped attitude not without a dash of arrogance. As part of the tough political repression to which the Germans in Rumania have been subjected, Herta Müller has been forced into silence.

Any German-Rumanian writer, with threats at his elbow, experi-ences those alienations, double-feelings and crises of identity which stimulate poetry. Deprived of a German world, he represents the facts of Rumanian life in a language which is foreign to them. On the other hand if he chooses to leave, and emigrates to West Germany, he will find himself in a country incredibly different from his own – and in a certain sense "less German". He will continue to write of the country he has left, which meanwhile, with the passing of years, changes and becomes foreign to him. Sometimes the intensity of this drama be-comes intolerable: Rolf Bossert, a young poet whom I met in

Bucharest while he was waiting for permission to leave the country, did in fact succeed in making his escape. But a few months later, in West Germany where he had found refuge and even success, he killed himself.

A general view of German-Rumanian literature bears witness to a variety of situations which in turn becomes a plurality of epochs, because to live in different situations and with different feelings means living at different times. The cultural association of the Germans of the Banat, which is fully integrated into the Rumanian Republic and the ideals of Socialism, is named after Adam Müller-Guttenbrunn, the nineteenth-century writer who championed German racial integrity in the Banat against Magyarization, and in terms which were decidedly nationalistic. In the upheavals of 1848 the Swabians of the Banat, like the Saxons of Transylvania, did not know how to act: they did not know who they were. With a leaning towards loyalty to the Hapsburgs, and surrounded by Hungarians, they were on the face of it threatened by the Hungarians, and therefore their enemies: as emerged quite clearly after the Compromise. But at Bela Crkva, for example, the tumultuous confusion of 1848 led to a downright military clash between the Germans and the Serbs. The latter besieged and ultimately captured the city. By fighting against the Serbs, the "Swabians of the Danube" were supporting the Hungarian rebels against Austria, because the Serbs were in conflict with the Hungarians and therefore allies of Vienna.

In Temesvár there were in 1902 twelve German newspapers, twelve Hungarian and one Rumanian. However, the process of Magyarization made deep inroads into the German presence. Adam Müller-Guttenbrunn describes this increasing loss of nationality, the shrinking of the German schools, the Magyarization of first names and surnames, and the way that portraits of Francis Joseph gradually vanished from the walls of Swabian houses. Whereas the Transylvanian Saxons pugnaciously defended their national identity, the Swabians of the Banat willingly allowed themselves to become assimilated, giving Hungarian names to their children or adopting a Magyar form of their own. In an amusing controversy in 1916, the burgomaster of Temesvár challenged Müller-Guttenbrunn and his claims for the rights of the German minority; but this burgomaster who championed Magyarization was a Swabian.

The events of 1848 still stand for confusion and pandemonium, by definition. As a boy Müller-Guttenbrunn used to play with the stones of a monument which had been knocked down – the carved heads of grinning animals. When the monument was first raised, to glorify the defence of Temesvár against the Hungarian rebels, these stone heads symbolized the demons of the national revolution overcome by virtue of the universal empire. It had then been demolished by the Hungarians, but for the youngster those demons scattered on the ground were still living and menacing. And even today, when Grandma Anka points out a building in Bela Crkva and says, "here, before the revolution, there was . . .", she means "before the revolution of 1848".

8. A GERMAN DESTINY

We are back in Bela Crkva. No. 35 Ulika 1 October used to be the home of a certain Vogter, a rich German industrialist and landowner who had stayed in the Banat even after the First World War. Grandma Anka told me that during the Second, at the time of the German occupation, he had a lieutenant in the *Wehrmacht* billeted on him, and used to treat him to sumptuous dinners. The *Wehrmacht* had entered Bela Crkva in 1941, and the German group, led by Dr Josef Janko, pursued the policy of an "Independent Banat". Its "Prinz Eugen" Division was intended to be a military force destined entirely to the defence of the Banat, to the extent that Janko – eager to keep the local *Deutschum* apart and distinct from Nazism – forcibly protested when it was proposed to deploy the Division for other purposes and in other areas.

The German army was mighty and much feared, the Reich was still very powerful, and the well-to-do Vogter lived in safety and opulence. During the summer his peasants would start for the fields at two in the morning, and work there until ten at night. This was when they got home and gathered in a hut behind the master's house to eat their only meal of the day. This was a watery broth with a few bits of bread and lard in it, and they all fed out of the same pot. One evening the lieutenant unwittingly came into the hut and asked them why on earth they were eating such stuff, at such a time of night. The farmhands leapt to their feet, cap in hand, and replied in trembling voices that they were having their supper. The officer kicked over the pot, summoned Vogter and yelled at him that he was a scoundrel and a disgrace to the name of German. He then told the peasants that from then on they would eat at the local inn, at his expense. I asked Grandma Anka what had become of that lieutenant. "Ah, who knows . . ." she said. "He was probably killed during the retreat by one of the partisans in the woods. It could have been one of the fellows he'd treated to meals at the inn."

9. THE TOMB OF OCTAVIÁN

Out of the blue Grandma Anka says that she would like to take a trip to the Siebenbürgen, to Sighişoara, to visit the tomb of Octavián. I ask about this Octavián – in view of the fact that she has mentioned his tomb, grammar might require me to ask who he *was*, but it always seems strange to me to speak of a person, any person, in the past tense. Grandma Anka's authoritarian and still-lovely face grows thoughtful, almost embarrassed, however hard it is to imagine that she knows what embarrassment is. "Well, he was a young lad, an officer, who came courting me. I was seventeen at the time, and I liked him, and we were sort of half engaged. Then – you know how it is – just for fun, or I don't know what, I dropped him." "And what about him?" "Him? He shot himself." I ask her if she was sorry at the time. "No," she replies without hesitation. "Not that time, not at all. I thought no more about it. But for some years now it has been in my head to visit him, to go and see his grave."

So it was that someone else's long-overdue debt took me to Transylvania, into a Rumanian-German-Hungarian multi-national mosaic, the dwelling-place for the last eight centuries of the Saxon colonists brought there by King Geza II of Hungary. Later, in 1224, King Andrew II gave them a patent assuring them special liberties and privileges. Their ancient presence in this part of the world is now in its declining years. German culture, side by side with Jewish culture, has been the unifying factor and germ of civilization in central Eastern Europe. The town squares of Sibiu-Hermannstadt and Braşov-Kronstadt, images of a German tradition that may well no longer exist in Germany itself, are like the ancient Roman arches and aqueducts: the seal and stamp of an integrated culture which bestowed a face on Central Europe.

The Saxons, though they are known as a whole by such a name, originally came from various parts of Germany, as we are told by the historian Friedrich Teutsch, "the Herodotus of the Saxons", in the course of regretfully correcting the monistic theory held by his father, Georg Daniel Teutsch, himself a scholar of note. For centuries the Saxons have preserved a proud independence. Together with the Hungarians and the Székely – a Magyar tribe claiming descent from Attila's Huns, the members of which all enjoyed the privileges of nobility – they were one of the three recognized nations against (or by the side of) which, especially during the nineteenth century, the Rumanians had to fight in order to establish their own national dignity. Independent farmers and solid bourgeois, the Saxons were very seldom either feudal lords or serfs. Isolated, cut off from their country of origin, they have always been a "cultural nation", inclined not towards joining their territory to that of Germany, but eager to preserve their own cultural identity.

Grandma Anka's main objective is the tomb at Sighişoara, but that does not prevent her from taking an interest in other detours and stops in Transylvania. The *Eminescu* bookshop in Sibiu bears witness to how rich and lively German literature still is in Rumania. As I am told in Braşov by Horst Schuller, editor of the *Karpathen-Rundschau*, it is widely differentiated. There are, of course, local poets such as Peter Barth, who died recently; he was a pharmacist in Blumenthal and wrote ten dialect poems a day. But there is also the *Neue Literatur* of Bucharest, an excellent, up-to-date periodical, which can stand comparison with reviews in the rest of Europe which have far greater means and far fewer restrictions. In the years 1970–5 there was a politico-literary group called the *Aktionsgruppe*, critical of the regime from a left-wing standpoint and pretty fiercely so. The work of Peter Motzan and Stefan Sienerth, to mention only a few, and above all of Gerhardt Csejka, a young critic and essayist living in Bucharest, give proof of a truly unusual vitality and wealth of enterprise, the spiritual growth of a community in decline. A few generations ago Erwin Wittstock gave us a delightful portrait of the Saxon province, today the poems of his son Joachim tell us "to pay attention to things that are yellowing". The literature, and above all the criticism, of the Germans in Rumania do not form an isolated suburb, but the living heart – intellectually varied and highly differentiated – of a body that is gradually dying.

Even among the emigrants there are considerable differences between those who left their homeland forty years ago (such as Heinrich Zillich) and continue to describe a country which no longer exists, and the successive waves of emigrants, each of which took with it a different piece of the homeland and a different time. A few years ago the time to leave came even for Alfred Kittner, poet and critic, the old patriarch, protector of generations of writers and friend of Paul Celan. The legendary Kittner believes in the eternity of poetry; each *nouvelle vague* of young experimental writers helped by him has smiled at him, considering him to be *passé*, but each time, ten years later, many of those ungrateful children have vanished from the map, while the old father was still there – as he still is.

It may be that Kittner was wrong to leave. Maybe his function, right until the end, was the guardianship of his world. When four or five more significant writers have left, Csejka tells me, I shall be writing my essays and critiques for no one. But it can also be an advantage in literature to write for no one, now that wherever one goes the machine of organized culture falsely claims to represent everyone.

10. AN AMBIGUOUS JOVE

In the Bruckenthal Museum in Sibiu there is a picture of Jove and Flora by Carlo Cignani. Samuel von Bruckenthal was Maria Theresa's governor of the Grand Principality of the Siebenbürgen, an extremely able politician clever enough to reconcile loyalty to the central enlightened despotism with attention to local particularities. To him we owe the art collection which today bears his name.

Cignani's Jove, who is seducing a predictable and appetizing "young thing", is a kind of repellent and unsettling hermaphrodite. The body is muscular and powerful, and the face, framed by thick white hair, is that of an old man who looks more like an old woman, lascivious and ambiguous. She reminds me of the ambivalent characters in Fellini's *Satyricon*, who exchange sexual roles, or of Frederick II in the play by Heiner Müller, acted by an imperious, sinister old woman. Cignani was a Bolognese, and a follower of Carracci, but his Jove seems rather to belong to the Graeco-Byzantine world of that Euxine Pontus towards which the waters of the Danube lead, a muddied world of undifferentiated pulsations, a Levantine bazaar of the mind.

The Black Church in Kronstadt (now called Braşov), the ancient walls of which call to mind Luther's hymn "A mighty fortress is our God", is a fortress of German faith and clarity, standing like a bulwark against the swarming and intermingling of which Cignani's Jove is the polymorphous god. Inside the church there is a tomb dated 1647. The inscription reads "I know and believe." The statue of a warrior, in full armour, helmet, gorget and all, and great moustaches, is reminiscent of Dürer's Knight, who proceeds straight along the path of life, yielding neither to the fear of Death nor to the gelatinous flatteries of the Devil.

Like the school opposite the church, called after Honterus, and the monument to Honterus himself, this German ethic is profoundly Protestant, with the sobriety, the straightforwardness and the toughness of the Reformation. Thanks to these keen, tenacious virtues the Germans have been the Romans of Mitteleuropa, and created a single civilization out of a melting-pot of diverse races. The splendid Turkish carpets in the Black Church, bearing witness to the Ottoman presence in Transylvania, speak of a different faith, but also one that was contrary to any sloppy ambivalence in its complete and utter abandonment to Allah, the one and only conqueror.

The poetry of these Saxon towns is the poetry of bourgeois craftsmen, solid and melancholy as the strict exactitude which Adolf Meschendörfer, the bard of Kronstadt – the "City in the East", which is to say the Civitas on the eastern frontiers of Europe – admired in his father and his grandfather, who was a schoolmaster. The Saxon tradition is proud of its statutes and ancient rights, of the quarrels between the various guilds, the tanners against the saddlers, and fiercely proud of the total independence from all the seats of power which in 1688 caused the Kronstadt shoemakers to declare war against the German Emperor, and (in the period of the dual monarchy) to resist the process of Magyarization. Even the Hungarian novelist Zsigmond Móricz, in his historical novels about the Siebenbürgen, makes mention of the statutes which forbade any army – sent from the Vojvoda or by the Emperor himself – to enter within the walls of Klausenburg (Cluj), and he also pays homage to the valour with which the Knights defended the privileges of their city.

This citizen poetry is a melancholy poetry of orderliness and repetition, a methodical passion for customs and places that attempts to rip some sort of guarantee and illusion of duration and stability from the impermanence of life. The ethos of the German bourgeois craftsman consists of love of the home, of the family, of friendships, and the rhythm that pulses out their universal-human: birth, copulation and death, the shop, the *Bierhaus*, the cigar, the game of cards, the church service, and sleep. In a short story by Heinrich Zillich, every evening at the same time old Bretz walks down the alley known as "The Suez Canal", spreads his legs, unbuttons his fly and pisses in all tranquillity, returning the greetings from the dark of the passers-by, the town councillor or the schoolmaster; and this inevitable vesperal rite is a firm assurance that in some way or other resists the bitter fleetingness of life and the unconsidered love of novelty.

The cheerful calm of evenings at the café soon slides and slips into melancholy, and little by little erases the lives of individuals and of the German community as a whole. Even as early as 1931, in Meschendörfer's *The City in the East*, the hero is in love with his hometown of Kronstadt, and in the end, when he is all alone, there is nothing for it but to write the story and the memories of his beloved town, and in this erudite and amorous pedantry, ever looking to the past, to search for comfort in the desert of his present life. One can always escape from the horrors of real life as Svevo's old dodderer did, by putting it down on paper and thereby keeping it at a distance. The fact is that Grandma Anka doesn't write, and has no need to do so.

12. TRANSYLVANISMUS

The pedantry of these German burghers, sometimes placid and sometimes melancholy, occasionally becomes quite ridiculous. During the troubles of 1848 the Saxons of Transylvania were undecided whether or not to accept union with Hungary. Kronstadt was in favour, Hermannstadt against it – so much against it that the sentries at the city gates asked any strangers who wanted to get in what side they were on: for the Emperor or for the rebels. If they replied "for the rebels" they were not allowed in. It appears that it never crossed anyone's mind that the candidate for entry might be lying.

The 1848 movement was chaotic amongst the Saxons, as it was everywhere else, seething with contradictions, with liberal and revolutionary movements which cancelled each other out, as in the case of the Hungarians rebelling against the Hapsburgs but hostile to the Rumanian rebellion of Iancu. The entire history of Transylvania is an intricate web of disagreements, cross-purposes, clashes, and the establishment and overthrow of national alliances. The novels of Möricz or of Miklós Jósika, for example, show how the Transylvanian princes steered a middle course between the Hapsburgs and the Turks, at the time when the Ottoman Empire was a powerful presence.

As sometimes happens in mixed-race frontier countries, this melting-pot of peoples and their various quarrels also brought about an awareness of having much in common, a special identity, entangled with contradictions but nonetheless unique in its clashes and clamour; such an awareness was proper to each and every one of the antagonists in the struggle. Transylvania has been a cradle of Hungarian culture, at least since the eighteenth-century autobiography of Miklós Bethlen or the *Confessions* and the *Memoirs* of Prince Ferenc Rakóczi II, the great leader of the rebellion of the *Kuruzzen* against the Hapsburgs. It is also the cradle of the Rumanian national consciousness, of the literary tradition that in the eighteenth and nineteenth centuries asserted the continuity of the Latin element in Dacia and the linguistic-national unity of the Rumanians.

Lucian Blaga, poet and translator of *Faust* into Rumanian, has devoted a vast amount of study to the culture of Transylvania during the eighteenth century, but his particular poetic Transylvania exists above all in the village celebrated in his prose: a village he loved without any sighing about his lost peasant ancestry, or any rancour against townspeople, but simply as a mythical, imaginative model for life, as an ideal "Mioritic space", which is to say the landscape of the Rumanian soul. In the Rumanian folksong the Miorița is the baby lamb which is the symbol of a sacrifice humbly accepted for the sake of others, in order that one's own death might not occasion reprisals and vengeance.

A dark, dramatic work, on the other hand, is *The Lost Village* (1919), by the Hungarian Transylvanian Dezsö Szabó, a curious, tortured intellectual. Much influenced by reading Nietzsche and obsessed by the purest and most absolute Magyar nationalism, Szabó preached the cult of the soil and of the race, going in for a Fascist-type, anti-townsfolk chauvinism, in which the uncorrupted Transylvanian village was for him the ideal. However, with the triumph of Horthy's counter-revolution, being a genuine Nietzschean, he realized that Democracy was not the only corrupting influence, but that Fascism also – and more than all else – corrupted and crushed the primitive purity of tradition beneath an artificial, falsifying process of modernization. He thereupon declared war on all and sundry, on the "German-Jewish-Slav bourgeoisie", on Fascism and finally on Nazism, those stranglers of the pure Magyar spirit.

The term "Transylvanismus" alludes to a multiplicity of peoples which is brought together by this feeling of belonging to a mixed, composite part of the world. The Saxons were certainly hard hit by the end of their independence, ratified by the Hungarian government in 1876 when they abolished the *Comes*, the "Sachsengraf", which is to say the earldom which represented their "Nationuniversität", and summed up their nation as a whole. Many novels and short stories, sometimes in a good-natured way and at other times in anger, describe the acceptance or rejection of the latter, and the Hungarian and German boys throwing stones at one another.

However, the Saxons had over the centuries developed such a feeling of their own independence as to induce their leader Rudolf Schuller to declare in 1908 that they did not wish to be "simply Germans, but Germans of the Siebenbürgen"; and that they were determined to defend their own distinct existence as Saxons, without moving a muscle in favour of the Swabians who were threatened by "Magyarization" – they coolly accepting the possibility that "the other Germans" in Hungary might go to the wall.

The German writers attempted to reconcile loyalty to Transylvanian independence with "Germanism" and the Hapsburg crown, loyalty to Francis Joseph as Emperor of Austria, not as King of Hungary. Adolf Meschendörfer, though by no means totally deprived of German nationalism, praises Germanism as universalism, the Holy-Roman-Imperial ideal which embraces all peoples, Germans, Celts and Slavs. He scoffs at the Teutomanic racists who invented the "Gothic man", because the concept of universalism – of which the bearers are of course the Germans – cannot in his opinion be bound down to one race or style, but is destined to extend throughout Europe, even into those parts of it which are Latin or Slav. But the German Emperor – as the parish priest of Kronstadt remarks in his book – is a traitor, because he abandons the Germans of the East, the true standard-bearers and advance-guard of the Germanic ideal, and lets them go to rack and ruin. According to Heinrich Zillich in his novel *Between Frontiers and Times* (1937), the Saxons, who have always "given" to their neighbours, feel abandoned by the court of Vienna.

In this work, which does have its chauvinistic and anti-Semitic side, Zillich describes the multi-national Transylvanian melting-pot and its quarrels, not without sympathy for its various ethnic ingredients. The friends of the hero, whose name was Lutz, are of a number of different nationalities, and though at the beginning Lutz is surprised to discover that a certain pastor is Rumanian, and can hardly credit the fact that beyond the mountains of his homeland there is another state – Rumania – at the end, one of his friends, Nicholas, has become a Rumanian lieutenant, and in the new Rumania, which annexed Transylvania after the First World War, he symbolizes not a break with tradition, but rather a hope for continuity.

For Zillich, who scorns the narrow-minded, rhetorical cult of the Teutons, the German people is great because (as he writes) it wishes to assert not merely itself, as do the little races which cannot see outside their own restricted circle, but also universal ideas and values, "what is great" and "what is right for everyone". For this reason it is a protagonist of "world history", the element which unites and binds together the peoples of Central and Eastern Europe, otherwise divided and heedless of each other; just as German, like Latin in the ancient world, is the common language, and therefore the universal tongue, beside which the particular languages of the other peoples must flourish, though none of them extends outside the confines of the people who speak it. This *gesamtdeutsch* (total German) attitude is a double-edged weapon. In Nazi times it opposed the barbarous racism of the National Socialist ethos in the name of universality, but it was also liable to provide Nazism with ideological weapons and passions that aided and abetted its dominion.

Zillich himself wavers between nationalistic tones and accents which are fraternally supra-national. At the end of his novel Lutz, the Transylvanian Saxon, does not emigrate to Germany, but stays at home in the new Rumanian motherland, the reason being (he says) that the task of the Saxons is now to give to Rumania what at one time they gave to Austria and to Hungary. This is their duty and their way of being German – no easy matter, because "it is difficult, infinitely difficult, to be a German in the East".

So difficult, indeed, that neither Vienna nor Berlin understand it: the Hapsburgs and the Hohenzollerns betrayed their most self-sacrificing sentinels. The relations between the edge of things and the centre is always difficult. Those who live on a frontier, geographical or cultural, feel themselves to be the true depositories and interpreters of the nation, and feel misunderstood by the rest of the nation, which seems to them to be unworthy of the name. If in a story by Erwin Wittstock the Vogt family of Hermannstadt religiously displayed a portrait of Bismarck in the house, in Zillich's novel Bismarck is condemned as the one who cynically abandoned the Germans of the East so as not to make enemies of the Hungarians. When I mention this question to Grandma Anka she simply says that that Bismarck fellow must have been a Jew.

13. ON THE CLOCK-TOWER

Octaviàn's tomb is at Sighişoara, the city that so entranced Enea Silvio Piccolomini, the pearl of the Siebenbürgen, the turreted, inaccessible "Nuremberg of Transylvania". With its Gothic houses and its towers named after the guilds – the farriers, the cobblers, the tailors, the tanners, the copper-smiths – and with the silence of its enchanting streets clambering up to the citadel, Sighişoara – Schässburg to the Saxons and Segesvár to the Hungarians – reminds one of Prague: the mystery of its stones and the gateways opening onto some other and secret space, on to an unsuspected side of things. The slender, pointed iron banners which surmount the towers are silhouetted clearly against the sky, intrepid in the wind, fearless knights in the arena, waiting for the tourney and an unknown destiny. The town is all peace and silence, but if we raise our eyes to those banners we expect a clarion call, the start of some imprecise but unavoidable battle.

Horror and slaughter have not spared this heraldic elegance. On March 31st 1785 the nobleman Andreas Metz wrote from Alba Julia to his brother Mihai, member of the senate of Sighişoara: he took pleasure in reporting the execution of Horea and Cloşca, leaders of the great peasant revolt of 1784. In their struggle against serfdom they appealed to the Emperor himself, the great Joseph II, and to the promises he had made. The Emperor was forced to quell the revolt with bloodshed, even though the allies of his reforms were those peasants, and not the nobles against whom they had risen. Much to the edification of Johannes Andreas Metz, Cloşca died broken on the wheel, whereas Horea, due to the intercession of Duke Jankovics, had the privilege of being run through twice with a sabre before being hoisted on the wheel. Their bodies were then quartered, their skulls displayed outside their houses, and the rest of their fragments hung up in the streets "as a warning to the other Wallachian rebels".

I don't go to the cemetery with Grandma Anka: these are things which should be done between two people alone, without a third party around, and she has to make her peace with her lieutenant. While she is with Octaviàn, I climb up the thirteenth-century clock-tower. High up, on the fourth floor of the tower, is the mechanism of the clock, with the figures of the days of the week, gaily coloured and about a metre tall, which shift at midnight, each occupying its place for the following day and appearing when its turn comes round. I am behind, or rather within the mechanism of the clock, with its pulleys and winches that mark the seconds, the clumsy, garishly painted wooden figures and all the rest – even the years that have passed since Grandma Anka saw Octaviàn. What does the Captain say in Büchner's *Woyzeck*? "My God, when I think that in a day the world turns all the way round – in one day, you understand! – it's something that gives me the shivers. All this time being lost, thrown away, and such waste . . . when I see my coat hanging on the wall I want to weep, and the coat is there, hanging . . ."

From such a vantage-point the whole of life appears as a waste and a loss of time, a perishable mechanism. Like the clock which ticks it out, reality is a mechanism, an organization of perpetual repetition, an assembly line moving ever and only towards the next phase. Anyone who loves life ought perhaps to love its interplay of cogwheels, and go into raptures not only about the voyage towards far distant islands, but also over the bureaucratic hassle to get a passport. Conviction, averse to the general mobilization of every passing day, consists in the love of something other, something that is greater than life, and flashes forth only in the gaps, the pauses, when the machinery has stopped, the government and the world are on vacation (thinking of the strong sense of *vacare*, vacancy, absence, lack), and nothing exists but the lofty, immovable light of summer. The world, as Borges says, is real, but why must it give us such a hard time? What one would like to do, after all, is not a great deal to ask: just to play truant from school now and then, while preserving one's respect for the teachers . . .

The figure of Monday has his back to me, but Sunday – and my guide-book suggests that it is not simply the day of the sun, but also of gold, of wealth – reveals a dull but rubicund face. I look down from the window: Grandma Anka has returned from her visit, and makes a brief signal to me to come down. The *Bierhaus*, recommended to us by a passer-by speaking German dialect, has – despite the food crisis in Rumania – some really worthwhile sausages.

14. ON THE BRINK OF SILENCE

Bistriţa owes its fame to Count Dracula. Not to the historical count, Vlad the Impaler, whose coffin is on display in Sighişoara, but to the invented one, the vampire in Bram Stoker's novel (in which, however, the town is named Bistritz, after the German manner). However, I am better protected than Jonathan Harker, Stoker's hero, because Grandma Anka is immune to all nocturnal monsters, and to anyone in general who wants to make anyone else afraid.

The literary clockwork in Stoker's novel is perfect, and reveals how seductive mechanisms can be. Besides this – and it is something that catches the interest of a traveller on the Danube – in Chapter Three Count Dracula sings the praises of the Székely, his own Hunnish tribe of border nomadic horsemen, for centuries on guard against the invasions of the Magyars, Lombards, Avars, Bulgars and Turks, and every one of them a nobleman because they are all equal in the saddle and avid for freedom. The Székely, at least since time immemorial, have been scarcely distinguishable from the Magyars. In recent years the Hungarian writer György Kovács and the Rumanian authoress Lucia Demetrius have portrayed these people in their novels. A collection of their folk-poetry, entitled *Wild Roses*, was published in 1863. Compared with the red of those roses, the blood which spurts so willingly in films and books about Dracula is simply coloured water.

According to Stoker's novel, Dracula's castle is close to the frontier of Bukovina, which is now Soviet territory. In 1865 Ferdinand Kürnberger, who in Vienna was the master of the *Feuilleton*, was expecting those remote, intact eastern provinces of the Hapsburg Empire to produce a fresh, brand-new literature, German in language but nourished by all the cultures of that Austro-Rumanian-Jewish-Russian-Ruthenian melting-pot. In the veins of the Austrians the virgin vines of Pruth must replace the bored, weary wine of the Rhine. This hope came true when the Empire which was to be refurbished from its eastern territories no longer existed. Czernowitz, the capital of the Bukovina, after 1918 became a lively, multi-racial literary centre, with such writers as Isik Manger, Rezzori, Alfred Margul-Sperber, Rose Ausländer, and others. In *The Hussar* Gregor von Rezzori, "homeless man" and "polyglot *homme tout à faire*", as are his characters, has given voice, with an elusive, melancholy poetry, to the teeming ambiguity of that Babel, its ironical interplay of truth and of falsehood, swapping parts back and forth.

That world has vanished, and its greatest spokesman, Paul Celan, expressed the ultimate truth about that disappearance, that death and sudden speechlessness. Celan's poetry is Orphic poetry pushed to the last extreme, a song which descends into night and into the realm of the dead, that melts into the blurry murmur of life and shatters every form, either linguistic or social, so as to find the magic, secret word which throws open the prison of history. In the most lofty parable of modern poetry the poet aims to be a redeemer, to take upon himself the evils of existence and to find once more the true names for things, which have been erased by the false language of communication. In the inextricable web of mediations which shroud the individual around, the poet is an anomalous creature who refuses to huddle down into the folds of that web, but struggles to tear through it and reveal the depths of being which it conceals. Often, as in the case of Hölderlin or of Rimbaud, the adventure is a deadly one, because beyond the net there is nothing, and the poet plummets into that nothingness.

Celan, also, sought for this "bottom non-bottom", as we read in one of his very last poems. Born at Czernowitz in 1920, Celan committed suicide in Paris in 1970. He experienced the holocaust of the Jews, in which his parents perished, as night in the most absolute sense, which annihilates any possibility of history or of real life, and later on he had to face the impossibility of putting down roots in Western civilization. It has been said that in himself he sums up a century of European poetry, born from that cleavage between reality and the individual, while also expressing those dreams of redeeming the world and destroying himself in this depiction of his own martyrdom.

His poetry leans out over the brink of silence. It is a word torn from wordlessness and flowering from wordlessness, from the refusal and impossibility of false, alienated communication. His arduous lines, cast into the boldest of lexical and syntactical formulations, are all woven of these negations, these denials, in which are expressed the only possible authenticity of feeling.

Celan experienced his own laceration, and the holocaust, as absolute evil. This evil, however, does not exist, and Eric Weil was perfectly correct to put us on our guard against its Medusa-like seductions. Even the most atrocious act has historical – and therefore relative – links with reality as a whole. But at the instant in which it is experienced, evil is thought of as violence most absolute, and even reflection, which attempts to understand its causes and motives, cannot make one forget the instant in which it was undergone with total suffering, unless the mind is willing to warp itself into a philistine reconciliation, which takes the edge off the sorrow and prevents a genuine understanding of the tragedy.

Celan, with searing immediacy and no trace of any reassuring conceptual mediation, puts himself on the side of the vanquished. He is probably the last Orphic poet, a religious reformer of Orphic poetry, bringing it to a blinding, primeval purity before it is snuffed out. For a century those radical linguistic and existential negations constituted a form of real resistance to social alienation. Now they are no longer scandalous, but have become precious objects of scandal. Anyone who trod that path today, even with personal integrity, would (according to an observation by Tito Perlini) in all probability face a pathetic destiny, all too easily absorbed by the mechanisms of alienated communication. Nevertheless, in Celan we are aware of this basic, deep-rooted renunciation, the gesture of one who puts an end to a tradition and at the same time erases himself.

Plato's condemnation of poetry is unacceptable but we are forced to come to terms with it. That sort of poetry which asks its salvation only of itself runs the risk of being satisfied with miming the contradictions, the distresses and perhaps the banalities of a person's own real state of mind, things which according to Plato make it impossible to pursue the quest for what is true and just. No one today, of course, can experience the problem as Plato experienced it, but poetry which feeds only on itself can even be a sin against poetry. Like rhymed quatrains and elaborate verse forms, even fragments of words groping in the darkness can repeat and regenerate themselves infinitely out of their own torment, turning to rhetoric, however lacerated that rhetoric might be. Celan's sacrifice is also the exorcism of this danger. Impossible conviction urged him to fall silent and to vanish, having left his "message in a bottle" to any contemporaries or descendants. Celan vanished in the night-time, into the waters of the Seine where he sought death. One of his lines reads, "I shed light behind me." Poetry is that dazzle which shows where he, with his poems, has vanished to.

15. HYPOTHESIS ABOUT A SUICIDE

A small intellectual disappointment caused by a temptation towards tidy solutions. Bukovina was the homeland of Robert Flinker, a psychiatrist and a writer influenced by Kafka, the author – in German – of stories and novels about enigmatical trials, obscure guilts and mysterious tribunals. Despite his obvious debt to Kafka, he was both personal and disquieting as a writer. Flinker was a Jew, and during the Nazi occupation he lived in hiding. When the Liberation came, in 1945, he killed himself. I had been fascinated by this man's fate. I imagined someone who could stand up to the very imminence of death, but eventually finds himself unaccustomed to freedom and the end of the nightmare, or else someone who could endure Nazism as Evil, but not Stalinism as the smiling face of Liberation; one who, faced with the notion that the alternative to Hitler was Stalin, takes his life.

But Wolfgang Kraus has informed me that Flinker killed himself for love, on account of an infatuation and a jilting that affected him like a schoolboy. A potential novel about the novelist thus goes up in smoke. But, on the other hand, could it not all come to the same thing? When someone is weary of life he gets rid of it by choosing methods that are even unconscious and indirect, such as cancer or a heart-attack. Why not an unhappy love-affair? Unable to come to the point at once, and kill himself because freedom was identified with Stalin, Flinker may have required some intermediary, and for this reason taken a girl at random, but one able to give him that little extra shove that was all he needed.

16. SUBOTICA, OR THE POETRY OF FALSEHOOD

On our return journey to Bela Crkva we make a very long detour which takes us into Hungary and thereafter into Jugoslavia, to Subotica, because Grandma Anka has stated that if I am going to get any idea of those regions I simply have to see it. Unpredictable, improbable, it appears to be a city of fascinating falsifications and infractions. At the beginning of the fourteenth century Gabriel Szamléni, confidential clerk to King Sigismund, conferred on it a patent of franchise laden with royal seals. This was later declared to be a forgery, along with other similar documents, and the clerk ended his days at the stake. Shortly before it fell into the hands of the Turks, in the sixteenth century, Subotica was for a brief period the residence and domain of the self-appointed Czar Iova, the Adventurer.

Made a free city by Maria Theresa, the place has that fiscal-cum-melancholy air of the architecture of her time, overlaid in the early years of the century, and perhaps overladen, with unbridled *Art nouveau*. The houses shriek out in notes of blue and yellow, they look like sea-shells, fretted with decorations and extravagant ornaments, crowns which look like pineapples, *putti* but with enormous breasts, gigantic bearded caryatids whose lower limbs become those of lions, which in turn dissolve in a formless swirl.

An abandoned synagogue appears to have popped out of Disney-land, with its swollen domes, glaring colours, fake bridges hanging between broken windows, steps overgrown with grass. The Town Hall is an orgy of stained-glass and staircases, a medley of friezes. This is a place where *Art nouveau* turned all the taps on. It is a distillation and superimposition of incompatible elements, as if each and every one of the aldermen, returning from Vienna, or Venice, or Paris, had sketched out a piece of what he had seen, and the Town Hall was the sum total of all this. Broch denounced the *fin de siècle* eclecticism of Vienna as an aesthetic representing a total lack of values and hidden behind sequins, which is to say kitsch; here he would have found a truly scandalous example of such kitsch. Fakery seems to be the poetry of Subotica. In the imagination of Danilo Kiš, the bewitching chronicler of the place, fakery becomes not only the appalling falsification of life brought about by Stalinism but also the clandestine split personalities of the revolutionaries who, to escape from the powers that be, change, multiply, disguise and lose their identities. The characters in *A Tomb for Boris Davidovich*, one of the most significant books in present-day Serbian literature, are figures in a world history which is entirely a gallery of fakers, victims and butchers.

One wonders why this kitsch broke out at Subotica in particular. In nearby Sombor the Committee building is the essence of composed and geometrical order, standing for the solidity of a town occupied with studying and planning the canals which linked the Danube to other rivers. Near Sombor lived the Schokatzi; at Subotica, on the other hand, were the Bunjewatzi, who had come in the course of centuries from Herzogovina, and of whom it is said in a book dating from the end of the last century that unlike the Magyars, who loved women to be round and rubicund, they had a preference for slender, pallid beauties. Being near the Hungarian frontier, Subotica is a border-town, lively and many-tongued. Sometimes, for an instant, one forgets whether one is in Jugoslavia or in Hungary. In Kidriceva Ulica, on a corrugated-iron fence erected because of roadworks, some careless but enamoured polyglot has written, "Jai t'ame."

17. NOVI SAD AND NEIGHBOURHOOD

Back to the Danube real and proper. Novi Sad was once the "Serbian Athens", a cradle of the cultural and political rebirth of Serbia. Today it is the capital of the Vojvodina. In the public offices and in Parliament there are five official languages (Serbian, Hungarian, Slovak, Rumanian and Ruthenian), even though the supremacy of Serbian is indubitable, and in the army total. The countryside is superb, the fortress of Petrovaradin, with its memories of Austrian and Turkish occupation, stands high above the Danube, while hidden in the nearby woods of the Fruška-Gora are the Orthodox monasteries with their icons and their immemorial peace.

In the market in Novi Sad one even sees peasant women in Slovak national costume. As in Novi Sad, the Vojvodina as a whole displays its multi-national character, almost a concentrated essence of that multi-plicity in unity which makes up Jugoslavia in general, and which economic crises and the centrifugal impulses of the various republics appear every so often to threaten. In interviews during the television programme mentioned earlier, Jon Petrović, a Rumanian in charge of the office for cultural self-management in Zitište, stated that when he goes to Rumania he feels he's in a foreign country. Bački Petrovac is a centre of the Slovaks, who have flourishing cultural traditions. After Tito's schism of 1948 some of these Slovaks had a hard time because they were suspected of being sympathetic to Stalinist Czechoslovakia, while others, who moved to Slovakia, were persecuted because they were suspected of Titoism. On the television, their bishop Joraj Struharik displays the red, gnarled snout of one with a healthy love for beer and sausages. The Ruthenians punctiliously distinguish themselves from the Slovaks and Ukrainians, looking to culture for their identity – according to their spokesman Julijan Rac.

Like the Slovaks, and even more so, the Hungarians have newspapers, magazines, publishing houses and a flourishing indigenous culture. A few years back Erwin Sinkó died, a great figure in Novi Sad. After playing a part in the republic of Béla Kun, he wrote his memoirs, *The Novel of a Novel*, as an exile in Moscow. In these he recounted the difficulty he had to get his novel *The Optimists* published in the Moscow of Stalin's purges – it was a 1,200-page fresco of the Hungarian revolution of 1919, and above all it evoked those terrible Stalin years. *The Novel of a Novel* is a remarkable testimony, the story of a writer who thinks that he has written for nobody, because both his book and his diary seem to be destined to remain forever unpublished, and Sinkó lives out the drama of a work addressed to no one, himself the phantom of a written text which seems to soak up life, but with neither purpose nor outlet.

In Stalin's Moscow, in the shadow of trials and purges and persecutions, Sinkó also suffered for being an "objective opportunist". He was not in the least inclined to complicity out of personal egoism, but – having clearly seen the infamy of tyranny – he objectively accepted its blackmail: he believed that it was impossible, in the struggle against Fascism, to take up arms at that time against the Stalinist regime and thereby weaken it, even though he realized that this belief was based on the conspiracy which supported and sustained terror.

In one marvellous passage, dated March 18th 1936, he recorded a conversation between Gorky and Malraux, who had come on a visit to the Soviet Union. It is a staggering snapshot of the downright obtuseness from which none escaped. The two of them were discussing Dostoyevsky. Gorky wrote him off as a preaching theologian, whereas Malraux, while admitting that the Dostoyevsky of the great "questions" about the world was a bit old-fashioned, did deign to observe that there was also a fine and worthy Dostoyevsky, concerned with solidarity and the future.

Never has a reader of Dostoyevsky, however simple and unprepared he was, however rotten the translation or botched the edition, given utterance to such idiocies. The wind bloweth where it listeth. At that moment Gorky and Malraux, two highly respected writers, achieved a world record: no one has ever understood less about literature than they did. They were not forced or justified by any threat: Stalin would not have sent them to Siberia if they hadn't talked about Dostoyevsky at all. What made them act as they did was, perhaps, a still grosser cowardice, an obscure desire to connive, to stand out, to set the tone for a cultural debate. They could claim to have achieved their object, and an enviable record.

In the Vojvodina there are plenty of gypsies, the Romanies, who are not just violinists, but also philologists, like Trifun Dimić, the author of a Romany dictionary. At Sibiu, in Rumania, moreover, they have a chief who (at least in the first instance) settles their disputes according to ancient tribal law. In official questionnaires in the Vojvodina an increasing number answer the question "Nationality?" by simply saying "Jugoslav". However, an Italian living in Novi Sad says that he feels like Lieutenant Drogo in *The Desert of the Tartars*, sunk in the slough of waiting for something that never happens.

18. FRONTIERSMEN

Grandma Anka is not very willing to talk about the *Grenzer*, the legendary, irregular troops of the Military Frontier, which were done away with by Francis Joseph about twenty years before she was born. But it seems that not long before that her grandmother had had an affair with a Chaikist and, in the small world of Bela Crkva in which hiding secrets and scandals was no easy matter, had caused something of a stir. The Chaikists, called after their boats the Chaikas in which they travelled swiftly and unpredictably up and down the Danube, were soldiers and river-pilots, Serbians for the most part. Their flotillas, intended for the struggle against the Turks, had officially become part of the Military Frontier, which had been established on regular lines as far afield as the Banat in the eighteenth century, with its "Chardake", or guard-houses. The Military Frontier, this long, autonomous strip which defended the Empire for a thousand kilometres between Carniola and the Balkans, was the soul of Danubian unity, a *limes* as solid as that of the Romans and as nomadic as the migratory peoples who came flooding into it in waves, fleeing from the Turks and the feudal overlords. Starting in Styria and Carniola in the sixteenth century, the Frontier unravelled like a serpent towards the south and east, a mobile wall which grew ever longer with the military strength of the Empire.

The Frontier enjoyed independent status, forming a single community of the soldiers and their families, obedient to their Knez or Vojvoda and to the distant, invisible Emperor, but not subject to any magnate or feudal overlord. In the course of its thousand kilometres it included various peoples, Wends, Germans, Illyrians and Wallachians, but its nationality was composite and undefined. The *Grenzer*, especially at the beginning, were largely Croats, but this term in itself embraced all sorts of different races. A considerable element consisted of Serbs, who lived in the *Zadruga*, a family community undivided in goods and blood, a confused unity of ties, love and property. The *Grenzer* defended the Empire against Turkish attacks and incursions, but their ranks also included some wild adventurers little short of being brigands, Haiduks and Uskoks, while large numbers of peasants joined them so as to escape from their feudal bondage.

The great magnates detested these freebooting soldiers who were independent of their power, and they complained more about the freedom of the militia than about the incursions of the Turks. But the *Grenzer* were not intimidated by them, any more than they were by the Crescent. A story by Heinrich Zillich tells of how the *Grenzer* gave a good whipping to an arrogant Hungarian baron whose property abutted on their territory. So as to avoid any troubles with the law, since their quarrels arose on the very border with the Frontier and it was hard to say which law prevailed, the feudal code or the one which obtained in their territory, they stretched the baron out on a bench set astride the border, paying tribute money into his very own hands on his side of the border, and on their own side giving his bottom a good thrashing.

Over the centuries the history of the Frontier, which also formed a *cordon sanitaire* against the plague, is a history of confusion and disorder, but also of discipline – of the iron links which bound together these peoples, whose country was a no-man's land between alien territories. It is a story of savagery, of cruel and barbaric sufferings, of loyalty, of course, of fearful toil and wild vitality, and of soldierly bragging – as in the tale of the imperial battalion of five hundred infantrymen given an escort of two Pandurs to guard them from being abducted. Above all it is a story of fierce, proud independence, jealously safeguarding its autonomy against any external authority. When in 1871, and once and for all in 1881, an imperial decree disbanded the centuries-old Military Frontier, placing it under Hungarian administration, the *Grenzer* felt betrayed. Svetozar Miletič, the uncrowned king of the Hungarian Serbs, publically denounced Francis Joseph, and Mihajlo Pupin recorded the fact that his father, an old-time Serbian *Grenzer*, told him: "Thou shalt never be a soldier in the Emperor's army. The Emperor has broken his word; the Emperor is a traitor in the eyes of the Frontiersmen."

The enterprising spirit of the Chaikist, which left such a disagreeable memory in Grandma Anka's family, is therefore one of the very last exploits of the Frontiersmen. Like many of those who give their lives in loyalty to a cause or a banner, these people were also betrayed by their banner. The great Austrian myth of the servant faithful to his master teaches us that the servant is indeed faithful, but the lord is often faithless.

19. A STALINIST WERTHER

As one can well imagine, Bela Crkva has a fine literature of its own. Each nationality can boast of its own culture, and the Serbs, for example, are justly proud of a particular jurist – and, incidentally, Minister of Justice – by the name of Gliša Gersić, an expert in public and international law, a student of Roman law and the laws of war, and the author of a most important work on the juridical aspects of the Balkan crisis of 1909. Professional bias, together with the narrowness of my linguistic resources, naturally lead me to take a special interest in the literature written in German. Germans were not lacking in Bela Crkva: in 1910 there were 6,062 of them, compared with 1,213 Hungarians, 1,994 Serbs, 42 Slovaks, 29 Croatians, 1,806 Rumanians, 3 Ruthenians, 312 Czechs, 42 Romanies and the 1,343 soldiers of the garrison or coming from elsewhere. Twenty-nine people were registered as "others", and 250 were "of the Jewish faith". Out of a total of 11,524, 8,651 could read and write.

German literature in Bela Crkva, it seems, was prevalently a feminine activity, exercised by the ladies of the privileged classes. "Even among the officers' daughters," we read in the voluminous history of Austrian literature by Nagl-Zeidler-Castle, in the chapter devoted to the Banat, "there are poetic talents." One of the most recent lyric voices to celebrate the town in nostalgic verses is that of a woman, Hilda Merkl. The poetess par excellence of Bela Crkva is, however, Marie Eugenie delle Grazie, the lone and plaintive nightingale of the "little white town" in the Banat. Born in Bela Crkva in 1864, this neurotic, introverted writer, sang the praises of her minuscule homeland, of the railwayman announcing the name of the station in a variety of languages, of the Turiczi pastry-shop which was the El Dorado of her childhood, of the sour-faced Herr Bositsch, proprietor of *Der schwarze Hund*, the Black Dog grocery store, of the ravishing Serbian lady, Mrs Radulovitsch, who would glide by in her carriage amid the admiration of all, of the Haiduks on horseback, the janissaries buried on the hill, the ice on the Danube breaking up in springtime – described also by Grandma Anka, with far greater intensity of expression – and the storks flying in from the lands of the Nile.

In her novel *Daughter of the Danube* the writer portrays herself in the character of Nelly, like her in love with her homeland and destined to an isolated and practically pathological solitude, the result of a proud, but far from happy, feeling of emancipation for women. In her story *The Gypsy*, written in 1885, she speaks about the ancient sorrow of a people whose sufferings arouse the pity or interest of absolutely nobody, and has nothing but the violin to speak of its own afflicted destiny.

Andreas A. Lillin, who in all probability will be the last German writer of Bela Crkva, died a few months ago. As a committed Stalinist he was, naturally, a narrator given to doing things on an epic scale, and a classic representative of the tenets of Socialist Realism. His novel *There Where the Wheat Is Milled* is a robust, forceful fresco of rural life, a hymn to the construction of Communist society and to the *Weltgeist* which, even when it appears in the garb of the Five-Year Plan, invariably operated for the good of each individual – for all that the individual may not know it, or may even fancy he's drawn the short straw.

Times change, alas, certitudes collapse, and in the rapid passing of things and of outlooks the life of those who are orthodox becomes ever more precarious and melancholy. As the guardian of totality, Andreas A. Lillin found himself increasingly isolated, the only one, or one of few, to defend the monolithic unity of the system and ideology which keeps the world compact. Around him events and people changed, Tito's Jugoslavia pulled out of the Cominform, Rumania (in which country he lived) chose its own national way to Socialism, Stalinism began to be questioned even in the Soviet Union, Communists throughout the world began to strike out new paths, and no one any longer swore that avant-garde art was simply bourgeois decadence and that everyone ought to write novels such as *And Quiet Flows the Don*.

Like many rigid custodians of immutable truth, I am told by Joachim Wittstock, Andreas A. Lillin was really a frail and sensitive person, a Stalinist Werther, a fine spirit who sought emotional invulnerability for himself within the armour of an unshakeable faith. Like everyone else he suffered on account of the world that changes and the truths that vanish, the loved faces that become strange to us and the incalculable loss of things. He wished to give an unchanging face, a reassuring order, to the indistinct and transitory seething of things. The more the world around him changed, and became foreign to him, the more he shut himself up in obstinate solitude, grieving and pathetic, even though rigid and inflexible on the face of it. His last book, *Our Dear Kinsfolk*, is written (1983) in opposition to the tendency of the Germans in Rumania to emigrate to the West. It is a work full of heavy-fisted preaching, which attempts to represent this tragic exodus as a sinister conspiracy set up by the capitalists.

Lillin died an isolated and forgotten figure, a tiny fragment of the mosaic which is the all but vanished Germanity of the Banat – a mosaic, however, which has its paradoxical aspects. In a study dated 1941 Milleker, who was curator of the Town Museum in Vrsắ, dealt with the ancient symbolism of the swastika: he wrote that the name of this symbol (traces of which have been found in the Banat dating back 6,000 years) is in fact a Slav word, and added that the Nazis could not have chosen a nobler sign than this venerable "symbol of love". Grandma Anka, who speaks excellent German, tells me that in her house they used to speak German to the dogs, but she – an admirer of Dr Kremling, leader of the German People's Party of Hungary – categorically denies that this had any disparaging significance.

20. A SAGA OF BELGRADE

As on one occasion he was looking from Pančevo at the right bank of the Danube, towards Belgrade and the castle of Kalemegdan, the Polish humorist Stanislav Jerzy Lec said that where he was standing, on the left bank, he still felt at home, inside the frontiers of his old Hapsburg monarchy, whereas for him the other side of the river was immediately "abroad", foreign parts. The Danube was, in fact, the border between the Austro-Hungarian Empire and the Kingdom of Serbia. In 1903 one of Grandma Anka's uncles was a member of King Alexander Obrenović's bodyguard. A few hours before the attempt on the sovereign's life, which he had got wind of but dared neither to oppose nor support, he threw off his uniform, plunged into the Danube, and was picked up some way downstream by Hungarian customs men. He lived the rest of his life in Bela Crkva, a Serbian deserter under sentence of death, but under the protection of the two-headed eagle.

Andrei Kuśniewicz, the Polish writer whose novels recalled the break-up of the double monarchy in terms of such urgent and spectral poetry, quotes Lec's words in agreement with the emotional and imaginative outlook of his colleague and countryman. He too looks out over that lost frontier, which for him is still the frontier of the world. For Lec and Kuśniewicz, Belgrade is on the other side, beyond the Pale.

It is difficult to say where and on what side of what Belgrade is, and to grasp the proteiform identity and extraordinary vitality of this incredible city which has been so many times destroyed, and so many times reborn, erasing all the traces of its past. Belgrade has had many periods of greatness, but each of these periods, writes Pedja Milosavljević in what amounts to a declaration of love for this chameleon of a capital city, "has disappeared with startling rapidity." The history and past of Belgrade do not live on in the few remaining monuments so much as in the invisible substratum, the epochs and civilizations crumbled like fallen leaves into the soil, the manifold, stratified, fertile humus in which this multiple city puts down its roots – a soil incessantly renewed, and which its literature has often represented as a great forge of metamorphoses.

In Belgrade a grandson of the Danubian empire ought really to feel at home and within his own borders. If Slovenia today is the most authentic Hapsburg landscape, Jugoslavia – and in the name of the country its capital, which controls the difficult, centrifugal equilibrium of the whole – is the heir of the two-headed eagle, of its composite, supra-national character, of its mediating function between East and West, between divergent or contrasting worlds and political blocs. Jugoslavia is a truly multi-national state, that is to say, built out of a multi-nationality which cannot be reduced to an unambiguous or predominant dimension. As in the case of the term "Austrian", maybe

"Jugoslav" is an imaginary concept in the manner of Musil, indicating the abstract force of an idea rather than the accidental concreteness of a fact; and perhaps it is the result of an operation of subtraction, and the lowest common denominator, once the individual nations have been removed, which shows what they all of them share but which is not to be identified with any of them.

Marshal Tito ended by resembling Francis Joseph more and more, and certainly not because he had fought beneath his banners in the First World War, but rather because of his awareness of inheriting a supra-national, Danubian legacy and leadership from him, and his desire to accept this legacy. But even, and indeed above all, Djilas, the great heretic of the Tito regime, has become practically the official representative of the old Mitteleuropa, one of the most authoritative and almost mythical voices of its rediscovery, of its rebirth as a political and cultural idea and perhaps even of a conciliatory idealization of it. Like the Hapsburg mosaic, that of Jugoslavia today is both imposing and precarious. It plays a very important role in international politics, and is determined to check and to annul its own internal tendencies towards dissolution. Its solidarity is necessary to the equilibrium of Europe, and its disintegration would be ruinous for this balance, as that of the double monarchy was for the world of yesterday.

Belgrade eludes portraiture, and its metamorphoses may be experienced or evoked rather than described. In his novel *The Fakers* (1974), Momo Kapor, a fifty-year-old Jugoslav novelist, narrated the saga of Knez-Mihailova Street, the finest and most epic street in the capital, and of the bewildered generation which, in the 1950s and 1960s, loses its youth and its life in the maelstrom of Old Belgrade in the process of disappearance and of the new – or rather of the several new – ephemeral Belgrades which come into being, exert their charm and vanish in turn at the ever-accelerating pace of history and society. His "Fakers" are engulfed in the promises which life flaunts on the real-life stage of Knez-Mihailova Street, caught between the left-overs of ideological rigidity and the glitter of Western prosperity, between anguishing truths and phoney emotional enticements, the suppressed crisis of Socialism and the myths of the celluloid. Kapor, in this book, wrote a small-scale *Education sentimentale* about the hopes and dreams of the post-war years in a country which is an advance patrol – sometimes to be considered "missing" – of the Third World. Belgrade is the background for this roundabout of disappointments, but also for the life which through them is reborn, and the astonishment which its

sudden changes of colour – such as the image of the model, Mima
Laševski, in Knez-Mihailova Street – leaves behind it.

21. AT THE IRON GATES

The hydrofoil for the Iron Gates leaves from Belgrade, near the point
where the Sava flows into the Danube. As we start off, Grandma Anka
casually points out the part of the city where, during the German
bombardment of April 6th 1941, she spent a day buried under the debris
with her second husband. She was, of course, unhurt; in fact they both
were. The sun hangs above the river, transforming the waters and the
mist to a dazzling shimmer. We speed down the Danube, between the
shores on which Trajan's memorial stone records his campaigns against
the Dacians of King Decebalus, on waters which were full of snares and
whirlpools and other dangers before the big dam and hydro-electric
power station were built at Djerdap, on the Jugoslav-Rumanian
frontier, and close to the border with Bulgaria. This gigantic undertak-
ing, which produces a considerable amount of electricity, has changed
the landscape and erased many traces of the past. Until a few years ago,
for example, the Danube still had its island of Ada Kaleh, populated by
Turks, complete with their cafés and their mosque; but now Ada Kaleh
has vanished, submerged by the river, and dwells in the slow, en-
chanted times of underwater things, like the mythical Vineta in the
Baltic.

At the Iron Gates in 74 B.C. the Roman general Gaius Scribonius
Curio expressed his unwillingness to penetrate into the dark forests on
the other side of the Danube; maybe as the representative of an
ordered, victorious civilization, he felt some obscure repulsion in the
face of the manifold stratification of peoples and cultures, intermingled
and indistinct, which is witnessed even today in the excavations at
Turnu-Severin. I make a tour of the hydro-electric plant, surrounded
by schoolchildren on an educational visit. The power-plant is possessed of an inexorable grandeur; it has a suggestion of menace, of
heroism. The documentary film served up to us on the tour recounts
the story of its construction, showing us titanic blocks of stone tipped
into the current, the cleaving of the waters, the irresistible advance of
the wheels of giant trucks. Accustomed as we are to the constant

criticism of progress, and concerned about ecological imbalances, we are rather taken aback by this Saga of the Five-Year Plan, by these pictures of the triumph of rationalization and technology over Nature, and we cannot help wondering whether those waters now harnessed by cement have really been tamed, or perhaps only suppressed for a moment, and are dourly meditating their revenge.

But this epic achievement, which recalls the Roman aqueducts, the roads which Tamburlaine cut through the mountains or Kipling's elephants, does have its grandeur and impersonal poetry, which is concealed from us by the anguished and certainly understandable objection to technology which pervades our culture. Maybe we ought to regard these modern pyramids with neither the progressive's rhetoric nor any sense of apocalyptic terror, giving to each his due, as Kipling in his *Bridge-Builders*, where he accords equal stress to British engineers and to Indian gods, praising, but at the same time setting limits to, the Labours of Hercules performed by Progress. The film was magnificent and incisive but not without a certain implicit rhetoric as employed by the regime. This was neutralized, however, by the schoolchildren who, for all the yells of their pretty, good-natured schoolmistresses, hurled fireworks into the dark corners of the hall, elbowed each other in the ribs, and generally re-established the balance between the solemnity of work and the impudence of life. Without the cheeky shindig set up by those children, I would probably have had less appreciation for that cyclopic endeavour.

We go by bus to Kladovo on the Bulgarian border. For a poorly prepared Westerner, geography gets vaguer and vaguer. Felix Hartlaub, the German writer whose fascinating notebooks were written "in the eye of the storm", which is to say in the special commando forces of the *Wehrmacht*, observed that to his mind, after Belgrade, there began a formless fog, which cast a vagueness over those Balkan lands in which he found himself, so that he wondered where on earth he was. I too, as I wait for the bus at Kladovo, wonder where I am.

EIGHT

Doubtful Cartography

1. "THEY SCORN THE TURKS"

In 1860 the French scientist and explorer Guillaume Lejean travelled up the White Nile as far as Gondokoro, and also up the Blue Nile, and (according to the encyclopaedias) drew one of the first dependable maps of these rivers. But in the years 1857–70 he also travelled in the Balkan peninsula, preparing an imposing mass of cartographical material on forty-nine large sheets, twenty of which were complete and finished in every detail. His Viennese friend and colleague, Felix Philipp Kanitz, however, travelling in Bulgaria in 1875, deplored the fact that the maps of that country were imprecise and unreliable; and that, as far as the lands near the Danube were concerned, they marked places that did not exist and failed to mark places that did. He agreed with Prof. Kiepert that Bulgaria was the most unknown country in Eastern Europe. Other cartographers used to invent towns or shift their locations by hundreds of kilometres. They drew maps which diverted the course of the rivers, and gave them purely arbitrary estuaries. Kanitz corrected Lejean's estimable maps; they were less precise than those of the Nile, and he was therefore in a position to define Bulgaria as "a perfectly unknown country". The Danube was more unknown than the Nile, and less was known of the peoples living on its lower course, Prof. Hyrtl insisted, than was known of the South Sea Islanders.

Cartography has without doubt taken some steps forward, but of all the countries of the East Bulgaria remains the most unknown, a place in which one rarely sets foot, and which comes into the limelight as the scene of improbable and unverifiable intrigues, imaginative trails of sensational conspiracies, accusations (denied) of genocide, interviews given by spokesmen of the Turkish minority which, according to the Western press, has been murdered to a man. Western Communists, when they hear that someone – especially if not a Party member – has been to Bulgaria, are quick to display a sort of aloof, ironic commiseration, and above all to marvel if he's retained any positive impressions.

The Bulgarians are eager to stress the positive side of things and their hospitality, as generous and cordial as one is likely to meet, is also a festive kind of indoctrination, a lesson in history, literature and culture to give the foreigner an understanding of their country and a love for it. Kitanka, our interpreter, is a lively, jovial girl who is fond of *rakia*, the excellent local aqua-vitae, and the small hours of the morning. She explains and illustrates the greatness of her country, amiably and inexorably compelling her guest to verify every detail of it, with the artlessness and enthusiasm of one who asks you to appreciate a beautiful day.

The traveller is not accustomed to this unreserved love of country. Almost everywhere some measure of scepticism is a thing everyone feels bound to display. To laugh at oneself, independent of the motives which justify it or otherwise, is not the privilege of Western decadence. Even in Hungary or Rumania those who represent official institutions feel obliged to express just a touch of dissent. Quite apart from concrete political or social motives, opposition is – regardless of frontiers – first of all dissidence expressed in the face of the prevailing reality. From rehearsals for the May Day parade to the crowded and well stocked restaurants and kiosks, Bulgaria on the other hand gives the impression of a robust epic quality, that of young recruits kept under a watchful eye, prepared to make a din in the dormitory, but affectionate towards their barracks and towards their country's flag.

At Vidin, Kitanka expatiates for ages about the ancient fortress of Baba Vida, which was first Roman, then Bulgarian and finally Turkish, but she cannot quite understand the excessive interest shown in the Mosque of Osman Pazvantoglu, topped by a heart-shaped emblem instead of the Crescent. In the late eighteenth century and the beginning of the nineteenth Osman, the powerful Pasha of Vidin, who had made his city more splendid than formerly, but also more modern and European, rebelled against Sultan Selim III, replacing the Crescent with his own personal symbol, which was a Heart. That rebellion, evoked in Vera Mutafčieva's novel *Chronicle of a Restless Time*, which appeared in 1966, is also a paradox. The Pasha, who was no conservative stick-in-the-mud himself, revolted against the enlightened Sultan, the promoter of many progressive reforms, and placed himself at the head of the janissaries, a body of men whom Selim III had dissolved; but at the same time he called upon the services of the Christians, the Bulgarian peasants oppressed by the Sublime Porte, and the Kardžălij, rebels and brigands who as occasion dictated became guerrilla fighters against the Turks, both in myth and in reality.

That dissent among the Ottomans does not in the least move

Kitanka, who confirms Lamartine's observation of 1833 during his stay in the charming town of Plovdiv, which was populated also by Turks, Greeks and Armenians, that the Bulgars "scorn and loathe the Turks." These passions are still intense, and the rancour is fresh. Bulgaria does not vaunt so much the building of Socialism as the rebirth, or rather the resurgence, of the nation, and the feeling of brotherhood between Bulgaria and Russia is based first and foremost on the struggle for liberation from the Turkish yoke in the last century.

Every battlefield and every episode is described with enthusiasm, down to the smallest detail. Lovely, learned, fervent girls lecture schoolchildren on every trench and every charge in the siege of Pleven, reproduced by a circular Panorama. The monument which rises on the height of Šipka, in memory of the decisive battle, always enjoys freshly picked flowers, as at Mohács. The mosques and minarets so plain and plentiful to see in pictures of the city at the end of the century have almost vanished; the peeling ruins before which people scurry, or the unreal, isolated shapes confirm the impression of Boscovich, the Ragusan astronomer and mathematician who founded the Brera Observatory, and who as early as 1762 was struck by the dilapidation of vestiges of the Ottoman Empire.

As far as it is possible to calculate their numbers, about seven hundred thousand Turks live in Bulgaria, though officially their existence is denied. Officially they are "Islamized Bulgars" – or Pomaks, as they used to be called – who have now been forced to adopt Bulgarian surnames. Every day the *Nouvelles de Sofia* publish interviews with Turks – or rather, with Pomaks – who according to Amnesty International or the newspapers of Ankara have mysteriously disappeared, whereas according to the authorities of the country they are alive and kicking. Today it is the turn of Damjan Christov, manager of a car and tractor station at Antonovo; wreathed in smiles he answers questions about his disappearance.

The five hundred years of the Ottoman yoke were certainly terrible times, with pillages and massacres, heads cut off and indolent exploitation. The splendid ikons preserved in Sofia, in the crypt of the church of Alexander Nevsky, which date back to the Bulgar Empire, have artistic and religious intensity enough to show us what a lofty and noble civilization the Turks overran at the end of the fourteenth century and submerged for five hundred years. In the nineteenth century, before attempting any form of resurgence, the Bulgars had to remember that they existed, to rediscover and repossess their own identity; like

Aprilov, who thought of himself as Greek (under the culturally de-nationalizing influence of the Greek Church, which was allied to the Ottomans), and only realized that he was a Bulgar when a book, *The Bulgars of Yesterday and Today*, was published in 1829 by the Ukrainian scholar Venelin. Books play an eminent role in the forming of the Bulgarian identity: a volume written and copied by hand many times over is the *Slaveno-Bulgarian History* by Paisy of Khilendar, which in 1762 marked its re-emergence after centuries of silence.

The centuries-long resistance of the submerged Bulgars is an extraordinary testimonial to a civilization. But every people remembers the violences to which it has been subjected by others, and if the Turks committed atrocities in Bulgaria, such as the Batak massacre in 1876, it is to be presumed that they were no more tender-hearted in the other territories of their dominions. Why, as soon as we cross this frontier, does rancour seem to be more long-lasting? The reason is certainly not to be found in the Bulgarian temperament, which is generous and hospitable. Kitanka resolves the problem by saying that Turks do not exist in Bulgaria, and that there is no consequent waning and oppressed minority. The opinions of those concerned count for nothing. The writer Anton Dončev, epic bard of the Rodhopi, tells that he once argued with an official living near Šumen because this fellow insisted that he was a Turk, whereas according to Dončev there was documentary evidence that he was descended from Genghis Khan. The distinction between nationality and citizenship seems unknown here. Anyone who lives in Bulgaria is a Bulgar, and that's that. When I mention the example of the much-admired Soviet Union – many different peoples united in a single state – our beautiful Kitanka says nothing, and is not in the least convinced.

2. AUTOBIOGRAPHY OF A HAIDUK

The soaring crags of Belogradčik are indistinguishable from the Turkish fortress which itself rises from Roman stonework of long ago. They loom over the landscape like a lone bird of prey – the harsh, melancholy landscape of the Balkans which has always impressed sentimental travellers, the inaccessible background to the exploits of the Kardžălij and the Haiduks. The entire Balkan peninsula was the theatre for the rebel Haiduk, whom one meets in song and story in Hungary, Serbia and Rumania; but his real homeland is perhaps Bulgaria in which, during the long centuries of the Ottoman yoke, he is practically to be identified with the torch of national freedom and independence. The Haiduks are celebrated in the works of Karavelov, the writer par excellence of the national resurgence, and those of Khristo Botev, revolutionary poet and martyr, the Petöfi of his nation. Surrounded by the indifference of the Pomaks and the hostility of the Čorbadž, the wealthy people who had not gone over to Islam but were nonetheless favourable towards Turkish rule, the Haiduks were half patriots and half brigands, and enemies of the Turks – to whom, all the same, they sometimes bore a striking resemblance. They were the eternal guerrilla fighters, the lords of the ravines and mountain gorges. Village troubadours, chroniclers and travellers agree in describing them as savage and indomitable, hunted in vain by the zaptiehs and bashibazouks (the Turkish police force) and by the "Arnauts", Albanians in the service of the Ottoman Empire.

Georg Rosen, who has written books about the Haiduks, and translated their folk-poetry, was inclined to wonder whether their incessant guerrilla warfare actually defended the Bulgarian nation, or held up its economic development, its trade and industry. Panajot Hitov is perhaps the most interesting of these patriot-outlaws; in his autobiography, written with all the freshness of life in the raw – we get a proper notion of the Haiduks' resistance to the despotism of the Ottoman Empire, and their contribution to the liberation of Bulgaria.

His Balkan background lends the Haiduk a picturesque air, and also something of chaos and barbarism, but this is purely a stereotyped convention. "Balkan" is an adjective with insulting overtones. Arafat, for example, once accused Syria of aiming at "the Balkanization of Lebanon and the whole Middle East". Anyone who has seen the streets of Sarajevo, and its bazaar, as sparkling as a mirror, or the spruce orderliness of Sofia, and compares these with what obtains in cities or countries held up as paragons of civilization, is inclined to use the term "Balkan" as a compliment, as others tend to employ the word "Scandinavian".

3. MANUSCRIPTS IN THE DANUBE

It was at Vidin that Petko Slaveykov, the first real modern Bulgarian poet, fell into the water and lost a number of manuscripts in a small river called the Cibăr. Other poetic works were by mischance reft from him by the Danube to which, as to a benevolent god of transience and forgetfulness, it seems necessary to offer a sacrifice of every work of river-literature, from the opus of Neweklowsky to the efforts of his imitators. Slaveykov squandered his life and his works with true magnanimity: he fought at Šika and ended up in prison in Istanbul; he celebrated his country, love and disappointment. That rather careless disappearance into the whirlpools of the Danube bears witness to the prodigality of his nature. The irony of the situation would have been perfectly rounded off if the poems of his son Pencho, a Nietzschean poet and therefore a Poet of Life, of the Future which drags us all along in its wake, had also been lost in the river.

In the later 1890s and the beginning of the present century Bulgaria had only recently acquired some measure of cartographical identity, and was still not only a remote province of Europe but one that remained an echo-chamber for the voices of the great cultural ferment which Europe has not even today fully outlived: the voices of Nietzsche, Stirner, Ibsen and Strindberg, the great heralds of contemporary thought and feeling, who tore from reality one mask and one foothold after another, pursuing life as it is and discovering its groundlessness. Coming once again to nationhood later than others, Bulgaria lives in various periods at the same time. According to Yana Markova, directress of the Jus Autor literary agency and an authority on cultural life, even after 1945 there were still villages which had never seen a theatrical performance; exactly as in a famous chapter of Ivan Vasov's *Under the Yoke*, the Bulgarian "national novel" par excellence published in 1889, the peasants, having for the first time in their lives witnessed a patriotic play, fêted the actor cast as the heroic intellectual Levski, hanged by the Turks, and gave extremely sour looks to the one who played the wicked pasha. If we observe the progress the country has made in the last forty years, its prosperity and the spread of education, it is hard not to admire the Socialism which has guided those giant strides.

But the Bulgaria which knew nothing of theatres, which is what we expect in lands under the dominion of Islam, was also the country of the turbulent Tolstoyan and Nietzschean intellectuals depicted by Emilyan Stanev in his novel *Ivan Kondarev*, written in the years 1958–64. Stanev brings the ideas of Nietzsche, the ethical rigour which pursues life while ignoring morality, to bear on his novels about the Bogomil heresy: this was the search for religious purity which rejected any kind of reassuring dogmatic mediation and ended by gazing upon the unfathomable river of life, which flows beyond good and evil and vanishes like water through one's fingers the moment one attempts to grasp it in its pure, amoral flow.

Kitanka, like anyone who is really and truly alive, is rather unfeeling about the terrible nostalgia of living. She is proud of her country and with perfect calm drinks an enviable quantity of *rakia*, which seems to have no effect on her. Maybe her robust cheerfulness is a legacy of the Ottoman yoke, to borrow the words of Vasov, one of the voices of the rebellion against that yoke. Oppression, he writes in his novel-epic of Bulgaria, has the privilege of making peoples happy; for when the political arena is closed, society seeks consolation in the immediate good things of life, in wine drunk under the trees, in love, in generation. "Enslaved peoples have their philosophy which reconciles them to life." Thus the great Vasov, in words which would very likely embarrass the powers that be in his country, who look up to him as a tutelary deity. But the fascinating thing about Bulgaria today consists also in the reconcilation with life – thanks to another and different yoke?

4. TARTARS AND CIRCASSIANS

Serving beneath Osman Pazvantoglu's rebel banners there was also a Tartar sultan, later defeated by the Pasha of Silistra. In the course of millennia the banks of the Danube received wave after wave of the most diverse migratory peoples, and Vidin was a historical blind-alley. There were Ragusans, Albanians, Kurdish exiles, Druses from Lebanon (whom Kanitz remembers seeing shut up in cages like birds of prey), gypsies, Greeks, Armenians, Spanish Jews and above all Tartars and Circassians. Tartars had arrived earlier, but many more arrived in the 1860s, during what might be called an exchange of peoples. Whereas many russophile Bulgarian families, as a result of the series of wars between the Russians and the Turks, had moved to Bessarabia and the Crimea, the Sublime Porte received and transferred to Bulgaria (especially in the years 1861–2) many Tartars and Circassians reluctant to live under the dominion of the Czar, in an odyssey tragic both for the new arrivals and for the Bulgarians who had to make room for them.

In the already accepted iconography, the Tartar, even in the eyes of the Bulgars and Bulgarophile travellers, is gentle, hard-working, polite and civilized. The Circassian, on the other hand, is a savage brigand, a horse-thief, a good-for-nothing and a ferocious watchdog for the Turks. In one of Vasov's stories it was the Circassian Džambalazat, as swarthy and terrifying as the Infidel champions in the chivalric romances, who fired the shot which killed Khristo Botev, the poet-martyr of the Bulgarian uprising. The proverbial beauty of the Circassian women is not denied by the Bulgarophiles, but it is shown in the light of a provocative and almost degrading sensuality, of savage, dominating bodies on litters of dirty hides.

This double exile, moving in both directions, of Bulgarians to the Crimea and Circassians to Bulgaria, is a ballad on the vanity of conquest. While the Circassians were settling in the villages of Bulgaria, spreading terror with their looting raids, they were experiencing a tragedy which touched the heart of Europe – which was touched again a few years later by the Turkish massacre of Bulgars in 1876. The exodus of the Circassians from the Caucasus is connected with their war against the Russians, led by Shamil, whom Tolstoy depicted in his *Hadji-Murad*, a masterpiece written near the end of his life, in which his instinctive poetry overcomes his stubborn determination to give poetry up. The Circassians were embarked at Trapezunte or at Samsun, herded together in appallingly unhygienic conditions, packed in with the animals, with the dying and the corpses, exposed to hunger and sickness, and epidemics which decimated their numbers to a terrifying extent. At Samsun, in September 1864, there were 60,000 live refugees and 50,000 dead ones, and the ships that transported them left a wake of bodies thrown into the water.

When they arrived in the Danubian territories which had been assigned to them, especially in the surroundings of Lom, the Circassian chieftains buried those of their dead who had not already been thrown away like refuse, hoping in this way to take possession of the land which received those mortal remains; and in that soil they planted their sabres, according to the ancient custom, in the belief that they were perpetuating the old tradition, whereas in fact they were setting a seal on the end of their myth. The legendary freedom of the people of the Caucasus ended with that wretched official procedure, which transformed the rebels of the Caucasus into a bewildered flock at an employment exchange.

In London committees were set up to support the Circassian cause; messages of protest were sent to the Russians, and Circassian chieftains were exhibited for the commiseration and exotic curiosity of members of the Whittington Club. Their tragedy was greater than the English philanthropists thought, because they were not simply expelled by the Russians, but (partly believing that they had chosen it) they set off on a migration that seemed also to be a triumphant march to a conquered land, offered them by the Sultan. Some ten years later the London clubs, which over the Circassian question had been anti-Russian and pro-Turkish, were protesting – like the whole of Europe – against the Turkish massacre of the Bulgarian rebels. The milestones of a journey across Bulgaria, wrote Kanitz, are the tumuli of vanished peoples.

5. AGENT ROJESKO

The bulk of the Circassian territory formed a strip along the Danube, near Lom. In that little town there was an agency of the Imperial Steam Navigation Company of the Danube, under the direction of Agent Rojesko, who for weeks on end opened none of his windows overlooking the river, to keep the house free from the stench of the sick and the corpses arriving on ships laden with Circassians suffering from typhus. Records and reports, as well as the testimony of travellers, show Rojesko toiling away tirelessly and courageously to prevent and forestall contagion, to help the refugees, to find them food and shelter, provide them with medicines and work.

Along the river, in these territories the geography of which was then still uncertain, one comes across a lot of these figures: traders, consuls, doctors and adventurers, the outposts of law and order or the vanguards which have pressed forward just a little too far, and been swallowed up in chaos. Such was the epic Rojesko, who combined the preciseness of an Austrian official with the initiative of a lost explorer; such were Dr Barozzi, sent on official missions on the vessels leaving

Samsun with their loads of Circassians, and the "Spaniard" (i.e. Sephardic Jew) Alexander Tedeschi, who ended up at Varna as consul for Austria-Hungary and France. Then there were officials and captains of the Lloyd Triestino Line, and the sinister St Clair, an English ex-captain who, with the name of "Sinkler", became a minor local satrap hostile to the Bulgarians and friendly with the Turks and brigands – a sort of mixture of Conrad's Kurtz, Kipling's man who would be king, and Lawrence of Arabia. Once their job or term of office is over these figures disappear, like sailors who go ashore and vanish among the crowds, leaving no trace other than in the rolls of some administration.

6. THE WAVE AND THE OCEAN

The crucible of Bulgaria is a great deal older than these picturesque Balkan-Caucasian mixtures, and it has very different mythical depths. In fact, its roots lie in the archaic encounter between the agricultural civilization of the South-East and the nomadic invaders of the steppes. Bulgaria is one of the chief nuclei of Great Slavia, and in fact is the territory in which the language of Cyril and Methodius was formed, a language known as Old Church Slavonic. For their part the Proto-Bulgars, coming from the Altai, crossed the Danube in the seventeenth century, led by Asparuh Khan, and established a powerful empire which several times proved the equal of the Byzantine Empire; but the Bulgars were gradually absorbed by the Slavs, who had arrived a century earlier, and whom they had subjugated. They amalgamated with their subjects and adopted their language, drawn in by the enormous assimilating and cohering force of Slav civilization, which sometimes, at its beginnings, seems to have delegated the guidance of its expansion to other peoples; when Slavification was entrusted to the Avars, for instance, the victorious conquerors soon disappeared because they advanced Slav culture but not their own.

But far deeper than this Slav undercurrent, which constantly comes to the surface, is the element of the Thracians, the vast community of peoples who form the substratum of the entire Carpathian-Danubian-Balkan culture. Anton Dončev, who has written epic and mythical accounts of his country's origins, with a *pietas* which embraces also the legacy of the Turks, says that the Thracians are an ocean, whereas the Unogonduri and Onoguri Proto-Bulgars, who came from the Caspian Sea and the Sea of Azov, are the waves which stir and swell that aboriginal ocean, while the Slavs are the earth, and the patient hand which moulds it and gives it form. The modern Bulgars are the fusion of all three elements.

Going back to one's origins, which Nietzsche unmasked as unimportant, is a commonplace in Bulgarian culture, and oscillates between real feeling and a sly tease. Someone of true Proto-Bulgar appearance will today be made the object of justified compliments. A century ago Prof. Rösler was convinced that the Proto-Bulgars were of Samoyedic stock. However this may be, there is a particular Bulgar look which the "naïve" painter Zlatio Bojadjiev has caught perfectly in his tall, melancholy huntsmen and his absorbed and massive Kharakachan nomads, leaning on their staffs like shepherd kings.

Bulgarian literature was produced under the sign of the epic until 1956, when the epic monumentality dear to Stalinism began to disintegrate. Dimitrov, whose mummy is displayed with Asiatic ritualism in Sofia as Lenin's is in Moscow, addressed a letter on May 14th 1945 to the Writers' Union in which he laid upon literature the duty to shape and educate. His aim was to direct the whole of the nation's literature into a single channel. Now the scene has changed: Bulgaria has not experienced "Prague Springs" or "Hungarian Autumns", and – at least officially – knows nothing of dissent or revisionism, but the Plenum of April 1956, the speech made by Zivkov to the youth of Sofia in 1969, and the 10th Party Congress in 1971, to mention only a few salient moments, have profoundly modified the situation in literature. Today, with Ivailo Petrov, the Bulgarian novel can even be good-naturedly humorous at the expense of the official optimism, as in his delightful short story *The Best Citizen in the Republic*, the tale of a decent fellow who is ground down by the bureaucratic procedures and the red tape tied up with the flattering honour which has been conferred on him. I wonder whether poor Uncle Ančo, encumbered and overwhelmed by the honours showered on him, and their concomitant duties, is a descendant of the Proto-Bulgars.

7. THE MACEDONIAN QUESTION

For a long time, as witness bloody pages of history and impassioned pages of literature, Bulgaria has claimed Macedonia, both politically and ethnically. The Macedonian question may be summed up in the story of Mr Omerić, which was told me by Adam Wandruszka. Omerić, who was so called under the Jugoslav monarchy, became Omerov during the Bulgarian occupation in the Second World War and then Omerski for the Republic of Macedonia, which is part of the Jugoslav federation. His original name, Omer, was Turkish.

8. GREEN BULGARIA

Kozlodúj. It was here in 1876 that Khristo Botev seized the steamship *Radetzky* as it made its way up the Danube, landed with two hundred men on Bulgarian soil, and gave the signal for insurrection, falling almost at once in battle, at the age of twenty-eight. This romantic, revolutionary poet invited one in his poems to listen, at eventide, to the Balkans chanting a Haiduk song; he dreamt of a liberation that was at once national and social, with the fraternal union of all the Balkan peoples and the religion of mankind. The revolutionary class, to his way of thinking, was the peasantry. This was in tune with the democratic tradition of Bulgar agrarian populism, far more widespread than in neighbouring countries oppressed by the large estates.

The Bulgarian agrarian movement has always been open and progressive by nature, as we see from the policy of its greatest leader, Stamboliski. It is free of the regressive and Fascist tones which we find in other "green" movements, for example the "green men" imagined by Codreanu, leader of the Rumanian legionaries. The Bulgarian progressivist intelligentsia largely came from the ranks of the village schoolmasters. The tiny town of Bozjenči, lost in the woods, intact and unchanged, gives us an idea of this modest, tranquil peasant dimension, free of ancestral barbarities. This emerges also in the house where Zivkov was born, in those small spaces of limited but clean life which gave birth to a vocation for revolutionary leadership. To steer clear of any sort of idyllic idealism, however, we should bear in mind what

Kanitz wrote . . . Observing the peasant women broken with toil, he said that only a few clues enabled one to guess what a woman of twenty had looked like as a girl of seventeen.

9. THE TALES OF ČERKAZKI

Village culture is dying everywhere, even in Bulgaria, but here it has found a poet to depict its disappearance into the abyss of time with an imagination which draws on its myth for the very last time, summoning forth the ironical magic which alone is capable of evoking its dissolution. Jordan Radičkov, sixty years old, belongs to the peasant world which in his stories has become a fairy-tale – the imaginary village of Čerkazki. Covered with snow and populated by hens and pigs at least as important as the men and women, Čerkazki is a village in which demons lurk in the most unexpected places, the sledges set off on their own, guns fire themselves, and the jays and the corn-cobs have as much to say as the mayor or the gamekeeper; and there is a captive balloon, whirled about by the wind, that gives battle to all the inhabitants including the police.

The bard of Čerkazki is the genuine voice of the oral tradition. The prodigious and absurd happenings of which he tells are the tales that pass by word of mouth in the inn, tales made up to ramble on about life and not be intimidated by History, downright lies that everyone tells to his friends and ends up by believing himself. As long as fairy-tales are told, life will survive. The tales of Čerkazki are hidden among the houses and in the implements of every day, the axe planted in the chopping-block and the bucket in the well; and it is the things themselves which whisper the tales and put them into circulation.

In his home in Sofia Radičkov writes about winters and about animals, about the Danube iced over and his father sending him to break the ice with a hatchet to fetch in some water. He writes about the gypsies and the Turks of his childhood, and Kitanka, who is acting as interpreter, adds that this is a case of poetic licence, because in Bulgaria there are no Turks, only Bulgarians. Radičkov is a poet of the cold, of the snow, of the whiteness of winter. He is a writer of refined irony, who changes the world into a soap-bubble; but he is also a sanguine peasant, rooted in that epic wholeness of which he narrates, embroiders and adjusts the outcome; he is familiar with death and capable of listening to all the voices of life, to the storks on the roof and the woodworm in the beam.

Radičkov is the most famous writer in Bulgaria today. He seeks for the wisdom that lies deep in everyday ingenuousness, intelligence concealed behind what seems foolish, poetic madness masquerading as simple-minded common sense and grumpy obstinacy, Don Quixote disguised as Sancho Panza. He is the poet of the wintry, frozen Danube, just as the ice on certain fountains assumes fantastic shapes; he is the wizard who sets free the characters and the stories imprisoned in that ice. He tell us that his father always used to go treasure-hunting with a divining rod; every evening he would get together with his friends to plan the next day's expedition. At the door, while we are saying goodbye to him, not without a touch of melancholy, I asked whether his father ever found any treasure. No, never, he replied without batting an eyelid.

10. THE WORLD CREATED BY SATANAIL

On the wall of a church in Eskus, which lies near the Danube and is now called Gigen, there is an inscription exhorting people to curse the heretics. It is probably earlier than the eleventh century. The curse is without doubt aimed at the Bogomils, against whom the 1211 synodal decree of the Czar issued a whole series of anathemas. The Bogomils first came into being in Bulgaria in the tenth century and were widespread throughout the Balkan peninsula until the fourteenth. They were brethren of the Cathars and Albigensians, and like these were savagely massacred and burnt at the stake. They declared that God had created the spiritual and celestial world, but that the terrestrial world of tangible and ephemeral appearances was the work of Satanail, the devil. The heirs of Manichaean and Gnostic dualism, which had even been the official religion in the Asiatic empire of the Uigurs, and was often confused with similar heresies, those of the Paulicians and Messalians, the Bogomils explained the incessant triumph of evil and sorrow by imagining that the world had been created by a perverse god. Satanail – the fallen angel, and according to some even a son of God, the evil elder brother of Christ – was the Cosmocrator, the lord of that part of creation which is cruel and unjust, the "steward" of the universe, the antagonist of the good God until the end of time or, according to the most radical dualists, throughout eternity. The whole of reality obeyed Satan; to procreate and perpetuate life meant obeying his commands, as Noah had done, thus becoming an accomplice in the survival of evil. The same was true of Moses and the prophets of the Old Testament, a book of glory and violence. Every prince and potentate on earth was a servant of the abyss, Jerusalem was demonic, and John the Baptist also was a messenger of darkness: icons in the crypt of the Alexander Nevski church show him with his hair on end, vibrating with malignant electricity, and wearing the irate expression of one who takes pleasure in announcing disasters.

The suffering and the death of creatures makes it impossible to thrust away into the archives of history the questions asked by the Bogomils: they ask who is to blame for the outrage inflicted on living things. The revolt against evil was also a protest against injustice: the Bogomils gave a voice to the oppressed peasantry and preached against social hierarchies, against all the lords of the earth. In two trenchant novels, *The Legend of Sibin, Prince of Preslav*, published in 1968, and *The Anti-Christ*, two years later, Stanev has depicted the tumultuous Bulgaria of the Bogomils, providing a historical fresco that is at the same time a parable of the questions, and the disorders, which the radical need for truth unleashes among men. Prince Sibin not only experiences the political upheavals caused by heresy and the persecution of it, but also the contradictions of a spirit torn by its mixture of good and evil, of creative and destructive forces, and by the impossibility of distinguishing between them.

The splendour of nature raises the mind to a religious sense of the eternal, but perhaps it is Satanail who rustles among these trees and breathes in those forces of life. The destructive principle denies the loftiest divine creation, but even this denial is necessary to the process of creation and to the moral life itself, and therefore can be good and divine, even if this very intuition could in turn be a temptation of Satanail, designed to raise men on high and show them the wheel of the world. Good and evil appear as the levers of motion. All seems necessary, the martyrdom of the heretics and the fury of those who martyr them.

Stanev depicts the dismay of the man who discerns this mixture of the true and false in everything, in the eyes of the mortally wounded stag, in sensuality, in asceticism, in the very attempt to understand and accept ambiguity. Disorder flares up in the hearts of men and among the masses of the heretics, fomenting social uprisings and producing other, antithetical heresies, and leading men to seek for God in purity as well as in depravity. The search for Absolute Truth burns up every truth and, paradoxically, arrives at the equivalence and indifference of all things, while the thirst for purity and the need to free oneself from sin end in the dullness of orgy. Life pursued in its essence continually negates all of its faces and converts them into their opposites.

Stanev approaches the drama of the Bogomils with a Nietzschean sensibility which has also enabled him to write wonderful stories about animals. Behind the look in the eyes of a dying stag the Christian conscience seeks to decipher the mystery of grief and of guilt, tormenting the spirit in this quest without end or answer. Drawn into this whirlpool of questions, Sibin sometimes feels nostalgic for Tangra, the laconic, indifferent deity of the Proto-Bulgars, the sky arched above the steppes, over things as they are, without torturing mind and spirit.

The "brambles of heresy" were widespread everywhere. They grew, and were rooted out, in Serbia, too, in Bosnia, Russia and the West, but Bulgaria was the land of heretics par excellence, the land of "the accursèd Bulgars". Kitanka is proud of this, but also a little vexed. This great historic role of Bulgaria, that of spreading such important religious movements all over Europe, fits in well with her patriotism, but not so well with the other theory, according to which "we Bulgars have always been atheists."

II. THE BIBLE OF THE GOTHS

Nicopolis. Near this town on the Danube, now reduced to a village, the Sultan Nayazid in 1396 annihilated a Christian army led by King Sigismund of Hungary. Contemporary chroniclers and the testimony of the traveller Schiltberger, the Marco Polo of Bavaria, chiefly stress the disdainful elegance with which the French cavalry, ignoring all strategic plans, dashed headlong in serried ranks to defeat. In the province of Nicopolis, ten centuries earlier, a group of Goths settled. One of these was Bishop Wulfila, whose translation of the Bible into Gothic marks the beginning of German literature. So these shores, on which there is no German presence whatever, were in a sense the starting point of Germanism, of its march towards the west, which so many centuries later would turn back eastward, like a river reversing its course, and then finally withdraw westwards again beneath the pressure of other epoch-making migrations.

12. RUSE

According to Elias Canetti, in Ruse (or rather, for him, in Rustschunk) the rest of the world was called Europe, and whenever anyone went up the Danube as far as Vienna he was said to be going to Europe. But if the truth be told, Ruse is very much "Europe", in fact a tiny reproduction of Vienna, with the yellow ochre of the nineteenth-century merchants' houses, spacious, attractive parks, the eclecticism of the *fin de siècle* buildings, laden with caryatids and other ornaments, and a late neo-classical symmetry. One feels at home there, in the familiar atmosphere of solid, hard-working Mitteleuropa, with the ancient, colourful mercantile prosperity of the river port and the dull impressiveness of heavy industry. Along the streets and in the squares one comes across corners of Vienna or Fiume, the reassuring uniformity of the Danubian style.

Until the years between the two world wars Ruse, known as "Little Bucharest", was the richest city in Bulgaria, and had witnessed the foundation of the first bank in the country. Midhat Pasha, the Turkish governor, had restored and modernized it, built hotels, brought in the railway, and broadened its streets and avenues according to the principles employed in Paris by Baron Haussmann, whom he had met in person. Two Italian sisters by the name of Elias (their father was representative of Lazar & Co., hatmakers), born in Ruse shortly before 1920, remember the winter snow as high as the houses and summer bathing in the Danube, the "Teteven" Turkish pastry-cook's shop, the French school run by Monsieur and Madame Astruc, the peasants bringing sacks of yoghurt and river-fish every morning, and the photographic studio of Carl Curtius, "Photographie Parisienne", where they went for their school photograph. They also remember the tendency to be cagey about one's wealth.

The city, however, was less restrained in the later nineteenth century. Consuls representing all sorts of European countries and merchants of divers nations animated its evenings. On one such night a famous Greek corn merchant gambled away his fortune, his red neo-classical palace near the Danube, and his wife. At the corner of the Square of September 9th the District Savings Bank has a symbolic façade depicting this world – voracious and chaotic but at the same time bogged down in decorum. Around the doors of the old bank are reliefs of leering masks, the head of a satyr, a Moloch of money, who flaunts a great moustache that stretches out and dissolves into *Art nouveau* flourishes. He glances sideways with lascivious Mongol eyes. Much higher up emerges a very different kind of head, a dignified inexpressive head circled with laurel: perhaps the founder of the bank, the father of the demons of finance who are now under the patronage of the archangels of state.

13. A STENTORIAN MUSEUM

During the last phase of Ottoman dominion, Ruse was a disembarkation point for the patriots and revolutionaries who were organizing themselves in Rumania, especially in Bucharest and Brăila. The Baba Tonka Museum, which overlooks the Danube, commemorates the heroic, tireless Bulgar woman who was the leading spirit in the patriotic conspiracy, and inspired the Revolutionary Committee founded in Ruse in 1871, as well as the insurrections of 1875 and 1876, which were crushed with great bloodshed. Baba Tonka has a stern face and a square jaw, the expression of one who is a bit too self-satisfied at having given four sons to the fatherland – two dead, two exiled – and declares herself ready to give another four. Also in the museum is a portrait of Midhat Pasha, wearing a fez, a dark double-breasted suit and glasses like the ones Cavour wore. He was a man of genius, mixed up in an impossible situation. He clearly saw the decline and even the injustice of the Ottoman regime, and laboured in favour of enlightened reforms and the modernization of the country, but he was determined to defend that Turkish dominion which he aimed to transform, and he passed from reform to the use of the gallows. On the banks of the Danube is a yellow house inlaid with black wood, where his mistress used to live.

The Baba Tonka Museum is stentorian. Ivan Vasov, who celebrated the 1876 uprising in his novel *Under the Yoke*, had the courage to call it "tragically inglorious", pointing out the contradictions in the revolutionary movement, and the inadequacy of the Bulgarian people, who at that time were not yet ready for liberation. For this very reason Vasov, whose work is today considered classic, is a genuine patriotic writer and his great novel – realistic, tragic, and occasionally even humorous – is the true epic of Bulgaria and the rebirth of the country.

14. GRAFFITI AT IVANOVO

Twenty kilometres from Ruse, near Ivanovo, high among inaccessible crags, is a fourteenth-century rock-hewn church. The grotto is frescoed in Giottoesque colours, with night-blue skies and landscapes out of Sienese paintings. A flagellated Christ looks calmly out at you. The frescos preserved in this eyrie, which overlooks an enchanting landscape of uncontaminated peace, are of marvellous beauty. Products of the Byzantine school of Târnovo, the ancient capital of the Bulgarian czars, they are the expression of a noble civilization constrained to five centuries of silence. The threat to those frescos comes no longer from the Turks, but – apart from the damp – from the names of visitors scrawled and scratched on the stone. The kind of hooliganism that yearns for immortality has illustrious precedents: Byron, for example, who sullied the Temple of Poseidon at Cape Sounion with his name. Time, however, ennobles even vandalism, and the writing with which certain eighteenth-century Greeks and Armenians ruined a magical blue sky are now objects of interest, and are cared for almost as much as that sky itself. "If there is one thing I can't stand," said Victor Hugo when present at something particularly bad or stupid, "it is to think that tomorrow all this will be history."

15. THE STORK AND THE LAMP-POST

In a little town between Ivanovo and Ruse there was once a stork which always built its nest on the lamp-post, unaware of the danger or the damage that might ensue. Having several times chased it away in vain, the Council, by official decree, erected another lamp-post, specially reserved for the stork, which indeed eventually chose it as its seasonal home. Bulgaria is also a country of such kindnesses – there is the famous valley of the roses, which distracted Moltke when he was on a tour of fortresses, and there is also the great attention paid to animals and to the poetry of animals.

16. THE HOUSE OF ELIAS CANETTI

In Ruse, beside the wrought-iron balcony at 12 Ulica Slavianska, a street running straight down to the port, there is still a large stone monogram with the letter C. The three-storeyed house was the business belonging to Canetti's grandfather, and is now a furniture shop. The quarter of the "Spanioli" (i.e. Sephardic Jews) – who in Ruse were at one time numerous, enterprising and somewhat exclusive – still consists, for the most part, of low houses surrounded by greenery, and generally single-storeyed. The Jews were well treated in Bulgaria: when its Nazi allies forced the Sofia government to make Jews wear the Star of David, the people demonstrated their sympathy towards those who were wearing it, says Hannah Arendt in her book on Eichmann, and in general attempted to obstruct or mitigate anti-Semitic measures.

In this quarter is the house where Canetti spent his childhood. Stojan Jordanov, director of the town museums, is a kind, educated man; he takes us to this house at 13 Gurko Street – an address which Canetti, in his autobiography, is careful not to reveal. The road in front of the gate is still "dusty and sleepy", but the garden-courtyard is no longer so spacious, having been partly built over. On the left of the courtyard one still goes up a few steps to reach Canetti's house. The building is divided into small apartments: in the first lives the Dakovi family, and at the last door we come to we are ushered in by Madame Vâlcova, the proprietress. The rooms are stuffed with objects of every sort, all crammed in higgledy-piggledy – carpets, blankets, boxes, suitcases, mirrors on the chairs, paper bags, artificial flowers, slippers, maps, pumpkins. On the walls are large, tattered photographs of film stars, a Marina Vlady, a young De Sica with his winning smile.

In these rooms one of the great writers of the century opened his eyes upon the world – a poet destined to divine and depict with exceptional power the delirium of the age, which dazzles and distorts the vision of the world. Amongst all these odds and ends, in the mystery that is always present in every space hewn out of the formless universe, something irrecoverable has been lost. Even Canetti's childhood has vanished, and his detailed autobiography does not succeed in grasping it. We send a postcard to Canetti in Zurich, but I know that he will not appreciate this intrusion into his dominions, this attempt to seek out his hiding place and identify it. In his autobiography, which was probably the determining factor in his winning of the Nobel Prize, Canetti goes hunting for himself, for the author of *Auto-da-fé*. The Nobel committee awarded prizes to two writers, the one of the past, who is in hiding, and the one of the present, who is reappearing. The first is a mysterious and anomalous genius, maybe vanished beyond recall; he it was who in 1935, at the age of thirty, published one of the great books of the century, his only truly great book, *Auto-da-fé*, which almost at once disappeared from the literary scene and remained forgotten for some thirty years. This impossible, unmanageable book makes no concessions and refuses to be assimilated by the cultural establishment; it is a grotesque parable of the delirium of the intelligence which destroys life, a terrible picture of the lack of love and of bewilderment. The republic of letters, with its benign historical approach, was the book's ideal mediator, but it rejected the work for the most obvious reason – the absolute and radical greatness was more than it could take. This book, which sheds light on our life as very few others do, was for a long time virtually ignored, and Canetti bore this neglect with a firmness of character which perhaps concealed, in its courteous modesty, a stubborn awareness of his own genius.

The author of *Auto-da-fé* would not have won the Nobel Prize on his own, not even with the aid of his other works of the past. For these to become accepted it perhaps needed another writer, the one who leapt into the limelight thirty years later, to accompany the fortunes of his book, now rediscovered by fame, just as if this fame were posthumous, and to guide us in our reading and interpretation and comment. It is as if Kafka's *The Trial* had been discovered decades late, and Kafka himself appeared, older and more well-mannered, to guide us through his own labyrinths.

The autobiography, which starts with his childhood in Ruse, is this construction of his own image, this enforced self-commentary; rather than narrate a living reality, he fixes it in description. Canetti sets out to tell us the genesis of *Auto-da-fé*, but he really says nothing about that grandiose book or about its unimaginable author, who must have been on the brink of catastrophe and the void. He does not even express the silence and absence of that author, of that other self, the black hole which has swallowed him up, though to have called him forth might well have given rise to another great book. On the contrary, he rounds off the corners and puts things to rights in tones of conciliatory authority, as if wishing to assure us that everything is really more or less as it should be. The result is that he says too little and too much at the same time.

I think it is difficult for him to accept this judgment, which is of course debatable like any other; but it is one based on love for him personally and for his lesson in what is truth. Occasionally Canetti resembles the power-figures in his books, with their desire to keep life under control, the ones he investigated and unmasked in *Crowds and Power*. Every great writer is besieged by the demons he has exposed, he knows them because he also runs the risk of being subjected by them. Sometimes it seems that he wants to hold the world, or at least his own image, in his fist in the unconfessed desire that only Canetti should talk about Canetti. When Grazia Ara Elias wrote to him that she too had been born and brought up in Ruse, and remembered the Canetti family and the Dr Menachemoff described in the autobiography, Canetti, who never answered her letter, was probably upset by the idea that someone else could claim rights over the image of Ruse, the doctor, and everything else – just because he had written about it, he thought of it all as his exclusive property.

With magnanimous generosity Canetti at one time allowed me to enter his life and helped me to enter upon mine by means of the letters he wrote to me; these, as indeed his whole person and his *Auto-da-fé* have formed constituent and essential parts of my being. My reception of his autobiography may have displeased him, but anyone who has learnt from him to perceive the thousand faces of power has the duty to resist that power in his name, even when he himself, for an instant, has assumed the face of that power. While Madame Vâlcova is shutting the door I look, probably for the last time in my life, around those jumbled rooms that witnessed the play and the maturing of an unknown boy, a poet whose lesson has been loyalty, and resistance to the unacceptable outrage of death.

NINE

Matoas

1. ON THE ROAD TO EVIL

The bridge which crosses the Danube and the Bulgarian-Rumanian frontier from Ruse to Giurgiu is named in honour of friendship, and proclaims that with its 2,224 metres in length it is the longest in Europe after the bridge crossing the Tagus at Lisbon. Grigore Ureche, the ancient chronicler, said that Rumanian territory lies "on the road to evil", meaning that it is in the path of the invasions which for centuries rolled over Eastern Europe. Not only the impact of the Jazyges, the Roxolans, the Avars, the Kumans and the Pechenegs, but also the banal misunderstandings and mistakes of everyday life can wound and draw blood. Rumanian peasants are able to shrug and say "That's life" in the face of every incomprehensible move on the part of destiny, and perhaps it would be as well to equip ourselves with that submissiveness to evanescent time which Zamfirescu, poet of the countryside, so admired in them.

Resignation seems to be a cliché of the Rumanian spirit, confirmed not only by facile orators and sentimental versifiers. Even Mihail Sadoveanu, the vigorous fiction-writer whose work comprises a national epic, writes in 1905 of his people as naturally inclined to accept their destiny, while Cioran praises the vocation of his people for wearing chains, for its restraint in bowing under the yoke, and "the nobility of our bondage". A bowed head, proudly announces a Rumanian proverb, is not cut off; and George Coşbuc, poet, peasant and patriot, states in his song *In oppressores* that, "abused, flogged, spat on, we accepted shame and ruin as a destiny."

Ever since the popular ballad *Miorița*, a song about mildness ready to be sacrificed, this "yes" to destiny has been extolled as the expression of an innate gentleness, a vocation for peace. The ideological *History of the Rumanian People*, written by a team under the direction of the academician Andrei Otetea, traces a "human feeling", the indication of a "hard-working, profoundly democratic" people who never had any desire to dominate other peoples, as far back as the Dacia of Decebalus, the awesome and brilliant adversary of the Emperor Trajan; the *History* does at the same time view the unification of Dacia by King Burebistas

in the first century A.D. as the first step in the direction not only
of Socialism in general, but of President Ceausescu's regime in
particular.

This gentle, melancholy idyll is dear to the hearts even of scholars
who show independence from the Party line. When it comes to
reconstructing the events of many centuries, the history of Rumania as
presented by Dinu C. Giurescu, with his fresh approach, is pervaded
with the harmony of the countryside and the odour of the woods
described at the beginning of the book, as if in accord with the eternal
flux of life and at the same time with the advent of history and the
continuing factor of transience. That gentle, harmonious landscape has
known tragedy and violence: in his novels Zaharia Stancu describes a
troubled, angry Danube, foaming with struggles and history; he
describes the hungry, bare-foot peasants coarsened by slavery but
capable of rising with fire and steel, as in the great rebellion of 1907, and
of displaying an intelligence that has not been dazzled by oppression
masquerading as destiny.

It is the road to evil, said the chronicler, the road of the curved sabre
when the Getae clash with Roman swords; of the Macedonian infantry
advancing beyond the Danube (in Arrian's account), bending down
the tall, thick-standing wheat with their long lances to open a passage
for the cavalry; of the iron sword worshipped as a god by the Scythians;
of young boys kidnapped by the Turks and the wooden yoke of the
Ottomans exchanged (in the words of the historian Michai Cserey) for
other yokes of iron. It is the road of the corn and the rushes burnt by
Stephen the Great of Moldavia to hold up the advance of Mohammed
II, of peasants oppressed and tortured, of slaughter and pillage,
bondage and violence. We have borne bridle and yoke, says a poem by
Coşbuc, and we bear them still.

The evil is that of having too much history, being a cross-roads, or at
least an optional stop on the route of universal history, along which the
slaughterhouses work overtime even in the minor centres. According
to a saying attributed some years ago to Chancellor Kreisky, Austria
has withdrawn from history and is very happy about it. Every good
heir or descendant of the Hapsburg Empire is disappointed to find
himself in the great theatre of the world, on the stage of world history
to which he has been sent to play a bit-part by powers as capricious as
the genies and spirits of the old folk-magic Viennese comedies.
Lacking Tamino's self-confidence, and doubtful of the protection
afforded him by benevolent higher powers, the walk-on actor would

dearly like to get off the stage and, without being too obvious about it, find an exit through the wings.

Rather than leading towards a hypothetical exit, our steps seem to sink into a yielding, friable soil, as when we put a foot on a layer of leaf-mould, that slips beneath our weight and traps our shoe in another, deeper layer, in the leaves that fell last year and have crumbled into damp earth. In order to reconstruct the complete course of his country's history and civilization, the great historian Nicola Iorga ventured into the most impenetrable depths of the people's lives, depths which have left no memory in written records, in the documents drawn up by the learned or by the upper classes of the past, but only in forms and customs, gestures and everyday actions which are rooted in the centuries.

Descending into the depths of this humus and, as it were, going back down the path taken by the sap that rises from the roots to the branches and the leaves, Iorga discovered layers that were ancient and buried, but still fertile in living substance, such as traces of the Ottoman migration and, still further back, that of the Turanian peoples from the heart of Asia towards the mythical "Land of Rum". Bianca Valota Cavallotti, his grand-daughter and the heir to his vocation as a historian, has written that he discovered a Byzantine-Turkish-Mongol unity and continuity flowing like an underground stream, the ancient, uninterrupted "Carpatho-Balkan community" stemming from the immemorial Thracian basis and followed by the multi-national Greek element which was so important, especially on the commercial level, in the history of the Danubian principates.

This melting-pot of races and cultures is a primordial medium of our history, a Nilotic slime in which there pullulate germs still confused and indistinct. If the Cimmerians, hard pressed in the eighth century B.C. by the Scythians, also – as suggested by Nestor – belong to the Thracians, and if the desert of the Getae (so called by Herodotus and Strabo) stretched so far as almost to merge with the ancient kingdom of the Odrisi which was lord of the Danube delta, then following the river to its mouth also means entering into a Cimmerian mist of origins, losing oneself in an ending that is really more of a return to the beginning.

Pompeius Trogus speaks of a "Histrianorum rex", King of the Getae and at war with the Scythians. At the time of Justinian, Dobrujia was called Scythia Minor – mere names for me until a short while ago. Fantasy words fill the mouth and awake an imprecise echo, as at school we used to say Trebizond without knowing whether or not it was the same as Trapezunte; we knew that Mithridates was King of Pontus and Prusias of Bithynia, but were unclear as to exactly where to find Pontus or Bithynia on the map; and we loved to say "Cilicia" or "Cappadocia" as I still love to roll high-sounding names over my tongue. But if in the learned writings of my fellow-townsman Pietro Kandler I read that in even earlier times Dobrudia-Scythia Minor was called Istria, then it becomes a different matter: the name takes on a colour and a smell, and is the red soil and white rock overlooking my sea.

Are the Istrians therefore Thracians, as Apollodorus thought, or Colchians, according to the views of Pliny and Strabo; or are they Gepids? Does the quest for the Golden Fleece lead therefore home, to the beach chosen on high to make me understand that one can be immortal, and have the Fleece and the amphora emerged from my sea? This is a joke played by the Danube, and the muddle arises from the mistake made by the ancients, who thought that the Danube – the Ister – split into two branches, one of which flowed into the Black Sea and the other, the Quietus or Timavus, into the Adriatic. Thus Istria was the land of Euxine Pontus, but also the white peninsula in the Adriatic.

Perhaps it was the Thracians who came from the Black Sea who brought with them rumours of the Danubian lands, or maybe the gold of these names was brought by the Colchians who followed the Argonauts as they rowed up the Danube, the Sava and the Ljubljana, and then carried their ships on their shoulders. There is an Absyrtis in the Black Sea which, like the Absyrtides of the Adriatic, originated in the scattered limbs of Absyrtis, the brother slain by Medea.

Scholars are very harsh with mythographers seduced by words: "Strabo and Pliny are inexcusable in stating that Absyrtis was murdered in the Absyrtides Islands which are in the gulf of Venice," says La Martinière's Dictionary. Is happiness therefore not ruled out wholly and absolutely, even if its promise glitters only in the errors of the ancient geographers? I am not, of course, thinking of lending them any credence, according to the manner of science, which periodically refutes the results attained and returns to long discarded hypotheses. Pomponius Mela, it is clear, cannot withstand the criticism made against him in this regard by Bernardo Benussi, published in 1872 in the Records of the "Imperial Ginnasio Superiore" of Capodistria when the author, though young, was (as the presentation put it) already "a regular teacher, librarian and head of the class".

Origins, unattainable and always uncertain, mean little, and not even Iorga is able to discover the primary substratum of his civilization. As Curtius said, "History does not know the origins of any people," because history does not exist: it is the historian who creates and produces it, by posing the question and then investigating it. Every genealogy goes back to the Big Bang. Discussions about the Latin origin of the Rumanians, or about the Dacio-Geto-Latino-Rumanian continuity, brought up time and time again by historians and by the nationalistic ideology of Rumania, are scarcely more important than the quarrel between Furtwangen and Donaueschingen over the sources of the Danube.

2. GODS AND PANCAKES

Bucharest. The Paris of the Balkans, apart from the economizing on electricity that of an evening does not exactly make it a Ville Lumière, represents, as one proceeds in a south-easterly direction, a further, and profane, emanation of the gradual decline of the image of the City, capital of France and of the nineteenth century, and indeed of Europe. As in the passage from one essential to another in neo-Platonic philosophies and religions, in this case, too, the descent from the One, from the Idea, on the various levels of matter is not simply a degeneration – it also implies some obscure impulse towards redemption.

The Franco-Balkan style grows heavier and more ornate, carried away by ornamentation and hounded by an abhorrence of vacuum; the balconies and the wrought iron of Parisian-type buildings flaunt exaggerated curves, flourishes and embellishments, the classicism is more massive, the eclecticism more marked and weighty, with bizarre columns and capitals and cheerful cupolas in *déco* style. *Art nouveau* is present with splendours and squalors, stained-glass windows and decrepit stairways.

The vast *Jugendstil* hallway of the Casa de Mode is thronged with gypsies, while not far off, the market stalls of Lipscani display evil-smelling cakes and brassières that look still warm from use. An exaggeratedly Parisian *passage* leads to a series of shops with exhibitions of pictures or handicrafts, but when they are closed their black iron doors become coffins leant up against the wall.

At 12 Lipscani there is a plaque commemorating the journalistic activities of Eminescu, the national poet, who wrote about living as if his existence were being narrated by a stranger. A critic, Zaharia, accused him of pathological "deambulatory automatism", so frequent were his changes of address. The street door opens into a courtyard rich in ornamental friezes and refuse; in one corner, in a niche, a statue of a woman, whose *Art nouveau* eroticism is anything but neutralized by the surrounding squalor, keeps watch over the sacks of rubbish piled up by the tenants. In the Hotel Hanul Lui Manuc, the hotel of Manuc Bey, built in 1808, red carpets cover the wooden stairs and a crush of clients drinks beer or coffee in the courtyard or on the upper storeys, near the arches and colonnades which are also made of wood. Among the tables on the ground floor there is a hen-run.

Bucharest is not only a city of crowds and bazaars, but also of great airy, elegant spaces, green parks and boulevards leading to secluded lakes, of nineteenth-century villas and the *fin de siècle* residences of Madame Lupescu, the king's famous mistress, and of neo-classical buildings and others in the style of the Stalin era. It is a real capital city: it has the atmosphere, the vastness, the majestic, careless waste of space. In spite of a few skyscrapers in the Soviet style of the 1950s, such as the Scînteia palace, it extends – like Paris – horizontally. It does not go upwards, like so many modern cities in the West, but stretches out towards the plains.

The stalls of Lipscani or the rubbish in front of the indulgent sinuosities of the statue in the courtyard are not the negation, but rather the continuity, of Parisian elegance, the last and lowest host of angels to announce and diffuse it, mingling with the most ephemeral everyday things. In this Plotinian procession the superior levels of being overflow from sheer superabundance, and spread over the lower levels; the soul descends into the pullulating stream of matter, and is dispersed beneath it: the Parisian *passage* becomes the *souk*, the market of the Levant. The noble, elegant style takes on an ambiguous appearance, like a face made up with vulgar colours, but it also acquires humanity with each incarnation, the humility of stench and sweat, the grubby, agonizing mortality that shouts and gesticulates, the damp breath of what Umberto Saba called warm life.

The Balkanization of Paris is a kind of Gnostic sensuality, which in the corruption of the flesh brings with it a longing for redemption, and wallows in the swarming baseness of the finite without forgetting its own origin and its own divine destiny. The indistinct biological substratum of the Rumanian melting-pot continually overwhelms the kaleidoscope of figures. It is no coincidence that in Rumanian culture there has been so much discussion of the contrast between basis and form. In backward, semi-capitalist countries, observes the Marxist Gherea, the social forms – as opposed to what happens in economically and politically developed countries – precede the social basis, and therefore remain weak, precarious superstructures, which the under-lying structure continually undermines and swallows up. In certain districts of Bucharest, even today, one gets the impression of witness-ing this incessant process of being engulfed, watching vitality dissolve all definite limits. The composite ethnic substratum is the multiple, changing face of this ancient amalgam: the dark olive-coloured eyes and the imperious noses of the beautiful Phanariot women, and the black, soiled hair of the great-grandsons of Aromuns or Kutzovlaks from Macedonia meander through the crowds like bubbles in a cauldron.

Like the fragments of crumbled ornaments, the lower level contains the higher and the memory of the higher; if the Byzantine tradition of painting has dissolved into Rumanian folk art and the votive illustra-tions of Wallachian peasant art, by diving deep into that folk culture we can perhaps find our way back up to the severity of sacred art. Thus in the imperial breasts of this gypsy woman, who is selling belts and buckles from her stall with brazen nonchalance, Grischa Rezzori, who waxes lyrical on the eroticism of Bucharest, would probably have seen the first step on the upward path of return, the harbingers of salvation which belong with the lowest level of the angelic hierarchy but for this very reason have survived into our own day, in the scrimmage of existence. In these streets in the Lipscani quarter I understand Grischa and the messianic nostalgia of sex which, in his writings about Bucharest, rises towards the heights and towards nothingness: to plunge into the broad pelvis of this gypsy woman, to be clasped between her thighs, to subject oneself to her despotic yet approachable queenliness would be to seek, or to find what has been vaguely promised.

In spite of her assuredly unforgettable blouse, I do not believe that the gypsy woman is a harbinger of the gods, though in this bazaar, where history and races of people are up for sale, there could be innumerable gods – just as until the last century, in the principates of Moldavia or of Wallachia, there were seventy different coinages in circulation, such as silver aspers, bani, kopecks, creitars, ducats, florins, galbens, groschen, levs, ortuls, thalers, pitaks, potroniks, schillings, timfi, ughii, zlotys, tults, dinars, and maybe even the Tartar dirhem. Inflation here is a disaster, but to some extent its rate contributes to the flow and exchange of life. Here many gods have been inflated and consumed, like the greasy pancakes displayed on the stalls. The latest, at the moment, is Ceausescu, whose portrait is everywhere.

This consumption of gods, rather like the letting of hotel rooms by the hour, reveals a basic lacuna in history, the march-past of the transient, the apotheosis of disenchantment. Cioran, with his open and total disillusionment, was born from these vegetable depths of the Rumanian world, even though not from Bucharest itself; or rather, as he himself writes, from that mixture of freshness and rottenness, of sun and dung. But real deep-rooted laughter scoffs not only at belief in order and values, but also at the presumption of chaos and nothingness; Cioran, dazzled by that nostalgic putrefaction, is incapable of this authentic scepticism, and also of humour. Tearing veil after veil from all philosophies and ideologies, Cioran deludes himself that he is watching all the bankrupt faiths parading before his eyes along the catwalk of world history, which is finished, without realizing that he too is taking part in this universal exhibition. A parasite of hardship, he takes refuge in absolute negation, splashing about comfortably among the contradictions of existence and of culture, and flaunting the frenzy of them, instead of trying to understand the far more arduous contest between good and evil, truth and falsehood, which every day brings with it.

The hucksters attempting to make ends meet among the stalls in Lipscani could teach the philosopher of absolute negation that this is a facile expedient for resolving all problems once and for all and putting oneself out of reach of all possible doubt. Cioran is a brilliant son of that market, but a son who has done the clever thing and, in his garret in Paris, put enough distance between himself and that merry, human poverty. Lipscani is also a feast of vulgarity, but the absence of value which produces this also generates the anguish of the void and of death, which that ambiguous frivolity tries to dull. That vulgarity also deserves respect: being squeamish, as Kafka so well knew, is a sin against life.

3. A DISPLACED CONFERENCE

The Writers' Union, at which the Italo-Rumanian literary conference is taking place, is a late nineteenth-century building in an eclectic *Art nouveau* style with a wealth of glaring decoration. Representing Italy – assuming that anyone can ever represent anything – there are four of us, Bianca Valota, Umberto Eco, Lorenzo Renzi and myself. An introductory report, perhaps as an act of homage to the close connection between the two cultures, is delivered by an illustrious academician, an *éminence* very far from *grise* in Rumanian science. He is a fine figure of a man and aware of the fact, and as he talks he clearly derives pleasure from running his large, slender hand through his long, thick, black hair that belies his pensionable age. He is very intelligent, affable, and endowed with a wealth of culture and originality. While some bigwig makes the inevitable stereotyped speech, the academician raises his eyes to the ceiling with a look of mock resignation which he does nothing to conceal; but when it comes to his turn, he gets up and imperturbably pronounces an analogous litany of commonplaces. He is stealthy and polished, benevolent but capable of sudden steely sallies. In personal relations he is open, solicitous, often diplomatically elusive, but also contemptuously bold in certain stinging judgments and statements, such as could put him in a dangerous situation. He has the art of slipping between difficulties as if he were only trying to avoid the storms, whereas in fact he leaps firmly into the saddle and grasps the reins.

The years he has lived through, from the Iron Guards to Stalinism, form an epoch worthy of the pen of Tacitus, but they have not ruffled his relaxed charm or his instinctive cordiality. In him, as in Rezzori's Mr Tarangolian, sincerity and falsehood are inextricably interwoven; but one feels that he is a man to be relied on. His culture is not just a personal quality, but reflects the level of the Rumanian intellectual class, the seriousness of its training, the breadth of its interests and knowledge, the rigour and the openness of its intelligence.

More important than the speeches and papers read are the conversations and informal chats which take place in the intervals, with their caution and allusive indiscretions. This ritual also is watched over by the cult of the satrap, Ceausescu, but even personal tyranny and the economic failures of the regime seem like vast progress compared with the Rumania of the Boyars and the misery of the peasants. A lot of people mince words in whispers; others, with great frankness, openly criticize Government, State and Party. In presenting me with one of his books, one academician tells me that I can read it with confidence up through the penultimate chapter, but should skip the last chapter, devoted to events since the Second World War. This, he is at pains to point out, is totally false from beginning to end. Bianca, who has read the most interesting paper, is troubled, though she gracefully dominates her feelings As the grand-daughter of the great Iorga, from whom she has inherited a historical awareness of national feelings. grafted onto a cosmopolitan consciousness, she would like to show us a different Rumania, the Rumania she loves, and which like all motherlands perhaps exists only in this love.

Our discussions are not immune to certain observations and leading questions posed by a number of young people. As a result, for the following day's work we are transported to a different building, the Iorga Institute. The large audience, not having been informed, naturally went back to the Writers' Union, as prescribed in the official programme. Only a few ingenious, enterprising young men got wind of the change and managed to join us. While the bulk of the people, attracted chiefly by the reputation of Umberto Eco, as well as by sympathy for Italy and general interest in contacts with foreign countries, waited in bewilderment somewhere else, we continued our work before an audience which we outnumbered.

4. THE MARSHAL'S WINDOW

"In that room," I am told by Grigore Arbore, poet and art critic, as he points out a window in the Royal Palace, now the Palace of the Republic, "King Michael arrested Marshal Antonescu, the military dictator of the country, at four in the afternoon of August 23rd 1944." Antonescu was a Mussolini who tried, in vain and too late, to become a Badoglio. In January 1941 he had eliminated the Iron Guard, the Fascist legionaries from his government and outlawed them. Allied to the Nazis and active at their side during the invasion of Russia in June 1941, Antonescu attempted to safeguard the politico-military independence of Rumania, and it is perhaps due in part to his tactics, or at least to his tendency to play a prudent waiting game, if – in spite of widespread anti-Semitism – there were no extermination camps in Rumania, and no deportations to camps in other countries.

His attitude, in substance, was aimed at convincing the Nazis that the Jews were forced to stay where they were and could not escape, so that their fate could be decided once the war was over. In 1944 he had started peace negotiations with the Russians, but these negotiations were still in progress and inconclusive on that August day when the marshal refused the king's demand that he should proclaim an immediate cease-fire. The dictator, who was on the point of detaching himself from his German ally, but did not think he yet had sufficient guarantees to support this step, was therefore arrested, totally unexpectedly, for his refusal to abandon the Nazis at once.

It seems that in Rumania today there is some very cautious suggestion of the slightest possible revision of the judgment on the *Conducator*, the "Duce" who was executed on June 1st 1946. The story of Antonescu is a classic parable of Fascism and of the cleavages within the Right Wing in Europe. Antonescu took an active part in the repression of the Hungarian Communist Revolution of Béla Kun, occupying Budapest, and he is a typical reactionary figure. As a dictator he allied himself to the Nazis, but he suppressed Fascism in Rumania. During those decades Fascism, up to a certain point, was a force that others thought they could exploit: the Western powers tried to use it to annihilate Communism and launch it against the Soviet Union, while the latter turned the tables, trying to gain time to consolidate itself by allying itself to Hitler. At a certain point the game collapsed, and Fascism no longer served any useful purpose, political or otherwise. It set itself against everything, and everything was against it, and its destiny became one last adventure of frenzy, infamy and desperation.

Certain branches of Fascism, or Right Wing groups associated with them, tried to jump off the band wagon when things began to fall apart, and to distinguish their militaristic nationalism from black ultra-radicalism; but Antonescu only succeeded in taking a step backwards.

It appears that his arrest took the Nazis completely by surprise, even the highly active German ambassador to Bucharest, Fabritius. The tragedy of those months, those days in Bucharest, also had some unreal and grotesque aspects, examples of absurd co-existence, paradoxical divergences. A certain Italian ex-carabiniere who has stayed on in Bucharest, where he has raised a family, reflects the whole story of those days. During the war he was serving at the Italian embassy. Mussolini, from Salò, appointed his new ambassador, choosing him from among the Italians of Bucharest. This new envoy went to introduce himself to Antonescu, who accepted his credentials as the ambassador of an allied power but told him that, as a gentleman, he could not bring himself to evict the ambassador of the King of Italy from his own embassy, though he now represented an enemy power. So it was that for the rest of the war, until the eve of the Russians' arrival, the ambassador of the king – of an enemy power – remained in his embassy, useless and undisturbed. Germans and Rumanians alike pretended not to notice, while, to keep up the formalities and make a show of confidence, the carabiniere mounted guard at the door with his rifle as enemy troops went marching by. He had not decided, he now says, what to do with that loaded rifle if one of those enemy detachments had assaulted the phantom embassy.

5. MAHALÁ AND AVANT-GARDE

The Mahalá, suburb of Bucharest, provided an inexhaustible fund of stories, intrigues, tricky situations and picaresque adventures for the plays of Ion Luca Caragiale, the classic of the Rumanian theatre. In the cafés of that part of the outskirts, at the end of the last century, he culled the destinies and parodies of the destinies, the individual griefs and compacts which reflected the tumultuous growth of the new Rumania (a recently unified state), of its social classes, and above all of its greedy, clumsy ruling class. He himself was not only the poet who depicted that world, but also a figure in it; this fertile author of comedies, short stories and sketches was also a journalist, theatre prompter and proof-reader. He founded periodicals, such as *The Rumanian Humbug* (1893), and opened beer-houses and restaurants at the station, which regularly went bust.

His vivacious and exhilarating comedies are perfect mechanisms of nullity, a vaudeville which clicks with instantaneous precision and dissolves the inconsistency of society and life. If Caragiale is a Rumanian Labiche, it is in his school that Ionesco learnt his trade. The Franco-Rumanian Ionesco, in fact, belongs to that avant-garde litera-ture which, in the view of many critics, and with particular reference to Dada, underwent a "Rumanian pregnancy" before coming to light in the West: Tzara, Urmuz with his self-destruction of the subject in language and his symbolic suicide, Virgil Teodorescu who wrote in the leopard language he invented: "Sobroe Algoa Dooy Fourod Woo Oon Toe Negaru . . ."

Even though his world is France, Ionesco has his roots in this Rumanian Dadaist soil, and also draws from it the taste for total parody which animates his dialogue and which is even stamped on his metaphysical clown face, *à la* Buster Keaton – a face which is his masterpiece. Perhaps Caragiale is a more subtle master of nonsense and the absurd than Ionesco, because in order to emphasize the solemn void of existence and of its social decalogues the latter is sometimes forced to underline this unreality in explicit terms, with that didactic schematization that might seem rather like the unwanted explanation of a joke.

Caragiale does not need to distort reality, to scoff at it explicitly, in order to reveal its falsity and vacuity. He only has to show it as it is, to quote the customary words that are actually uttered to lay bare its nothingness, which is all the more disquieting for being so normal. His characters are not explicitly absurd in their remarks, but they make perfectly reasonable statements that are all the more absurd for that. They are not a caricature of the soap-bubble of which we are made, but a faithful portrait.

Ionesco, in spite of the stereotyped mechanics of the absurd which prevent him from attaining true greatness, is certainly greater than Caragiale because he gives a voice also to the anguish of death, the darkness of existence and its frustrated but insuppressible longing for eternity. His most ferocious sarcasm strikes above all at the parasites of the absurd, the verbose, supposed theorists of paradoxical sophistries and trendy quips. The bourgeois philistinism of the Smith family in *The Bald Primadonna*, as it repeats catch-phrases from the newspapers and common parlance, is no different from the philistinism of the intellectuals in the swim, who scoff at the bourgeois and declare that true sincerity lies in ambiguous double-speak and that "only the ephemeral endures."

The avant-garde, out of loyalty to itself, does away with that merry-go-round of avant-garde novelties which has by now become the most inevitable of repetitions. Bartholomeus I – one of the Masters of Letters who, in his *Impromptu of the Soul*, dictate laws to the poor author – does not like the word "creator". As an honest representative of respectable experimentalism, which is to say Rhetoric, he cherishes the word "mechanism". I wonder whether Ionesco, thinking of him and his real-life models, called to mind the lapidary saying of the Rumanian Dadaist Mihai Cosma: "Literature: the best toilet-paper of the century."

Rumanian culture now administers its great avant-garde tradition with caution and not without benevolence. As early as 1964 there was a performance of *Rhinoceros* by Ionesco, a writer notoriously and viscerally anti-Communist. In the late 1940s, however, the regime was heavy-handed – in the name of a vulgar Marxist pseudo-Classicism – against authors suspected of the nihilistic "dissolution of poetry", and even the great revolutionary poet Tudor Arghezi had his troubles. With a mixture of provocation and prudent exorcism Nina Cassian, as early as 1945, entitled a collection of poems *I Was a Decadent Poet*. But not even such a poet as Marin Sorescu succeeds as he would wish to (with *Jonas*, written in 1968) in giving an adequate, positive reply to Ionesco's *The King Dies*, let alone to Beckett's far greater *Waiting for Godot*.

6. THE SLOT-MACHINE OF POETRY

In a district almost in the outskirts lives Israil Bercovici, the Yiddish poet. Literature, he tells me, is a slot-machine: life and history drop in – or hurl in – a storm of events, the unique light of a certain evening, troubles in love or world wars, but one can never tell what is going to come out, a few meagre coins or a regal fistful of money, a waterfall of poetry. Timid and discreet as a person, Bercovici is a delicate poet; he is swathed in that family gentleness and stubborn *pietas* that have vanquished centuries of violence and of pogroms. The library in his neat, modest little house is a miniature ark of east European Jewry, and when he reads one of his poems – for example *Solovej*, the Nightingale – while his wife, just back from the hospital where she works as a doctor, prepares the lunch, we get a better understanding of certain of Singer's stories, their mystery of marriage and the impassioned epic quality of Jewish family life.

Among the books is an album of Isahar Ber Rybak, a portfolio of engravings and drawings entitled *Shtetl*, the name of a small eastern Jewish town. This is the world of Chagall, equally magical and indelible, but stronger, more poetic. Rybak is a greater artist than the great Chagall, though in spite of his time in Paris – which gave him a place in Western culture, with all the poetry of his Eastern homeland, and also a certain reputation – he has never got into international circulation as he deserves to, and perhaps now never will. Some years ago, time and posterity might have done him justice, revising its merits and giving him better marks. But time can no longer be the gentleman, and discover the message that lies beyond the medium. Today the media are the message; they alter and erase history, in the manner of Big Brother in Orwell's *1984*. The cultural industry has destroyed posterity; there will be no re-examinations of present triumphs, and Rybak's hour will never really arrive: at the most some half-hearted, momentary rediscovery by a handful of enthusiasts. "For whosoever hath, to him shall be given . . . but whosoever hath not, from him shall be taken away even that he hath." But if the great world forces one to bow, one can always, like Bertoldo, do it facing in the wrong direction. The exceptional grandeur of Rybak shines forth in shadow.

Yiddish literature in Rumania is in an unusual position. The Jews, including the Jewish writers, have for the most part left the country, and most of the remainder are getting on in years. "We have new forces," says Bercovici with a smile, as he shows me the Yiddish literary review. "New poets. It may be that they start writing rather late, and are in no hurry to discover their vocation. This one here, for example, is a beginner at seventy-nine, while this fellow, who has now published two volumes of verse, brought out his first at the age of seventy-six."

In the majority of cases it is not a matter of sentimental, pathetic effusions, of that literary second adolescence that occasionally seizes the old when they are on the brink of the poetry of their Last Will and Testament. These lyrics are restrained and subtle, shorn of second-hand feelings, and reveal awareness and mastery of the formal exploits of contemporary poetry. So what does "new poets" mean? The slot-machine of literature has continual surprises in store, and makes fun even of the generation gap.

7. AT THE VILLAGE MUSEUM

The Village Museum, on the shores of Lake Herăstrău, is not only one of the most famous attractions of Bucharest, but also a compendium of centuries of Rumanian life. The latter is at one and the same time measured by the repetitions and by the slow evolution of the peasant world: the wooden huts and churches, the roofs of straw and mud, the beds with their huge coloured blankets, form a universe which appears to be static and unchanging, like nature, but which in fact does change with patient slowness, like the growth and aging of great trees. Rumanian civilization is one of wood, of the goodness and strength of wood, of the firm, religious mildness of everyday utensils, of the tables and benches in the house which preserve the memory of the great woods in which the original population sought safe refuge, in ancient times, from the invader of the moment.

In a great deal of Rumanian literature the village is the centre of the world and the point of view from which the world is regarded. Coşbuc, who wished (he claimed) to extol the spirit of the people, wanted to compose the epic of the Rumanian village; while Mihail Sadoveanu, who has in fact created this epic, also sinks the roots of his protesting, rebellious art – albeit within the broad and tranquil scope of his narrative power – in the political and cultural movement born in 1901 with the magazine *Semănătorul*, which championed a type of revival and progress rooted in loyalty to the peasant tradition. Rumanian populism, in the words of Ion Mihalache, leader of the Ţaranista Party, proclaimed the compactness of the peasant masses, and affirmed that it was "the only homogeneous class" in the country.

The champions of the rural world were able to defend themselves with much hardened political sense against feudal-capitalist exploitation, but they idealized the past. The expansion of the large estates, and the tiny size of properties insufficient to support a single family, were the paradoxical result of the agrarian laws passed during the nineteenth century, and in particular the Organic Regulations of 1831. The latter had broken with traditional law of custom and asserted private property in the modern sense. The ancient peasant communities had thus lost their control on the village, and the new agrarian contracts imposed on the rural masses had delivered them to the tender mercies of the landowners.

Iorga, writing just after the 1907 Revolution, and contesting the boyar claim to have possessed the land since time immemorial, conjured up the harmonious image of an ancient village community, in which at one time the boyar played his part on equal terms with the others. Even Mihail Sadoveanu, a democratic and revolutionary writer, depicts an archaic world in which peasants and masters are free men with equal rights; however Panait Istrati, the rebel anarchist who extolled the bloody, brigandish vendettas of the Haiduks against the feudal lords, the governors and the cruel, corrupt prelates, refers to a primitive era of collective harmony, when the boyars were not land-owners but the chief men in the various communities, while the land belonged only to the community. Even Eminescu defends "the ancient classes" against "modern" capitalistic exploitation and Zamfirescu, in *Country Life* (1894), praises the healthy traditional orders of the nation, peasant and nobleman, as against the new, brutal class of *nouveau riche* farm bailiffs, who use their money to destroy the link with the land.

This romantic anti-capitalism over-idealizes the archaic peasant world, the warm cowshed atmosphere of the community, which was so often permeated with gloomy poverty and black violence. Urban society, so often and so factiously accused of alienation, has liberated the individual, or at least has laid the foundations for his liberation. But the intellectuals who transfigured the peasant world, as Iorga did, had no intentions of restoring the lost idyll. This idealization gave them the impetus not to return to the past, but to fight against the evils of the present. Nostalgia for times past made them look to the future. The houses, churches, farms, windmills and presses in this Village Museum are genuine, though transplanted and put together in an artificial com-plex such as a museum inevitably is; but to walk through this pretend village, enter these real cabins, look at antique bread-chests and at the leaves of this early June, is certainly no less genuine than "country life", as Zamfirescu called it. In the real villages today there is probably nothing that isn't a fake. If you want to find nature, go to the museum.

8. HIROSHIMA

"Hiroshima" is the name bestowed by the people of Bucharest on the quarter of the city which Ceausescu is gutting, levelling, devastating and shifting with a view – maybe in competition with President Pompidou, as befits the Paris of the Balkans – to building his Centre, the monument to his glory. Shi Huang Ti, the Chinese Emperor who was uncertain whether to destroy or to construct, divided himself equally between these two conflicting passions by building the Great Wall and burning all the books. Ceausescu's megalomania, at least as far as this pharaonic building project is concerned, appears to take a peculiar form of demolition, which is to say transference from one place to another. He does not demolish buildings, in fact he frequently preserves them, but he shatters the landscape by moving edifices to some other nearby site, sometimes tens of metres away and sometimes hundreds, in order to create a new space that is his own.

He shifts an eighteenth-century church, complete with its foundations fifty metres further over; he moves houses and blocks of flats; he sticks a chapel onto a tenement building put up a century and a half later, and if the two blocks are not a perfect fit he lops a bit off one and a bit off the other and throws them away; he modifies the town planning with the judgment of a child playing sand-castles. In order to magnify the impact of their dominance, the powerful portraits of Ceausescu need to be surrounded by a human void, they need to depopulate cities, as the Sultan Muhammad Tughlak did with his Delhi. Ceausescu, for his part, takes delight in these removals, and is the proprietor of the Pantechnicon firm which crates up the scenario of the centuries.

Squares, streets, avenues and alleyways in the environs of the panoramic levelled space in which arise the building of the National Assembly and the patriarchal church are one vast, dynamic building site, with holes and cracks, great heaps of earth and stone, mobile cranes and rubble and ruins. Squalor has a mysterious majesty of its own, and in the desolation of this prolonged removal there is the magic of dullness, the larval regality of the subsoil, of the blind, grey life that crawls through underground passages and cracks, and flows, along with the liquid draining from refuse, towards the hidden treasures at the centre of the earth.

Those cellars stripped bare to the sky are like moles and bats thrust violently into the light or insects turned onto their backs, but this irruption of the daylight into the realm of darkness does not dispel the secret of that lower kindgom otherwise still lying hidden. That moist dark, now dug up, upon which the house once rose, is the swamp of origins, now forced further down, in which are sunk the roots of life itself. The house soars upwards, with its luminous dining-rooms, playrooms for the children, libraries, all of them equally forgetful of that faceless layer which underpins them. Existence does not remember, and does not wish to remember, the dark depth from which it originated and, together with its own secretions and refuse, consigns to the drains even the very thought of its essentially terrestrial nature. An archaeology of dumps and drainage would perhaps render us a secret, upside-down history of cities, like the grandiose history created by Ernesto Sábato in his novel *Of Heroes and Tombs*.

But that world is not simply the infernal sewer depicted by this Argentinian author. Amongst the rubbish and refuse there shine certain treasures, mined by gnomes in the bowels of the earth. When we were children, and a lead soldier or tinfoil chocolate wrapping mysteriously disappeared for ever, one thought that it had slipped into some crack and descended into that unknown country, there to be welcomed and put on the throne, like the fishermen lured by mermaids to the bottom of the sea.

Literature is attracted by depths and refuse, which appear not in the form of wretchedness to be redeemed as much as a corner in which a vanished enchantment has taken refuge. Journeys downwards, from those of Jules Verne to the more modest ones of Sussi and Biribissi in the drains, are more fabulous than others, because they penetrate the most secret, inaccessible core, the mythical fiery centre that recalls the ages in which the earth was an incandescent sphere, or else the discarded things of existence, never to be seen again.

In his novel *The Old Man and the Officer* Mircea Eliade descended into the cellarage of old Bucharest, in which his characters mysteriously disappear, just as the arrows they shoot into the air never come down again. The state secret police, in the novel, attempt to decipher the political significance of these fabulous accounts of disappearances and magic, but they get lost in the labyrinth of the mythical narrative. The old schoolmaster Zaharia Farâma, who tells these stories, survives the powers-that-be, who interrogate him in order to tear supposed state secrets from his lips, and the much-feared Anna Pauker who commands him to account for these fantasies.

For Mircea Eliade the genuine, immortal mythology of the people conflicts with the false, technocratic mythology of power. This great student of myths the world over may be mistaken; perhaps he exalts the past too much. It is probable that every archaic myth, that appears to us today as an uncorrupted truth, was originally a technocratic power-trick, a mystery hoarded by the forces of power, the enigma surrounding the secret police. The centuries erase this and that body of secret police and their power, so that all that remains is the story of their mystery, as pure and genuine as any fable that has no axe to grind, but is simply there to be told. When enough time has gone by, the various re-emergings and swallowings-up caused by the works undertaken at the command of Ceausescu will perhaps become a source of poetry and myth, like the destructions wrought of old.

9. THE TRIUMPH OF TRAJAN

Adamclisi is the site of the *Tropaeum Traiani*. Of the original monument, built by the Roman Emperor in 109 A.D. to celebrate his victory over the Dacians and the Sarmatians, there remains only the cylindrical base. The present building, a reconstruction of the ancient model, was erected in 1977. Trajan put up his to commemorate his triumph over Decebalus, King of the Dacians, whom the Rumanian nation numbers among its heroes and the great men of its history, and the descendants of Decebalus have rebuilt it as an act of homage to the glory of both of them, the victor and the vanquished.

Decebalus is a historic character and at the same time a symbolic figure, a political strategist of genius who over the centuries has become the hero of poems and folksongs, the emblem of the freedom of Rumania. But the Rumanians, who honour him as the champion of their oppressed identity, consider themselves in equal measure sons of his and of his enemy, of the invaded Dacians and of the Latin invaders. The Dacio-Roman synthesis and the continuity of this synthesis over the centuries is, in Rumania, the foundation of the idea and feeling of nationhood. In his *Illustrated History of the Rumanian People*, Dinu Giurescu mentions a stone erected near the *Tropaeum Traiani* by the sons of a certain Daizus, who fell in battle against the Kostoboks. From the stone we learn that Daizus, like his father Comozus, had a Dacian name, but that his sons already had Latin names, Iustus and Valens. The historian is pleased to note this process of Romanization within the space of three generations, and it is pleasing also to Rumanian patriotism, proud of the nation's Latinity – proud of being a wedge in the Slavic sea, a fact deprecated by the Czarist minister Gorchakov but a cause of satisfaction to Cavour.

10. BLACK SEA

According to Nestor the name "black", given to the internal sea by the indigenous peoples living round it, was interpreted by the Greeks as inhospitable, *axeinos*. They later proceeded to describe it as hospitable, *euxeinos* or Euxine, when they had founded their cities along the coasts and transformed it into a Hellenic sea. But even today the power of words projects on the Black Sea the image of a waste of waters, a vast oppressive pond, a place of exile, of winters and solitudes. Weininger associated it with Nietzsche, with a face ever clouded over and incapable of serenity. The bathing season on the famous beaches between Constanţa and Mamaia, with its hotels and tourists, does not succeed in vanquishing the magic of the name, of "those waters which sometimes look black, as if night had her cradle there," writes Vintila Horia. The heavy atmosphere, the lazy, oleaginous sea, the fake, would-be luxury of the big hotels, are all at one with the lethargic, obscure fascination of the name itself and the archaic and barbaric myths which it evokes.

Constanţa, the ancient Tomis, where Ovid lived in exile, is now a place bustling with heavy industry, trade and shipping. The architectural eclecticism is heavy, even leaden, the *Art nouveau* looms gloomy and monumental, the sea today is really black and grey beneath rain-laden clouds, and the cranes in the harbour area engrave a rusty sadness on the horizon. Horia, in a novel about Ovid, imagines the exiled poet listening to the harsh cry of the gulls and thinking they were crying "Medeaaa!", strident and piercing as the barbarian sorceress herself. Even without arbitrary urgings from the imagination, the moist wind weighs on the heart and the effect of the barometer on the blood pressure is no less than that of the magic and poisonous herbs known to Medea.

Does a high humidity mixed with certain literary reminiscences result in the emptying out of life? Do they combine to reveal its dullness, its lack of meaning, its flaccid solitude – a flag after the wind has dropped? The cranes are the metal masts of a huge, desolate ship, Charon's boat launched from a state-owned shipyard, while the whole of the city is a gigantic, anonymous vessel which got under way before there was time to wave goodbye, floating in a dead calm, that takes away even regret and the nostalgia of farewells. The waters are a pagan shroud, an ultimate passage beyond which there is no knowledge, no answer to so many questions, but only a dim limbo, the same reality as before, equally imperfect but more larval and indifferent, with attenuated desires and feelings, as if the only secret were that of blunting the edge of things, and truth were nothing but interest abated.

The Christian other world contains souls and bodies, the pagan one only shades. Maybe for this reason the pagan one is more modern and credible: it is a cinema repeatedly projecting the film of a reality already non-existent, the mere silhouettes of life. Perhaps these have little to say for themselves; they are weary of the script that used to be stimulating. Mute, apathetic, they brush against each other like the photos of two lovers side by side but not embracing. In this sirocco even the face of the beloved we saw disappearing round the corner would cause us no grief, and it would be Avernus.

When the Black Sea winds brought on this melancholy, Ovid, after whom the main square is named, would have recourse to Eros, whom it is not inopportune to invoke against the pointless ebb of time. But the honest medicine of that thrill could not have sufficed him, not in Tomis, for he was not the poet of love or of sex, but of eroticism, and eroticism requires the big city, the mass-media, the gossip of the salons and publicity. The skilful erotic writer, whether Ovid or D'Annunzio, has a genius for marketing, he lays down codes of behaviour and invents slogans and advertising formulas, like D'Annunzio, or else he prescribes fashions and cosmetics, like Ovid. This does not prevent him from being a great poet, as both of these were at times. But in any case he needs an important stage to perform on, and above all a complex, many-faceted society, a network of social intermediaries and a mechanism for reproducing reality that renders the medium indistinguishable from the message, the experience from the information, the product from the advertisement. The poet of eroticism, in order to exist as such, has to be in the swim of things; he needs Rome, or imperial Byzantium, or Paris, or New York. It was difficult or even impossible to practise eroticism in the provincial, domestic Germany of the nineteenth century, and it was even worse among the Getae. Those Sarmatian winters must have been really chilly for Ovid. Augustus showed great cunning in selecting his revenge.

II. THE THRACIAN HORSEMAN

The gods in the Constanţa Museum wear enigmatic masks in which the Cimmerian indifference of their origins shades off into a promiscuous decadence. An Apollo dating from the first century B.C. has a beautiful female head, far more feminine and seductive than the head of Aphrodite just a little way beyond; Isis has a fleshy, sensual mouth; the Eleusinian triad remind us of the cycles of death and rebirth, Pontus submits to Fortuna, and in a frieze Eros, out on a lion hunt, has the face and expression of a naughty child. The encouraging exhortations of Ceausescu, prominently displayed in large letters on the walls, assault three-headed Hecate and attempt to subject even the Great Mother Cybele and her orgiastic mysteries to the good, clean sentiments of Socialism.

These figures, as elusive as their shady eroticism, take us back to the multiple, composite substratum of this civilization, to races, epochs and gods that have become jumbled together as in the slums of dockland. Iorga thought that the remote, primal basis of this community, a Carpathian-Balkan-Byzantine mix, was to be found in the Thracians, "the greatest people in the world, after the Indians", in the view of Herodotus; they could, he felt, have been the most powerful, if they had been united and ruled by a single chief, rather than dispersed into many peoples under different names.

In the museum, in fact, the figure which dominates the menagerie of the gods is the Thracian Horseman. He doesn't have a name of his own, and is not a god. He is, rather, the symbol of a hidden god who is not profaned by effigies, perhaps because, like God, he is undepictable and ineffable, the Horseman being his dauntless soldier. Astride his horse, the sacred animal, the Thracian Horseman charges forward, and his cloak flies out behind him in the wind. In one figure, ravaged by time, horse and rider have suffered the mutilation of their heads, but another retains all intact, with the face and expression of one who fights valiantly.

Tradition attests to the serenity of the Thracians and the Getae, and their calm acceptance of death: like the luminous aura which in the *Iliad* surrounds Rhesus, his golden weapons and his horses, white as snow and swift as the wind. This tranquillity is familiarity with death, freedom from the fears and anxieties that cause all blind idolatry of life. The Thracians wept for the birth that brought man so many troubles, and celebrated the end, which delivered him from ills or brought him to beatitude. The Getae did not fear death, and indeed chose it freely, rather than imprisonment or slavery.

Where did this serenity come from? From familiarity with the pulse of nature, inducing in them a feeling like the leaves of the trees, which grow and fall as they do? Or from faith in immortality, from the conviction that death is the beginning of the true, eternal life by the side of Zalmoxis, the hidden god? Rhesus was attacked and killed in his sleep; the gold and the white surrounding him are the nimbus of a "conviction" immune from that nocturnal slaughter, and which Homer, the descendant of his enemies, causes to shine down through the millennia. Maybe the Thracian Horseman is a figure of conviction and death has no power over him, so that he rides in total safety in the saddle of his horse, an infernal animal which has become his faithful companion. Where is he going on that horse, beyond what mountain pass? In the Pomočnjaki clearing, on Mount Snežnik, one morning the freshly risen sun, with the vapour lifting from the grass, had created an impenetrable curtain of light which concealed the woods beyond. The figure which rose up and moved towards that tent of light, entering it and vanishing into the dazzle of it, beyond that threshold, had withdrawn from my sight, but there was no sense either of fear or of loss in the accomplishment or the perception of that disappearance.

True mystery is as luminous and pure as that morning; it disdains tricks and miracles, the junk of sensationalism and the occult. In the museum there is a statue of Glýcon, a triform monster with the head of a dog or an antelope with human eyes and hair, the body of a snake and the tail of a lion. Glýcon was worshipped in Paphlagonia in the second century A.D., as an incarnation of Aesculapius, and his cult reached as far as Rome. He could well be a *genius loci* of this blurred scenario of metamorphosis. But, much more prosaically, he is a reminder of a confidence trick. Alexander of Abonuteichos, a swindler, trained a snake and disguised it. The snake then provided the faithful with auguries and oracles at a high price. The followers and the generations of followers do not know how to believe in God or to look atoms or the void in the face. Incapable of understanding the Gospels and Lucretius, their ethos turns to cheap intellectual trinkets with sophisticated pretensions, and seeks comfort from the booth of the supernatural. The mystery of life, of death and of destiny merges with the woman sawn in half inside a crate, who then skips out and bows to the audience.

The cult of Glýcon is a mark of their own inability to understand the trick. And what an unfathomable mystery lies, a few yards further on, in the amphoras which have emerged from the sea and in the sea to which they refer us, or in the really beautiful head of a mourning woman, which tells us all that is inexplicable in grief. Is it hard to imagine this enchanting, sorrowing woman asking – as the nonchalant Alexander of Abonuteichos would very likely have done – "What sign are you?"

For Hölderlin the voyage of the forefathers of the Germans along the Danube was the movement towards days of summer, towards the land of the sun, Hella and the Caucasus. I arrive at Histria – Istria – the dead city that for me bears the name of summer and familiar places. It feels odd to arrive at this time of day – in the evening – and even odder to arrive alone: the word Istria is connected with absolute light, the zenith of day, and a closeness that knows no solitude.

Here, on the other hand, in this archaeological metropolis, it is a desert. The gate is already shut, while a few extinct smokestacks and trucks look as abandoned as the ruins of the ancient Milesian colony. I climb over the wall, and walk amidst thistles and stalks of wild oats, among the remains of the temple of Zeus and the basilica, massive doorways and columns standing up like stelae, and soundless Baths. The still, diaphanous evening overarches this tomb of the centuries, a grass-snake disappears among the stones, the birds shrill on the crumbling walls. The ruins slope down to a sea that is reddish with sea-weed and ooze.

The dead city has the eternity of destruction, the stones do not tell of the moment when the ships of the Milesian colonists arrived on these shores to found the city, but rather of the waves of erasure, of Goths, Slavs and Avars, the moments when life stopped. A cross among the stones commemorates Panait Emil, Simion Mihai and Platon Emil who died (drowned?) on March 12th 1984, but in that silence of the centuries the remains of a temple raised to a local, unknown deity quite overshadow those of the Christian basilica, in spite of the fact that it is the hour of the Angelus.

The city is big, the roads run criss-cross, radiating outwards or getting lost in mazes, and for a moment or two it is hard to find the way back. Like the White Cobra in Kipling's dead city, in this limpid air, which likewise preserves each single sound intact, one gets the impression of having somehow gone deaf, of no longer hearing the voice of reality. The centuries of death amassed among these ruins are not a shadow, a darkness that swallows up the images. They are, on the contrary, a clear, immutable light in which the eye descries every object. They are also a wall of glass, separating one from the sounds of the outside world. Through this rubble of the past we step, not so much blind as deaf, enwrapped in that unreality, sometimes even clumsy and comical, which surrounds those who are hard of hearing.

We feel defenceless, easy prey to an attack which would catch us unawares. In detective stories there are blind men who make perfectly terrifying murderers or excellent detectives; but deaf men, no. Even old age seems more deaf than blind. Though even in these debilitations the dictionary is merciful, and one can always persuade oneself, as the doctor reassuringly told one of Gigi's uncles, that it isn't really a matter of deafness, but simply of hypoacoustic receptivity. To which the uncle replied: "Can't hear a word you're saying."

13. AT THE FRONTIER

Soon I shall be back beside the river again, not to leave it until the very end. Beyond, to the west, stretches the Bărăgan, the Rumanian steppe, a place of desolation and of exile, with fiery summers and freezing winters and horizons that never end. This is the place to which the Antonescu regime deported the gypsies, in an exodus to which Zaharia Stancu has raised a monument in the shape of his novel, *The Camp*. Here too, after 1945, the Germans of Rumania were sent. Sadoveanu and Panait Istrati have sung of the sunsets over the boundless ocean of the plains, of the thistles and the struggles of the peasants, of the gypsy violin and the song of the thrush attuned to a heartfelt nostalgia.

At the foot of the hill of Denis Tepe, not far north of Babadag, is the bay where the Argonauts are supposed to have anchored on their return from Colchis. The offshore waters are empty, the sea is wan, and on the colourless hillside a few sporadic industrial plants display a suburban squalor. The Danube is beginning to split up and spread out, like wine from a broken *krater*, as the poem says when a wounded hero falls from his chariot. This presage of the end is, however, tranquil and majestic, rich with fertile vitality. In the Baltă the Danube merges with the meadows in a vast, inextricable jungle of water, dense trees overhanging the river to form liquid caverns, deep flowing lairs, dark green and as blue as the night, in which it is impossible to tell the soil from the water and the sky. Vegetation covers everything, climbing and twisting everywhere in an exuberant proliferation, a play of mirrors reflecting one another.

The island of Brăila, sixty kilometres long and lying between the main branch of the Danube and the "old" Danube, is a liquid Eden, an island of Alcina, reigned over by canebrakes. It was near here, as we read in Gibbon, that the Goths agreed to hand over their women and children to the Romans, but not their weapons. At Brăila the river comes together again into one powerful stream, as befits a city with such flourishing trade and industry, and a river-port that is almost as busy and bustling as the nearby one at Galaţi.

This ancient commercial emporium is now a great centre of metal-working and ship-building. The yellow-ochre of a noble though heavy nineteenth-century style, with its neo-classical decorousness adorned with *Art nouveau* scrolls and caryatids, yields to an undefined levantine ambiguity, like an Eastern port, a ferment of all the elements which the sea washes up on the beach. During the nineteenth century Brăila was also a centre for Bulgar exiles preparing for the Revolution. Vasov described these patriots, the Chǎšovi, and their interminable nocturnal discussions in the taverns of the town.

In the *Danube* restaurant in Lenin Square the walls are pompously papered in red, with a pretence of *fin-de-siècle* décor, but the light is dim, and the alliance between a cloudless noon and the electric light in the confined space of the room is not sufficient to read the menu. The Strada Republicii, which I have just travelled along, is one of those streets flanked by eclectic buildings, often coloured yellow-ochre to orange, which I have traversed so many times in the course of these last few years, in Hungary, in Slovakia, in the Banat, in so many towns large and small of the Pannonian Sea. In the semi-darkness of this restaurant I get the impression that all these roads converge on this square and end here, for ever, as if this were the frontier of my Danubian world – my frontier.

Turks have left their mark on Brăila, or Ibrail, but even more so have the Greeks, from the merchants whose wealth is flaunted in the Greek Orthodox Church to Markos's partisans who arrived here in 1948 after the civil war. The poet of Brăila, Panait Istrati, who is commemorated and shown off in his native city, was son of a Greek smuggler, and never known to his father. In the museum there is a photograph of him in a street in Nice in 1921, wearing a broad-brimmed hat and reading *Humanité*, in a pose reminiscent of Scott Fitzgerald which tells us everything about the tortured insolence, the harmless and sly naïvety of that lost generation – crying out its own perdition – to which Panait Istrati belonged.

Having attempted to cut his throat, he sent a letter to Romain

Rolland from the hospital in Nice, a desperate cry for help written on the eve of his attempt; in his letter he twice interrupted his laments to recount funny episodes from his childhood. Rolland went into raptures about this "narrator from the Orient" who had travelled over half the world doing the most impossible jobs, this "Gorky of the Balkans", the poet of vagabonds and derelicts, and proceeded to promote him and publicize his works in France. A few years later Panait Istrati was world-famous; his works, almost always with Rumanian-Balkan themes, though sometimes written in French, which he had taught himself, were translated into twenty-five languages; and a master of criticism such as Georg Brandes, to whom at one time Thomas Mann had in fear and trembling sent the manuscript of *Buddenbrooks*, imprudently declared that he loved Istrati more than any other contemporary novelist in the whole of Europe. Obstructed for his Communism, the writer incurred the wrath of the orthodox Left for his criticisms of the Soviet regime. In 1925 he dropped all his literary projects in order to devote himself to helping the people living between the Dniester and Tibiscus rivers, who were being oppressed by the Rumanian government.

Rolland compared his stories, which uncoil endlessly from one into another, to the twists and turns of the Danube, to that tangle of streams and banks which Panait Istrati has described in his novel *Kyra Kyralina*, caught by their glitterings, their disappearances, and daunted by the trickeries, the misfortunes, the cruelty in ambush round those bends. He is the poet of the promiscuity and ambivalence of the East, of that disorder from which we seem to expect redemption and violence at the same time. His rebellious anarchism makes him a brother to the victims and the vanquished, and from a literary point of view he is not at his best when he narrates their resurgence or preaches of their revenge, as in the *Haiduks*.

As often occurs with men in revolt against false morality, Panait Istrati, the defender of the weak and the humiliated, eventually falls prey to the naïve temptations of vitalism, without realizing that it inscrutably decrees the abuse of power by the strongest. Sex under many forms is extolled as free pleasure, but it too becomes a trap which draws its victims into the whirlpool of life and the hands of the persecutors. For Panait Istrati, a poet when he harkens to suffering and a rhetorician when he celebrates life without law or progress, existence resembles an oriental brothel, with its inviting curtains in the entrance and its greasy interior.

Brăila and nearby Galați – the licentiousness of which was branded by the Antiquarius, with special mention of the throng of prostitutes at every corner – are two places well suited to his way of yarn-spinning, reminiscent of a story-teller in a bazaar. Today the two cities, and especially the second – a Danubian Hamburg – do not display carpets but shipyards, cranes, a steel Hades; though it is true that these appear as such only to those with short memories who have forgotten the human holocaust that happened in the multi-coloured world of yesterday. If anything the two cities, especially Galați, are the symbol of the Rumanian ambition to become independent of the Soviet Union, and also the symbol of the economic crisis into which those ambitious projects have emerged.

The Pruth, the waters of which were at one time lauded as pure and salubrious, for kilometres on end marks the border with Russia, beyond which the Danubian co-ordinates no longer function. The frontier reeks of insecurity, fear of being touched, like the fear that grips Canetti's characters: an obscure terror of the Other. Like every other frontier, including the confines of our own selves, the Pruth is an imaginary line, beyond which the grass is identical to the grass growing on this side. It may be that Danubian culture, which seems so open and cosmopolitan, also creates these feelings of anxiety and shutting things out. It is a culture which for too many centuries was obsessed with the dyke, the bulwark against the Turks, against the Slavs, against others in general. "The Danube is therefore the great base for every operation, in whatever direction this may move, just as it is the line of defence par excellence, fitted to resist attack from whatever direction it may come . . ." (*Essay on Strategic Geography* by Col. G. Sironi, Turin, 1873, p. 135.)

14. AT THE DELTA

Count István Szécheny, the pioneer of communications in south-eastern Europe, as well as the patriarch of the Hungarian national resurgence, wrote on October 13th 1830 to his friend Lazar Fota Popovich expressing pleasure at having met Miloš Obrenović, Prince of Serbia, and having found him a convinced supporter of the "Regulation", that is, of the projects and works needed to ensure the

navigability of the Danube. Szécheny was returning from Constantinople and from Galaţi, where he had gone to promote the accomplishment of his grandiose plans. He had gone as far as the delta and way
beyond the delta, beyond the limits of the great watercourse which he
had in mind, and during the return journey he had fallen seriously ill;
so ill, in fact, that from the vessel on which he was homeward-bound he
wrote Count Waldstein a letter which he thought would be his political
last will and testament.

During those months, therefore, and for various reasons, Szécheny
had undergone the experience of the End. The *Regulation* is well suited
to the End, or to the approach of it. The actual conclusion is a task for
engineers, notaries and others adept at calculations, accounts and
precise registration. Death restores to life, which is so very approxi-
mate, the dignity of order: the heedless flow of money settles into the
clear terms of a Will, those irregular *liaisons* vanish into thin air, and
give place, in obituaries and condolences, to the legitimate spouses,
while the death throes are watched over and measured like no other
moment in a lifetime. On page 745 of his weighty monograph on the
Danube, published in 1881, Alexander F. Heksch takes the trouble to
retrace his steps, and to correct certain details in earlier descriptions,
which have been dated by changes made while he was proceeding with
his description. Until that moment he had not been worried, and had
gone ahead swiftly and thoughtlessly; but as he neared the end he felt
the need to put everything in order.

There is solidarity between the centrifugal slowing-up which is
proper to an ending and the map which records it. The delta, into
which the boat drifts and is lost like a floating log, is one great
dissolution, with branches and rivulets and ramifications that wander
off on their own, like the organs of a body on the point of succumbing,
each of which shows a decreasing interest in any of the others. All the
same, the delta is a perfect network of canals, a precise work of
geometry, a masterpiece of "Regulation". It is a great death kept under
control, like that of Marshal Tito or of other protagonists of world
history – a death that is incessant regeneration, an exuberance of plants
and animals, reeds and herons, sturgeon, wild boar and cormorants,
ash-trees and canebrakes, a hundred and ten species of fish and three
hundred species of bird – a laboratory of life and the forms of life.

An uprooted oak-tree lies rotting in the water, a vulture swoops like
lightning on a little coot. A girl takes off her sandals and dangles her
legs over the side of the boat. The delta is a labyrinth of the *ghiol*, the

watery paths that wind among the canes, and is the map of the canals which regulate the flow of water and the routes through the labyrinth. The story of the delta is to be found in the anonymous tales centred among the reed and mud cabins of the Lipovenian fishermen, in the ice and in the thaws which flood them, but it also exists in the records of the *Commission Européenne du Danube*, established in 1856; a body which in the years 1872–9 allotted 754,654 francs to the construction of the dykes at Sulina.

In a travelling notebook it is easier to scribble down something about the canal rather than about the *ghiol*, about Engineer Constantin Barsky, an expert commentator on the project for the Canara canal between the Danube and the Black Sea and the author, a century ago, of lectures on the subject, rather than about Kovaliov Dan, a Lipovenian boatman and fisherman living at the 23rd milestone on the branch of the river leading to Sulina; or about little Nikolai, of whom I knew nothing except the shy smile he gave when a girl kissed him as she got off the boat. In order to justify its existence a book ought to be the story of Nikolai, of his bashfulness before that face which leant above him. Unequal to Nikolai, books slip away and fall back on summaries, on a précis of conquests and the fall of empires, anecdotes from the Council Chamber, conversations at court or in Parnassus, the minutes of international commissions.

The boat glides over the water, the canebrakes slip by on the banks. Perched on a tree, a cormorant that has opened its wings to dry off is etched against the sky like a crucifix, the gnats swarm like an uncaring handful of the loose coinage of life; and the German scholar who specializes in Danubian literature does not envy Kafka or Musil, with their genius for depicting dark cathedrals or inconclusive committees, but rather Fabre or Maeterlinck, the bards of the bees and the termites; and he understands how Michelet, having written the history of the French Revolution, would have liked to write the history of the birds and the sea. Linnaeus is a poet, when he urges us to count the bones of a fish and the scales of a snake, and to observe and distinguish between the flying-feathers and the steering-feathers of a bird. The murmur of summer and of the river would require of the person committed to putting it into words, while lost in its enchantment, all the particular punctuation of the Swedish classifier, the commas which mark his phrases, the semi-colons which subdivide his sentences, and the full stops which conclude his distinctions.

Admittedly, the catalogue of the Museum of the Delta in Tulcea, the last town on terra firma, from which the boat-trip started, facilitates the description of greenfinches, jackdaws, plovers, storks, herons, pelicans, otters, stoats, wild-cats, wolves, blackthorn, dog-roses, euphorbias, willows. After all, among phytologists, or rather scientists, Linnaeus numbers not only botanists in the proper sense, but also the most chancy amateurs, including poets, theologians, librarians and miscellaneous others. But the miscellany is a summary of the world, while all around is the real world, and the amateur armchair botanist realizes that if one is a naturalist purely by order of the King, like Buffon, one is awkwardly placed when confronted with the ancient mother herself; and it may be that in order to describe the motion of a running hare one has recourse, as that French gentleman did, to a digression on the migration of peoples in the age of barbarians.

Yesterday I was in the Museum of the Delta, and today I am on the delta with its odours, colours, reflections, changing shadows on the current, wings flashing in the sun. The liquid life runs through the fingers and forces one – even in the joy of today as one stands on the deck of the vessel like a Homeric king on his chariot – to be aware of all the inadequacies of our perceptions, our senses atrophied by millennia, our sense of smell and of hearing unequal to the messages that come from every waving tuft of grass, our antique severance from the flow of life, our lost and rejected brotherhood. We are like a Ulysses who no longer needs to be tied to the mast, like sailors who no longer have to stop their ears, because the song of the Sirens is entrusted to ultrasonic waves which His Majesty the Ego cannot discern. A cormorant flies over with open beak and neck outstretched, resembling a prehistoric bird over the primitive marshes, but the immense chorus of the delta, the whole of its deep *basso continuo*, is to our ears only a murmur, a voice we cannot catch, the whisper of life which vanishes unheard, leaving us behind with our "hypoacoustic receptivity".

The fault does not lie with the Danube, which here clearly shows that it does not come from the fairy-tale tap near Furtwangen. The fault lies rather with one who, faced with the glitter and music of these waters, feels the need to grasp hold of that bit of nonsense, if only to reject it in scorn, and even to digress about the hypothetical dripping of the tap so as to elude the song of the river. It is probable that even the ship's logbook, written by a plumber rather than a Ulysses, also leaks, rather than slipping along swift and sure like the little boat that Nikolai certainly knows how to make out of scraps of bark and paper. Books, one knows, are heavily insured risks, for literary society is a far-sighted insurance company, and it is rare to find poetic disasters that are not handsomely protected. But to take notes with a tranquil mind on this deck, amid the meanderings of this delta, one would need the maritime "all risks" clause, which includes particular damage to goods in transit, damage from hooks, contact with contaminating substances in the cargo, theft, illegal opening, failed delivery, dispersal, breakage and/or leakage.

It is a glorious day, and the boat wanders like an animal among the various branches of the river. In the old delta, near Chilia, the mud is gradually becoming transformed into dry land, the bottomless ooze turns to soil on which to build, plant and harvest, water-courses and canals form a delta within the delta, willows and poplars rise above the undergrowth of brambles and tamarisk, great white and yellow water-lilies lie like islands on the primaeval ocean in antique cosmographies. Close to the Soviet frontier lies Chilia Veche, a Greek colony and Genoese trading-post where in the fourteenth century the notary Antonio di Ponzo recorded the sales of carpets, wine, salt and twelve-year-old slaves and in the seventeenth century the monk Niccolò Barsi mentioned the two thousand sturgeon caught daily. Now it displays the lofty towers of its church, which so impressed the Lipovenian fishermen in the novel *The Endless River*, written in the 1930s by Oskar Walter Cisek.

The branch leading to Sfîntu Gheorghe which, at 110 km, is the longest, in the vicinity of Mahmudia runs right by the fortress of Salsovia, in which Constantine had Licinius put to death. On the left-hand side it leaves a tropical forest and low-lying sandy dunes, the realm of frogs and snakes in which summer temperatures reach 60° Centigrade. The literature of the delta, in fact, leans more towards the frosts than to the scorching summers. Cisek describes the fishermen breaking the winter ice on the river to reach their prey, while Stefan Bânulescu writes about the Crivâţ, a freezing, piercing wind; he describes the howling snowstorms and the creaking of the ice as it begins to crack and melt. The great standby of the literature of the delta, its epic scenario par excellence, is of course the flood, the Danube overflowing and submerging villages, the tide overwhelming cattle-sheds, huts and shelters in the forest, carrying away animals both domestic and wild, oxen, stags and boar, in its swirling waters.

For Sadoveanu the delta is also a catchment area for peoples, as if the Danube carried to the sea the detritus of centuries and civilizations, fragments of history, and, in overflowing, scattered them about. These vestiges have short lives, though; they are swept from the banks at flood-time and disappear into the soil, like leaves and other dross brought down by the river. The stories of the Danube, says Sadoveanu, are born and die in a moment, as a puddle dries out in the sun. In one of his short stories Stefan Bănulescu describes the funeral of a child during a winter storm, the boat which carries its body here and there in search of a hillock or a dune in which to dig a grave, the raging waters which threaten to wash away the humble burial-place, the winter which erases even that tragedy and sorrow, that precarious tomb, that story without a name.

In the stories of Sadoveanu and Bănulescu we often come across gypsies, as if this wandering people on the fringes of society were a tribe well-suited to dwelling in the archaic and forgotten world of the delta. A century ago this really was the realm of irregulars and fugitives, a no-man's land which gave refuge to outlaws from all over the place. The Turks, who were lords of the region, did not keep any regular garrison here, but only a haphazard, undisciplined militia press-ganged from amongst the peasants. These men joined forces with the deserters and brigands hiding in the marshes, whom they were supposed to be fighting and keeping under control, but from whom they were barely distinguishable. The guide-books of the last century, the monumental one by Baron Amand von Schweiger-Lerchenfeld, for example, speak of a jungle of men of every type and race, Turks and Caucasians, gypsies and negroes, Bulgars and Wallachians, Russians and Serbs, sailors from half the globe, adventurers, delinquents and escaped criminals. "Murder was the order of the day." After the Crimean War, on their way to Bulgaria, there was an influx of Nogai, Tartars and Circassians decimated by disease.

The delta today, with a population of twenty-five or thirty thousand, is chiefly the land of the Lipovenians, the fishermen with long patriarchal beards who left Russia in the eighteenth century to avoid religious persecution. The Old Believers, the followers of the monk Philip, had left Moldavia and taken refuge in Bukovina. They rejected the priesthood, the sacraments, marriage and military service, and above all they refused to swear allegiance to or pray for the Czar, while as the supreme act of expiation they selected death at the stake or by fasting. In Austrian Bukovina Joseph II granted them freedom of worship and exemption from military service. The enlightened Emperor probably despised the principles which forbade them to be vaccinated or to take any medicine, but he is sure to have admired their qualities of mildness and hard work, their respect for the law and above all their ingenuity, which made them the most highly qualified craftsmen and farmers, well ahead on the technical level. Towards the middle of the century many Lipovenians decided to accept the hierarchy and to celebrate the Mass according to the ancient liturgy; and at the end of the century some of them entered the Greek Orthodox Church.

The Lipovenians in the delta are fishermen today, but elsewhere they do all sorts of jobs in the factories and industries of Rumania. However, they remain above all the people of the river; they live in the water like dolphins or the other sea-mammals. Along the banks their black boats look like animals resting on the beach in the sun, seals ready to dive and disappear in the water at the slightest sign. On the water also are their houses of wood, mud and straw, roofed with canes, their cemeteries with blue crosses, and the schools which their children get to by canoe. The Lipovenian colours are black and blue, as mild and clear as the eyes of Nikolai beneath his blond hair. As the boat passes their houses, people come to the doorways and windows, and with cheerful hospitality beckon us to stop and pay them a visit. Some of them, with a few strokes of the paddle, come alongside us offering fresh fish in exchange for *rakia*.

There is no clear distinction between land and water. In the villages the thoroughfares between one house and another are sometimes grassy paths and sometimes canals, with rushes and water-lilies. Dry land and river merge one into the other, the *plaur* with their cane roofs either float like drifting treetrunks or are fixed to the bottom like islands. It is no coincidence that the delta has its Venice: Valcov, with its church of many cupolas.

On the old course of the Danube, on the double bend near Mile 23, in the vicinity of the canal which leads to Sulina, lives Zaharia Haralambie, keeper of the pelican reserve. His whole life long he listens to their cries and the flapping of their wings. Like the other Lipovenians, he has a frank, open face, a fearless innocence. The children, who flocked round us as soon as we disembarked, dive into the river and drink the water, and chase one another here and there without making any distinction between land and water. The women are talkative, amiable, inclined to easy-going familiarity which caused Cisek, in his novel, to foster encouraging amorous fantasies. The delta is the great abandonment to the flow, the liquid universe that frees and loosens things, leaves that let go and surrender to the current.

Where does the Danube end? In this endless flowing there is no end, there is only a verb in the present participle. The branches of the river go their own way, die when they choose to die, one a little sooner, one a little later, like the heart, the nails and the hair, which the death certificate releases from the bonds of reciprocal fidelity. In this maze the philosopher would have a hard time to point a finger at the Danube, and his ostentation of exactitude would become an uncertain, circular gesture, vaguely all-embracing; for the Danube is everywhere, and also its end is everywhere, throughout the 4,300 square kilometres of the delta.

Büsching mentioned seven mouths, as did Ammianus in ancient times; Kleemann – in 1764 – counted five, like Herodotus and Strabo; Sigmund von Birken listed them according to the names which he found in Pliny: Hierostomum or the Sacred mouth, Narcostomum or the Lazy, Calostomum or the Beautiful, Pseudostomum or the False, Boreostomum or the Northern mouth, Stenostomum or the Narrow, and Spirostomum, the mouth with the spirals.

The official branches of the river, starting from Tulcea, are three: that of Chilia to the north, which in turn enters the sea by way of forty-five mouths, in Soviet territory, and carries two thirds of the water and detritus of the Danube; the central channel of Sulina, which discharges directly into the Black Sea thanks to the canal-works carried out between 1880 and 1902, which make it both navigable and symbolically straight and resolute in its course; and the branch of Sfîntu Gheorghe to the south, which twists and turns, and gives the Danube the official length attributed to it in the manuals. Strictly speaking there is a fourth, the Dunavăt canal: this splits off from the above branch, turns back towards the south-west, and flows into the great Lake Razin, which also receives the waters of the Dranov canal, which divides from the same branch.

To establish the mouth of the river, it would not be proper to pursue squabbles such as exist in the case of the sources. Men, animals and rivers should be allowed to die in peace, without even being asked their names. Maybe it is permissible to choose the mouth of the Danube according to the name, for the love of a lazy, wandering conclusion such as is promised by Narcostomum, or out of attraction to that last word in shuffling, that ace up the sleeve suggested by Pseudostomum, the false mouth. Both consistency and magic ought to make me plump for the sacred mouth because, according to Sigmund von Birken, near it there once stood a town anciently called Istropolis.

Confusion is becoming worse confounded, as when old men muddle up names and dates, erring by decades and confusing the dead with the living. The choice, therefore, can only be the conventional one, the arbitrary one, as befits the age of perfect nihilism. If there is no truth, the operative criterion may be determined at will, like the rules of chess or the roadsigns in the highway code. The straight line leading to Sulina is an aid to decision, while its efficient navigability, attained thanks to canalization, is a strong lure for all admirers of "Regulation". Let it be accepted, therefore, that the Danube ends at Sulina.

15. "INTO THE GREAT SEA"

Art, the sign-language par excellence, bears out the choice of Sulina. On the banks of the domesticated Danube, which flows tranquil and slow towards its end, women kneel in the water washing carpets and stretching them out to dry. Ships of iron and rust rock on the current, suggesting the movement of an active port, but the town is dozing in a vague sort of dismantlement, a prolonged and apathetic confinement to bed, the reason for which it can't quite remember. In the shops and stores there is practically nothing, a bit of lard and some tinned food; even the market stalls are empty, though a superfluous supply of radishes in profusion hints at a parody of abundance.

A haphazard, colourless process of modernization has demolished the old Turkish town, now dotted here and there among dusty streets, rubble and stunted trees. The doors of the station which regulates passenger traffic on the river are shut, and a small, hesitant crowd is vaguely queueing up, without anyone knowing if and when they can buy tickets. A few soldiers, half dressed in uniform, are busying themselves about some indeterminate task. At the Hotel Farul one can find something to munch at, but to get a drink one has to sit in the courtyard, where no food is served.

Sulina is an emblem of evacuation, of desertion, a film set in which the takes were made quite a while ago, and the troupe, on leaving, abandoned the scenery and costumes and wings, as being of no further use to them. Constantin Frantz, the jurist who was an opponent of Bismarck and champion of a federal, multi-national Mitteleuropa in which the German element was to make for unity but not trans-gression, dreamt of a Danubian federation which included – taking his words absolutely literally – also the mouths, the delta, and this lighthouse at Sulina which marks the point where the river flows into the sea. A lot of water has flowed under the bridges since then, say the ripples on the banks. The film that is already on the reel is that of the old Europe of the Danube; it tells stories of love, of diplomatic intrigues and of the fashionable life of the *belle époque*, set in the environment of the *Commission Européenne du Danube* which, with all the felt-padded caution and even, perhaps, the secret affairs of the heart so inseparable from nineteenth-century politics, presided over the works undertaken to enlarge and organize the port of Sulina.

This history has now packed its bags and cleared out of Sulina, leaving behind it a few Turkish houses, the lighthouse built with the proceeds of the tolls levied on shipping using the harbour, and one or two façades vaguely *Art nouveau* in style. What arrives at Sulina today is the rubbish floating on the Danube. In his novel *Europolis* (1933) Jean Bart, alias Eugen P. Botez, sees human destinies also arriving at Sulina, like wreckage from a sunken ship. The town, as suggested by its imaginary name, is still living in an aura of opulence and splendour, a port situated on the great trade-routes, a place where one meets people from distant countries, where one dreams of wealth, and catches a glimpse of it, even handles it, but above all where one loses it.

In the novel, the Greek colony, with its cafés, is the background for this declining prosperity for which the Danube Commission supplies the political and diplomatic dignity – or at least the reflection of it. The book, nonetheless, is a story of dashed hopes, of decadence, of deceit, solitude, unhappiness and death. It is a symphony of the End, in which the town that sets itself up as a miniature capital of Europe turns into a slum and an abandoned roadstead.

I walk towards the sea, curious to see the river-mouth, to dip my hand and my foot in the mixture of transition or else to touch the solution of continuity, the hypothetical point of dissolving. The dust turns to sand, the soil beneath me is already the dunes of the beach, my shoes get muddy in puddles which may themselves be mouths, tiny crooked mouths through which the Danube bleeds away. In the background I can see the sea. Side by side in the tow-coloured hearthland, among the abandoned shipyards, are the rubble of works in progress, clumps of heather and the smell of tar; and cemeteries – Orthodox, Turkish, Jewish, Old Believers' – only a stone's throw from one another. Simon Brunstein, on that May 17th 1924 which for him had no sequel, was sixty-seven years old; like lances in rout on the open plain, a forest of railings guards the remains of a nameless Turk; a stone column commemorates Captain David Baird, drowned at Sulina in 1876, at the age of forty-six. Margaret Ann Pringle, on May 21st 1868, was twenty-three, and is buried close to William Webster, Chief Officer of the *Adalia* who was drowned trying to save her.

Margaret and William like Paul and Virginie, Hero and Leander, Senta and the Flying Dutchman, other figures in the fable binding together love, death and the sea. Every cemetery a continual epos, to beget and suggest every possible novel. Illegally fencing in a small plot of this sandy terrain, planting there all the signs and plaques of every pub, restaurant and café I have seen closed down, being evicted each time without batting an eyelid. Keeping the score is reassuring in any case: it gives the illusion of restraining and dominating loss, forces the pathos of the funeral march into the sedate prose of the register.

Afternoon is still at its fullest, and the air is crowded with gulls and herons, masses of herons making loud, harsh, monotonous cries; large, shaggy pigs are rooting about in the puddles, and occasionally, for an instant, their shadows stretched and fractured upon the dunes make them appear enormous. It is a big beach, the figures on it abstract outlines. A number of abandoned radar installations are huddled there like the hulks of ships or gigantic birds, the old cranes with yellowed and rust-coloured feathers which used to carry the Taoist sages up to heaven. The sea is greasy and opaque, it smells of petroleum and cradles the usual, predictable refuse. One cannot make out the dividing line, at which – according to Ammianus – the fish coming from the open sea crashed up against the barrier formed by the current of the Danube. And it is even more unlikely that we shall discover the current of the river which, if we are to believe Salomon Schweiger, threw itself bodily into the Black Sea, crossed it in a straight line and arrived two days later at Constantinople still intact and still perfectly pure and drinkable.

The air is sultry; I am thirsty; someone shouts something at me from a distance, but I don't understand him. The pigs are still rooting around the big metal birds. The Danube is the slough they are digging their snouts into; nowhere does the sea receive that clear water of which that old book speaks. Why must our journey end in nothing? Question from a line of Arghezi's. The horizon is immense and greyish, a breached though lofty wall; the sun pierces the sea with white spears, the edge of a cloud glides across and sinks lower; her eyelashes, when she half closed her eyes . . . if we were not in a wearisome East European country I would call to her from some bar on the beach. The

delta, according to the guide-books, is a meeting-point for the migrations of birds, six migratory routes in spring and five in autumn; if only
one could follow the complete trajectory and career of even one
nomadic bird, as Buffon wanted to, one would know everything –
Platonic nostalgia, the eroticism of distance. According to Eustathios
and Stephanos of Byzantium the Scythians called the lower reaches of
the Danube Matoas, river of happiness. The gulls and herons cry out. A
pig uproots a tuft of grass with its tusks, chews it and reduces it to
fragments, and looks at me with stupid, cruel, close-set eyes.

There is no river-mouth, one does not see the Danube. There is no
assurance that the muddy creeks among the canebrakes and dunes
come from Furtwangen or ever lapped the shores of Margaret Island.
But a mouth, any one of the many, the countless mouths, is essential to
the "Regulation" of a punctilious note-book on the Danube, and I
search for it, as one searches for a key, a word which won't come, a
missing page, rummaging through pockets and drawers. A stamp is
missing from your passport and without a stamp you cannot leave.
There is no tall-masted, sea-going vessel, no sea-shanty in the heart.

The world of papers, office documents, bureaucratic procedures
suffers from its very nature from bottle-necks, but then, at the last
moment, no one knows how, all comes out right. The mistake was to
look for the mouth in this direction, in the open, undefined spaces of
the dunes and the beach, the horizon and the sea, instinctively following the spread and dispersal of the little rivulets. A kind, if shabbily
dressed, soldier is halted and questioned while he is making his way
between the puddles on a bicycle. One has, it seems, to turn back: his
gesture resembles that of the pallid, kindly necromancer Tadzio-
Hermes as he waves at a distant point in the immensity, in the oceanic
infinite that withers up all that is empirically finite. But what the
smiling, dishevelled soldier is showing me, as he stretches his arm in
that direction, is the entrance to the port, and the sentry-box where the
sentry, behind a badly painted barrier which blocks the road, checks on
people going in and asks for entry permits.

The Danube, properly channelled, reaches the sea in the harbour
area reserved for dock personnel, and loses itself in the sea under the
surveillance of the Harbour Master. To get to the end one requires a
pass, but the controllers are men of the world: they don't really
understand what this foreigner wants, but they see that he is inoffensive, and allow him to take a turn around and see the nothing there is to
see, a canal running into the sea in a setting of ships, winches, beams,

crates piled-up on jetties, rubber stamps on packages, certificates of Customs clearance.

Is that all, then? After three thousand kilometres of film we get up and leave the cinema, looking for the popcorn vendor, and absent-mindedly wander out at a back exit. There are few people to be seen, and even they are in a hurry to leave, because it's already late and the docks are emptying. But the canal runs on, runs on, calmly and confidently into the sea, and it is no longer a canal, a limitation, a Regulation, but a flowing outwards that opens and abandons itself to all the waters and oceans of the entire globe, and to the creatures living in their depths. Lord let my death – says a line of Marin's – be like the flowing of a river into the great sea.

INDEX

Aach, River, 29, 33
Abdias (Stifter), 129, 148
Abnoba, Mount, 19, 27
Abraham (preacher), 63, 177
Absyrtis, 364
Achternbusch, Herbert, 117
Ada Kaleh, 333
Adam, 301
Adamclisi, 380
Adorno, 144, 270
Adriatic, 19, 137, 364
Adriatic Sea Described and Illustrated, The (Menis), 136
Ady, Endre, 242, 250, 256–7, 261, 265, 275, 282, 291
Aeneid, 279
Aetius, 43
Agnelli, Arduino, 31
Ahasverus, 82
Aktionsgruppe, 310
Alba Julia, 317
Albert, Duke of Bavaria, 110–11, 112
Albertus Magnus, 83
Aleichem, Sholem, 121–2, 286
Alemanni, 83
Alexander Obrenovic, King, 331
Alexander of Abonuteichos, 384
Altdorfer, Albrecht, 149
Altenberg (village), 159
Altenberg, Peter, 167, 168, 184
Altman, 168
Amedeo, 19–25, 27, 73, 85, 94, 95, 202, 227, 234, 270, 282, 286, 287
Amery, Carl, 114, 115
Ammianus, 396, 399
Andrew II, King, 309
Andrian-Werburg, Baron, 30
Andrić, Ivo, 179
Anghel, Dimítrie, 279
Anka, Grandma, 292, 293, 294, 296, 297, 298, 301–3, 308, 309, 310, 313, 317, 318, 319, 322, 326, 328, 329, 330, 331, 333
Annunzio, D', Gabriele, 103, 215, 382
Anti-Christ, The (Stanev), 351
Antipolitics (Konrád), 268
Antiquarius, 27, 66, 110, 111, 283, 286, 293, 304, 389
Antonescu, Marshal, 370–1, 372, 386
Apollodorus, 364
Apologia (Magin), 223

Aprilov, 340
Apuleius, 109
Aquileia, 116
Aquinas, St Thomas, 61, 83
Arany, János, 244, 267–8
Arbore, Grigore, 370
Arendt, Hannah, 356
Arghezi, Tudor, 374, 399
Argonauts, 19, 364, 386
Arnauts, 341
Arnim, Achim von, 105
Arpad, 258, 264
Arrian, 362
Arstetten, 150, 151, 152, 154
Artmann, 192
Asparuh Khan, 346
Áts, Erika, 281
Attila, 119, 120, 158, 310
Augustin, Anna, 200–201
Augustine, St, 23
Aurelius, Marcus, 210–12, 237
Auschwitz, 46, 63, 90, 91, 92, 142, 143, 145
Ausländer, Rose, 320
Ausonius, Decimus Magnus, 42–3
Austria/Austrians, 28, 29, 30, 31, 38, 78, 80–1, 116, 183, 203, 222, 243, 362
Austrian Literary Association, 187
Austro-Hungarian Empire, 244, 245, 254, 331
Austro-Hungarian Monarchy Described and Illustrated (Mikszáth), 283
Austro-Slav movement, 222, 223
Auto-da-Fé (Canetti), 175, 357–8
Avars, 346, 385
Aviano, Marco d', 177
Azov, Sea of, 347

Baar, the, 41
Baba, Gül, 266
Baba Tonka Museum, 354–5
Baba Vida fortress, 338
Babits, Mihály, 250–1, 259
Bačka, the, 294, 296
Bački Petrovac, 324
Bad Dürmheim, 28
Bagatelles pour un massacre (Céline), 51
Baioni, Giuliano, 164, 225
Baird, Captain David, 399
Baja, 277–9
Baksay, Alexander, 280

Balassi, Bálint, 258
Balász, Béla, 262
Bald Primadonna, The (Ionesco), 373
Balkans, 334, 337, 340, 348, 350
Ballad of the Hundred Days, The (Roth), 81
Baltă, the, 386
Banat, the, 65, 74, 137, 291–300, 304–8, 326, 328, 330
Bánffy, Prime Minister of Hungary, 245
Banners (Krleža), 255
Bânulescu, Stefan, 393, 394
Bărăgan, the, 386
Baranya, 280, 281, 282, 286
Barbarossa, Frederick, 102
Barozzi, Dr, 345–6
Barraclough, 102
Barsi, Niccolò, 393
Barsky, Constantin, 391
Bart, Jean, 398
Barth, Peter, 310
Bartholomeus I, 373
Bartók, Béla, 265, 291
Batak massacre, 340
Baudelaire, 15, 211
Bauer, Karl, 102, 103
Baumgartner, Joseph, 114, 115
Baumgartner, Herr, 182–6
Bavaria/Bavarians, 59, 61, 69, 83, 99, 113–16
Bavarian Party, 114, 115
Bayer, Konrad, 154, 192, 196
Beck, Karl Isidor, 175
Beckett, Samuel, 374
Becskerek, 294, 295
Beethoven, 137, 206
Befreiungshalle (Kehlheim), 98–9
Behkalam, Akbar, 178
Bela Crkva, 293–4, 296–8, 302, 303, 307, 308, 322, 326, 328, 329, 331
Belated Reportages (Mňačko), 232
Belgrade, 29, 74, 176, 177, 295, 330–3
Belle Époque, 39
Belogradčik, 340
Belvedere palace, Vienna, 153, 180
Bencsik, Michal, 223
Benn, Gottfried, 16
Benussi, Bernardo, 364
Bérard, 252
Berblinger, Albrecht Ludwig, 74
Bercovici, Israel, 287, 374, 375
Berlin, 96
Bernanos, Georges, 52
Bernauer, Agnes, 110–12, 113
Bernese Oberland, 19
Bernini, 41
Bertoldo, 44
Berwanger, Nikolaus, 306

Best Citizen in the Republic, The (Petrov), 347
Bethlen, Miklós, 314
Bettiza, Enzo, 232
Between Frontiers and Times (Zillich), 315–16
Bevilacqua, Giuseppe, 68
Biribissi, 379
Birken, Sigmund von, 34–5, 396
Biserica Albă *see* Bela Crkva
Bismarck, 99, 317, 397
Bissula, 41–3
Bistriţa, 319
Black Forest, 17, 20, 38, 45, 47
Black Sea, 19, 20, 21, 25, 27, 29, 97, 122, 278, 364, 380–2, 391, 396, 399
Blaga, Lucian, 314
Blau, River, 73
Bleyer, Jakob, 281, 282
Blindheim, Battle of, 93
Bloch, 40, 160, 274, 275
Blomberg, Barbara, 106
Bloody Sonnets (Hviezdoslav), 224
Bloy, Léon, 81
Blue Nile, 337
Blum, Léon, 50
Boboroni, 303
Bogen, 113
Bogenberg, 113
Bogomil heresy, 343, 350–1, 352
Bohemia, 81, 82
Bojadjiev, 347
Bombaci, Alessio, 178
Bonyhád, 281, 282
Bordeaux, 42
Borges, 43, 62, 120, 318
Bortstrieber, Gertrud, 272, 273, 274
Boscovich, 339
Bositsch, Herr, 329
Bosnians, 297
Bossert, Rolf, 306–7
Botev, Khristo, 341, 344, 348
Botez, Eugen P., 398
Bozjenči, 348
Bozzi, Paolo, 22
Brăila, 354, 386–7, 389
Brandes, Georg, 388
Braşov (Kronstadt), 305, 309, 310, 312–13
Bratislava, 29, 219–21, 224, 226, 228, 230, 232
Braudel, F., 39
Brecht, Berthold, 96, 97, 106, 142
Breg, River, 16, 19–28, 35–8, 42
Breitwieser, 200
Brera Observatory, 339
Breu, Professor Josef, 213
Breuninger, M. F., 43, 44
Bridge-Builders (Kipling), 334

Brigach, River, 20, 21, 28, 42, 43–4
Brion, Friederike, 131
Broch, 173, 263, 323
Brodarics, István, 285
Bruckenthal, Samuel von, 311
Bruckner, Anton, 130, 146, 148
Brunngraber, Rudolf, 72, 73
Brunstein, Simon, 398
Bucharest, 365–79
  Case de Mode, 365
  "Hiroshima", 377–9
  Hotel Hanul Lui Manuc, 366
  Lipscani, 365, 366, 368
  Mahalá, 372
  Palace of the Republic, 370
  Village Museum, 375–7
  Writers' Union, 369–70
  mentioned, 305, 307, 310, 354
Büchner, 318
Budapest, 261–75, 276
  castle of Vajdahund, 262
  Danube Fountain, Engels Square, 41
  Fortuna Utca, 270
  Gresham Insurance Buildings, 263
  Lukács' library at Belgràd Rakpart,
    271–5
  Margaret Island, 270–1
  Musée de l'Hôtellerie, 270
  Opera House, 262
  Parliament buildings, 262
  Petöfi Square, 264
  Post Office Savings Bank, 263
  Roosevelt Square, 263–4
  Square of the Heroes, 264
  Stalin's statue, 276
  statue commemorating Kazinczy,
    269–70
  tomb of Gül Baba, 266
  mentioned, 29, 242, 252, 255, 256, 282, 371
Buddenbrooks (Mann), 388
Buffon, 109, 161, 392, 400
Bukovina, 306, 319, 322, 394
Bulgaria/Bulgarians, 40, 337–481, 352, 355, 356
Bulgars of Yesterday and Today, The
  (Venelin), 340
Bülow, Heinrich Dietrich von, 140
Bunjewatzi, 295, 300, 323–4
Burebistas, King, 361–2
Burton, Richard, 24
Büsching, 396
Byron, 355

Caesar, Julius, 19
Camp, The (Stanau), 386
Canara canal, 391
Canetti, Elias, 35, 109, 127, 140, 161, 175, 353, 356–8, 389

Caracalla, 62
Caragiale, Ion Luca, 372, 373
Carducci, G., 228
Carniola, 326
Carnuntum, 210–12
Carol I of Rumania, 48
Carracci, 311
Casa, Monsignor Della, 26
Caspian Sea, 347
Cassian, Nina, 374
Castelli, 183
Castle, The (Kafka), 89
Castle to Castle (Céline), 49
Cathedral of Ulm (Thrän), 75
Caucasus, 344, 345
Cavallari, Alberto, 164, 251–2, 253, 275, 276
Cavallotti, Bianca Valota, 363
Ceausescu, President, 305, 362, 368, 369, 377–8, 379, 383
Cecconi, Maurizio, 15
Celan, Paul, 47, 306, 311, 320, 321
Céline, L.-F., 49–52, 53–4, 57, 58, 66
Čerkazki (imaginary village), 349–50
Cervantes, 156
Chaikists, 326, 328
Châlons-sur-Saône, 42
Charles IV, Emperor, 66
Charles V, 106
Charles VI, Emperor, 220
Charles, last Emperor of Austria, 209, 277
Charles of Lorraine, 176, 177, 179, 180
Cherrapunji, 57, 58
Chesterton, G. K., 160
Chilia, 393, 396
Chilia Veche, 393
Chotkowa und Wognin, Sophie von *see*
  Sophie, Duchess
Christian Democrat Party (Italy), 39
Christlich-Sozial Union (CSU), 114, 115
Christov, Damjan, 339
Chronicle of a Restless Time (Mutafčieva),
  338
Cibăr, River, 342
Cignani, Carlo, 311, 312
Cimmerians, 363
Cioran, 242, 361, 368
Circassians, 344–5, 346, 394
Cisek, Oskar Walter, 393, 395
Cisleithania, 245
City in the East, The (Meschendörfer), 313
Cloşca, 317–18
Cluj (Klausenburg), 306, 312
Codreanu, 348
Cohen, Chaim, 63
Comenius, 228
Commission Européenne du Danube, 391, 398
Communism, 63, 197, 198, 231–2, 248, 254, 273, 275, 297, 329, 337, 371

Confessions (Ferenc Rakóczi II), 314
Conrad, Joseph, 137, 155, 346
Constance, Lake, 29, 33
Constanţa (ancient Tomis), 381, 382
Constantine, 393
Constantinople, 390, 399
Čorbadž, 341
Corpechet, 50
Coşbuc, George, 361, 362, 376
Cosma, Mihai, 374
Cosmographia (Münster), 35
Country Life (Zamfirescu), 377
Crimea, 344
Crnojević, Arseniji, 259
Croats, 212–13, 295, 327, 328
Croce, Benedetto, 302
Crowds and Power (Canetti), 161, 358
Csejka, Gerhardt, 310, 311
Csepel, 275
Cserey, Michai, 362
Curtius, 365
Cuvier, 260
Czechs/Czechoslovakia, 222–6, 232, 235, 324, 328
Czernowitz, 306, 319–20

Dachau, 152
Dacia, 29, 314, 361
Dacians, 333, 380
Dada, 372
Daizus, 380
Dan, Kovaliov, 391
Dante, 228, 237
Danube et Adriatique (Demorny), 136
Danubius (god), 28
Danubius Pannonico-Mysicus, Observationibus, etc. (Marsili), 41
Daughter of Sláva, The (Kollar), 223
Daughter of the Danube (Grazie), 329
De animalibus (Albertus Magnus), 83
De conflictu hungaorum, etc. (Brodarics), 285
Death on the Instalment Plan (Céline), 52
Decebalus, King, 333, 361, 380
Deep Roots (Áts), 281
Deigele, 83
Demetrius, Lucia, 319
Demorgny, G., 136
Dénes, Anton, 304
Denis Tepe hill, 386
Déry, Tibor, 248, 257
Descartes, 23, 94
Desert of the Tartars, The (Buzzati), 326
Desiderium aureae pacis (Institoris), 224
Destruction of Reason (Lukács), 188
Deutsche Einheit (Srbik), 30
Diegerlen, Prof, 77
Dillingen, 85, 86, 87, 88, 89

Dimić, Trifun, 326
Dimitrov, 347
Dionysus, 114
Diósy, Ödön, 265
Djerdap, 333
Djilas, M., 254, 255, 332
Dobrujia, 363
Doderer, 174, 175
Döderlein, Johann Alexander, 97, 98
Dollfuss, 177, 191, 197, 198
Dömölky, János, 253
Don John of Austria, 106
Donauer, Sigismund Christoph, 108
Donaueschingen, 19, 20, 28, 41, 43
Donauwörth, 93
Dončev, Anton, 340, 346–7
Dor, Milo, 301
Dostoyevsky, 81, 246, 274, 325
Dózsa, György, 283, 304
Dranov canal, 396
Drave, River, 41
Dunavăt canal, 396
Dunay, Frau, 163
Dürer, 312
Duse, Eleonora, 215
Dyment, Dora, 163

Eckhartsau, 209
Eco, Umberto, 369, 370
Edda, 119, 120
Éducation sentimentale (Flaubert), 129
Eichendorff, 150, 160
Eichmann, Adolf, 46, 114, 142–4, 186, 356
Einstein, Albert, 74
Eisenstadt, 189, 212–14
Elchingen, 78
Eliade, Mircea, 379
Elias, Grazia Ara, 358
Elias family, 353
Elizabeth Empress (Sissy), 206–9, 258, 259
Elizabeth, St, 219
Embser, 141
Eminescu, 366, 377
Encomium of Absent Mindedness (Amedeo), 21
Encyclopédie, 37
Endless River, The (Cisek), 393
Engelmann, Paul, 169
Eötvos, Baron József, 256
Eratosthenes, 19
Ernest, Duke of Bavaria, 110, 111, 112
Eskus, 350
Essay on Strategic Geography (Sironi), 389
Esterházy, Celsissimus Princeps Nicolaus, 221
Esterházy family, 251
Esterházy palace, 212
Esztergom, 258

Ethica catholica (Kachník), 235–7
Eugène, Prince of Savoy, 29, 78, 138, 146, 180, 294, 304
Europolis (Bart), 398
Eustathios, 400

Fable of Friendship (Gütersloh), 149
Fabre, 391
Fabritius, 371
Fakers, The (Kapor), 332
Family Strife in Hapsburg (Grillparzer), 80
Fascism, 30, 39, 45–6, 50, 170, 197, 199, 224, 249, 250, 254, 263, 281, 314–15, 325, 370, 371
Faulkner, W., 159
Faurisson, Prof, 143
Faust (Goethe), 36, 37, 83, 281
Faust (Lenau), 300
Favoretto, Monica, 100–1
Fehértemplon *see* Bela Crkva
Fekete, Franz (Czar Ivan), 283–4
Felbinger, 185
Ferdinand of Hapsburg, Emperor, 284
Ferenc Rakóczi II, Prince, 314
Fertoöd, 251
Fever (Kot), 232
Ficker, Julius, 102
Fidus Achates or the Faithful Travelling Companion (Zeiller), 58
File of Rudenesses Received (Thrän), 75
Flaubert, Gustave, 129, 160, 173, 202, 203
Fleisser, MarieLuise, of Ingolstadt, 95–7, 111
Flinker, Robert, 322
Forty, de, 94
France, 69, 94 *see also* Napoleon
Francesca, 37, 73, 86, 95, 140, 202, 264
Francis Ferdinand, Archduke of Austria-Este, 150–4, 181, 223
Francis Joseph, Emperor, 28, 40, 135, 141, 150, 159, 174, 205–9, 307, 315, 326, 328, 332
Frank, Bruno, 96
Frantz, Constantin, 397
Franz, 31
Franzel the Negress (Schmid), 65–6
Frederick II of Swabia, 106
Frederick II the Great, of Prussia, 29, 30, 141
Frederick III, Emperor, 135
Freud, Sigmund, 160–1, 203–4, 214
Friedell, Egon, 187
Friedrich, O., 41
From the Watermen to the Steamers (Watzinger), 62
Fruška-Gora, 324
Fürstenberg Castle, 20
Furtwangen, 19, 20, 21, 22, 38, 392

Gadda, C. E., 211
Gaius Scribonius Curio, 333
Galați, 387, 389, 390
Garbai, 242
Gaulle, De, 95
Gazette of San Vito, 100
Gellert, 214
Genet, Jean, 92
Gentis Slavonicae lacrimae, suspira et vota (Jacobeus), 224
Gepids, 364
Gerhardinger, Dr, 119
German Clock Museum, 21, 38
Germany/Germans, 29–32, 49, 67–9, 74, 99, 178, 235, 281, 282, 295–8, 304–17, 328, 330, 352–3, 372, 385, 386
Gersić, Gliša, 328
Getae, 362, 363, 382, 383
Geza, Prince, 258
Geza II, King of Hungary, 309
Gherea, 367
Gian, Dr Jon, 294
Gibbon, 387
Gide, André, 52
Gigen, 350
Gigi, 35, 36, 37, 50, 73, 94, 95, 140, 202, 227, 234, 246, 260, 268, 280, 386
Giotti, Virgilio, 53
Giuditta, Maria, 22, 23, 24, 36, 37, 95, 140
Giurescu, Dinu C., 362, 380
Giurgiu, 361
Glambayas, The (Krleža), 253, 254
Glýcon, 384
Göd, 291
Goethe, 36, 37, 83, 84, 85, 100, 131–5, 213, 237, 267, 281, 299, 300
Golden Ass (Apuleius), 109
Goltz, Von der, 140
Gondola Ilica, 228
Gönyü waterfall, 59
Gorchakov, 380
Gorizia, 40
Gorky, 325
Goths, 28, 352, 385, 387
Göttweig monastery, 146
Götz Von Berlichingen (Goethe), 299
Grabenko, Jelena, 273
Gradisca, Eulambio di, 260, 261
Gran, 176
Gratian, 42
Grazie, Marie Eugenie delle, 329
Great Moravia, 221
Great Slavia, 346
Greece, 99, 117
Greeks, 363, 387
Green Party, 36
Grein, 150
Grenzer, 326, 327, 328

Grillparzer, 38, 77, 78–82, 98, 112, 113, 130, 135, 186, 201, 202–3
Grimm, Hermann, 133
Griselini, Francesco, 33, 294, 304
Grotthus, F. Wilhelm C. L. von, 82
Gudhrun, 119, 120
Gumpelzhaimer, Christian Gottlieb, 102, 103
Günzberg, 90
Gustavus Adolphus, 93, 95, 137
Gütersloh, 149
Györ, 256
Gypsy, The (Grazie), 329

Hadji-Murad (Tolstoy), 344
Hafiz, 132
Haiduks, 327, 329, 340–1, 376–7
Haiduks (Istrati), 388
Hainburg, 36, 37
Hamsun, 40, 53
Hapsburgs/Hapsburg Empire, 29, 30, 31, 39, 58, 78, 79, 81, 82, 90, 102, 106, 135, 146, 150, 151, 178, 207, 209, 215, 220–4, 241–5, 254, 255, 257, 259, 277, 278, 294, 314–16, 319, 362
Haralambie, Zaharia, 395
Hartlaub, Felix, 334
Hauser, Arnold, 305
Haussmann, Baron, 353
Haydn, 214
Hebbel, Friedrich, 100, 110, 111, 112, 113
Hecataeus, 19
Hegedüs, André, 248
Hegel, 16, 60, 61, 79, 84, 111, 113, 139, 213, 267
Heidegger, 44–7, 61
Heine, 67, 69, 208
Heksch, Alexander F., 390
Hemingway, E., 52
Henry IV, 102
Heraclitus, 23, 147
Herăstrău, Lake, 375
Hercynian Forest, 19
Herczeg, Ferenc, 299, 300–1
Herder, 32, 33
Hermannstadt *see* Sibiu (Hermannstadt)
Herodotus, 19, 24, 102, 363, 383, 396
Herzogovina, 324
Hesiod, 25
Hesperia, 19
Hidrographia Helvetiae (Scheuchzer), 122
Hieronymi, Otto, 244
Hindemith, 20
Histoire physique de la mer (Marsili), 160
History, Legends and Wonders of Regensburg (Gumpelzhaimer), 102
History of the Rumanian People, 361–2
Histria, 385–6

Hitler, 50, 57, 70, 71, 127, 128, 152, 281, 282, 322, 371
Hitov, Panajot, 341
Höchstädt, Battle of, 78
Hodža, Milan, 223
Hoffmann, 16, 68
Hofmannsthal, 30, 188, 194, 207
Hohenzollern-Sigmaringen, princes of, 48, 50
Hohenzollerns, 316
Hölderlin, 17, 18, 100, 160, 278, 279, 320, 385
Hole, The (von Arnim), 105
Holotík, L'udovít, 222
Holy Roman Empire, 31, 32, 66, 67, 81, 83, 84, 102, 105, 106
Holzkirchen, 113
Homebook of the City of Weisskirchen in the Banat (Kuhn), 298
Homer, 109, 121, 384
Honterus, 312
Horea, 317–18
Horia, Vintila, 381
Horkheimer, 162, 270
Hörnigk, 241
Horthy, 250, 259, 281, 291, 314
Höss, Rudolph, 142, 143, 144, 145
Huber, Wolf, 149
Hudetz, 185
Hugo, Victor, 26, 355
Humboldt, 99
Hundred Years of Solitude, A (Marquez), 121
Hungaric Gate, 210
Hungary/Hungarians, 116, 137, 212, 220, 221, 222, 241–4, 248, 249, 252, 255, 256–7, 261, 269, 276, 281, 282, 284, 295, 304, 307, 308, 310, 313–17, 325, 328
Hungary in the Year 1677 (Montecuccoli), 243
Hunger Artist, The (Kafka), 163
Huns, 42, 119, 120, 310
Hunyadi, János, 262, 264, 304
Hussar, The (Rezzori), 320
Hviezdoslav, 224
Hyperboreans, 19
Hyrtl, Prof., 337

I Confess That I Have Lived (Neruda), 53
I Was a Decadent Poet (Cassian), 374
Iancu, 314
Ibsen, 136, 342
Idris, 157
If This Is a Man (Levi), 142
Iller, River, 59, 60
Illmitz, 212
Illustrated History of the Rumanian People (Giurescu), 380

Illyés, Gyula, 286
Ilz, River, 117, 122
Immendingen, 28, 33
Impromptu of the Soul (Bartholomeus I), 373
In oppressores (Oşbuc), 361
Inferno (Strindberg), 150
Ingolstadt, 95–7
Inn, River, 117, 122
Institoris, Michal, 224
Institutiones Poeticae in usum Gymnasiorum, etc., 266–7
Ionesco, E., 372, 373, 374
Iorga, Nicola, 363, 365, 370, 376, 377, 383
Iova, Czar, the Adventurer, 323
Iron Gates, 59, 333
Iron Guard, 370
Isonzo, 209
Istanbul, 342
Ister (as name for Danube), 18, 278, 364
Ister (god), 28
Istrati, Panait, 376–7, 386, 387–8
Istria, 364, 385
Istrian exodus, 40
Istropolis, 396
Italian Neo-Fascist Party, 39
Italy, 39, 183, 199, 369, 371, 372
Ivan, Czar (Franz Fekete), 283–4
Ivan Kondarev (Stanev), 343
Ivanovo, 355

Jacobeus, Jakub, 224
Jacomuzzi, Stefano, 141
Janata, Christa, 192, 196
Janko, Dr Josef, 308
Jankovics, Duke, 317
Janos, Apaczai Cseri, 284
Jaroš, Peter, 224
"Jes" group, 192
Jewess of Toledo, The (Grillparzer), 112–13
Jews, 52, 53, 144–5, 177, 189–90, 213, 225, 230, 320, 328, 356, 371, 375
Johnson, Doctor, 26
Jókai, Mór, 243, 256, 257–8, 263
Jonas (Sorescu), 374
Jordanov, Stojan, 356
Jorg, 179
Joseph II, 31, 80, 81, 191, 294, 317, 394
Jósika, Miklós, 314
József, Attila, 250, 257, 279
Journey to the End of the Night (Céline), 51
Jugoslavia, 254, 324, 329, 331–2
Jünger, 53
Juvenal, 255

Kachník, Dr Josepho, 235–7
Kádár, 248, 249, 252, 257

Kafka, Franz, 44, 46, 52, 54, 77, 79, 88, 89, 122, 140, 162–4, 188, 202, 203, 213, 225, 234, 246, 322, 357, 368, 391
Kallbrunner, Josel, 295
Kalocsa, 276–7
Kalteherberg inn, 27
Kandler, Petro, 364
Kanitz, Felix Philipp, 337, 343, 345, 349
Kapor, Momo, 332
Kappus, Franz Xaver, 304–5
Kara Mustapha, 176–7, 179
Karavelov, 341
Kardelj, 296–7
Kardzălij, 338, 340
Karl Alexander, Duke of Württemberg, 65
Karl and the Twentieth Century (Brunngraber), 72–3
Károlyi, Count, 33, 40, 244–5
Karpathen-Rundschau, 310
Kaufmann family, 44, 47
Kazinczy, Ferenc, 269
Kehlheim, 98
Kemény, Zsigmond, 242, 267
Kepler, 25, 74, 107–8
Kery, Theodor, 212
Ketterer, Franz Anton, 38
Khevenhüller, Count von, 62
Kidriceva Ulica, 324
Kiepert, Prof., 337
Kierkegaard, 41, 60
Kierling, 162–4
King Dies, The (Ionesco), 374
King Ottocar: His Rise and Fall (Grillparzer), 79, 81–2
Kipling, 334, 346, 385
Király, 286
Kis, Danilo, 323
Kiss, 286
Kitanka, 338, 339, 340, 343, 349, 352
Kittner, Alfred, 311
Kladovo, 334
Klapka, 256
Klausenburg *see* Cluj (Klausenburg)
Kleeman, Nicolaus Ernst, 259, 396
Klimó, Bishop Georg, 280
Klopstock, 100
Klosterneuburg, 159, 162
Klösz, György, 261
Knabel, Wilhelm, 281
Kñiggtätz, 245
Kö, Pál, 286
Köchel, 157
Kocsis, 247–51, 259
Koerber, Prime Minister of Austria, 245
Koestler, Arthur, 63
Kollár, Ján, 223
Költschitzky, 180

Kommandant at Auschwitz (Höss), 143
Komorn, 256, 258
Konrád, György, 268
Kossuth, 243, 264, 269
Kot, Jozef, 232
Kovács, György, 319
Kovács, Margit, 260
Kozlodúj, 348
Krafft, Ludwig, 67
Kraus, Karl, 79, 175, 255
Kraus, Wolfgang, 187, 322
Krčméry, Štefan, 225, 231
Kreisky, Chancellor, 362
Kremling, Dr, 330
Krems, 157
Kriemhild, 116, 119, 120, 158
Krleža, Miroslav, 253–5
Kronstadt *see* Brasov (Kronstadt)
Krúdy, Gyula, 251
Kubrik, 205
Kuhn, Alfred, 298
Kun, Béla, 250, 269, 325, 371
Kunz, 191
Kürnberger, Ferdinand, 319
Kuśniewicz, Andrei, 331
Kyra Kyralina (Istrati), 388
Kyselak, Josef, 154–7

La Martinière's Dictionary, 364
La Vigue, 49
Lafitte, 72
Lajos, Dóczi, 281
Lamartine, 18, 339
Lang, Fritz, 92, 119
Larisch, Countess, 172
"Las Castas" (Museum of Mexico City), 34
Lászloné, Kakony, 277
Late Summer, The (Stifter), 129
Latour d'Auvergne, Théophile Malo
    Corret de, 94
Laube, Heinrich, 103
Laufen, 65, 66
Lauingen, 83, 85
Laval, Pierre, 49, 50
Lavergnolle, Gaston, 175
Lec, Stanislav Jerzy, 330–1
Lechner, 263
Lecture illustrée, 235, 237
Legend of Sibin, Prince of Preslav (Stanev),
    351
Léhar, Franz, 258
Leitha, River, 210, 212
Lejean, Guillaume, 337
Lenau, 299, 300
Lenclos, Ninon de, 260
Lengyel, Géza, 263
Leopardi, Giacomo, 160
Leopold, Emperor, 180

Lepanto, Battle of, 106
Less, Captain, 46
Lettere odeoporiche (Griselini), 294
Letters to a Young Poet (Rilke), 305
Letters to Milena (Kafka), 89
Levi, Primo, 142
Lichtenberg, 261
Licinius, 393
Liebhard, Franz (Reiter Róbert), 291–2,
    296
Life of Quintus Fixlein (Jean Paul), 87, 88
Lillin, Andreas A., 329, 330
Limes, 97–8
Linnaeus, 160, 161, 391, 392
Linz, 60, 62, 104, 107, 127, 128, 130, 131, 135,
    137–8, 142
Lipovenians, 394–5
Ljubljana, River, 364
Loewinger, Herr, 297
Lom, 344, 345
Loos, Adolf, 184, 195
Lorenz, Konrad, 159, 161
Lost Village, The (Szabo), 314
Louis II of Hungary, 286
Louis XIV, 69, 78, 137
Louis XVI, 90
Louis the Great, 285
Louis Philippe, 72
Lowlands (Müller), 306
Luccheni, 207
Lucretius, 160
Ludwig I of Bavaria, 98, 99, 117, 207, 208
Lu-Hsün, 181
Lukács, G., 68, 187–8, 248, 261, 262, 263,
    267, 271–5, 291
Luner, Josefine, 200, 201
Lungu, Lazar, 302
Lupescu, Madame, 366
Lupi, Sergio, 146
Luther, 68

Ma, 292
Macedonia/Macedonians, 297, 348, 362,
    367
Machiavelli, 139, 140
Mack, General, 78
Maddalena, 22, 23, 25, 73, 75, 85, 86, 95, 147
Maeterlinck, 391
Magic Flute, 113
Magin, Jan Baltazár, 223
Magyars, 220, 222, 242, 243, 256, 257, 263,
    310, 314, 315, 319, 324
Mahmudia, 393
Maierosch, 303
Makart, Hans, 206
Malraux, André, 325
Mamaia, 381
Mandách, 281

Manger, Isik, 320
Mann, Golo, 70
Mann, Thomas, 32, 42, 68, 77, 142, 188, 388
Mao Tse-tung, 139
March, River, 59, 210
Marcomanni, 210
Marcus Aurelius *see* Aurelius, Marcus
Margul-Sperber, Alfred, 320
Maria, Empress, 62
Maria Sonia, tomb of, 158–9
Maria Taferl monastery, 146
Maria Theresa, 30, 74, 150, 209, 220, 259,
    294, 304, 311, 323
Marianna, Szendy, 264
Marie Antoinette, 90
Marin, 401
Markos, 387
Markova, Yana, 342
Marlborough, Duke of, 78
Maros, River, 282
Marshal, the, 103–5
Marsili, Marshal Luigi Ferdinand, 41, 140,
    159–60
Marx/Marxism, 188, 197, 198, 248, 249, 250,
    254
Master of Messkirch, 53
Master of the Thalheim Altar, 53
Mates, Ben, 296
Matiašovce, 233
Matliary, 234
Matoas, 359–401
Maurice, Duke of Saxony, 61
Mauthausen, 60, 142–5, 149
Maximilian I, Emperor, 101, 103
Maximilian of Mexico, 208
Mayerling, 168, 171, 172, 174
Medgyessy, Ferenc, 270
Meditations (Aurelius), 210
Mela, Pomponius, 19, 364
Melk, 146, 149
Memoirs (Ferenc Rakóczi II), 314
*Memories, impressions, reflections and
    landscapes on a voyage to the Orient*
    (Lamartine), 18
Menachemoff, Dr, 358
Mengele, Josef, 90–93, 143
Menis, Dr Gugliemo, 136
Mercy, General, 294, 295
Merian magazine, 19
Merkl, Hilda, 328
Mérode, Cléo de, 237
Meschendörfer, Adolf, 312, 313, 315
Messkirch, 44–7
Metternich, 94, 100, 241
Metz, Andreas, 317
Metz, Mihai, 317
Metzger, Dr, 122
Michael, King of Rumania, 370

Michelet, 391
Michelsburg Hill, 98
Michelstaedter, 64, 147
Midhat Pasha, 353, 354
Mihalache, Ion, 376
Mihálik, 224
Mikszáth, Kálmán, 261, 282, 283
Milesian colonists, 385
Miletič, Svetozar, 327–8
Military Condition of the Ottoman Empire,
    etc. (Marsili), 159–60
Military Frontier, 326–8
Milleker, 330
Millenial Bee, The (Jaroš), 224
Milosavljević, Pedia, 331
Mináč, Vladimir, 221, 222
Mindszenty, Cardinal, 253
Minucci, Count, 116
Miorița, 361
Mitteleuropa, 20, 28–33, 155, 183, 245, 249,
    255, 268–9, 332, 397
Mittner, Ladislao, 83
Mňačko, 232
Modern Midas, A (Jókai), 257–8
Mohács, 284–7
    Battle of, 220, 257, 283, 284, 285
Mohammed II, 362
Mohr, Adam, 109
Moidle-Schiff (vessel), 65
Moltke, Field Marshal, 356
Moltke, Count Helmuth James von, 57, 70
Montecuccoli, Raimondo, 137–40, 141,
    243
Montez, Lola, 98
Montgelas, 114–15
Moricz, Zsigmond, 312, 314
Moscow, 325
Möser, 67
Mosonmagyaróvár, 251
Mother Danube (Friedrich), 41
Motzan, Peter, 310
Mozart, 100, 157, 190
M'Queen, James, 24
Mühlhiasl, the, 114
Müller, Heiner, 311
Müller, Herta, 306
Müller-Guttenbrunn, Adam, 281, 293, 300,
    307–8
Münster, Sebastian, 35
Musel, River, 28
Musil, R., 28, 89, 130, 133, 159, 161, 168, 170,
    194, 195, 246, 297, 391
Mussolini, 371
Mutafčieva, Vera, 338

Näf, Werner, 106
Nagl-Zeidler-Castle, 328
Nagy government, 248, 256

Napoleon, 39, 78–81, 94, 98, 99, 256
Nashville, 168
Naumann, 31
*Navigation and Rafting on the Upper
   Danube* (Neweklowsky), 59–64
Nayazid, Sultan, 352
Nazism, 30, 32, 47, 50, 68, 69, 70, 71, 90,
   93, 144, 145, 161, 187, 199, 200, 235, 281,
   282, 296, 315, 316, 322, 330, 356, 370, 371
Nedel'a (Novomeský), 230–1
Németh, László, 257
Neruda, Pablo, 53
Nestor, 363, 380
Neuberg, 23, 94
Neudiedel, lake of, 212
Neu-Eck, 17
Neue Literatur, 310
New Squire, The (Jókai), 243
Neweklowksy, Ernst, 59–65, 342
Ney, Marshal, 78
Nicopolis, 352
Niebelungs, The, 119
Nietzsche, 188, 223, 314, 342, 343, 347, 381
Nikolai, 391, 392, 395
Nile, River, 19, 24, 282, 337
Ninon de Lenclos (opera), 260
Noce, Auguste del, 188
Nodier, Charles, 68
Nogai, 394
North (Céline), 49
Nothing Other Than the Memory (Dor), 301
Nouvelles de Sofia, 339
Novel of a Novel, The (Sinkó), 325
Novi Sad, 324–6
Novomeský, Ladislav, 221, 230–2, 233

Oberhausen, 93–4
Obrenović, Miloš, 389
Octavián, 309, 317, 318
Octavián, Stefán, 279
Odrisi, 363
Of Heroes and Tombs (Sábato), 378
Ofen, 284
Öhrlein, Dr, 20, 22, 23
Old Church Slavonic, 346
Old Man and the Officer, The (Eliade), 379
Olmütz, 235
Omerić, Mr, 348
Ontology of Social Being (Lukács), 271–2
Optimists, The (Sinkó), 325
Opus Danubiale (Marsili), 140, 159
Oravský Podzámok, 221, 226
Orbis Pictus (Comenius), 228
Ormánság, 280
Osman Pazvantoglu, 338, 343
Osnabrück, 67
Otava valley, 221
Otetea, Andrei, 361

Otto, Archduke, 151
Otto, King of Greece, 99, 117
Otto, Uncle, 199–200
Otto the Great, 102
Ottocar of Bohemia, 79, 80, 81–2
Ottoman Empire *see* Turks
Our Dear Kinsfolk (Lillin), 330
Ovid, 18, 381, 382

Pabst family, 184
Pácirta, 271
Padua, 15
Pagans, The (Herczeg), 299, 300
Paisy of Khilendar, 340
Pálfy, Blasius, 283
Pálné, Apostol, 277
Pančevo, 295, 330
Pannonia, 29, 116, 119, 211, 212, 239–87
Pannonius, Janus, 242
Pan-Slavism, 223, 224, 226
Paphlagonia, 384
Paracelsus, 219
Parsifal, 20
Passarowilz, Peace of, 65
Passau, 59, 62, 114, 116–19, 122–3
Paul, Jean (Richter), 18, 68, 83–5, 86–8, 89
Paul, St, 67
Pechenegs, 258, 299
Pécs, 279, 280, 285
Perlini, Tito, 321
Pessoa, 52
Pétain, Marshal, 49, 50
Petöfi, 222, 242, 244, 250, 256, 264, 282
Petrov, Ivailo, 347
Petrovaradin fortress, 324
Petrović, Jon, 324
Pezinok, 226
Piccolomini, Enea Silvio (later Pius II),
   116, 317
Pilgrim, Bishop, 116, 119
Pioneers of Ingolstadt (Fleisser), 95–6
Pischinger, Oskar, 152–3, 154
Pius II *see* Piccolomini, Enea Silvio
Piwonka, Leopoldine, 190
Planten, 106
Plato, 211, 261, 321
Pleven, Siege of, 339
Pliny, 18, 19, 136, 364, 396
Plovdiv, 339
Podbiel, 227
Polkar, Alfred, 190
Pollack, Martin, 212, 213
Pölškei, József, 286
Pomaks, 339, 341
Ponzo, Antonio di, 393
Poor Street Musician, The (Grillparzer), 201
Popa, Vasko, 299, 301
Popescu, President, 296, 298, 303

Popovich, Lazar Fota, 389
Popovici, Aurel, 31, 269
Pottenbrunn, 141
Pound, Ezra, 261
Prague, 101, 107, 223, 226, 231, 232, 317
Preusmann, Dr, 122
Priest, The (Svantner), 224
Pringle, Margaret Ann, 399
*Problematical Report of Jakob Bühlmann,
   The* (Hauser), 305
Propositions on the Danube (Tumler), 279
Proto-Bulgars, 346, 347, 352
Prussia, 30, 99
Pruth, River, 389
Pseudo-Scymnus, 19
Ptolemy, 18, 19
Puchenau, 60
Pupin, Mihajlo, 328
Purgatory at Ingolstadt (Fleisser), 96
Purgstall, Joseph von Hammer, 132

Quadi, 210
Quieto/Quietus, River, 136, 137, 364
Quine, 24, 64
Quittner, Zsigmond, 263

Raba, River, 137, 256
Rac, Julijan, 325
Radetzky, 348
Radičkov, Jordan, 349–50
Radulovitsch, Mrs, 329
Rajk, 247
Rakoczi rebellion, 257
Rákosi, 247, 248
Razin, Lake, 396
Recluse, The (Stifter), 129
Reder, Christian, 170, 186
Regensburg, 59, 62, 99, 101–5, 106, 107, 108
Reiter, Robert, 291–2, 296
Renzi, Lorenzo, 369
Repubblica di Salò, 39
Return of Filip Latinovicz, The (Krleža),
   254
Rezzori, Gregor von, 306, 320, 367
Rhaetia, 28
Rheingold (Wagner), 170
Rhine, River, 26, 27, 29, 30
Rhinoceros (Ionesco), 374
Richter, Jean Paul *see* Paul, Jean
Riedling, 58
Rilke, 38, 305
Rimbaud, 91, 211, 292, 320
Ritter, Gerhard, 140
Road to Damascus, The (Strindberg), 150
Robak, Fritz, 213
Róbert, Reiter, 291–2, 296
Roes, Alexander von, 103
Rojesko, Agent, 345

Rolland, Romain, 387–8
Romanies, 326, 328
Rome/Romans, 41, 42, 43, 97–8, 210, 362,
   380, 384, 387
Rommel, Field Marshal, 70–1
Roreto, General Petitti de, 199
Rose, The (Monica Favoretto), 100
Rosen, Georg, 341
Rosenberger, Franz X., 117
Rösler, Prof, 347
Roth, Joseph, 81, 93, 174, 189, 191, 193, 196,
   215
Róth, Miksa, 263
Rudhard, Minister, 117
Rudolph I of Hapsburg, 79, 81
Rudolph II, 80
Rudolph, Archduke of Hapsburg, 170,
   171, 172, 174
Rudolphine Tables (Kepler), 74
Rufus, Milan, 233
Rühm, Gerhard, 154, 192
Rumania/Rumanians, 295, 296, 305, 306,
   310, 314, 316, 328–30, 354, 361, 362, 365,
   367, 370–2, 376, 380
Rumanian Humbug, The, 372
Rumi, Jalal ud-Din, 179
Rundstedt, von, 70
Ruse, 353–4, 355, 356, 357, 358, 361
Rusperger, Emmeram, 111
Russia, 167, 226, 232, 249, 251, 275, 297, 306,
   325, 329, 339, 340, 344, 345, 371, 389, 394
Rusticus, 211
Ruthenians, 223, 295, 324–5, 328
Rybak, Isahar Ber, 374–5

Saba, Umberto, 144, 211, 366
Sábato, Ernesto, 378
Sade, 160
Sadoveanu, Mikhail, 361, 376, 386, 393–4
St Clair, 346
Salomé, Lou Andreas, 97
Salomon, Ernst von, 117
Salsovia, fortress of, 393
Salvadori, Massimo, 249
Salzburg, 61, 297
Samsun, 344, 346
Sándor, Moritz, 263
Sandrin, 229–30, 237
Sankt Florian, 146, 147, 148, 149
Sarajevo, 150, 151, 152, 153, 181, 341
Sarmatae, 210
Sarmatic Sea, 20
Sartre, 75–6, 254
Satanail, 350–1
Sauter, Ferdinand, 203
Sava, River, 41, 364
Savigny, 67
Saxons, 281, 304, 307, 309–310, 312, 313, 315

Scheiffele, Johann Matthäus, 74
Schescherko, 298
Scheuchzer, Jacob, 122
Schikaneder, 113
Schiltberger, 352
Schmeller, Johann Andreas, 101
Schmeltzl, Wolfgang, 176
Schmid, Hermann, 65, 66
Schmidt of Krems, 157
Schmitz (pharmacist), 303
Schokatzi, 280, 295, 323
Scholl, Hans and Sophie, 70
Schönberg, 184, 261
Schönbrunn, 152
Schorske, 129, 194
Schratt, Katherine, 174
Schubart, Christian Friedrich Daniel, 74
Schubert, 133, 203
Schuller, Horst, 310
Schuller, Rudolf, 315
Schultes, J. A., 62–3
Schultz, 58
Schumpeter, 193–5
Schweiger, Salomon, 399
Schweiger-Lerchenfeld, Baron Amand
    von, 394
Schwicker, 284, 293, 295
Scythia Minor, 363
Scythians, 19, 243, 362, 363, 400
Sédan, Battle of, 40, 57
Seidler, Irma, 272–3, 274
Selim III, Sultan, 338
Semănătórul, 376
Seneca, 19
Serbs/Serbia, 259–60, 280, 295, 296, 298,
    304, 305, 307, 324, 326–8, 331
Seven Swabians, The (Herczeg), 300–1
Sfîntu Gheorghe, 393, 396
Shakespeare, 136, 206
Shamil, 344
Shi Huang Ti, 377
Shtetl (Rybak), 374
Sibiu (Hermannstadt), 305–6, 309, 310, 311,
    313, 317, 326
Siebenbürgen, 304, 305, 306, 309, 311, 312,
    315, 317
Siebenkäs (Jean Paul), 85
Siegfried, 29, 119
Sienerth, Stefan, 310
Sighişoara, 262, 309, 310, 317–19
Sigmaringen, 48–54
Sigurdhr, 119, 120
Šika, 342
Šikula, Vincent, 224
Silistra, Pasha of, 343
Singer, I. B., 57, 88, 89, 113, 121, 265, 374
Sinkó, Erwin, 325
Sinowatz, Chancellor, 212

Šipka, 339
Sironi, Col. G., 389
Slataper, 136
Slaveno-Bulgarian History (Paisy of
    Khilendar), 340
Slaveykov, Pencho, 342
Slaveykov, Petko, 342
Slavia and the World of the Future (Štur),
    223
Slavs, 32, 98, 220–4, 346, 347, 385, 389
Slovaks, Slovakia, 220–6, 231–3, 295, 324,
    328
Smatlák, Štanislav, 223–4, 231
Smithies, Arthur, 194, 195
Snežnik, Mount, 47, 185, 215, 384
Sobieski, Jan, 176, 177, 180
Sofia, 339, 341, 347, 349
Solovej (Bercovici), 374
Sombor, 323
Song of The Niebelungs, 20, 29, 116, 119, 120,
    158
Sophie, Duchess (Sophie Chotek von
    Chotkowa und Wagnin), 150–3
Sopron, 245–6, 247
Sorescu, Marin, 374
Soul and Form (Lukács), 272
Soviet Union see Russia
Speer, 127
Speke, Captain John, 24, 282
Sperber, Manès, 197, 198
Sperber, Margul, 306
Srbik, Heinrich von, 29, 30, 31, 32
Srem, the, 294
Stalin/Stalinism, 197, 231, 232, 248, 254, 273,
    274, 276, 322, 323, 325, 329, 347
Stamboliski, 348
Stancu, Zaharia, 362, 386
Stanev, Emilyan, 343, 351–2
Stauffenberg, Von, 71
Steidl, Imre, 262
Stein, 157
Steinbrunn-Štikapron, 213
Stendhal, 26, 81
Stephanie, Archduchess, 171
Stephanos of Byzantium, 400
Stephen, St, King of Hungary, 258
Stephen the Great of Moldavia, 362
Sterne, Laurence, 28, 156
Stifter, Adalbert, 117, 128–31, 146, 147, 148
Stilicho, 43
Stirner, 342
Stojacskovics, 284
Stoker, Bram, 319
Strabo, 18, 19, 363, 364, 396
Strada, 274
Straubing, 109, 113
Strauss, Franz Josef, 114
Strauss, Johann, 122, 175, 205

Straža, 296
Strena seu De Nive Sexangula (Kepler), 107
Strindberg, 150, 342
Struharik, Joraj, 324
Studies in European Realism (Lukács), 273
Štur, L'dovit, 223
Sturm und Drang, 33, 37
Styria, 326
Subotica, 322–4
Suleika (Marianne Willemer), 131–5
Suleiman the Magnificent, 179, 283, 285, 286
Sulina, 27, 391, 395, 396, 397, 398, 399
Sunday (Noromeský), 230–1
"Sunday Circle", 262, 263
Sussi, 379
Švantner, František, 224
Svevo, 52, 86, 137, 313
Swabian Chronicle (Reiter Robert), 292
Swabians, 65, 74, 83, 281, 295, 297, 305, 307, 315
Systema Naturae (Linnaeus), 160
Szabó, Dezsö, 314
Szabó Jnr, 286
Szabolcsi, Miklós, 250, 279, 291
Szamléni, Gabriel, 322–3
Széchenyi, Count István, 242–3, 263, 269, 389, 390
Szeged, 282, 283, 284
Székely, 295, 310, 319
Szekszárd, 251
Szende, Béla, 281
Szentendre, 259–61
Szigetvár, siege of, 179
Szilágy, Ladislaus, 283
Szilassy, Baron, 269

Tales of Hoffmann, 68, 82
Talmud, 44
Târnovo, school of, 355
Tartars, 243, 343–4, 394
Tatranska Lomnica, 234
Tatras, the, 227, 234–5
Taxa Pharmaceutia Posoniensis (Torkos), 219–20
Tedeschi, Alexander, 346
Temeschburg *see* Temesvár
Temesvár (Timişoara, Temeschburg), 291, 293, 294, 304–8
Teodorescu, Virgil, 373
Teutsch, Friedrich, 310
Teutsch, Georg Daniel, 310
Theory of Colours (Goethe), 85
Theory of the Novel, The (Lukács), 272
There Where the Wheat is Milled (Lillin), 329
Thibaut, 67
Thracian Horseman, 383–4

Thracians, 346–7, 363, 364, 383
Thrän, Ferdinand, 75–8
Tilly, 94, 95
Timişoara *see* Temesvár
Tipoweiler, Herr, 298
Tisza, Istvan, 245, 300
Tisza, River, 41, 282, 283
Tito, 213, 254, 297, 303, 324, 329, 332, 390
Tolstoy, 78, 344
Tomb for Boris Davidović (Kis), 323
Tomis *see* Constanţa
Tomori, Archbishop, 286
Torkos, Ján Justus, 219
Tractatus (Wittgenstein), 17, 275
Tragedy of Man (Mandách), 281
Trajan, 333, 361, 380
Trani, Professor, 228–30, 237
Transylvania, 243, 262, 304, 305, 309–16
Transylvanismus, 313–17
Trapezunte, 344
Trauttmansdorf castle, 141
Travels on the Danube (Schultes), 62
Treatise on War (Montecuccoli), 138, 139
Trenčin, 227
Trieste, 39, 95, 198, 199, 209, 301
Trogus, Pompeius, 363
Tropaeum Traiani, 380
Trost, 93, 114
Trotsky, 167
Trunz, Erich, 133
Tschantschendorf, 213
Tübingen, 15, 16
Tukachevsky, Marshal, 95
Tulcea, 391–2, 396
Tulln, 158–9
Tumler, Franz, 279
Turanian peoples, 363
Turenne, 137
Turks, 35, 74, 99, 137, 138, 176–80, 220, 242, 243, 258, 259, 284, 286, 294, 295, 304, 312, 314, 323, 326, 327, 333, 337–49, 354, 362, 387, 389, 394
Turmalin (Stifter), 148
Turnu-Severin, 333
Tuttlingen, 34, 48
2001: A Space Odyssey, 205

Ulm, 33–4, 57–8, 59, 61, 66–78, 82
    Bread Museum, 72
    cathedral, 66–7, 74
    Fischerviertel, 73
    pig-market square, 74
    site of capitulation to Napoleon, 78
    Town Hall, 70, 72, 74
Under the Yoke (Vasov), 342, 354
Unity, Identity and Chance (Bozzi), 22
Upper Danube, extent of, 59–60
Urban, St, 221

Urdonau, 19, 20
Ureche, Grigore, 361
Urmuz, 372–3
Urzidil, Johannes, 29
Uskoks, 327

Vác, 259
Vajdahund castle, 262
Valcov, 395
Vâlcova, Madame, 356, 358
Válek, 224
Valentinian I, Emperor, 42
Valóság, 248
Valota, Bianca, 369, 370
Varna, 346
Vásárhelyi, Paul, 244
Vasov, Ivan, 342–4, 354–5, 387
Vazul, Dimšić, 260
Venelin, 340
Venice, 15
Verdi, 260
Verlaine, 91
Verne, Jules, 157–8, 175, 379
Versailles, Treaty of, 71
Verschuer, Prof. Otran van, 90
Vetsera, Helene, 171, 172
Vetsera, Maria, 170–4
Vichy government, 48, 49
Vidin, 338, 342, 343
Vienna, 167–209, 215
  Army Historical Museum, 181
  Augarten, 201–2
  Belvedere palace, 153, 180
  Bergasse, 203–4
  Café Central, 167, 168
  Cemetery of the Nameless, 190–1
  Cemetery of Sankt Marx, 190
  Central Cemetery, 181–6
  Chamber of Workers and Employees, 186
  Crime Museum, 41, 200–201
  Dorotheum, 175
  Gasthaus Fuchs (Rogergasse), 192–3
  Gentzgasse, 187
  Hermesvilla, 206, 208
  Himmelstrasse, 204
  I.B.M. Centre, 205
  Jews in, 189–90
  Josephinum, 191–2
  Karl-Marx-Hof, 197–9
  Kundmanngasse, 169
  Künstlerhaus exhibition "The Turks Before Vienna", 176–80
  Mariahilfestrasse, 199
  Museum of the Twentieth Century, 180
  Rembrandtstrasse, 193
  Schwarzpanierstrasse, 206
  Strudlhof Steps, 174–5

Wiener Gruppe, 154, 192, 195–6
  mentioned, 19, 29, 36, 59, 60, 62, 78, 104, 137, 214, 241, 245, 251, 252, 261, 279, 323, 353
Vignale Monferrato, 40
Village on the Plain (Stifter), 146–7, 148
Villány, 280
Villerual, Countess, 62
Vilshofen, 114, 115
Vindobona, 211
Vineta, 157
Virgil, 278–9
Visit, The (Konrád), 268
Vlad the Impaler, 319
Vlasits, 213
Vogter, 308
Voices of Marrakesh (Canetti), 109
Vojvodina, 294, 295, 306, 324, 326
Völkischer Beobachter, 282
Volksbuch, 101
Vörösmarty, 250
Vršac, 299, 300, 301, 330
Vuković, Milan, 293

Wachau, the, 125–64
Wackenfels, Johannes Matthäus Wackher von, 107
Wagner, Ferdinand, 119
Wagner, Richard, 170
Waiting for Godot (Beckett), 374
Waldstein, Count, 390
Walhalla, 99–100
Wandruszka, Adam, 135, 348
War and Peace (Tolstoy), 78, 121
Wastlhuber, von, 117
Watzinger, C. H., 62
Weber, Max, 46, 71, 112
Webster, William, 399
Weil, Eric, 320–1
Weininger, 18, 40, 206, 381
Weissenburg, 97
Weisskirchen, 293, 297 *see also* Bela Crkva
Weissmuller, Johnny, 304
Werfel, Franz, 135
Wesselényi, Baron Miklos, 269
West-Östlicher Divan (Goethe), 132–3, 135
White Nile, 337
Whittington Club, 345
Wiener Gruppe, 154, 192, 195–6
Wienerisches Diarium, 214
Wild Roses, 319
Wilhelm of Germany, 99
Willemer, Marianne (née Jung), 131–5
Windberg, monastery of, 114
Wittgenstein, 17, 169, 188, 194, 275
Wittstock, Erwin, 310, 317
Wittstock, Joachim, 310, 330
Wolfgang, Count of the Palatinate, 83

Wood (Reiter Róbert), 292
Wotton, Sir Henry, 107
Woyzeck (Büchner), 318
Wulfila, Bishop, 352

Yalta, 268, 269, 275
Ybl, Miklós, 41, 262
Yellow Island, 282

Zagreb, 253, 255
Zaharia, 366
Zamfirescu, 361, 377

Zápolya, John, 284
Zeiller, Martin, 58
Zeno, 40
Zerer, Stefan, 62
Ziller, 317
Zillich, Heinrich, 310, 313, 315–16, 327
Zimmer, 303
Zita, Empress, 172, 278
Zitište, 324
Zivkov, 347, 348
Zoltan, Kis, 264
Zríny family, 242